American Poetry

THESE ARE BORZOI BOOKS, PUBLISHED BY
ALFRED A. KNOPF

Faust

Johann Wolfgang von Goethe

Faust

PARTS
ONE AND TWO

TRANSLATED FROM THE GERMAN BY

George Madison Priest

PROFESSOR OF GERMAN LITERATURE

PRINCETON UNIVERSITY

1941: ALFRED A. KNOPF
NEW YORK

TO
DAVID MAGIE

Preface

THE FOLLOWING translation embodies several good intentions. Primarily it is meant to enable American and English readers whose knowledge of German is feeble or non-existent to obtain some idea of the content and meaning of Goethe's masterpiece. The translation is not meant for professors of German literature or for other masters of the German language. No one who can read Goethe's own lines will ever be contented with the poor surrogate that a translation of *Faust* will always be.

The time seems auspicious for the publication of a new translation of *Faust*. In this centenary year of Goethe's death it is well for other countries besides Goethe's fatherland to be reminded, by some presentation of the poet's work, that such a man once trod this earth. To meet this situation no other work of Goethe's could be chosen as fittingly as *Faust*. Into no other work did Goethe put so much thought and poetry and artistry. No other work contains so much of the rich heritage that Goethe left, not merely to Germany, but to the world.

No account, except an occasional suggestion in the Notes, is given here of the composition of *Faust*. It is not told how Goethe began the writing of *Faust* in his early twenties, continued it at several periods in his life, and did not finish the play until he was nearly eighty-two years old. Nor is there any comparison of the three more or less different versions of the First Part which are in existence. As this publication is intended, first of all, as an introduction to *Faust*, it omits deliberately all account of the many moot and knotty problems involved in a presentation of the origins and composition of Goethe's play. *Faust* is presented, as nearly as possible, in the form, and only in that form, in which Goethe finally wished it to be known.

The translation follows the text of the standard edition of Goethe's works, the "Jubiläumsausgabe," or "Jubilee Edition," in as many respects as lie in the power of the translator. The numbering of the lines is the same and the metrical and rhyming systems of the original have been preserved in the more formal, more elevated passages. In straightforward dialogue the translator has followed Goethe's example in taking liberties with the sequence of rhymes, in leaving a number of lines unrhymed, and in not straining after absolute purity of rhyme. Lines in the translation which may seem to be improperly stumbling and irregular are in many cases reflections of the same characteristics in the German, a device of Goethe's to vary the metre or to suggest the

[iii]

momentary restlessness or confusion of spirit of the speaker. In general, the translator has aimed to change nothing, to omit nothing, and, above all, to add nothing. He harbours the increasing conviction that Goethe can not be improved upon.

Many other English translations of *Faust*, especially of the First Part, have long since been in existence. "Long since." With the exception of one of but little importance no translation of the whole of *Faust* has appeared in many years and in the meantime men have attained to a far better understanding of the whole as well as of its major and minor elements. The present translation attempts to avoid the misconceptions of its predecessors and to utilize, as far as possible, the wisdom and research of recent and contemporary students of *Faust*.

To all these and to many others the translator feels under great obligation. First of all, he became indebted to Karl E. Weston, the literary executor of William Page Andrews, who generously gave him the privilege of using Mr. Andrews's translation of the First Part as if it were the translator's own. Numerous passages — the songs of the Archangels and Faust's Curse, for example — have been taken over from Mr. Andrews's work virtually intact. Without the impetus which he received from Mr. Andrews's manuscript the translator would hardly have had the courage to attempt his translation at all.

It was impossible, as it would have seemed foolish, to ignore earlier translations and they too have suggested many rhymes and wordings, especially the translations by Bayard Taylor, Anna Swanwick, and Albert G. Latham. Items involving interpretation and explanation, to be found in the Introduction and Notes, have been derived chiefly from works by German scholars — Heinrich Rickert and Georg Witkowski especially, and Erich Schmidt and K. J. Schröer among other Germans — as well as from Calvin Thomas's edition of Goethe's text.

In addition to all these, many friends have aided the translator in the preparation of his manuscript, especially Harvey W. Hewett-Thayer, Alan Holske, Denver Lindley, Robert N. Cunningham, and Faith Greene, but gratitude is due, most of all, to Morris W. Croll and Hans Jaeger who spent many hours in reading and rereading the manuscript to its great improvement and the translator's lasting indebtedness.

Lastly, the translator wishes to express his cordial thanks to the publishers and various members of their staff for all their generous, unfailing coöperation.

GEORGE M. PRIEST

PRINCETON, NEW JERSEY,
February 20, 1932.

Second Preface

In preparing this new version of his translation of *Faust* the translator has reviewed and re-studied every line and every paragraph of his previous version with as keen a vision as he possesses. He has in consequence changed the translation of many lines of the play and altered numerous paragraphs in the Introduction and the Notes — to their betterment, he hopes, in respect of accuracy and clarification, perhaps also in respect of poetic sensitivity and expression. The translator claims responsibility for all the faults of this revision of his former translation, but he must assure his readers that the merits of this new version are largely due to Ernst Beutler, one of the most competent Goethe scholars of the present time, and to Hans Jaeger and Samuel B. Bossard who have given him most generously of their time and acumen. He also acknowledges gratefully his renewed indebtedness to Morris W. Croll and Denver Lindley and a new obligation to Bayard Q. Morgan and Herman Salinger.

GEORGE M. PRIEST

PRINCETON, NEW JERSEY,
September 29, 1941.

Contents

CONTENTS

Introduction

FAUST IN FACT AND FICTION

DR. GEORG, later called Johannes, Faust, a famous practitioner of the black arts, was born about 1480, possibly in Knittlingen, a village in Württemberg, possibly in Helmstedt, a hamlet near Heidelberg. After he had acquired what seems to have been the education of a learnèd man of that time, Faust led a highly irregular life, appearing as a philosopher, astrologer, prophet, or physician, as seemed at the moment most advantageous, in Würzburg, Kreuznach, Erfurt, Heidelberg, and numerous other places. Several towns, Nuremberg and Ingolstadt among others, ejected him. The last historical information about Faust was set down in a letter written in America in 1540 and saying that the "philosopher" Faust had correctly foretold the writer that 1540 would be a bad year for him. Meanwhile, between 1536 and 1539, Faust had died at Staufen in Baden a sudden, if not violent death.

This historical Faust boasted mightily if he did not deliberately swindle his fellow-men. He claimed that if the works of Plato and Aristotle were lost, he could restore them out of his own inner consciousness. Christ's miracles were not astonishing, he said, because he could perform them as often as he liked. He boasted also that all the victories of the German Empire's troops in Italy in 1525-7 had been won by him and his arts. It was widely told and believed that he had accomplished many extraordinary feats of magic. It was said, for example, that when lecturing on Homer to students in Erfurt, he produced Homeric heroes in the flesh, and another story related how he conjured up the illusion of grape-laden vineyards. Men believed that he was indeed "the lucky one," as the name Faust or Faustus means.

Besides the feats always associated with the name of Faust, numerous works of magic originally ascribed to Simon Magus, Albertus Magnus, Paracelsus, and others of similar repute were later attributed to Faust. Thus Faust's reputation grew and spread and in that credulous age leading men of the time, Melanchthon for example, believed in the reality of Faust's powers. Melanchthon, who is said to have known Faust personally, tells in a sermon that Faust once swallowed another magician in Vienna and that after a few days the magician's body was found in a cave.

When these powers were explained as having been conferred

through a compact which Faust had made with the Devil, belief in Faust became crystallized. For all men then believed that the Devil sometimes appeared on earth in person. Luther believed that he did, whether or not Luther once threw his ink-well at the Devil. Melanchthon mentions as a fact that the Devil accompanied Faust in the form of a dog.

After Faust's death men could easily credit the report that the Devil had come for Faust and snatched him away in fire and smoke. For many years this and other exciting stories about Faust must have passed from mouth to mouth, and it was inevitable that soon or late the Faust legend would find a way into print.

The first known printed account of Faust's life and deeds is contained in the anonymous chap-book, *Historia von Dr. Johann Fausten,* which Johann Spies published in 1587 at Frankfort-on-the-Main. It ascribes many different tricks of magic to Faust and includes extracts from popular text-books on natural sciences, moral treatises, and the like, thoroughly Lutheran in its point of view. According to it, Faust acquired the degree of doctor of theology at Wittenberg and then became a man of the world, doctor of medicine, astrologer, and mathematician. In the course of time he signed his soul away to the Devil, Mephistopheles, for the power to perform all sorts of wonders and for the sake of having a rich and varied life on earth. Thus devilish arts enabled Faust to evoke the shade of Helena (Helen of Troy). Later he was united with her, begetting a son, Justus Faustus. After the expiration of twenty-four years Faust bequeathed his possessions to his student servant, Wagner, and came to a horrible end. As a whole the Spies chap-book is a clumsy compilation, but it emphasizes Faust's thirst for knowledge, and his defection from God is compared with the rashness of the heaven-storming Titans of Greek mythology and with the arrogance of Lucifer.

New printings and pirated editions of Spies's publication spread the story of Faust with great rapidity. Revised and enlarged versions also appeared, adding an account of Faust's riding on a cask out of an unnamed wine-cellar in Leipsic and another of a time when Faust bored four holes in a table and caused four kinds of wine to flow out of them. By 1592 Spies had issued at least fourteen printings of his original text, and translations into Low German, English, Dutch, and French were already in circulation.

But the Spies Faust-book was crowded out of popularity by a new version of the story which Georg Rudolff Widman published in Hamburg in 1599. A stern, orthodox Lutheran, Widman was deeply interested in presenting Faust as a shocking example. He therefore told the story to suit his religious purposes, lengthening the chapters with many pious exhortations and admonitions. Widman showed little appreciation of Faust's daring spirit and he failed to hand down items that had interested the readers of the earlier chap-book. He relegated the evocation of Helena, for instance, to a footnote as of too unchaste a character for his readers. Widman was the first to tell that the Devil appeared to Faust from behind the stove in Faust's study and that Faust visited the court of Emperor Maximilian.

Widman's version of the Faust story maintained its standing as the best for the greater part of a century, but in 1674 it was superseded by the account which was written by Nikolaus Pfitzer, a Nuremberg physician. Pfitzer's work derives from that of Widman, but he was less orthodox than Widman, less interested in preaching, and more entertaining, even piquant. Pfitzer introduced the story of a sixteenth century Gretchen whom Faust vainly sought to seduce.

Pfitzer's Faust-book went through numerous editions, but in 1725 or earlier some person who called himself " a man of Christian sentiments " (Christlich Meynenden) published an abbreviated edition which became and remained the standard version. This chap-book was much more to the point. It was much better written than its predecessors and it maintained a critical, rationalistic point of view. It was sold all over Germany at all seasons of the year throughout the eighteenth century.

Of greater importance for the genesis of Goethe's *Faust* than the chap-books, however, were the independent literary treatments, especially the dramatic versions, of the Faust story. Only a year after the first appearance of the Spies Faust-book a dramatic version of the history of Faust was performed in London, and it is generally accepted that the English translation of the Spies Faust-book inspired Christopher Marlowe about 1588–9 to write and publish *The Tragical History of the Life and Death of Doctor Faustus,* a play that was performed twenty-three times in London within the years 1594 to 1597. Through Marlowe's *Faustus* or the English chap-book, or through both, the name and story of Faust became widely known in England, giving rise to a versified *History of Doctor John Faustus* (1664) and to various English farces in the seventeenth and eighteenth centuries, but none of these attracts anybody now except the literary historian. Nor can anything be said in praise of the English puppet-play. In England Marlowe's *Faustus* was and remained the first, last, and fairest fruit of the story of Faust.

Within a few years after the composition and production of Marlowe's *Faustus* in England, that is, near the end of the sixteenth century and down into the seventeenth, so-called "English Comedians" played numerous English dramas, various Shakespearean plays and almost certainly Marlowe's *Faustus,* in many German towns. It is less certain but highly probable that Marlowe's play furnished the substance and much of the form of the German folk-play which arose at an unknown date and which was produced all over Germany by strolling players until the second half of the eighteenth century. The content of the folk-play varied greatly in the course of time. The clown, Hans Wurst (Pickelhäring), was introduced to satisfy the crude taste of the time, and Faust's death became more and more boisterous and lurid. By the middle of the eighteenth century when superstition had largely given way before the assaults of rationalism, the folk-play did little more than appeal to popular fondness for the morbid and gruesome or for the fantastic and clownish. Meanwhile the story of Faust had been turned into a puppet-play which achieved great popularity among old and young. It is hardly conceivable that any German of the eighteenth century did not see either the folk-play or the puppet-play. Most Germans very probably saw both. The puppet-play has survived to the present day and may still be seen occasionally in German marionette theatres.

Many well-known modern German authors besides Goethe tried their hands on the Faust story. The earliest and most important of these was Lessing, who outlined a complete play in 1759 but executed only a few scenes. Like Goethe and in the spirit of the Age of Rationalism Lessing could not believe that man was born with a thirst for knowledge only to be damned for attempting to slake his thirst, and Lessing also planned that Faust should be saved. A Viennese, Paul Wiedmann, published his "allegorical" drama, *Johann Faust,* in 1775, and Friedrich (Maler) Müller his two fragmentary plays, *A Situation from the Life of Faust* and *Faust's Life,* in 1776 and 1778. Another contemporary of Goethe's, Maximilian Klinger, treated the story in the form of a novel, *Faust's Life, Deeds, and Journey to Hell* (1791). The nineteenth century witnessed the publication of numerous Faust dramas besides Friedrich Theodor Vischer's *Faust: The Third Part of the Tragedy* (1862), the best of several parodies of Goethe's work. Only a few of the later Faust dramas exhibit real literary merit: Christian Dietrich Grabbe's attempt to fuse Mozart and Goethe in one grandiose play, *Don Juan and Faust* (1829), Heinrich Heine's sketch for a ballet,

Doctor Faustus: A Dance Poem (1851), and, above all, Nikolaus Lenau's drama, *Faust* (1836).

The First Part of Goethe's *Faust* has been translated into English by some forty-four different translators, the Second Part also by as many as sixteen translators. The most satisfying of these translations are specified on p. 425.

After various scenes from the First Part of *Faust* had been performed in Breslau and Berlin between 1810 and 1828, the whole of the First Part was staged for the first time in Braunschweig in January, 1829; the whole of the Second Part in Hamburg in April, 1854; the whole of the two Parts in Weimar in May, 1876.

Of the various Faust operas those by Spohr (1814) and Busoni (1920) are based on the chap-book. Gounod's *Faust* (1859) derives from Goethe's play, but it gives the story of only a portion of the First Part and in Germany it is fittingly called *Faust and Margaret* or merely *Margaret*. Boïto's *Mefistofele* (1868) comprises in a very condensed form the essence of the whole of Goethe's *Faust*. Other music inspired by Goethe's work includes a choral composition by Schumann entitled *Scenes from Goethe's Faust,* symphonies by Berlioz and Liszt, and the *Faust Overture* by Wagner, besides incidental music by almost every composer of renown since the time of Goethe.

The most famous representation of the historical Faust in art is the etching by Rembrandt. Goethe's *Faust* has been illustrated with varying success by Cornelius, Retzsch, Delacroix, Nehrlich, Slevogt, and many others.

AN OUTLINE AND INTERPRETATION
OF GOETHE'S "FAUST"

THE DRAMATIC action of Goethe's *Faust* begins with the "Prologue in Heaven." The Archangel Raphael praises the harmony of the universe and the glory of the ever-active, ever-vivifying sun, the symbol of eternal, heavenly light, and the archangels Gabriel and Michael give voice to their contemplation of the earth, the fitting home of man in its alternation of light and darkness, in its restless tides and raging storms. The three archangels join together in praising the Lord God's "lofty works" that still are "sublime as on the first of days."

Mephistopheles, a Prince of Darkness, now steps forth as one of the Lord's "retinue." Mephistopheles knows that the Lord has drawn near to "ask how all is getting on," and although the Devil realizes that he can not make "fine speeches" such as those of the archangels, he is ready to tell the Lord about the "downright bad" condition of everything on earth. He finds "earth's little god" as "singular as on the first of days"; man is indeed so pitiable that the Devil himself is "reluctant to torment him."

The case becomes concrete. The Lord tacitly acknowledges that some men may be as Mephistopheles has described men in general, but He asks: "Do you know Faust, my servant?" That is, Faust is a special case, not a typical man but a capable man of good intent who serves God "confusedly" but shows withal assuring signs of life and activity. Yes, Mephistopheles knows Faust and proves it in saying: "He asks of heaven every fairest star and of the earth each highest zest." Nothing can satisfy Faust because he is striving after the unattainable. To Mephistopheles Faust seems singularly vulnerable to devilish temptations. Mephistopheles believes confidently that Faust will finally despair of realizing his aspirations and that he then will gladly turn to a life of sensual pleasure; the Devil prophesies: "Dust shall he eat, and that with zest." Mephistopheles therefore offers to bet with the Lord that he can win Faust away from His service. The Lord enters into no wager with Mephistopheles. In His omniscience He foreknows of course how Faust will live and die and He knows that He can rely on the Heaven-sent aspiration in the soul of Faust; but He does grant Mephistopheles permission to lead Faust downward if Mephistopheles can lay hold upon him. "Man errs as long as he doth strive," says the Lord; in striving man shows at least that he is active and has a goal in view, and the Lord adds: " A good man, though his striving be obscure, remains aware that there is one right way."

The " Prologue in Heaven " thus lays bare the problem of the play. We are to witness a struggle between the forces of light and those of darkness, between the positive and the negative, between the affirmation and the negation of the boon of life on earth. *Faust* is of necessity a " tragedy," for Faust fights a losing fight as all men do who strive to break the bonds of humankind, to attain the unattainable and to know the unknowable. But Faust will be saved because with all his errings he returns again and again to his striving to find and remain on the " one right way."

The vast spaciousness of Heaven gives way to a narrow, cluttered, disharmonious room, a perfect environment for Faust, the man who is occupying the room. He too is restless and out of harmony with himself and with living. He has not been satisfied by all the learning he has acquired and he possesses none of the honours and splendours of the world. For these reasons he has turned to magic arts. Through them he has hoped, though in vain, to satisfy his longing to perceive " whatever holds the world together in its inmost folds."

Shifting restlessly from mood to mood, Faust opens a book of magic and sees the sign of the Macrocosm, the symbol of the universe. Thrilled by the sight of the perfect harmony of the cosmos, he exclaims: " Ah, what rapture at the sight of this! Am I a god? In these pure lineaments I see creative Nature's self before my soul appear." Faust thus attains to a lofty view of the Eternal Mind and Will but such a cosmic world is sufficient unto itself and too vast for Faust. He can not enter into it and play a part in it. He can only contemplate it, and so the symbol of the Macrocosm soon suggests to him only " pageantry, mere pageantry." Feeling himself as much an outcast as ever, he has learned only one thing: man's incapacity.

And he learns little more when he turns another page of the magic book and sees the sign of the Earth-Spirit. He hails this spirit: " Thou, Spirit of the Earth, I feel, art nigher." In its presence he who has invoked the Spirit, feels himself to be a superman. But the all-permeating, ever-creating Spirit of the Earth reveals Faust's complete lack of comprehension of the motive spirit and of the meaning or purpose of life on earth. Again Faust realizes his own insignificance and that he is a very tiny part of a great gigantic whole. The Earth-Spirit vanishes, Faust collapses in despair.

The despair in which the Earth-Spirit leaves Faust is broken by the entrance of Faust's student servant, Wagner, whose Philistine worship of learning and utter satisfaction with pedantry and the pedant's complacent attitude towards life stand out in sharp contrast with Faust's state of mind. Faust can not resign himself to the world as he has found it. He has found nothing within himself to satisfy him, learning and knowledge have failed him, magic has failed him — what is there for him but despair and suicide? Suicide may open the door to a new, more understanding life. Though it may lead to nothingness, Faust decides upon suicide in the hope that he may thus escape from an intolerable existence on earth into "other spheres of pure activity."

Nevertheless Faust can not strip off "the son of earth." As he puts the death potion to his lips, the Easter hymns from a nearby church proclaim the resurrection of Christ, reminding Faust of the celebration of spring and the new life that spring foretells. Perhaps, he thinks, he can find a new life on this earth after all. He puts the potion aside. The earth has him again.

In this "earthly" mood Faust takes a walk with Wagner on the following day, Easter Sunday afternoon. The people he meets are not of Faust's kind, they know no striving beyond the things of this earth; they are contented in their limited spheres, undisturbed by the problems of how and why men should live. Nevertheless Faust shares their joy in nature as he once was thrilled by the glamour of moonlight; here he is no longer a superman, he is a very human person. But the people praise Faust more than he thinks he deserves. "The crowd's applause now sounds like scorn to me," he says, and conscious of his shortcomings he slips back into his former pessimism; he reverts to the conflicts and disharmonies within him. He does not like to be pessimistic, but he sees night and darkness coming on and he longs for the wings of a bird that he may follow the light of the sun on and on, "eternal brightness drinking." Wagner does not understand such an aspiration and hence Faust proceeds to lay bare the two souls within his breast, the one cleaving to the things of earth, the other aspiring to its supersensual origins but to which it can never attain as long as it continues to dwell in human flesh. Faust is ready to accept any aid which will bear him away to a new life, whether it be the aid of spirits or that of a magic mantle.

Faust's state of mind is now amply presented. In Faust's own recognition of his twofold nature we see that he is aware of his own "confusion," and the ideal time for Mephistopheles to enter his life has come. Faust suspects that an evil spirit is lurking in the poodle that comes leaping about him and his companion, but Wagner dissuades

[xvi]

him from his fears and Faust takes the poodle (Mephistopheles) home with him. The Devil thus enters Faust's life in the form of a poodle in accordance with the Faust-book tradition.

Again in his study, Faust appears far more calm; "the love of all mankind, the love of God are stirred anew" in him. The thoughtful professor feels reason and hope blooming once more and so he turns to a professorial occupation, the study and translation of the Gospel of John. There he finds: "In the beginning was the Word," that is, the ark of the world or the world principle, but to Faust who has longed "to cease word-threshing," "Word" is not enough. The Apostle must have meant the "Thought" or "Meaning" behind the "Word" as the guiding principle of all things. But "Thought" in turn does not satisfy Faust either; "Is it then Thought that works, creative, hour by hour?" he asks. "Thought" can lead only to inactive contemplation which is inadequate, as Faust learned from gazing at the Macrocosm. Faust therefore proceeds to his own free interpretation of the text and says not "It is written" but "It should stand: 'In the beginning was the Power!'" But "Power" too does not suffice unless it be used and produce something. Hence Faust formulates a world principle which springs directly out of his own personality and writes "assured: 'In the beginning was the Deed.'" This conclusion embodies the very core of Faust, of the man who turned from the contemplation of the Macrocosm, who derided Wagner's contentment with mere perception, who resolved upon suicide as an avenue of escape to "other spheres of pure activity," who soon will abjure "a bed of sloth," who toward the end of his life will say: "The Deed is everything."

From the beginning of this scene the poodle has growled whenever Faust has mentioned God. When Faust arrives at "Deed" as the supreme life principle, thus revealing himself as "aware that there is one right way," Mephistopheles realizes that the time has come for him to step into action and he issues from the poodle. Faust, at this time in a calm state of mind, is "not afraid of devil or hell" and he maintains such coolness in the presence of Mephistopheles (whom he recognizes at once as a spirit from Hell) that Mephistopheles has to adjust himself to the situation. A stirring, highly dramatic dialogue ensues in which Mephistopheles discloses himself much more clearly than he has yet appeared. Just as Faust has been dealing with the beginning of things, Mephistopheles tells of his own beginning and what for him is the world principle. He is "part of the Power which would the Evil ever do, and ever does the Good," "the Spirit that denies," a "spirit of negation," as the Lord has already described him, or the spirit of destruction which is evil in the eyes of Faust and men in general, but good in the eyes of Mephistopheles. Mephistopheles declares himself with startling frankness to be a confirmed nihilist, a demonic power, bent upon the destruction of all things. Faust as a "servant" of God takes the side of creative might. The debate comes to a standstill. Seeing that Faust is too calm and serene in his present mood for the Devil to get at him, Mephistopheles begs permission to go away. When Faust demurs, Mephistopheles resorts to a trick which will enable him to leave and which at the same time, he hopes, will lead Faust downward on the Devil's way. He summons spirits who conjure up before Faust's dreaming eyes a vision of sensual pleasure and while Faust dreams on about enrapturing forms and flowing wine and Isles of the Blest, Mephistopheles vanishes.

When Mephistopheles revisits Faust, he finds him far more amenable. Faust, the calm observer, has disappeared; he has given way once more to the Faust who despairs of earthly existence with all its limitations and its "never-ending song": "Thou shalt renounce! Renounce shalt thou!" Faust feels his unsatisfied struggling as something divine and compelling but he can not convert it into tangible accomplishment against the hindering forces of his environment. "So," he exclaims, "Being like a load on me is pressed, I long for death, existence I detest." Faust curses all that seems to most men to make life desirable. He denies or negates the world with Mephistophelian fury and hence, in spite of the song of spirits who admonish Faust to build up a new life within himself, Mephistopheles finds Faust in exactly the proper mood to enter into an agreement with the Devil.

Mephistopheles suggests first the compact of the Faust chap-book, that he be Faust's slave in this world and Faust be his in the world beyond, but Faust rejects this offer flatly. He is not interested in the other world that Mephistopheles has in mind; he has surrendered the thought of suicide and the impulse to seek "other spheres of pure activity." Faust doubts profoundly that there is any sense in an earthly life that does not have personal enjoyment as its goal, and yet Faust knows that this very enjoyment is senseless because its highest ecstasy does not offer real satisfaction. But Faust remains interested in the problem of living on this earth. Only when Mephistopheles suggests that they soon can feast in "peace" is Faust stirred to contradict him and to offer him a wager. Irritated by the word "peace" in perfect accordance with his nature, Faust makes the conditions of the wager unmistakably clear: "If ever I lay me on a bed of sloth in peace, that instant let for me existence cease! If ever with lying flattery you can rule me, so that contented with myself I stay, if with enjoyment you can fool me, be that for me the final day! "

The balance of the play therefore revolves around certain questions: will Mephistopheles "fool" Faust with "enjoyment" which Faust suggests as a possibility? will Faust lay himself "on a bed of sloth" as Mephistopheles expects? will Faust's "activity languish" as the Lord knows it will not? will Faust "eat dust, and that with zest," as Mephistopheles has confidently asserted? In view of Faust's character as the play has revealed it, the future answer to each of these questions would seem to be certainly "No." But Faust goes still farther.

Faust has cursed the world and all that seems to make life worth living. He does not believe that any experience in life deserves to endure, and he adds: "If to the moment I shall ever say: 'Ah, linger on, thou art so fair!' then may you fetters on me lay, then will I perish, then and there!" Faust thus makes a wager that has two facets: he must lose either if he "stagnates," that is, if he lays himself "on a bed of sloth," or if he ever finds life worth living. Mephistopheles must lose unless he can "fool" Faust with "enjoyment." The association of the two thus centres around a wager, not a compact. In no sense, never, does Faust agree to cede his soul to the Devil after a definite period of enjoyment as he does agree in the chap-book stories of his career.

Faust is now ready for whatever Mephistopheles may offer him. As before, he does not desire merely passive joys; he also seeks restless activity whether it involves pain or pleasure, and he seeks to know and to enjoy all that is a part of human experience. After he has experienced all this, he will be willing to die without any thought or care for what may happen to him beyond this life. Mephistopheles is aghast at the range of Faust's desires, but he assures Faust of his readiness to serve him and he promises to show him " the little world and then the great."

The following dialogue between Mephistopheles and a student in which Mephistopheles discusses branches of learning may have been included in the drama to suggest what Faust was like in his younger years, perhaps to scourge the obscurantism of university faculties in Faust's and Goethe's student days, but in the story of the life of Faust the scene is nothing more than an amusing interlude.

The scene in Auerbach's Cellar has slightly greater value. Faust is obviously bored by the bibulous students and he remains a passive spectator throughout. Even Mephistopheles could hardly have expected that sensual pleasure of this kind would tempt Faust seriously. Indeed, this experience can scarcely be called a temptation at all, however great the merits of the scene as a *genre* picture. It does present, however, how easily Mephistopheles dominates a scene in which he appears.

Having failed to tempt and win Faust in Auerbach's Cellar, Mephistopheles decides to lose no more time but to proceed at once to the temptation that involves the strongest of all sensual passions, man's sexual love for woman. He thinks, however, that the sensual desires of Faust's young manhood should first be restored, and he therefore takes him to the Witch's Kitchen to work the charm by means of a magic potion. There Faust's passion is aroused when he sees in a magic mirror the recumbent form of a woman beautiful as a Titian or Giorgione Venus. It would be strange indeed if such a vision could not stir the sexual nature of a man who has manifested such uncontrolled, such passionate desires as Faust has expressed. Here too Faust remains Faust. The potion is not needed for Faust's passion, but his physical appearance must be rejuvenated. He must appear of an age suitable to win the love and adoration of a girl of Gretchen's age. Hence the hocus-pocus continues, Faust drinks the magic potion which transforms him completely externally, and he is ready to "see a Helena in every girl" he meets.

Faust sees Gretchen first as she is returning home from church, from an act of religious devotion that is characteristic of Gretchen throughout our knowledge of her. As soon as Faust sees her, he reveals the strength of his sexual nature in demanding that Mephistopheles procure Gretchen for him without delay, but when Faust stands in Gretchen's own "neat little room," surveying a scene of childlike purity, his better nature asserts itself. "Away," he says, "I'll never come back here again." Mephistopheles, not Faust, leaves a casket of jewels for Gretchen. But Gretchen shows the jewels to her mother and the mother gives the "unrighteous" goods to the Church. Another jewel-casket must be smuggled into Gretchen's room, and she is showing them to her neighbour, Martha, resolving to keep them without the knowledge of her mother when Mephistopheles appears in order to ingratiate himself and Faust into the good graces of Martha and Gretchen. He suggests that he bring Faust to confirm his fictitious report of the death of Martha's vagabond husband. Faust objects to bearing false witness, but his desire to see and know Gretchen has grown so strong that Mephistopheles persuades him to lie. Faust and Gretchen meet in Martha's garden and their love for each other develops. Faust declares it and then Gretchen.

Faust soon realizes that his passion and desire for Gretchen are getting the better of him and, as he has done in his earlier life, he goes off alone into nature to regain his control of himself, and as he gazes upon nature, he seems to gain the object for which he came out. But his thoughts revert to the companion who is goading him on to the consummation of his love for Gretchen. When Mephistopheles appears and pictures Gretchen in her loneliness and longing, Faust's desire overwhelms him and he resolves to give up the struggle and to return to her.

Meanwhile Gretchen has been sitting alone, dreaming only of Faust, longing for his return, longing for a perfect love life. Two souls are not dwelling in Gretchen's breast. But her soul includes her simple religious belief and her faith in Mother Church. She must ask Faust if they are one in religious belief as well as in love. Faust can not give her an answer that will satisfy her. He is deeply religious, so deeply that he can not express his belief in time-worn, stereotyped phrases, and yet he will not offend Gretchen nor disturb her belief. He evades the issue. Gretchen feels that her religion is not Faust's, and in that she is right. She is also right in her feeling of horror and loathing toward Mephistopheles, but she casts her aversion aside and turns to talk with Faust of their love for each other. Feeling that she is only yielding to a normal, God-given impulse, she grants without real hesitation Faust's plea for " one calm, little hour " upon her bosom. It is Faust who " falls," not Gretchen.

After her surrender to Faust Gretchen is at first benumbed. She knows that she has offended a convention of society, but she is not conscious of any guilt. She does not feel that she has sinned in doing what nature led her to do; she has only followed an impulse of love. Nor in her prayer to the Mater Dolorosa does she express any real consciousness of guilt; she expresses only her terror of the shame that society will visit upon her. That shame her brother makes her see with crushing effect.

Meanwhile Faust sinks to lower depths. In front of Gretchen's house he flippantly thinks of more jewels for his love, he listens without apparent offence to a " moral " song which Mephistopheles sings as a serenade to Gretchen, and finally he kills Gretchen's brother in cowardly fashion and flees.

Gretchen's collapse is at hand. Gretchen who had not felt that she was sinning, seeks refuge from her haunting fears in the churchly worship her faith prescribes. But there all the more she feels herself responsible for the death of her mother and for the death of her brother. The Evil Spirit voices her condemnation of herself as well as her world's condemnation of her, and the merciless chant of the Judgment Day, breathing not a breath of Christian love, leaves her no hope of the world beyond. To Gretchen her fate is sealed.

Planning to draw him down still lower, Mephistopheles takes Faust to a gathering of witches high up on the Brocken (cf. note to "Walpurgis Night," p. 371 f.), to a scene of excesses which may appeal to Faust's reckless character. At first they pass through the beauties of night in the spring-time, beauties which appeal even to Mephistopheles, but the approach of the witches soon becomes audible, and the beauties of nature are forgotten or blotted out. For a time the crowding and pressing of the witches leave no time or place for calm reflection. Faust's thirst for knowing things awakens, he wants to be at the top of the Brocken, but Mephistopheles diverts him and, just as he tempted Faust away from his contemplation of nature by reminding him of Gretchen, he calls his attention now to the sight of witches nearby. Faust fears that he is going to lose himself altogether: " If I'm not to forget myself, I must watch out! " Nevertheless he follows Mephistopheles's suggestion and proceeds to dance with a young witch while Mephistopheles is dancing with an old one.

The climax of the incident is reached. The remembrance of Gretchen suddenly stirs in Faust as a vision of her rises before him in which she " seems to move with shackled feet." Faust gazes at the vision with increasing conviction that it really is Gretchen, that Gretchen is in prison, and Mephistopheles can not banish the idea from his mind. Mephistopheles has not triumphed. Faust's better nature has asserted itself again. Faust has allowed his sexual passion to entangle him and he has incurred great guilt, but he has not become a slave of his passion. His remembrance of Gretchen has saved him, in a sense a foreshadowing of the end of the play, for even now " the Eternal-Womanly " (love in its purest, most selfless earthly manifestation) is drawing Faust above his baser self. Mephistopheles's failure to capture Faust through his sexual nature is a turning-point of the play. Never again is Faust so ensnared by machinations of the Devil.

The balance of the First Part concludes Faust's experience with Gretchen. Mephistopheles can not restrain Faust from returning swiftly to save Gretchen if he can, but he can not, for she will not let him. However mad she seems at times, she knows that she has killed her child and she is determined that she *will* not be saved; she will atone. When she sees Faust's hated companion again, she shrinks away even from Faust who has given himself to the Devil, as it seems to her, whereas she will give herself over to the judgment of God.

Faust has done what he could and he has acted finally not as a sensual lover but as a man. Gretchen's tragedy has become a tragedy for Faust. " Can I survive this misery? " he groans and at the culmination of the scene he exclaims: " Oh, had I never been born! " Faust thus expresses his remorse and anguish consummately in cursing his very existence.

When the Second Part of the play begins, Faust is seen to be lying in the midst of a dimly lighted Alpine scene, " weary " from the turmoil of his recent life, " restless " from the pangs of conscience. Kindly elves hover about him to erase the memory of the past, not to blot out Faust's guilt but to enable him, through consciousness of guilt and suffering in the past, to regain new, atoning zest for life and to be ready for further experiences. When Faust awakens, he is " refreshed anew," his " pulses beat and waken," and he feels within him a vigorous resolve to strive unceasingly toward a supreme existence; but he has conquered the sexual element within him and he has turned his back forever upon all attempts to solve the metaphysical (cf. note to 4679–4727). Faust is renouncing more and more, but meanwhile he is ready for a new experience.

In the First Part of the drama Faust saw the " little world," himself playing the leading role in it. It was a world with Faust as its centre, the world of the subjective, self-centred Faust, a world in which for Faust love was the primal element. In the " great world " which Mephistopheles is now to show him, Faust has overcome his subjectivity. He is only a part of a far larger world in which he is to learn to know Beauty and Power.

With his former promise of the " great world " in mind, Mephistopheles takes Faust to the Emperor's court where he may weary and break Faust's striving spirit with the " shallow stuff " that is to be found there. But Mephistopheles must first gain a footing in the court for himself and when this has been accomplished, he introduces Faust in the guise of Plutus at a masquerade. Various figures appear at first, allegorical and satirical figures which have little or nothing to do with the story of Faust. Then Faust enters, the God of Wealth, attended by Poetry and by Stinginess (Mephistopheles), and displays before the Emperor (who appears in the guise of Pan) a magic chest of molten gold. Fascinated by the sight of much-needed gold, the Emperor is induced to lend his signature for the issuance of paper money based on treasure which Mephistopheles has assured him is lying buried in the ground. Thus, as we learn in the following scene, Faust wins as a wonder-worker a foremost place in the Emperor's favour and court, and ascribing this reputation to him, the Emperor can properly request Faust to show him the most beautiful male and female figures that fact or story has ever known, the images of Paris and Helena. When Faust seeks the aid of Mephistopheles in gratifying the wishes of the Emperor, Mephistopheles acknowledges that he can not evoke the images desired: "The heathen-folk do not concern me. They occupy a hell that's all their own." He can only reveal to Faust the way to their abiding-place, the realm of the "Mothers" (cf. note to "A Dark Gallery," p. 385 f.). Mephistopheles tries in vain to deter Faust from proceeding on the errand, fearing that he will lose all control of Faust. In other words, Mephistopheles is no longer the active, controlling agent that he was in the First Part of the play; he is falling more and more into the background. Faust is becoming more and more independent.

Faust secures the means of evoking phantom forms, and in the presence of the court he practises with conscious zest the creative power which he has discovered within himself. He evokes a scene of classical beauty in which the images of Paris and Helena appear. With the appearance of Helena a turning-point of prime importance in Faust's life is reached. To Faust the image of Helena is not a vision such as that in the Witch's Kitchen which stirred his physical senses but a vision of restrained, ideal beauty. To Faust, long since purified of physical passion by the horrors of his experience with Gretchen, Helena is now the one thing to be desired. Still the old, eager, reckless Faust, he can not merely observe beauty, he must possess it. He attempts to seize the phantom but it vanishes and he falls into a swoon. Mephistopheles's plan to ensnare Faust with pleasure at the Emperor's court has worse than merely failed. Faust has not only not shown any liking for court life; he has taken the first step on his way to Helena, to an ideal that lies far outside the realm of Mephistopheles, a goal for which Mephistopheles can have no understanding and not even an avenue of approach and which must lead Faust farther and farther away from him.

Mephistopheles knows that the vision of Helena has "paralyzed" Faust, but the Christian Devil is not at home in the world of the ancients and he does not know anything better to do with Faust than to take him back to his old study. Here various incidents occur but none in which Faust, who is still in his swoon, is an actor. Mephistopheles holds another conversation with the student of the First Part, now an arrogant, know-it-all young Bachelor of Arts, and Mephistopheles helps Wagner vitally in creating a spiritual creature whom Mephistopheles needs. This creature, Homunculus, is a spark of life which is without corporeal form but which is endowed with vast knowledge and extraordinary perception. He can help Mephistopheles greatly by reding Faust's mind and spirit (cf. note to " Laboratory," p. 389 f.). Homunculus sees at once that Faust is dreaming of Helena and that he can recover from his swoon only on Helena's native soil. The three — Homunculus attended by Mephistopheles and Faust wrapped in Mephistopheles's magic mantle — start off for Greece.

They arrive in Greece just as the spirits of Greek history and mythology are gathering to celebrate the Classical Walpurgis Night (cf. note p. 391 f.), a scene made glamorous by the gentle light of the moon. Homunculus goes off in search of the best way in which to acquire corporeal existence. Mephistopheles seeks congenial adventures in dallying with the fantastic and grotesque figures of classical antiquity. Fascinated by the sight of the Phorkyads, images of the supremely ugly, he prevails upon them to lend him one of their forms for a time. Thus Mephistopheles becomes, as it were, a part of the antique, classical world and may appear in the following act in contrast with the supreme beauty of Helena and as an integral part of the action of the play.

As soon as his feet touch the soil of Greece, Faust awakens to full consciousness. " Where is she? " he asks, and with restless energy, unaided by Mephistopheles, he starts on a search for Helena. He is still not prepared for a union with her; he must first traverse the ascending scale of the life of classical times from the lowest, most repulsive forms up to perfect beauty. Through diligent, persistent inquiry, still true to basic elements in his native character, Faust finally comes to the seeress Manto who consents to conduct him to the throne of Persephone where he may obtain permission to bring the shade of Helena to earth. Through trial and testing Faust's conception of beauty is clarified and his spirit ennobled for the union with Helena (cf. note to the " Classical Walpurgis Night," p. 391 f.).

Helena appears with a group of captive Trojan women before the palace of Menelaus at Sparta. She thinks that she has just returned from the siege of Troy, but she does not know the whole intent of Menelaus when he bade her precede him to his palace to prepare for a sacrifice. Her supreme beauty is scarcely extolled by her women before Mephistopheles, in the guise of supreme ugliness, appears on the threshold of the palace and warns her that Menelaus intends to sacrifice her and her women and that she can be saved only by a nearby lord, Faust. Helena can not dispute these assertions, and she and her women are transported to Faust's castle where Helena is united to Faust. Faust has reached the new goal toward which he has been striving. Helena has become a reality to him, and in the happiness which Faust now enjoys, we may expect him to bid the moment: " Ah, linger on, thou art so fair! " But a fateful son, Euphorion, is born to Faust and Helena, a child of his mother in beauty, a son of his father in his boundless aspiration and in his impulse to activity. Euphorion attempts to fly to the aid of others, displaying a spirit of altruism which his father, Faust, displayed when a young man (cf. lines 1001 ff.), but Euphorion is " a genius without wings." He falls dead, calling to his mother to return to the spirit world.

Faust now realizes that the inactive enjoyment of beauty could be only a transitory episode in the course of his experience. In this realization Faust again wins a victory through the insight and strength of his own nature, just as his own nature rescued him from the sensual in his experience with Gretchen. Idle enjoyment could again not satisfy him. He renounces the enjoyment of beauty as a goal in life. Nevertheless the union with Helena has wrought a great change in Faust. He has been imbued with a new sense of the beauty of form; he has learned the benefits of restraint and control; and a will to dominate has been aroused in him from his association with a beauty that dominated all who came under its spell. Thus newly equipped and with a reinvigorated impulse to activity Faust turns to seek a new goal. Still the old Faust and yet a new Faust, still an imperfect man and prone to err, Faust turns to seek an undertaking which will offer free play to all the powers and potentialities that he now feels within himself. He seeks it and he will find it, not in some world-embracing sphere of action but in the long-familiar, restricted environment of his native land.

On his flight back to his native soil Faust has had a vision of a great work that he might accomplish. He has observed the restlessness of the tides, the fruitless beating of the waves upon the shore, and he has conceived a triumph over one of nature's greatest forces in thrusting the sea back from the shore. This is the ambitious, daring Faust again, who would conquer nature. Activity, achievement, is Faust's only goal. " The Deed is everything." Thus Faust again takes the initiative, and in aiding Faust to reach his goal Mephistopheles can be nothing more than a servant; at most he can only enable Faust to attain his objective the sooner. But Mephistopheles assumes his task cheerfully, as he hopes to satisfy Faust with mere domination. Under the infatuation of paper money the Empire has gone from bad to worse, a rival Emperor has arisen, and Mephistopheles suggests that he and Faust rescue the legitimate Emperor from his enemies. To this Faust agrees, as he may draw profit from having lent aid. The decisive battle is won, and the Emperor grants to Faust a long stretch of barren seashore.

Faust proceeds at once to carry out his great scheme and when we see him again, years of successful accomplishment lie behind him. Where once stretched only barren seashore, fertile fields are now to be seen, protected by dunes and dikes erected at Faust's command. Faust rules over a large territory as he desired when he said: "Lordship, possession, are my aim and thought." But Faust is still unsatisfied. Just as he longed for knowledge and love and beauty in the past and was never satisfied, so now he craves the possession of all that he can see from his palace. He instructs Mephistopheles to remove an aged couple from their cottage (which impairs his view) to another place which he has reserved for them; then he will be lord of all he surveys. But Mephistopheles hopes to break Faust's spirit through sin and guilt and he brutally causes the death of the old people, though indirectly. Faust curses the act but he knows himself guilty, guilty through his striving after unbounded dominion and power.

The last turning-point in Faust's life follows immediately. Faust puts the thought of guilt out of his mind because, however great his fault, he can not be deterred from completing his great undertaking. But he has heard three grey spirit-women speak of "Death." He must take stock of his life. In calm meditation he realizes that he has not yet fought his way into freedom, that in his striving to be more than a mere man, he has employed supernatural means, first in evoking spirits, then in employing Mephistopheles as a guide and as a servant. He now longs to banish all magic from his path, above all, to stand "a man only" before Nature; "then were it worth the pain to be a man." Formerly he cursed life as having no worth; now with the renunciation of magic arts he confesses that life has worth and value. He curses his curse. As the Lord foretold, Faust is coming out "where all is clear."

But a grey figure, Worry, steals close to Faust, symbolizing fear that he may not complete his undertaking, that his activity may languish. Faust has known Worry in the past but since he has been experiencing life, he has "only flown through the world." He has dismissed Worry from his life. Now when he is an aged man, he can lose his physical sight but this can not affect Faust's will to activity. Blinded, he calls upon his men to "seize shovel and spade" so that what he has planned may happily be accomplished.

Mephistopheles reappears and, knowing that Faust's end is near, proceeds to order his minions to dig Faust's grave, while Faust undaunted renews his urging that his own undertaking be brought to completion. With this end in view the vision of his "highest, best achieving" rises before Faust. He sees his newly wrested, broad domain occupied by a people who will be ever active and alert to ward off the danger from without, earning thus as of their own free will their right to life and freedom. Renouncing now his craving for dominion, he sees himself as only a man among men, standing free and active among a free and active people. To the moment in which this vision might become reality Faust says that he might say: "Ah, linger on, thou art so fair!"

For Faust these words mean that he has reached a heroic height of renunciation, the hardest ascent that life ever presents to high-spirited, capable, ambitious men. Gone is Faust's reckless egoism. Gone are his longing and demand for all-embracing experience and self-expansion. Faust sees the possibility of the "bliss" of life in "a little span," and he welcomes it with open arms, renouncing with finality all that was once his goal in life. With this renunciation the egoist in Faust's character remains unchanged. In the life that he envisages, Faust would retain that characteristic that sets him off not as typical of men in general but typical only of those who are capable and of good intent: his impulse to constant, aspiring activity. Basically Faust would change only in directing this impulse with confident, enduring assurance. Faust is now not only aware that there is one right way; he is assured that he is on the one right way. He has come out "into the clear."

In the times that are past, activity implied to Faust a goal of subjective self-satisfaction. Now the goal of his activity has become objective; it has assumed a definitely communal, social, altruistic aspect. Faust's "love of man is stirred anew" and this time lastingly. Free activity in behalf of one's own self as well as in behalf of one's fellowmen has become Faust's motive force and this he sees as the motive force of all the people of his vision.

Faust's vision includes immediately only the domain which he has wrested from the sea, but it implies a far larger realm. It implies the beginning of a new world. In such a world the individual does not lose himself. He benefits himself but in so doing, he benefits also his fellowmen. And what is the good of all is also the good of the one. What Faust's vision implies is a world of perfected, far-seeing coöperation. In such a world men deserve the right to the boon and privilege of living.

As long as Faust was striving toward the goal of an ambitious egoist, he found no satisfying moment. To no moment could he say: "Ah, linger on, thou art so fair!" Now, as one of many free and active men, he knows that there can be such a moment. Foreseeing its coming, he speaks the fateful words and falls back dead. Faust has affirmed life; he has done what he thought he would never do. He sees that life can be worth living, that such a life as he foresees is worth living. Faust has lost his wager. He committed a fundamental mistake in negating life on earth, in denying its worth and its capacity to satisfy an aspiring, active man. He has found a solution of the problem of living.

Mephistopheles claims Faust's soul but he too has lost. Faust has never laid himself " on a bed of sloth "; he has never been fooled by enjoyment. He has found supreme happiness in constructive activity, the antithesis of Mephistopheles's aim for Faust and a goal for which Mephistopheles, the spirit of negation and destruction, has neither sympathy nor understanding.

The Lord was right. Faust erred indeed throughout his life, but he always remained aware that there was one right way.

At heart Mephistopheles, too, knows that the Lord was right, but he blusteringly attempts to prevent the ascension of Faust's soul to Heaven. Angels appear, renewing the struggle that Heaven and Hell, or the forces of light and darkness, wage for the spirit of man. The angels triumph, strewing rose leaves, symbols of heavenly love, and bear Faust's soul to Heaven.

With the victory of the angels over Mephistopheles the ascent begins, an ascent through regions where all is helpful activity inspired and permeated by " Almighty Love which fashions all and cherishes all." No other kind of after-life could satisfy Faust's ever-active spirit. No other after-life could Goethe imagine, he who saw all things in the process of ever-becoming, ever-developing.

Angels bearing Faust's immortal part sing as they soar aloft:

> Lo! rescued is this noble one
> From evil machination;
> " Who, ever aspiring, struggles on,
> For him there is salvation."
> And if to him Celestial Love
> Its favouring grace has given,
> The Blessèd Host comes from Above
> And welcomes him to Heaven.

In other words, Faust has ever aspired and ever struggled on, however confusedly and erring. Thus he has earned the right to a life beyond this one, and because love which is divine in origin has been manifest in his earthly life, he has also won a loving, welcoming reception from those who like Faust have lived on earth a life of aspiring endeavour. The purest, most selfless form of love that Faust has known on earth, the Eternal-Womanly now too in the world beyond draws Faust " on and on."

Faust

Dedication

Ye wavering forms draw near again as ever
When ye long since moved past my clouded eyes.
To hold you fast, shall I this time endeavour?
Still does my heart that strange illusion prize?
Ye crowd on me! 'Tis well! Your might assever
While ye from mist and murk around me rise.
As in my youth my heart again is bounding,
Thrilled by the magic breath your train surrounding.

Ye bring with you glad days and happy faces.
Ah, many dear, dear shades arise with you;
Like some old tale that Time but half erases,
First Love draws near to me and Friendship too.
The pain returns; the sad lament retraces
Life's labyrinthine, erring course anew
And names the good souls who, by Fortune cheated
Of lovely hours, forth from my world have fleeted.

They do not hear the melodies I'm singing,
The souls to whom my earliest lays I sang;
Dispersed that throng who once to me were clinging,
The echo's died away that one time rang.
Now midst an unknown crowd my grief is ringing,
Their very praise but gives my heart a pang,
While those who once my song enjoyed and flattered,
If still they live, roam through the wide world scattered.

And I am seized with long-unwonted yearning
Toward yonder realm of spirits grave and still.
My plaintive song's uncertain tones are turning
To harps aeolian murmuring at will.
Awe binds me fast; tear upon tear falls burning,
My stern heart feels a gentle, tender thrill;
What I possess, as if far off I'm seeing,
And what has vanished, now comes into being.

PRELUDE ON THE STAGE

MANAGER   DRAMATIC POET   JESTER

Manager.   Ye two that have so often stood by me
    In time of need and tribulation,
    Come, say: what hope in any German nation   35
    For what we undertake have ye?
    I much desire to give the crowd a pleasure,
    In chief, because they live and let us live.
    The posts, the boards are up, and here at leisure
    The crowd expects a feast in what we'll give.   40
    They're sitting now with eyebrows raised,
    Quite calmly there, would gladly be amazed.
    I know how one can make all minds akin,
    Yet so embarrassed I have never been.
    In truth, accustomed to the best they're not,   45
    But they have read a really awful lot.
    How shall we plan that all be fresh and new
    And with a meaning, yet attractive too?
    For I do like to see them crowding, urging,
    When toward our booth the stream sets in apace   50
    And with its powerful, repeated surging
    Pours through the strait and narrow gate of grace,
    When still in broad daylight, ere it is four,
    They fight and push their way up to the wicket
    And as the famine-stricken at the baker's door   55
    They nearly break their necks to get a ticket.
    This miracle, upon such varied folk, the poet
    Alone can work; today, my friend, oh, show it!
Poet.   I beg you, of that motley crowd cease telling
    At sight of whom the spirit takes to flight!   60
    Enveil from me the billowing mass compelling
    Us to its vortex with resistless might.

[5]

No, lead me to the tranquil, heavenly dwelling
Where only blooms for poets pure delight,
Where Love and Friendship give the heart their blessing, 65
With godlike hand creating and progressing.
       Ah, all that from the bosom's depths sprang flowing,
All that from shy and stammering lips has passed,
Sometimes success and sometimes failure knowing,
To each wild moment's power a prey is cast. 70
Oft only after years, in credit growing,
Doth it appear in perfect form at last.
What gleams is born but for the moment's pages;
The true remains, unlost to after-ages.

Jester.   Could I but hear no more of after-ages! 75
Suppose the thought of them *my* mind engages,
Who'd give the present world its fun?
That will it have and ought to have it too.
The presence of a gallant chap, revealed to you,
I think, is also worth while being shown. 80
Who pleasantly can just himself impart,
Is not embittered by the people's whim;
He likes to have a crowd surrounding him,
More certainly to stir and thrill each heart.
So do be good, show you can set the fashion. 85
Let Fantasy be heard with all her chorus:
Sense, Reason, Sentiment, and Passion;
Yet mark you well! bring Folly too before us!

Manager.   But, more than all, do let enough occur!
Men come to look, to see they most prefer. 90
If, as they gaze, much is reeled off and spun,
So that the startled crowd gapes all it can,
A multitude you will at once have won;
You then will be a much-loved man.
You can compel the mass by mass alone; 95
Each in the end will seek out something as his own.
Bring much and you'll bring this or that to everyone
And each will leave contented when the play is done.
If you will give a piece, give it at once in pieces!
Ragout like this your fame increases. 100
Easy it is to stage, as easy to invent.
What use is it, a whole to fashion and present?
The Public still will pick it all to pieces.

[6]

Poet.   You do not feel how bad such handiwork must be,
     How little that becomes the artist true!   105
     I see, neat gentlemanly botchery
     Is now a sovereign rule with you.
Manager.   Reproof like this leaves me quite unoffended!
     A man who does his work, effectively intended,
     Must stick to tools that are the best for it.   110
     Reflect! You have a tender wood to split;
     And those for whom you write, just see!
     If this one's driven hither by ennui,
     Another leaves a banquet sated with its vapours;
     And — what the very worst will always be —   115
     Many come fresh from reading magazines and papers.
     Men haste distraught to us as to the masquerade,
     And every step but winged by curiosity;
     The ladies give a treat, all in their best arrayed,
     And play their part without a fee.   120
     Why do you dream in lofty poet-land?
     Why does a full house make you gay?
     Observe the patrons near at hand!
     They are half cold, half coarse are they.
     One, when the play is over, hopes a game of cards;   125
     A wild night on a wench's breast another chooses.
     Why then, with such an aim, poor silly bards,
     Will you torment so much the gracious Muses?
     Give only more and ever, ever more, I say.
     Then from the goal you nevermore can stray.   130
     Seek to bewilder men — that is my view.
     But satisfy them? That is hard to do. —
     What is attacking you? Pain or delight?
Poet.   Go hence and seek yourself another slave!
     What! shall the poet take that highest right,   135
     The Right of Man, that Right which Nature gave,
     And wantonly for your sake trifle it away?
     How doth he over every heart hold sway?
     How doth he every element enslave?
     Is it not the harmony that from his breast doth start,   140
     Then winds the world in turn back in his heart?
     When Nature forces lengths of thread unending
     In careless whirling on the spindle round,
     When all Life's inharmonic throngs unblending

In sullen, harsh confusion sound,   145
Who parts the changeless series of creation,
That each, enlivened, moves in rhythmic time?
Who summons each to join the general ordination,
In consecrated, noble harmonies to chime?
Who bids the storm with raging passion lower?   150
The sunset with a solemn meaning glow?
Who scatters Springtime's every lovely flower
Along the pathway where his love may go?
Who twines the verdant leaves, unmeaning, slighted,
Into a wreath of honour, meed of every field?   155
Who makes Olympus sure, the gods united?
That power of Man the Poet has revealed!

Jester.   Then use these handsome powers as your aid
And carry on this poet trade
As one a love-adventure carries!   160
By chance one nears, one feels, one tarries!
And, bit by bit, one gets into a tangle.
Bliss grows, then comes a tiff, a wrangle;
One is enrapt, now one sees pain advance,
And ere one is aware, it is a real romance!   165
So let us also such a drama give!
Just seize upon the full life people live!
Each lives it though it's known to few,
And grasp it where you will, there's interest for you.
In motley pictures with a little clarity,   170
Much error and a spark of verity,
Thus can the best of drinks be brewed
To cheer and edify the multitude.
Youth's fairest bloom collects in expectation
Before your play and harks the revelation.   175
Then from your work each tender soul, intent,
Absorbs a melancholy nourishment.
Then now one thought and now another thought you start;
Each sees what he has carried in his heart.
As yet they are prepared for weeping and for laughter;   180
They still revere the flight, illusion they adore.
A mind once formed finds naught made right thereafter;
A growing mind will thank you evermore.

Poet.   Then give me back the time of growing
When I myself was growing too,   185

[8]

When crowding songs, a fountain flowing,
Gushed forth unceasing, ever new;
When still the mists my world were veiling,
The bud its miracle bespoke;
When I the thousand blossoms broke,   190
Profusely through the valleys trailing.
Naught, yet enough had I when but a youth,
Joy in illusion, yearning toward the truth.
Give impulse its unfettered dower,
The bliss so deep 'tis full of pain,   195
The strength of hate, Love's mighty power,
Oh, give me back my youth again!

Jester.   Youth, my good friend, you need most in the fight
When enemies come on, hard pressing,
When, clinging to your necks so tight,   200
The dearest maidens hang caressing,
When, from afar, a wreath entrances,
Luring to hard-won goal the runner's might,
When, after madly whirling dances,
A man carousing drinks away the night.   205
But on the lyre's familiar strings
To play with grace and spirit ever
And sweep with lovely wanderings
Toward goals you choose for your endeavour,
That is your duty, agèd sirs,   210
And we revere you for it no less dearly.
Age makes not childish, as one oft avers;
It finds us still true children merely.

Manager.   Words have been interchanged enough,
Let me at last see action too.   215
While compliments you're turning — idle stuff! —
Some useful thing might come to view.
Why talk of waiting for the mood?
No one who dallies, ever will it see.
If you pretend you're poets — good! —   220
Command then, poets, poetry!
What we're in need of, that full well you know,
We want to sip strong drink, so go
And start the brew without delay!
Never is done tomorrow what is not done today   225
And one should let no day slip by.

[9]

With resolution seize the possible straightway
By forelock and with quick, courageous trust;
Then holding fast you will not let it further fly
And you will labour on because you must. —   230
    Upon our German stage, you are aware,
Each tries out what he wishes to display,
So in your work for me today
Scenes, mechanism you are not to spare.
Use both the lights of heaven, great and small;   235
The stars above are yours to squander;
Nor water, fire, nor rocky wall,
Nor beasts nor birds are lacking yonder.
Thus in our narrow house of boards preside
And on through all Creation's circle stride;   240
And wander on, with speed considered well,
From Heaven, through the world, to Hell!

PROLOGUE IN HEAVEN

The LORD   The HEAVENLY HOSTS

Afterwards MEPHISTOPHELES

The three ARCHANGELS *come forward*

Raphael.   The Sun intones, in ancient tourney
  With brother-spheres, a rival song,
  Fulfilling its predestined journey,   245
  With march of thunder moves along.
  Its aspect gives the angels power,
  Though none can ever solve its ways;
  The lofty works beyond us tower,
  Sublime as on the first of days.   250
Gabriel.   And swift, beyond where knowledge ranges,
  Earth's splendour whirls in circling flight;
  A paradise of brightness changes
  To awful shuddering depths of night.
  The sea foams up, widespread and surging   255
  Against the rocks' deep-sunken base,
  And rock and sea sweep onward, merging
  In rushing spheres' eternal race.
Michael.   And rival tempests roar and shatter,
  From sea to land, from land to sea,   260
  And, raging, form a circling fetter
  Of deep, effective energy.
  There flames destruction, flashing, searing,
  Before the crashing thunder's way;
  Yet, Lord, Thy angels are revering   265
  The gentle progress of Thy day.
The Three.   Its aspect gives the angels power,
  Since none can solve Thee nor Thy ways;
  And all Thy works beyond us tower,
  Sublime as on the first of days.   270

Mephistopheles.   Since you, O Lord, once more draw near
     And ask how all is getting on, and you
     Were ever well content to see me here,
     You see me also midst your retinue.
     Forgive, fine speeches I can never make,   275
     Though all the circle look on me with scorn;
     Pathos from me would make your sides with laughter shake,
     Had you not laughter long ago forsworn.
     Of suns and worlds I've naught to say worth mention.
     How men torment them claims my whole attention.   280
     Earth's little god retains his same old stamp and ways
     And is as singular as on the first of days.
     A little better would he live, poor wight,
     Had you not given him that gleam of heavenly light.
     He calls it Reason, only to pollute   285
     Its use by being brutaler than any brute.
     It seems to me, if you'll allow, Your Grace,
     He's like a grasshopper, that long-legged race
     That's made to fly and flying spring
     And in the grass to sing the same old thing.   290
     If in the grass he always were reposing!
     But in each filthy heap he keeps on nosing.
The Lord.   You've nothing more to say to me?
     You come but to complain unendingly?
     Is never aught right to your mind?   295
Mephistopheles.   No, Lord! All is still downright bad, I find.
     Man in his wretched days makes me lament him;
     I am myself reluctant to torment him.
The Lord.   Do you know Faust?
Mephistopheles.   The Doctor?
The Lord.   Yes, my servant!
Mephistopheles.   He!
     Forsooth, he serves you most peculiarly.   300
     Unearthly are the fool's drink and his food;
     The ferment drives him forth afar.
     Though half aware of his insensate mood,
     He asks of heaven every fairest star
     And of the earth each highest zest,   305
     And all things near and all things far
     Can not appease his deeply troubled breast.
The Lord.   Although he serves me now confusedly,

I soon shall lead him forth where all is clear.
The gardener knows, when verdant grows the tree,   310
That bloom and fruit will deck the coming year.
Mephistopheles.   What will you wager? Him you yet shall lose,
If you will give me your permission
To lead him gently on the path I choose.
The Lord.   As long as on the earth he shall survive,   315
So long you'll meet no prohibition.
Man errs as long as he doth strive.
Mephistopheles.   My thanks for that, for with the dead I've never got
Myself entangled of my own volition.
I like full, fresh cheeks best of all the lot.   320
I'm not at home when corpses seek my house;
I feel about it as a cat does with a mouse.
The Lord.   'Tis well! So be it granted you today!
Divert this spirit from its primal source
And if you can lay hold on him, you may   325
Conduct him downward on your course,
And stand abashed when you are forced to say:
A good man, though his striving be obscure,
Remains aware that there is one right way.
Mephistopheles.   All right! But long it won't endure!   330
I have no fear about my bet, be sure!
When I attain my aim, do not protest,
But let me triumph with a swelling breast.
Dust shall he eat, and that with zest,
As did the famous snake, my near relation.   335
The Lord.   In that too you may play your part quite free;
Your kind I never did detest.
Of all the spirits of negation
The wag weighs least of all on me.
Mankind's activity can languish all too easily,   340
A man soon loves unhampered rest;
Hence, gladly I give him a comrade such as you,
Who stirs and works and must, as devil, do.
But ye, real sons of God, lift up your voice,
In living, profuse beauty to rejoice!   345
May that which grows, that lives and works forever,
Engird you with Love's gracious bonds, and aught
That ever may appear, to float and waver,
Make steadfast in enduring thought!

[13]

Heaven closes, the ARCHANGELS *disperse*

Mephistopheles alone.   I like to see the Old Man not infrequently,   350
    And I forbear to break with Him or be uncivil;
    It's very pretty in so great a Lord as He
    To talk so like a man even with the Devil.

First Part
OF THE TRAGEDY

Night

In a high-vaulted, narrow Gothic chamber F A U S T, *restless in his chair by his desk*

Faust.   I've studied now Philosophy
And Jurisprudence, Medicine,   355
And even, alas! Theology
All through and through with ardour keen!
Here now I stand, poor fool, and see
I'm just as wise as formerly.
Am called a Master, even Doctor too,   360
And now I've nearly ten years through
Pulled my students by their noses to and fro
And up and down, across, about,
And see there's nothing we can know!
That all but burns my heart right out.   365
True, I am more clever than all the vain creatures,
The Doctors and Masters, Writers and Preachers;
No doubts plague me, nor scruples as well.
I'm not afraid of devil or hell.
To offset that, all joy is rent from me.   370
I do not imagine I know aught that's right;
I do not imagine I could teach what might
Convert and improve humanity.
Nor have I gold or things of worth,
Or honours, splendours of the earth.   375
No dog could live thus any more!
So I have turned to magic lore,
To see if through the spirit's power and speech

[15]

Perchance full many a secret I may reach,
So that no more with bitter sweat   380
I need to talk of what I don't know yet,
So that I may perceive whatever holds
The world together in its inmost folds,
See all its seeds, its working power,
And cease word-threshing from this hour.   385
      Oh, that, full moon, thou didst but glow
Now for the last time on my woe,
Whom I beside this desk so oft
Have watched at midnight climb aloft.
Then over books and paper here   390
To me, sad friend, thou didst appear!
Ah! could I but on mountain height
Go onward in thy lovely light,
With spirits hover round mountain caves,
Weave over meadows thy twilight laves,   395
Discharged of all of Learning's fumes, anew
Bathe me to health in thy healing dew.
      Woe! am I stuck and forced to dwell
Still in this musty, cursèd cell?
Where even heaven's dear light strains   400
But dimly through the painted panes!
Hemmed in by all this heap of books,
Their gnawing worms, amid their dust,
While to the arches, in all the nooks,
Are smoke-stained papers midst them thrust,   405
Boxes and glasses round me crammed,
And instruments in cases hurled,
Ancestral stuff around me jammed —
That is your world! That's called a world!
      And still you question why your heart   410
Is cramped and anxious in your breast?
Why each impulse to live has been repressed
In you by some vague, unexplainèd smart?
Instead of Nature's living sphere
In which God made mankind, you have alone,   415
In smoke and mould around you here,
Beasts' skeletons and dead men's bone.
      Up! Flee! Out into broad and open land!
And this book full of mystery,

From Nostradamus' very hand,   420
Is it not ample company?
The stars' course then you'll understand
And Nature, teaching, will expand
The power of your soul, as when
One spirit to another speaks. 'Tis vain   425
To think that arid brooding will explain
The sacred symbols to your ken.
Ye spirits, ye are hovering near;
Oh, answer me if ye can hear!

He opens the book and perceives the sign of the
Macrocosm

What rapture, ah! at once is flowing   430
Through all my senses at the sight of this!
I feel a youthful life, its holy bliss,
Through nerve and vein run on, new-glowing.
Was it a god who wrote these signs that still
My inner tumult and that fill   435
My wretched heart with ecstasy?
Unveiling with mysterious potency
The powers of Nature round about me here?
Am I a god? All grows so clear to me!
In these pure lineaments I see   440
Creative Nature's self before my soul appear.
Now first I understand what he, the sage, has said:
" The world of spirits is not shut away;
Thy sense is closed, thy heart is dead!
Up, Student! bathe without dismay   445
Thy earthly breast in morning-red! "

He contemplates the sign

Into the whole how all things blend,
Each in the other working, living!
How heavenly powers ascend, descend,
Each unto each the golden vessels giving!   450
On pinions fragrant blessings bringing,
From Heaven through Earth all onward winging,
Through all the All harmonious ringing!
   What pageantry! Yet, ah, mere pageantry!
Where shall I, endless Nature, seize on thee?   455
Thy breasts are — where? Ye, of all life the spring,
To whom both Earth and Heaven cling,

Toward whom the withering breast doth strain —
Ye gush, ye suckle, and shall I pine thus in vain?
> *He turns the book over impatiently and per-*
> *ceives the sign of the* EARTH-SPIRIT

How differently upon me works this sign!   460
Thou, Spirit of the Earth, I feel, art nigher.
I feel my powers already higher,
I glow already as from some new wine.
I feel the courage, forth into the world to dare;
The woe of earth, the bliss of earth to bear;   465
With storms to battle, brave the lightning's glare;
And in the shipwreck's crash not to despair!
Clouds gather over me —
The moon conceals her light —
The lamp fades out!   470
Mists rise — red beams dart forth
Around my head — there floats
A horror downward from the vault
And seizes me!
Spirit invoked! near me, I feel, thou art!   475
Unveil thyself!
Ha! how it rends my heart!
To unknown feeling
All my senses burst forth, reeling!
I feel my heart is thine and to the uttermost!   480
Thou must! Thou must! though my life be the cost!
> *He clutches the book and utters the sign of the*
> SPIRIT *in a tone of mystery. A ruddy flame*
> *flashes up; the* SPIRIT *appears in the flame*

Spirit.   Who calls to me?
Faust turning away.   Appalling apparition!
Spirit.   By potent spell hast drawn me here,
Hast long been tugging at my sphere,
And now —
Faust.   Oh woe! I can not bear thy vision!   485
Spirit.   With panting breath thou hast implored this sight,
Wouldst hear my voice, my face wouldst see;
Thy mighty spirit-plea inclineth me!
Here am I! — what a pitiable fright
Grips thee, thou Superman! Where is the soul elated?   490
Where is the breast that in its self a world created

[18]

And bore and fostered it? And that with joyous trembling
Expanded as if spirits, us, resembling?
Where art thou, Faust, whose voice rang out to me,
Who toward me pressed with all thy energy?   495
Is it thou who, by my breath surrounded,
In all the deeps of being art confounded?
A frightened, fleeing, writhing worm?

Faust.   Am I, O form of flame, to yield to thee in fear?
'Tis I, I'm Faust, I am thy peer!   500

Spirit.   In the tides of life, in action's storm,
Up and down I wave,
To and fro weave free,
Birth and the grave,
An infinite sea,   505
A varied weaving,
A radiant living,
Thus at Time's humming loom it's my hand that prepares
The robe ever-living the Deity wears.

Faust.   Thou who dost round the wide world wend,   510
Thou busy spirit, how near I feel to thee!

Spirit.   Thou art like the spirit thou canst comprehend,
Not me!

Vanishes

Faust collapsing.   Not thee!
Whom then?   515
I, image of the Godhead!
And not even like to thee!

Somebody knocks

O death! I know it — 'tis my famulus —
Thus turns to naught my fairest bliss!
That visions in abundance such as this   520
Must be disturbed by that dry prowler thus!

<small>WAGNER in dressing-gown and night-cap, a
lamp in his hand. FAUST turns round impa-
tiently</small>

Wagner.   Pardon! I've just heard you declaiming.
'Twas surely from a Grecian tragic play?
At profit in this art I'm also aiming;
For much it can effect today.   525
I've often heard the boast: a preacher
Might take an actor as his teacher.

[19]

Faust.   Yes, if the preacher is an actor, there's no doubt,
As it indeed may sometimes come about.
Wagner.   Ah! if thus in his study one must stay,   530
And hardly sees the world upon a holiday,
Scarce through a telescope, and far off then,
How through persuasion shall one lead one's fellow-men?
Faust.   Unless you feel, naught will you ever gain;
Unless this feeling pours forth from your soul   535
With native, pleasing vigour to control
The hearts of all your hearers, it will be in vain.
Pray keep on sitting! Pray collect and glue,
From others' feasts brew some ragout;
With tiny heaps of ashes play your game   540
And blow the sparks into a wretched flame!
Children and apes will marvel at you ever,
If you've a palate that can stand the part;
But heart to heart you'll not draw men, no, never,
Unless your message issue from your heart.   545
Wagner.   Yet elocution makes the orator succeed.
I feel I am still far behind indeed.
Faust.   Seek for the really honest gain!
Don't be a fool in loudly tinkling dress!
Intelligence and good sense will express   550
Themselves with little art and strain.
And if in earnest you would say a thing,
Is it needful to chase after words? Ah, yes,
Your eloquence that is so glittering,
In which you twist up gewgaws for mankind,   555
Is unrefreshing as the misty wind,
Through withered leaves in autumn whispering.
Wagner.   Ah, God! how long is art!
And soon it is we die.
Oft when my critical pursuits I ply,   560
I truly grow uneasy both in head and heart.
How hard to gain the means whereby
A man mounts upward to the source!
And ere man's ended barely half the course,
Poor devil! I suppose he has to die.   565
Faust.   Parchment! Is that the sacred fountain whence alone
There springs a draught that thirst for ever quells?
Refreshment? It you never will have won

If from that soul of yours it never wells.

Wagner.   Excuse me! But it is a great delight   570
    To enter in the spirit of the ages and to see
    How once a sage before us thought and then how we
    Have brought things on at last to such a splendid height.

Faust.   Oh, yes! Up to the stars afar!
    My friend, the ages of aforetime are   575
    To us a book of seven seals.
    What you call "spirit of the ages"
    Is after all the spirit of those sages
    In which the mirrored age itself reveals.
    Then, truly, that is oft a sorry sight to see!   580
    I vow, men do but glance at it, then run away.
    A rubbish-bin, a lumber-garret it may be,
    At best a stilted, mock-heroic play
    With excellent, didactic maxims humming,
    Such as in puppets' mouths are most becoming.   585

Wagner.   But, ah, the world! the mind and heart of men!
    Of these we each would fain know something just the same.

Faust.   Yes, "know"! Men call it so, but then
    Who dares to call the child by its right name?
    The few who have some part of it descried,   590
    Yet fools enough to guard not their full hearts, revealing
    To riffraff both their insight and their feeling,
    Men have of old burned at the stake and crucified.
    I beg you, friend, it's far into the night,
    We must break off our converse now.   595

Wagner.   I'd gladly keep awake for ever if I might
    Converse with you in such a learnèd way;
    Tomorrow, though, our Easter-Sunday holiday,
    This and that question you'll allow.
    I've studied zealously, and so   600
    I know much now, but all I fain would know.   *Exit*

Faust alone.   How strange a man's not quitted of all hope,
    Who on and on to shallow stuff adheres,
    Whose greedy hands for hidden treasure grope,
    And who is glad when any worm appears!   605
        Dare such a human voice resound
    Where spirits near me throng around?
    Yet still I thank you, poorest one
    Of all the sons of earth, for what you've done.

Torn loose by you, from that despair I'm freed   610
That nearly drove my senses frantic.
That vision, ah! was so gigantic,
I could but feel myself a dwarf indeed.
    I, image of the Godhead, and already one
Who thought him near the mirror of the Truth Eternal,   615
Who revelled in the clearness, light supernal,
And stripped away the earthly son;
I, more than cherub, whose free force
Presumed, prophetic, even now to course,
Creating, on through Nature's every vein,   620
To share the life of gods: that! — how must I atone!
A voice of thunder swept me back again.
    I may not dare to call myself thy peer!
What though I had the might to draw thee near,
To hold thee I possessed no might.   625
At that ecstatic moment's height
I felt so small, so great;
Thou cruelly didst thrust me back as one
Doomed to uncertain human fate.
Who will instruct me? And what shall I shun?   630
Shall I that impulse then obey?
Alas! the deeds that we have done —
Our sufferings too — impede us on life's way.
    To what the mind most gloriously conceives,
An alien, more, more alien substance cleaves.   635
When to the good of this world we attain,
We call the better a delusion vain.
Sensations glorious, that gave us life,
Grow torpid in the world's ignoble strife.
    Though Fantasy with daring flight began   640
And hopeful toward Infinity expanded,
She's now contented in a little span
When in Time's eddy joy on joy's been stranded.
For Worry straightway nestles deep within the heart,
There she produces many a secret smart.   645
Restlessly rocking, she disturbs both joy and rest.
In new disguises she is always dressed;
She may appear as house and land, as child and wife,
As fire, as water, poison, knife.
What never will happen makes you quail,   650

And what you'll never lose, always must you bewail.
  I am not like the gods! Feel it I must.
I'm like the worm that burrows through the dust,
That in the dust in which it lived and fed,
Is crushed and buried by a wanderer's tread.   655
   Is it not dust that narrows in this lofty wall
Made up of shelves a hundred, is it not all
The lumber, thousandfold light frippery,
That in this world of moths oppresses me?
Here shall I find what is my need?   660
Shall I perchance in a thousand volumes read
That men have tortured themselves everywhere,
And that a happy man was here and there? —
Why grinnest thou at me, thou hollow skull?
Save that thy brain, confused like mine, once sought bright day   665
And in the sombre twilight dull,
With lust for truth, went wretchedly astray?
Ye instruments, ye surely jeer at me,
With handle, wheel and cogs and cylinder.
I stood beside the gate, ye were to be the key.   670
True, intricate your ward, but no bolts do ye stir.
Inscrutable upon a sunlit day,
Her veil will Nature never let you steal,
And what she will not to your mind reveal,
You will not wrest from her with levers and with screws.   675
You, ancient lumber, that I do not use,
You're only here because you served my father.
On you, old scroll, the smoke-stains gather,
Since first the lamp on this desk smouldered turbidly.
Far better had I spent my little recklessly   680
Than, burdened with that little, here to sweat!
All that you have, bequeathed you by your father,
Earn it in order to possess it.
Things unused often burden and beset;
But what the hour brings forth, that can it use and bless it.   685
   Why does my gaze grow fixed as if a spell had bound me?
That phial there, is it a magnet to my eyes?
Why does a lovely light so suddenly surround me
As when in woods at night the moonbeam drifts and lies?
   Thou peerless phial rare, I welcome thee   690
And now I take thee down most reverently.

In thee I honour human wit and art.
Thou essence, juice of lovely, slum'brous flowers,
Thou extract of all deadly, subtle powers,
Thy favour to thy Master now impart!   695
I look on thee, and soothed is my distress;
I seize on thee, the struggle groweth less.
The spirit's flood-tide ebbs away, away.
I'm beckoned out, the open seas to meet,
The mirror waters glitter at my feet,   700
To other shores allures another day.
  A fiery chariot floats on airy pinions
Hither to me! I feel prepared to flee
Along a new path, piercing ether's vast dominions
To other spheres of pure activity.   705
This lofty life, this ecstasy divine!
Thou, but a worm, and *that* deservest thou?
Yes! turn thy back with resolution fine
Upon earth's lovely sun, and now
Make bold to fling apart the gate   710
Which every man would fain go slinking by!
Here is the time to demonstrate
That man's own dignity yields not to gods on high;
To tremble not before that murky pit
Where fantasies, self-damned, in tortures dwell;   715
To struggle toward that pass whose narrow mouth is lit
By all the seething, searing flames of Hell;
Serenely to decide this step and onward press,
Though there be risk I'll float off into nothingness.
  So now come down, thou goblet pure and crystalline!   720
From out that ancient case of thine,
On which for many a year I have not thought!
Thou at my fathers' feasts wert wont to shine,
Didst many a solemn guest to mirth incline,
When thee, in pledge, one to another brought.   725
The crowded figures, rich and artful wrought,
The drinker's duty, rhyming to explain them,
The goblet's depths, at but one draught to drain them,
Recall full many a youthful night to me.
Now to no neighbour shall I offer thee,   730
Upon thy art I shall not show my wit.
Here is a juice, one's quickly drunk with it.

With its brown flood it fills thy ample bowl.
This I prepared, I choose this, high upborne;
Be this my last drink now, with all my soul,   735
A festal, lofty greeting pledged to morn!
>*He puts the goblet to his lips*

>*The sound of bells and choral song*

Chorus of Angels.

>Christ is arisen!
>Joy to mortality,
>Whom earth's carnality,
>Creeping fatality,   740
>Held as in prison!

Faust.   What a deep humming, what a clarion tone,
Draws from my lips the glass with mighty power!
Ye deep-toned bells, make ye already known
The Easter-feast's first solemn hour?   745
Ye choirs, do ye the hymn of consolation sing,
Which angels sang around the grave's dark night, to bring
Assurance of new covenant and dower?
Chorus of Women.

>Rare spices we carried
>And laid on His breast;   750
>We tenderly buried
>Him whom we loved best;
>Cloths and bands round Him,
>Spotless we wound Him o'er;
>Ah! and we've found Him,   755
>Christ, here no more.

Chorus of Angels.

>Christ is ascended!
>Blessèd the loving one
>Who endured, moving one,
>Trials improving one,   760
>Till they were ended!

Faust.   Ye heavenly tones, so powerful and mild,
Why seek ye me, me cleaving to the dust?
Ring roundabout where tender-hearted men will hear!
I hear the message well but lack Faith's constant trust;   765

The miracle is Faith's most cherished child.
I do not dare to strive toward yonder sphere
From whence the lovely tidings swell;
Yet, wonted to this strain from infancy,
Back now to life again it calleth me.   770
In days that are no more, Heaven's loving kiss
In solemn Sabbath stillness on me fell;
Then rang prophetical, full-toned, the bell;
And every prayer was fervent bliss.
A sweet, uncomprehending yearning   775
Drove me to wander on through wood and lea,
And while a thousand tears were burning,
I felt a world arise for me.
Of youth's glad sports this song foretold me,
The festival of spring in happy freedom passed;   780
Now memories, with childlike feeling, hold me
Back from that solemn step, the last.
Sound on and on, thou sweet, celestial strain!
The tear wells forth, the earth has me again!

Chorus of Disciples.

    Though He, victorious,   785
    From the grave's prison,
    Living and glorious,
    Nobly has risen,
    Though He, in bliss of birth,
    Creative Joy is near,   790
    Ah! on the breast of earth
    We are to suffer here.
    He left His very Own
    Pining for Him we miss;
    Ah! we bemoan,   795
    Master, Thy bliss!

Chorus of Angels.

    Christ is arisen
    Out of Corruption's womb!
    Burst bonds that prison,
    Joy over the tomb!   800
    Actively pleading Him,
    Showing love, heeding Him,
    Brotherly feeding Him,
    Preaching, far speeding Him,

Rapture succeeding Him,   805
To you the Master's near,
To you is here!

Outside the Gate of the Town

All sorts of people are walking out

Some Young Workmen.   Why are you going off that way?
Others.   We're going to the Hunters' Lodge today.
The Former.   But toward the Mill we'd like to wander.   810
Workman.   Go to the River Inn, that's my advice.
A Second.   The road that way is far from nice.
The Others.   What will you do?
A Third.   Go with them yonder.
A Fourth.   Come up to Burgdorf! There you'll surely find
    The prettiest girls and beer, the finest kind,   815
    Besides a first-rate sort of scrap.
A Fifth.   How you do swagger! What a chap!
    Does your skin itch a third time for a row?
    I will not go, I fear that place somehow.
Servant-Girl.   No, no, I'll go back toward the town.   820
Another.   We'll find him by those poplars certainly.
The First.   But that is no great luck for me!
    At your side he'll go walking up and down;
    He never dances but with you.
    With your fun what have I to do?   825
The Second.   Today he's surely not alone; he said
    His friend would be with him, the curly-head.
Student.   By thunder! how the whacking wenches stride!
    We must go with them, brother, come along.
    Strong beer, tobacco with a bite, and, on the side,   830
    A servant-maid decked out, for these I long.
Citizen's Daughter.   I say, just see those fine young blades!
    It really is an insult. See!
    They could have had the best of company
    And run here after serving-maids!   835
Second Student to the first.
    Not quite so fast! There come two others, there behind,
    Quite neatly dressed and rather striking.

[27]

One of them is my neighbour too, I find,
And she is greatly to my liking.
They go their way now quite demurely,   840
Yet, in the end, they'll take us with them surely.
The First.   No, friend! To feel constrained is too depressing.
Quick then! lest we should lose the wilder prey.
The hand that wields the broom on Saturday
Will Sunday treat you with the best caressing.   845
Citizen.   No, that new burgomaster I don't like a bit.
Now since he's in, he's daily bolder every way,
And for the town, what does he do for it?
Are things not growing worse each day?
Now more than ever we must all submit,   850
And more than ever must we pay.
Beggar sings.

> Good gentlemen and ladies pretty,
> So flushed of cheek and fine of dress,
> May it please you, look on me with pity,
> And see and soften my distress!   855
> Let me not vainly grind here waiting!
> Who likes to give, alone is gay.
> A day all men are celebrating,
> Be it for me a harvest day.

Another Citizen.   I know naught better on a Sunday or a holiday   860
Than chat of wars and warlike pother,
When off in Turkey, far away,
The people clash and fight with one another.
We stand beside the window, drain our glasses,
And see how each gay vessel down the river passes,   865
Then in the evening homeward wend our ways,
Blessing with joy sweet peace and peaceful days.
Third Citizen.   Yes, neighbour! I would leave things so;
Each other's skulls they well may crack,
And everything may topsyturvy go,   870
If only things at home stay in the old, old track.
Old Woman to two CITIZENS' DAUGHTERS.
My! How dressed up! You beautiful young dears!
Who would not gape now if he met you?
But not so haughty! Have no fears!
What you desire I know well how to get you.   875

Citizen's Daughter.　　Come, Agatha, away! I take great heed
　　That with such witches no one sees me go;
　　Yet to me on St. Andrew's Night, indeed,
　　My future lover she did really show.
The Other.　　She showed me mine too in the crystal ball,　　　　880
　　So soldier-like, with others swift to dare;
　　I look about, I seek him everywhere,
　　But I can't find him, not at all.
Soldiers.

　　　　　　　Castles with lofty
　　　　　　　Ramparts retaining,　　　　　　　　　　885
　　　　　　　Maids who are haughty,
　　　　　　　Scornful, disdaining,
　　　　　　　Fain I'd be gaining!
　　　　　　　Bold is the venture,
　　　　　　　Grand is the pay!　　　　　　　　　　890
　　　　　　　　　We let the trumpet
　　　　　　　Summon us, wooing,
　　　　　　　Calling to pleasure,
　　　　　　　Oft to undoing.
　　　　　　　That is a storming!　　　　　　　　895
　　　　　　　Life in its splendour!
　　　　　　　　　Maidens and castles
　　　　　　　Both must surrender.
　　　　　　　Bold is the venture,
　　　　　　　Grand is the pay!　　　　　　　　　　900
　　　　　　　Then are the soldiers
　　　　　　　Off and away.

FAUST *and* WAGNER

Faust.　　From the ice they are freed, the stream and brook,
　　By the Spring's enlivening, lovely look;
　　The valley's green with joys of hope;　　　　　　　905
　　The Winter old and weak ascends
　　Back to the rugged mountain slope.
　　From there, as he flees, he downward sends
　　An impotent shower of icy hail
　　Streaking over the verdant vale.　　　　　　　　910
　　Ah! but the Sun will suffer no white,
　　Growth and formation stir everywhere,

'Twould fain with colours make all things bright,
Though in the landscape are no blossoms fair.
Instead it takes gay-decked humanity. 915
Now turn around and from this height,
Looking backward, townward see.
Forth from the cave-like, gloomy gate
Crowds a motley and swarming array.
Everyone suns himself gladly today. 920
The Risen Lord they celebrate,
For they themselves have now arisen
From lowly houses' mustiness,
From handicraft's and factory's prison,
From the roof and gables that oppress, 925
From the bystreets' crushing narrowness,
From the churches' venerable night,
They are all brought out into light.
See, only see, how quickly the masses
Scatter through gardens and fields remote; 930
How down and across the river passes
So many a merry pleasure-boat.
And over-laden, almost sinking,
The last full wherry moves away.
From yonder hill's far pathways blinking, 935
Flash to us colours of garments gay.
Hark! Sounds of village joy arise;
Here is the people's paradise.
Contented, great and small shout joyfully:
" Here I am Man, here dare it to be! " 940
Wagner.   Doctor, to walk with you is ever
An honour and a profit, though
I'd here not care to stray alone, — no, never, —
Because to all that's vulgar I'm a foe.
This fiddling, shrieking, bowling, — all this revel 945
To me's a sound detested long;
They riot as if driven by the Devil,
And call it a pleasure, call it a song.
Peasants under the linden tree. Dance and song.
            The shepherd decked him for the dance,
        In ribbons, vest, and wreath to prance, 950
        Adorned with fine arraying.
        Now round the linden lass and lad

[30]

Were thronging, dancing there like mad.
Hurrah! Hurrah!
Hurrah-a-rah-a-rah!   955
Thus fiddle-bow was playing.
     He crowded and he pushed in haste,
Then bumped into a maiden's waist,
Elbow against her laying.
The lively damsel turned her head: 960
"I find that stupid, now!" she said.
Hurrah! Hurrah!
Hurrah-a-rah-a-rah!
"Don't be so rude and swaying!"
     Then round and round they winged their flight,   965
They danced to left, they danced to right,
All petticoats displaying.
They grew so red, they grew so warm,
Then rested panting, arm in arm,
Hurrah! Hurrah!   970
Hurrah-a-rah-a-rah!
On hip the elbow staying.
     "I say, don't make so free with me!
How many fooled his bride-to-be,
Deceiving and betraying!"   975
And yet he coaxed her to one side,
And from the linden far and wide:
Hurrah! Hurrah!
Hurrah-a-rah-a-rah!
Rang shouts and fiddle-playing.   980

Old Peasant.   Good Doctor, this is fine of you,
  That you don't scorn us here today,
  And now amid this crowding throng,
  A highly-learnèd man, you stray.
  Hence take in turn the finest mug   985
  That with a fresh, cool drink we've filled.
  I pledge you, sir, and wish aloud
  Not only that your thirst be stilled:
  For every drop the mug conveys,
  A day be added to your days!   990
Faust.   I take the refreshing drink and thus I too
  Return the health with thanks to all of you.

The people gather round in a circle

Old Peasant.   Forsooth, it is indeed well done
        That you on happy days appear.
        You have aforetime with us too   995
        Been kind when days were evil here!
        Full many a one stands here alive,
        Whom your good father still did wrest
        From burning fever's deadly rage
        When he set limits to the pest.   1000
        And you as well, a young man then,
        To every sick man's house you went around.
        Many a corpse did men bring forth,
        But from within you came out sound,
        Withstanding many a test severe;   1005
        The Helper over us helped our helper here.
All.   Health to the man whom we have tried,
        Long may he be our help and guide!
Faust.   To Him on High with reverence bend,
        Who teaches help and help doth send!   1010

He goes on with WAGNER

Wagner.   Oh, what a feeling you must have, great man,
        Thus venerated by this multitude!
        Oh, happy he who, through his own gifts, can
        Draw such a gain, such gratitude!
        The father shows you to his brood,   1015
        Each asks and hastes and nearer draws;
        The fiddle stops, the dancers pause.
        You go, they stand in rows to see.
        The caps are quickly lifted high;
        A little more and they would bend the knee   1020
        As if the Holy Sacrament came by.
Faust.   Only a few steps farther, up to yonder stone!
        Here let us rest a little from our straying.
        Here often, wrapped in thought, I sat alone
        And tortured me with fasting and with praying.   1025
        In hope full rich, firm in the faith possessed,
        With tears, sighs, wringing hands, I meant
        To force the Lord in Heaven to relent
        And end for us the fearful pest.
        The crowd's applause now sounds like scorn to me.   1030
        Oh, could you but within me read

How little, son and father, we
Were worthy such a fame and meed!
My father was a simple, worthy man,
Who over Nature and her every sacred zone,   1035
Quite honestly, in his odd plan
Mused with a wayward zeal that was his own,
Who, with adepts their presence lending,
Shut him in that black kitchen where he used,
According to receipts unending,   1040
To get the contraries together fused.
There was a lover bold, a lion red,
Who to the lily in a tepid bath was wed.
Both, tortured then with flames, a fiery tide,
From one bride-chamber to another pass.   1045
Thereon appeared, with motley colours pied,
The youthful queen within the glass.
Here was the medicine; the patients died,
And no one questioned: who got well?
Thus we with hellish nostrums, here   1050
Within these mountains, in this dell,
Raged far more fiercely than the pest.
I gave the poison unto thousands, ere
They pined away; and I must live to hear
The shameless murderers praised and blessed.   1055

Wagner.   How can you give yourself to such lament?
Does not a good man do his part
In practising transmitted art
Exactly and with good intent?
If you revere your father as a youth,   1060
Gladly from him you will receive;
If as a man you further knowledge and the truth,
Then can your son a higher goal achieve.

Faust.   Oh, happy he who still hopes that he can
Emerge from Error's boundless sea!   1065
What man knows not, is needed most by man,
And what man knows, for that no use has he.
But what fair blessing that this hour can show
Let's not with mournful thoughts like these embitter!
Behold how in the evening sunset-glow   1070
The green-encircled hamlets glitter.
The sun retreats — the day, outlived, is o'er —

[33]

It hastens hence and lo! a new world is alive!
Oh, that from earth no wing can lift me up to soar
And after, ever after it to strive! 1075
I'd see in that eternal evening beam,
Beneath my feet, the world in stillness glowing,
Each valley hushed and every height agleam,
The silver brook to golden rivers flowing.
The mountain wild with all its gorges 1080
Would hinder not the godlike course for me;
Before astounded eyes already surges,
With bays yet warm, the open sea.
And yet at last the god seems to be sinking;
But new impulse awakes, to light 1085
I hasten on, eternal brightness drinking,
Before me day, behind me night,
Above me heaven, and under me the billow.
A lovely dream, the while the glory fades from sight.
Alas! To wings that lift the spirit light 1090
No earthly wing will ever be a fellow.
Yet 'tis inborn in everyone, each fancies
His feeling presses upward and along,
When over us lost amid the blue expanses
The lark sings down his showering song, 1095
When over rough heights of firs and larches
The outspread eagles soaring roam,
And over lakes and over marshes
The crane strives onward toward his home.
Wagner.   I've often had capricious, odd hours of my own, 1100
Yet such an impulse I have never known.
One's sated soon if on the woods and fields he look;
I'll never envy any bird his wing.
How differently the joys of spirit bring
Us on from page to page, from book to book! 1105
Then winter nights become so sweet and fair,
A blessèd life warms up our every limb;
And ah! if one unrolls a parchment really rare,
The whole of Heaven descends on him.
Faust.   By one impulse alone are you impressed. 1110
Oh, never learn to know the other!
Two souls alas! are dwelling in my breast;
And each is fain to leave its brother.

[34]

The one, fast clinging, to the world adheres
With clutching organs, in love's sturdy lust;   1115
The other strongly lifts itself from dust
To yonder high, ancestral spheres.
Oh, are there spirits hovering near,
That ruling weave, twixt earth and heaven are rife,
Descend! come from the golden atmosphere   1120
And lead me hence to new and varied life!
Yea! were a magic mantle only mine,
To bear me to strange lands at pleasure,
I would not barter it for costliest treasure,
Not for the mantle of a king resign.   1125

Wagner.   Oh, call them not, the well-known swarms
That streaming spread throughout the murky air;
In every quarter they prepare
A danger for mankind in a thousand forms.
Sharp spirit-fangs press from the north   1130
Upon you here with arrow-pointed tongues;
And from the east, now parching, they come forth
And feast themselves upon your lungs;
And when the south wind from the desert drives
Those that heap glow on glow upon your brain,   1135
The west wind brings the swarm that first revives,
Then drowns you and the field and plain.
They like to hear, on mischief gaily bent,
They like to hearken, for they like to try
To fool us, pose as if from Heaven sent,   1140
And lisp like angels when they lie.
But let us go! The world's already grey,
The air grows chill, the mists of evening fall!
'Tis now we treasure home the most of all. —
Why do you stand and stare? What is the trouble?   1145
What in the gloaming seizes you in such a way?

Faust.   You see that black dog streaking through the grain and stubble?

Wagner.   I saw him long since; not important did he seem to me.

Faust.   Observe him well! What do you take the beast to be?

Wagner.   Why, just a poodle; in his way he's worrying   1150
In his attempt to find his master's traces.

Faust.   But do you note how in wide spiral rings he's hurrying
Around us here and ever nearer chases?
And if I err not, there's a trail behind him!

[35]

Along his path a fiery eddy flies. 1155

Wagner.   Only a plain black poodle do I see. Don't mind him!
I think it's an illusion of your eyes.

Faust.   He seems in magic nooses to be sweeping
Around our feet, a future snare to bind.

Wagner.   I see he doubts, he's timidly around us leaping, 1160
Two strangers — not his master — does he find.

Faust.   The circle narrows; he's already near!

Wagner.   You see a dog! It is no spectre here.
He snarls and doubts, now on his belly see him crawl,
He wags his tail, dog-habits all. 1165

Faust.   Come here! And be a friend with us!

Wagner.   It is a beast and, poodle-like, ridiculous.
Stand quiet and he'll sit up too;
Speak to him and he'll scramble up on you;
Lose something and he'll bring it back again, 1170
Leap into water for your cane.

Faust.   You're likely right. I find no trace remaining
Of any spirit; it is all mere training.

Wagner.   By any dog, if he but be well trained,
Even a wise man's liking may be gained. 1175
Yes, he deserves your favour thoroughly,
A clever pupil of students, he.

They go into the gateway of the town

Study

Faust entering with the poodle.

Meadow and field have I forsaken,
That deeps of night from sight enroll;
A solemn awe the deeps awaken, 1180
Rousing in us the better soul.
No wild desires can longer win me,
No stormy lust to dare and do;
The love of all mankind stirs in me,
The love of God is stirred anew. 1185

Be quiet, poodle! Don't make such a riot!
Why at the threshold do you sniff the air?
Lie down behind the stove in quiet!

[36]

My best of cushions I will give you there.
As on the hillside pathway, leaping   1190
And running about, you amused us best,
So take now too from me your keeping,
But as a welcome, silent guest.

     Ah, when the friendly lamp is glowing
     Again within our narrow cell,   1195
     Through heart and bosom light comes flowing
     If but the heart knows itself well.
     Then Reason once again discourses
     And Hope begins to bloom again;
     Man yearns to reach life's flowing sources,   1200
     Ah! to the Fount of Life attain.

Snarl not, you poodle! To the sacred strain
That now doth all my soul surround,
Is suited not that bestial sound.
We know full well that men deride whate'er   1205
They do not understand
And that before the Good and Fair,
Which oft is hard for them, they grumble;
And will the dog, like them too, snarl and bumble?
    But ah! I feel already, with a will the best,   1210
Contentment wells no longer from my breast.
But wherefore must the stream so soon run dry
And we again thus thirsting lie?
I have experienced this in ample measure.
And yet this feeling has its compensation;   1215
We learn the supernatural to treasure.
Our spirits yearn toward revelation
That nowhere glows more fair, more excellent,
Than here in the New Testament.
To open the fundamental text I'm moved,   1220
With honest feeling, once for all,
To turn the sacred, blest original
Into my German well-beloved.
                He opens a volume and applies himself to it
'Tis written: " In the beginning was the Word! "
Here now I'm balked! Who'll put me in accord?   1225
It is impossible, the *Word* so high to prize,

[37]

I must translate it otherwise
If I am rightly by the Spirit taught.
'Tis written: In the beginning was the *Thought!*
Consider well that line, the first you see,   1230
That your pen may not write too hastily!
Is it then *Thought* that works, creative, hour by hour?
Thus should it stand: In the beginning was the *Power!*
Yet even while I write this word, I falter,
For something warns me, this too I shall alter.   1235
The Spirit's helping me! I see now what I need
And write assured: In the beginning was the *Deed!*
    If I'm to share this room with you,
Poodle, then leave off howling,
Then leave off growling!   1240
Such a distracting fellow I can't view
Or suffer to have near me.
One of us two, or I or you,
Must quit this cell, I fear me.
I'm loath your right as guest thus to undo.   1245
The door is open, you've a passage free.
But what is this I now must see!
Can that happen naturally?
Is it phantom? Is it reality?
How long and broad the poodle grows!   1250
He rises up in mighty pose,
'Tis not a dog's form that he shows!
What spectre have I sheltered thus?
He's like a hippopotamus
With fiery eyes, jaws terrible to see.   1255
Oh, mine you are most certainly.
For such as your half-hellish crew
The Key of Solomon will do.
Spirits in the corridor.
        Captured is someone within!
        Stay without, none follow in!   1260
        Like a fox in a snare
        Quakes an ancient hell-lynx there.
        But now give heed!
        Hover hence, hither hover,
        Under, over,   1265
        And he soon himself has freed.

[38]

Can ye avail him,
Oh, do not fail him!
For he has already done
Much to profit us, each one.   1270

Faust.   First, to deal with this beast's core,
I will use the Spell of Four:

Salamander must be glowing,
Undine self-coiling,
Sylph vanish in going,   1275
Kobold keep toiling.

Who would ignore
The elements four,
Their powers
And dowers,   1280
No master he
Over spirits can be.

Vanish in fiery glow,
Salamander!
Gurgling, together flow,   1285
Undine!
In meteoric beauty shine,
Sylph!
Bring homely help,
Incubus! Incubus!   1290
Step forth and end the charm for us.

None of the Four
Hides in the beast.
He lies quite calmly, grins evermore;
I've not yet hurt him in the least.   1295
Thou'lt hear me longer
Conjure thee stronger!

Art thou, fellow, one
That out of Hell has run?
Then see this Sign!   1300
Before which incline
Black cohorts e'er!

[39]

It swells up now with bristling hair.

> Thou reprobated,
> Canst rede His token? 1305
> The Ne'er-originated,
> The Never-spoken,
> Who every Heaven has permeated,
> He! wantonly immolated!

Behind the stove, held by my spells, 1310
Like an elephant it swells,
And all the space it fills complete.
In vapour it will melt away.
Mount not up to the ceiling! Lay
Thyself down at thy Master's feet! 1315
I threaten not in vain as thou canst see.
With holy fire I'll shrivel thee!
Do not await
The light thrice radiate!
Do not await 1320
The strongest art at my command!

> MEPHISTOPHELES *steps forth from behind*
> *the stove while the vapour is vanishing. He is*
> *dressed as a travelling scholar*

Mephistopheles. Wherefore this noise? What does my lord command?
Faust. So this, then, was the kernel of the brute!
A travelling scholar is it? The *casus* makes me smile.
Mephistopheles. To you, O learnèd sir, I proffer my salute! 1325
You made me sweat in vigorous style.
Faust. What is your name?
Mephistopheles. The question seems but cheap
From one who for the Word has such contempt,
Who from all outward show is quite exempt
And only into beings would delve deep. 1330
Faust. The being of such gentlemen as you, indeed,
In general, from your titles one can read.
It shows itself but all too plainly when men dub
You Liar or Destroyer or Beëlzebub.
Well now, who are you then?
Mephistopheles. Part of that Power which would 1335
The Evil ever do, and ever does the Good.

Faust.   A riddle! Say what it implies!
Mephistopheles.   I am the Spirit that denies!
    And rightly too; for all that doth begin
    Should rightly to destruction run;   1340
    'Twere better then that nothing were begun.
    Thus everything that you call Sin,
    Destruction — in a word, as Evil represent —
    That is my own, real element.
Faust.   You call yourself a part, yet whole you're standing there.   1345
Mephistopheles.   A modest truth do I declare.
    A man, the microcosmic fool, down in his soul
    Is wont to think himself a whole,
    But I'm part of the Part which at the first was all,
    Part of the Darkness that gave birth to Light,   1350
    The haughty Light that now with Mother Night
    Disputes her ancient rank and space withal,
    And yet 'twill not succeed, since, strive as strive it may,
    Fettered to bodies will Light stay.
    It streams from bodies, it makes bodies fair,   1355
    A body hinders it upon its way,
    And so, I hope, it has not long to stay
    And will with bodies their destruction share.
Faust.   Now I perceive your worthy occupation!
    You can't achieve wholesale annihilation   1360
    And now a retail business you've begun.
Mephistopheles.   And truly thereby nothing much is done.
    What stands out as the opposite of Naught —
    This Something, this your clumsy world — for aught
    I have already undertaken,   1365
    It have I done no harm nor shaken
    With waves and storms, with earthquakes, fiery brand.
    Calm, after all, remain both sea and land.
    And that accursèd trash, the brood of beasts and men,
    A way to get at them I've never found.   1370
    How many now I've buried in the ground!
    Yet fresh, new blood forever circulates again.
    Thus on and on — one could go mad in sheer despair!
    From earth, from water, and from air
    A thousand germs evolving start,   1375
    In dryness, moisture, warmth, and cold!
    Weren't it for fire which I withhold,

I'd have as mine not one thing set apart.

Faust.   So to that Power never reposing,

Creative, healing, you're opposing   1380

Your frigid devil's fist with might and main.

It's clenched in spite and clenched in vain!

Seek something else to undertake,

You, Chaos' odd, fantastic son!

Mephistopheles.   We'll really ponder on what can be done   1385

When my next visits here I make.

But may I for the present go away?

Faust.   Why you should ask, I do not see.

Though we have only met today,

Come as you like and visit me.   1390

Here is a window, here a door, for you,

Besides a certain chimney-flue.

Mephistopheles.   Let me own up! I can not go away;

A little hindrance bids me stay.

The witch's foot upon your sill I see.   1395

Faust.   The pentagram? That's in your way?

You son of Hell explain to me,

If that stays you, how came you in today?

And how was such a spirit so betrayed?

Mephistopheles.   Observe it closely! It is not well made;   1400

One angle, on the outer side of it,

Is just a little open, as you see.

Faust.   That was by accident a lucky hit!

And are you then my captive? Can that be?

By happy chance the thing's succeeded!   1405

Mephistopheles.   As he came leaping in, the poodle did not heed it.

The matter now seems turned about;

The Devil's in the house and can't get out.

Faust.   Well, through the window — why not there withdraw?

Mephistopheles.   For devils and for ghosts it is a law: 1410

Where they slipped in, there too must they go out.

The first is free, the second's slaves are we.

Faust.   Does Hell itself have its laws then?

That's fine! A compact in that case might be

Concluded safely with you gentlemen?   1415

Mephistopheles.   What's promised, you'll enjoy with naught subtracted,

With naught unduly snipped off or exacted.

But that needs more than such a brief consideration

[42]

And we'll discuss it soon in further conversation.
But now, most earnestly I pray, 1420
For this time let me go away.
Faust.   One moment longer do remain;
Tell me at last some pleasant news.
Mephistopheles.   Let me go now, I'll soon be back again;
Then you may question as you choose. 1425
Faust.   I've never set a snare for you;
You walked, yourself, into this net tonight.
Let him who holds the Devil hold him tight!
He'll not so soon catch him anew.
Mephistopheles.   If it so please you, I'm prepared, indeed, 1430
To lend you company, but take good heed:
It's on condition that my arts beguile
The time for you in worthy style.
Faust.   I'll gladly see your arts, in that you're free,
Though only if you please with artistry! 1435
Mephistopheles.   More for your senses, friend, you'll gain
In this one hour than you'd obtain
In a whole year's monotony.
All that the tender spirits sing you,
The lovely images they bring you, 1440
Are not an empty sorcery.
They will delight your sense of smell,
They will refresh your palate well,
And blissful will your feeling swell.
Of preparation there's no need, 1445
We're here together, so proceed!
Spirits.

Vanish, ye darkling
Vaultings above him!
More lovely gleaming,
Blue ether beaming, 1450
Gaze down, benign!
Now are the darkling
Clouds disappearing!
Faint stars are sparkling,
Gentler suns nearing 1455
Hitherward shine.
Graces, adorning
Sons of the morning,

[43]

Spirit-like, bending,
Wavering, hover.   1460
Yearning unending
Follows them over;
Ribbons a-trailing,
Fluttering, veiling,
Wide spaces cover,   1465
Cover the bower,
Where, with deep feeling,
Lovers are dreaming,
Life-pledges sealing.
Bower by bower!   1470
Tendrils out-streaming!
Heavy grape's gushing,
In the vats plunging;
Out from the crushing
Winepresses lunging,   1475
Wine-streams are whirling;
Foaming and purling
Onward o'er precious
Pure stones they wind them,
Leave heights behind them,   1480
Broad'ning to spacious
Fair lakes, abounding
Green hills surrounding.
Wingèd creation,
Sipping elation,   1485
Sunward is fleeting,
Bright islands meeting,
Flying to meet them
On the waves dancing,
Rhythmic, entrancing,   1490
Where we, to greet them,
Hear a glad chorus,
See o'er the meadows
Dancers like shadows,
Flitting before us,   1495
Playing, regaling,
Hills some are scaling;
Others are swimming,
Lakes swiftly skimming;

Playfully trailing,   1500
Other ones flitter,
All for existent,
All for the distant
Stars as they glitter
Rapturous Love.   1505

Mephistopheles.   He sleeps! Well done, ye tender, airy throng!
Ye truly lulled him with your song,
And for this concert I am in your debt.
You're not the man to keep the Devil captive yet!
Enchant him with a dream's sweet imagery,   1510
Plunge him into an ocean of untruth!
But now, to break this threshold's sorcery,
I have to get a rat's sharp tooth.
To conjure long I do not need;
Already one is rustling and it soon will heed.   1515
      The lord of all the rats and mice,
Of flies and frogs and bugs and lice,
Bids you now venture to appear
And gnaw upon this threshold here
Where he is dabbing it with oil.   1520
Already you come hopping forth. Now to your toil!
Quick to the work! The point that held me bound
There on the outer edge is found.
Just one bite more — 'tis done! Begone!
Now, Faustus, till we meet again, dream on!   1525
Faust awakening.   Am I again a victim of delusion?
That streaming throng of spirits — gone are they?
Dreamt I the Devil through some mere illusion?
Or did a poodle only leap away?

Study

FAUST   MEPHISTOPHELES

Faust.   A knock? Come in! Who now will bother me?   1530
Mephistopheles.   'Tis I.
Faust.   Come in!
Mephistopheles.   Full three times must it be.
Faust.   Come in, then!

Mephistopheles.   Fine! I like that! All is well!
    I hope we'll bear with one another and agree!
    For I, your every crotchet to dispel,
    Am here all dressed up like a noble squire,   1535
    In scarlet, gold-betrimmed attire:
    A little cloak of heavy silk brocade,
    Here on my hat a tall cock's-feather too,
    Here at my side a long and pointed blade;
    And now, to make it brief, I counsel you   1540
    That you too likewise be arrayed,
    That you, emancipated, free,
    Experience what life may be.
Faust.   I'll feel, whatever my attire,
    The pain of life, earth's narrow way.   1545
    I am too old to be content with play,
    Too young to be without desire.
    What can the world afford me now?
    Thou shalt renounce! Renounce shalt thou!
    That is the never-ending song   1550
    Which in the ears of all is ringing,
    Which always, through our whole life long,
    Hour after hour is hoarsely singing.
    I but with horror waken with the sun,
    I'd fain weep bitter tears, because I see   1555
    Another day that, in its course, for me
    Will not fulfil one wish — not one,
    Yea, that the foretaste of each joy possessed
    With carping criticism half erases,
    That checks creation in my stirring breast   1560
    With thousands of life's grinning faces.
    I too, when darkness sinks down o'er me,
    Must anxious stretch me on my bed;
    There, too, no rest comes nigh my weary head,
    For savage dreams will rise before me.   1565
    The god that dwells within my soul
    Can stir to life my inmost deeps.
    Full sway over all my powers he keeps,
    But naught external can he ever control.
    So Being like a load on me is pressed,   1570
    I long for death, existence I detest.
Mephistopheles.   And yet Death never is a wholly welcome guest.

Faust.   Ah, happy he around whose brow Death binds
    The blood-stained wreath mid victory's blaze,
    Whom in a maiden's arms Death finds   1575
    After a dance's maddening maze.
    Oh, would that I, beneath the lofty Spirit's sway,
    Enrapt, had rendered up my soul and sunk away!
Mephistopheles.   And yet that night, those juices brown
    A certain man did not drink down.   1580
Faust.   Spying is your delight, is that not so?
Mephistopheles.   Omniscient am I not, yet many things I know.
Faust.   Though, from the frightful frenzy reeling,
    A sweet, familiar tone drew me away,
    Though what remained of childlike feeling   1585
    Was duped by echoes of a happier day,
    I now curse all that, round the soul, enfolds it
    With dazzling lures and jugglery,
    And, banned within this cave of sorrows, holds it
    With blinding spells and flattery.   1590
    Cursed, before all, the high adherence
    To some opinion that ensnares the mind!
    Cursed be the blinding of appearance
    That holds our senses thus confined!
    Cursed be dissembling dream-obsessions,   1595
    The fraud of fame, a name's enduring life!
    Cursed all that flatters as possessions,
    As slave and plough, as child and wife!
    Cursed too be Mammon, when with treasures
    He stirs us on to deeds of might,   1600
    When he, for lazy, idle pleasures,
    Lays down for us the cushions right!
    Cursed be the grape's sweet juice deceiving!
    Cursed Love's supreme, delicious thrall!
    A curse on Hoping! on Believing!   1605
    And cursed be Patience most of all!
Chorus of Spirits invisible.
             Woe! Woe!
             Thou hast destroyed
             The beautiful world,
             With powerful fist;   1610
             'Tis smashed, downward hurled!
             A demigod dashed it to bits!

We're trailing
The ruins on to the Void,
And wailing   1615
Over the beauty lost and gone!
Mighty one
Midst the sons of earth,
Splendider
Build it again,   1620
Build it aloft in thy breast!
And life's new quest
Commence
With clearer sense,
And songs of cheer   1625
Anew shalt hear!

Mephistopheles.

These are the little folk
Of those whom I evoke.
Hark how they to joy and deed
Sagely bid you to give heed!   1630
Into life they would,
Far from solitude
Where stagnate sap and sense,
Persuade and lure you hence.

Cease with your brooding grief to play   1635
That, like a vulture, eats your life away.
The worst of company will let you find
That you're a man among mankind.
But yet I don't mean that I'll thrust
You midst the rabble men don't trust.   1640
I'm not one of the Great;
Still, if through life you'll go with me,
In that case I'll agree
With pleasure to accommodate
You, on the spot belong to you.   1645
I'll be your comrade true
And if to your liking I behave,
I'll be your servant, be your slave!
Faust.   And what in turn am I to do for you?
Mephistopheles.   That is a long way off! Pray don't insist.   1650
Faust.   No, no! The Devil is an egoist

[48]

And not "for God's sake!" only will he do
What will another's needs assist.
Tell me your terms both plain and clear!
Such servants in the house bring danger near.   1655
Mephistopheles.   *Here* to your service I will bind me;
Beck when you will, I will not pause or rest;
But in return when *yonder* you will find me,
Then likewise shall you be at my behest.
Faust.   The *yonder* is to me a trifling matter.   1660
Should you this world to ruins shatter,
The other then may rise, its place to fill.
'Tis from this earth my pleasure springs,
And this sun shines upon my sufferings;
When once I separate me from these things,   1665
Let happen then what can and will.
And furthermore I've no desire to hear
Whether in future too men hate and love,
And whether too in yonder sphere
There is an *under* or *above*.   1670
Mephistopheles.   In this mood you can dare to go my ways.
Commit yourself; you shall in these next days
Behold my arts and with great pleasure too.
What no man yet has seen, I'll give to you.
Faust.   Poor devil! What have you to give?   1675
Was any human spirit, struggling to ascend,
Such as your sort could ever comprehend?
Still, have you food on which no man can live?
Have you red gold that runs through, without rest,
Quicksilver-like, the hand it's in?   1680
A game at which men never win?
A maiden who while on my breast
Will with my neighbour ogle and conspire?
The joys divine of honour, once possessed,
Which vanish like a meteor's fire?   1685
Show me the fruit which, ere it's plucked, will rot,
And trees that every day grow green anew!
Mephistopheles.   Such a commission frights me not;
Such treasures I can serve to you.
But, my good friend, the time approaches when we could   1690
In peace and quiet feast on something good.
Faust.   If ever I lay me on a bed of sloth in peace,

That instant let for me existence cease!
If ever with lying flattery you can rule me
So that contented with myself I stay,   1695
If with enjoyment you can fool me,
Be that for me the final day!
That bet I offer!
Mephistopheles.   Done!
Faust.   Another hand-clasp! There!
If to the moment I shall ever say:
"Ah, linger on, thou art so fair!" *   1700
Then may you fetters on me lay,
Then will I perish, then and there!
Then may the death-bell toll, recalling
Then from your service you are free;
The clock may stop, the pointer falling,   1705
And time itself be past for me!
Mephistopheles.   Consider well, we'll not forget it.
Faust.   Your perfect right to that I'll not deny.
My action was not rash, I'll not regret it.
As soon as I stagnate, a slave am I,   ·   1710
And whether yours or whose, why should I ask?
Mephistopheles.   Then at a Doctor's-feast this very day
I'll act as servant and fulfil my task.
But one thing still: in case of life or death, I pray,
Give me a written line or two.   1715
Faust.   What, pedant! Something written do you ask of me?
Was neither man nor word of man yet known to you?
Is it not enough that this my spoken word
Disposes of my days for all eternity?
Does not the world rush on, in all its currents stirred,   1720
And should a promise have a hold on me?
Yet to our hearts we've taken this conceit.
Who gladly would its hold undo?
Blest he whose bosom is with breachless faith replete,
No sacrifice will that man ever rue.   1725
But any stamped and written parchment sheet
Is like a ghost that all men shrink to view.
The spoken word dies forthwith in the quill;
Leather and wax remain our masters still.
What, Evil Spirit, do you want of me?   1730
Brass, marble, parchment, paper? Name it then!

Am I to write with graver, chisel, pen?
I offer you your choice quite free.
Mephistopheles.   How can you talk so heatedly,
   Exaggerate in such a way?   1735
   Just any little sheet will do, it's all the same.
   With one wee drop of blood you sign your name.
Faust.   If this will satisfy you, then I say:
   Let us agree and put the farce to this odd use.
Mephistopheles.   Blood is a quite peculiar juice.   1740
Faust.   Fear not! This league with you I shall not break!
   The aim and goal of all my energy
   Is to fulfil the promise I now make.
   I've puffed myself too high, I see;
   Only within your ranks do I deserve to be.   1745
   The Mighty Spirit spurned me with a scoff,
   And Nature turns herself away from me.
   The thread of thought is broken off,
   To me all learning's long been nauseous.
   In depths of sensuality   1750
   Let us our glowing passions still!
   In magic's veils impervious
   Prepared at once be every marvel's thrill!
   Come, let us plunge into Time's rushing dance,
   Into the roll of Circumstance!   1755
   There may then pain and joyance,
   Successes and annoyance,
   Alternately follow as they can.
   Only restlessly active is a man!
Mephistopheles.   To you no goal is set, nor measure.   1760
   If you should like to nibble everything,
   To snatch up something on the wing,
   May all agree with you that gives you pleasure!
   Fall to, I say, and don't be coy.
Faust.   You hear indeed, I do not speak of joy.   1765
   Life's wildering whirl be mine, its painfulest enjoyment,
   Enamoured hate, and quickening annoyment.
   My bosom, of all thirst for knowledge cured,
   Shall close itself henceforth against no woe;
   Whatever to all mankind is assured,   1770
   I, in my inmost being, will enjoy and know,
   Seize with my soul the highest and most deep;

Men's weal and woe upon my bosom heap;
And thus this self of mine to all their selves expanded,
Like them I too at last be stranded.   1775
Mephistopheles.   Oh, trust me who for many a thousand year
Have chewed this crust, it is so hard at best
That twixt the cradle and the bier
That ancient leaven no man can digest.
Trust one like me: this Whole is wrought   1780
And fashioned only for a God's delight!
He dwells in an eternal light;
Us into darkness He has brought;
To you are suited only day and night.
Faust.   Ah, but I will!
Mephistopheles.   Well said and right!   1785
And yet I fear there is but one thing wrong;
For life is short and art is long.
I'd think you'd let yourself be taught.
Associate you with a poet; then, in thought,
You leave the gentleman full sweep,   1790
Upon your honoured head to heap
Each good and noble quality:
The lion's mood,
The stag's rapidity,
The fiery blood of Italy,   1795
The Northman's hardihood.
The secret for it? Let him find
How magnanimity and cunning are combined,
How with a youth's hot impulse you may fall
In love according to a plan.   1800
Might I myself know such a gentleman,
Him Mr. Microcosm I would call.
Faust.   What am I if I strive in vain
To win the crown of all mankind which, though **afar,**
All senses struggle to obtain?   1805
Mephistopheles.   You at the end are — what you are.
Put on your head perukes with a million locks,
Put on your feet a pair of ell-high socks,
You after all will still be — what you are.
Faust.   I feel that I have made each treasure   1810
Of human mind my own in vain,
And when at last I sit me down at leisure,

No new-born power wells up within my brain.
I'm not a hair's-breadth more in height
Nor nearer to the Infinite.   1815
Mephistopheles.   My good sir, you observe this matter
As men these matters always see;
But we must manage that much better
Before life's pleasures from us flee.
Your hands and feet too — what the devil! —   1820
Your head and seed are yours alone!
Yet all with which I gaily revel,
Is it on that account the less my own?
If for six stallions I can pay,
Aren't all their powers added to my store?   1825
I am a proper man and dash away
As if the legs I had were twenty-four!
Quick, then! Let all reflection be,
And straight into the world with me!
A chap who speculates — let this be said —   1830
Is very like a beast on moorland dry,
That by some evil spirit round and round is led,
While fair, green pastures round about him lie.
Faust.   But how shall we begin?
Mephistopheles.   We'll just get out, so come!
Bah! what a place of martyrdom!   1835
What kind of life is this you lead?
Boring the youngsters and yourself indeed!
Leave that to Master Paunch, your neighbour!
Why plague yourself by threshing straw?
The best that you can know with all your labour,   1840
You dare not tell the striplings raw.
Right now I hear one in the passageway.
Faust.   I can not possibly see him today.
Mephistopheles.   He's waited long, the poor young chap;
Uncomforted, he must not go away.   1845
Come, let me have your gown and cap;
I in that costume? What a precious fit!
                    He dresses himself up
Now you can leave things to my wit!
I only need a quarter of an hour.
And then our lovely tour, meanwhile prepare for it!   1850
                    Exit FAUST
                    [53]

Mephistopheles in F A U S T's *long robe.*

    Humanity's most lofty power,
    Reason and knowledge, pray despise!
    Let but the Spirit of all Lies
    With works of dazzling magic blind you;
    Then, absolutely mine, I'll have and bind you!—   1855
    To him has Fate a spirit given
    That, uncurbed, ever onward sweeps,
    Whose striving, by too hasty impulse driven,
    The joys of this earth overleaps.
    Him will I drag through wild life whirling past,   1860
    Through all that is unmeaning, shallow stuff;
    I'll see him struggle, weaken, and stick fast!
    Before his greedy lips that can not feast enough
    Shall hover food and drink as if for some grand revel;
    Refreshment will he all in vain implore;   1865
    And had he not surrendered to the Devil,
    Still were he lost forevermore.

A S T U D E N T enters

Student.   I've been here just a little while or so
    And come to pay an humble call,
    To talk with you, a man to know,   1870
    One who is named with reverence by all.
Mephistopheles.   You please me greatly by your courtesy!
    A man like many another one you see.
    Have you already looked about elsewhere?
Student.   I beg you, take me in your kindly care!   1875
    I come with every good intention,
    Fresh blood, and money, though not much to mention.
    My mother scarcely would permit my going.
    I'd fain learn here abroad something worth knowing.
Mephistopheles.   Well, now you're at the proper place.   1880
Student.   Yet, frankly, would I could my steps retrace!
    Within these walls, the lecture hall,
    I do not like it here at all.
    It is a space that's so confined;
    One sees no green nor any tree,   1885
    And in the halls with benches lined,
    Sight, hearing, thought, all go from me.
Mephistopheles.   That only comes with habit, so
    A child takes not its mother's breast

[54]

Quite willingly in the beginning, though 1890
Soon nourishes itself with zest.
So at the breasts of Wisdom nursed,
Each day you'll lust for them the more athirst.
Student.   I'll cling about her neck with joy,
But say what means thereto I shall employ. 1895
Mephistopheles.   Ere you go on, explain your views.
Which is the faculty you choose?
Student.   I'd like right learnèd to become; what is
On earth I'd gladly comprehend,
To heaven itself my range extend, 1900
Know all of nature and the sciences.
Mephistopheles.   Then you are on the proper way
But must not let yourself be lured astray.
Student.   Body and soul I'm for it bent;
Yet there would please me, I must say, 1905
A little freedom and divertisement
Upon a pleasant summer holiday.
Mephistopheles.   Make use of time, its course so soon is run,
Yet system teaches you how time is won.
I counsel you, dear friend, in sum, 1910
That first you take *collegium logicum.*
Your spirit's then well broken in for you,
In Spanish boots laced tightly to,
That you henceforth may more deliberately keep
The path of thought and straight along it creep, 1915
And not perchance criss-cross may go,
A-will-o'-wisping to and fro.
Then you'll be taught full many a day
What at one stroke you've done alway,
Like eating and like drinking free, 1920
It now must go like: One! Two! Three!
In fact, when men are fabricating thought,
It goes as when a weaver's masterpiece is wrought.
One treadle sets a thousand threads a-going,
And to and fro the shuttle flies; 1925
Quite unperceived the threads are flowing,
One stroke effects a thousand ties.
Then some philosopher steps in, and he
Will demonstrate to you it so must be:
The first was so, the second so, 1930

[55]

And thus the third and fourth are so;
And if no first nor second had been there,
The third and fourth one would be never.
All students prize that everywhere,
But are they weavers? No, they're not that clever.   1935
Who'll know aught living and describe it well,
Seeks first the spirit to expel.
He then has the component parts in hand
But lacks, alas! the spirit's band.
Encheirisis naturae, Chemistry names it so,   1940
Mocking herself but all unwitting though.

Student. I can't quite understand you, I confess.

Mephistopheles. Next time, be sure, you will have more success,
When you have learned how to reduce
And classify all by its use.   1945

Student. I feel as stupid after all you've said
As if a miller's wheel were whirling in my head.

Mephistopheles. And next — the first of all worth mention —
To Metaphysics you must give attention,
And see that you profoundly strive to gain   1950
What is not suited for the human brain.
For what goes in or won't go in the head,
A brilliant phrase will serve you in good stead.
Yet, first of all for this half-year,
Observe the best of systems here.   1955
You take five lectures daily — understand?
And when the clock strikes, be on hand!
Be well prepared before the start,
With paragraphs well got by heart,
So later you can better look   1960
And see he says naught save what's in the book;
But write away as unabated
As if the Holy Ghost dictated!

Student. You will not need to say that to me twice!
I can foresee how much I'll gain from this advice;   1965
Because what one has down in black and white
It is a comfort to take home at night.

Mephistopheles. But come now, choose a faculty!

Student. I can't adjust myself to Law — not possibly.

Mephistopheles. I can't blame that in you, it's no demerit.   1970
This science as it really is I see.

Statutes and laws that we inherit
Like an eternal malady
Go trailing on from race to race
And furtive shift from place to place.   1975
To nonsense reason turns, and benefit to worry.
Woe unto you that you're a grandchild, woe!
For of the law that was born with us, no!
Of that, alas! there never is a query.
Student.   You have increased my own disgust. The youth   1980
Whom you instruct is blessed in sooth!
I'm now almost inclined to try Theology.
Mephistopheles.   I would not wish to lead you so astray.
In what this science teaches, it would be
So hard to shun the false, misleading way;   1985
So much of hidden poison lies therein,
You scarce can tell it from its medicine.
'Tis best here too that only one be heard
And that you swear then by the master's word.
Upon the whole — to words stick fast!   1990
Then through a sure gate you'll at last
Enter the templed hall of Certainty.
Student.   Yet in each word some concept there must be.
Mephistopheles.   Quite true! But don't torment yourself too anxiously;
For at the point where concepts fail,   1995
At the right time a word is thrust in there.
With words we fitly can our foes assail,
With words a system we prepare,
Words we quite fitly can believe,
Nor from a word a mere iota thieve.   2000
Student.   Pardon, I keep you here with many a question,
But I must cause more trouble still.
Concerning Medicine as well you will
Not make some pithy, keen suggestion?
Three years! how quickly they are past!   2005
And, God! the field is far too vast.
If but some sign is indicated,
A man can sooner feel his way.
Mephistopheles aside.   With this dry tone I am now satiated;
The downright devil I must once more play.   2010
                              Aloud
Medicine's spirit one can grasp with ease.

[57]

The great and little world you study through,
To let things finally their course pursue
As God may please.
It's vain that you in search of knowledge roam and drift,   2015
Each only learns what learn he can;
Yet he who grasps the moment's gift,
He is your proper man.
You are moreover quite well built, beside,
Will never lack for boldness too;   2020
And if you only in yourself confide,
All other souls confide in you.
Learn chiefly how to lead the women; be assured
That all their "Oh-s" and "Ah-s," eternal, old,
So thousandfold,   2025
Can at a single point be cured;
And if you half-way decorously come,
You have them all beneath your thumb.
A title first must make them comprehend
That your art many arts doth far transcend.   2030
By way of welcome then you touch all matters
For sake of which, long years, another flatters.
Learn how the little pulse to squeeze
And then with sly and fiery glances seize
Her freely round the slender hips to see   2035
How firmly laced up she may be.
Student.   Now that looks better! Now one sees the where and how!
Mephistopheles.   Dear friend, all theory is grey,
    And green the golden tree of life.
Student.   I vow,
    It's all just like a dream to me.   2040
    Another time I'll bore you, if I may,
    To hear your wisdom through and through.
Mephistopheles.   All that I can I'll gladly do.
Student.   It is impossible for me to go away
    Before I hand my album here to you.   2045
    Will your grace grant this favour to me too?
Mephistopheles.   Oh, very well!
                        He writes and gives it back
Student reads.   Eritis sicut Deus, scientes bonum et malum.
                        *He closes the book reverently and takes his
                        leave*

[58]

Mephistopheles.   Follow the ancient text and heed my coz the snake;
  With all your likeness to God you'll sometimes tremble and quake.   2050

F A U S T enters

Faust.   Now whither shall we go?
Mephistopheles.   Whither it pleases you.
  We'll see the little world and then we'll see the great.
  With how much joy and how much profit too
  You'll sponge the whole course through until you graduate.
Faust.   But with my beard so long I may   2055
  Quite lack life's free and easy way.
  In this attempt no luck will come to me;
  I never fitted in society at all.
  With other men I feel myself so small;
  I'll feel embarrassed constantly.   2060
Mephistopheles.   For that, good friend, this is the remedy I give:
  Just trust yourself, then you'll know how to live.
Faust.   We'll leave the house but how shall we set out?
  Have you a horse, a servant, carriage, anywhere?
Mephistopheles.   We'll only spread this mantle out   2065
  And have it bear us through the air.
  You'll take upon this daring flight
  No heavy luggage, only light.
  A bit of fiery air — I'll have it ready here —
  Will lift us from this earth without ado,   2070
  And if we're light, we'll go up swiftly too.
  I must congratulate you on your new career.

Auerbach's Cellar in Leipsic

DRINKING–BOUT OF JOLLY COMPANIONS

Frosch.   Will no one drink? and no one laugh?
  I'll teach you how to look so wry!
  You're everyone like sodden chaff   2075
  And always used to blaze sky-high!
Brander.   That's your fault; you don't add a single stroke,
  No beastliness and not one silly joke.
Frosch pours a glass of wine over B R A N D E R ' S *head.*
  There you have both!

Brander. You twofold beast!

Frosch. That's what you asked me for, at least! 2080

Siebel. If any quarrel, throw 'em out!
Come, sing with all your lungs, boys, swill and shout!
Up! Holla! Ho!

Altmayer. My God! I'm done for! Here!
Some cotton wool! The fellow bursts my ear.

Siebel. When vaulted ceilings echo back our song, 2085
Then first we feel the bass is deep and strong.

Frosch. Quite right! Then out with him who takes a thing amiss!
Ah! tara lara da!

Altmayer. Ah! tara lara da!

Frosch. The throats are tuned for this!
He sings
Dear Holy Roman Empire! Say, 2090
How does it stick together?

Brander. A nasty song! Shame! a political song!
A wretched song! Thank God each morning, brother,
That for the Roman Empire you don't need to bother!
There is at least one gain I am most thankful for, 2095
That I'm not Kaiser and not Chancellor.
And yet we must not fail to have a ruler. Stay!
Let us elect a Pope! What do you say?
You know the kind of quality that can
Bear down the scale and elevate the man. 2100

Frosch sings.
Soar aloft, Dame Nightingale,
Ten thousand times my sweetheart hail!

Siebel. No greeting to a sweetheart! I'll not hear of this!

Frosch. You will not hinder me! My sweetheart, hail! A kiss!
He sings
Lift the latch! In silent night. 2105
Lift the latch! The lover wakes.
Drop the latch! The morning breaks.

Siebel. Yes, sing on, praise and brag of her with all your might!
I will in my own time be sure to laugh at you.
She once led me astray, she'll do it to you too. 2110
Give her a kobold for her lovesick yearning!

[60]

At some cross-road let him go woo her.
Let some old buck, from Blocksberg homeward turning,
Still on the gallop, bleat "Good Evening!" to her.
A gallant fellow of real flesh and blood   2115
Is for that wench a deal too good.
I'll hear no greetings to that lass
But such as smash her window-glass.

Brander pounding on the table.

Give heed! Give heed! Lend me your ear!
You, sirs, confess that I know what is what.   2120
Some lovesick folk are sitting here,
And so in honour due their present lot
I must contribute to their night's good cheer.
Give heed! A brand-new song 'twill be!
And sing the chorus lustily!   2125

He sings

There once in a cellar lived a rat,
Had a paunch could scarce be smoother,
For it lived on butter and on fat,
A mate for Doctor Luther.
But soon the cook did poison strew   2130
And then the rat, so cramped it grew
As if it had love in its body.

Chorus shouting.

As if it had love in its body.

Brander.

It flew around, and out it flew,
From every puddle swilling,   2135
It gnawed and scratched the whole house through,
But its rage was past all stilling.
It jumped full oft in anguish mad,
But soon, poor beast, enough it had,
As if it had love in its body.   2140

Chorus.

As if it had love in its body.

Brander.

By anguish driven in open day
It rushed into the kitchen,
Fell on the hearth and panting lay,
Most pitiably twitchin'.   2145

[61]

Then laughed the poisoner: "Hee! hee! hee!
It's at its last gasp now," said she,
"As if it had love in its body."

Chorus.

"As if it had love in its body."

Siebel.　　How these dull chaps enjoy themselves! Now that's　　2150
A fine old art, so it would seem,
To scatter poison for poor rats!

Brander.　　They stand so high in your esteem?

Altmayer.　　See the old tub, so bald and fat!
Misfortune makes him mild and tame;　　2155
He sees in any bloated rat
His very own image, quite the same.

FAUST *and* MEPHISTOPHELES *enter*

Mephistopheles.　　Before all else I now must let you view
The doings of a jovial crew,
That you may see how smoothly life can flow along.　　2160
To this crowd every day's a feast and song.
With little wit and much content,
Each, on his own small round intent,
Is like a kitten with its tail.
While no sick headache they bewail　　2165
And while their host will still more credit give,
Joyous and free from care they live.

Brander.　　Those people come directly from a tour,
You see it in their strange, odd ways;
They've not been here an hour, I'm sure.　　2170

Frosch.　　In truth, you're right! My Leipsic will I praise!
A little Paris, one that cultivates its people.

Siebel.　　Who are these strangers, do you think?

Frosch.　　Leave it to me! Give me a brimming drink
And from these chaps I'll worm the truth　　2175
As one draws out a young child's tooth.
To me they seem of noble family,
So proud and discontented they appear to be.

Brander.　　They're mountebanks, I'll lay a bet with you!

Altmayer.　　Perhaps!

Frosch.　　　　　　　　Pay heed, I'll make them feel the screw!　　2180

Mephistopheles to FAUST.　　These chaps don't scent the Devil out
And would not if he had them by the snout!

Faust.　　We greet you, sirs!

[62]

Siebel.   Thanks and to you the same!
                          In a low tone, looking at MEPHISTOPHELES
                          askance
      Why is that fellow's one foot lame?
Mephistopheles.   We'll sit with you if you'll permit the liberty.   2185
      Instead of some good drink which is not here,
      We shall enjoy your company's good cheer.
Altmayer.   A very pampered man you seem to be.
Frosch.   I guess you started late from Rippach on your way.
      Can you have supped with Master Hans tonight?   2190
Mephistopheles.   We passed him by without a stop today!
      We spoke with him last time. He'd quite
      A lot about his cousins to convey,
      Charged us with greetings to each one.
                          He bows toward FROSCH
Altmayer in a low tone.   You got it then! He knows!
Siebel.   A cunning fellow, he! 2195
Frosch.   Just wait a bit, I'll get him on the run.
Mephistopheles.   If I mistake not, didn't we
      Hear practised voices sing in chorus?
      In truth, a song must perfectly
      Reëcho from this vaulted ceiling o'er us!   2200
Frosch.   Are you perchance a virtuoso?
Mephistopheles.   Oh no! The zest is great, ability but so-so.
Altmayer.   Give us a song!
Mephistopheles.   A lot, if that way you incline.
Siebel.   But let it be a brand-new strain!
Mephistopheles.   We have returned quite recently from Spain,   2205
      The lovely land of melody and wine.
                          He sings
                  A king there once was reigning,
                  Who cherished a great big flea —

Frosch.   Hear that! A flea! Did you quite grasp the jest?
      I say, a flea's a tidy guest.   2210
Mephistopheles sings.
                  A king there once was reigning,
                  Who cherished a great big flea;
                  No little love attaining,
                  As his own son loved he.
                  He called his tailor hireling,   2215

The tailor to him flew:
" Ho, measure now the squireling
For coat and breeches too."

Brander.   Be sure to tell that man of stitches
    That he must measure to a hair,   2220
    And if his head is dear to him, I swear,
    No wrinkles must be in those breeches!
Mephistopheles.

        In silk and velvet splendid
        He now was always dressed,
        By ribbons gay attended,   2225
        A cross upon his breast.
        Was minister created,
        A mighty star did sport;
        Then all his kin, elated,
        Became great lords at court.   2230

        Lord, lady, and dependent
        Were plagued and sore distressed;
        The queen and her attendant
        Were bitten by the pest.
        And yet they dared not whack them   2235
        Nor scratch by day or night.
        We smother and we crack them
        Whenever we feel them bite.
Chorus shouting.

        We smother and we crack them
        Whenever we feel them bite.   2240

Frosch.   Bravo! Bravo! That was splendid!
Siebel.   And so should every flea be ended!
Brander.   Point your fingers and squeeze them fine!
Altmayer.   Long live freedom! Long live wine!
Mephistopheles.   A glass to honour freedom I would gladly clink   2245
    If but your wines were better fit to drink.
Siebel.   We do not want to hear such talk again!
Mephistopheles.   I only fear the landlord might complain;
    Else I would treat each worthy guest
    With what our cellar offers of the best.   2250
Siebel.   Do bring it on! The risk be mine.

Frosch.   Produce a good glass and we'll praise your wine.
But don't give us a sample all too small;
If I'm to play the solemn judge at all,
A right good mouthful I require.   2255
Altmayer in a low tone.   They're from the Rhine, I scented that before.
Mephistopheles.   Fetch me a gimlet!
Brander.   Say, why that desire?
You haven't got the casks outside the door?
Altmayer.   Back there the landlord keeps his tool-kit placed.
Mephistopheles, taking the gimlet, to Frosch.
Now say, what do you want to taste?   2260
Frosch.   What do you mean? Have you so many kinds?
Mephistopheles.   I leave the choice to each. Make up your minds!
Altmayer to Frosch.
You're licking your chops now! Be careful, steady!
Frosch.   'Tis well! If I'm to choose, it's Rhine wine I propose.
The best of gifts is what the fatherland bestows.   2265
Mephistopheles, boring a hole in the edge of the table at the place where
Frosch *is sitting.*
Get us some wax at once, to have the stoppers ready!
Altmayer.   Ah! These are tricks! It's jugglery!
Mephistopheles to Brander.   And you?
Brander.   Champagne's the stuff for me,
And bubbling, sparkling, must it be.
                                    Mephistopheles *is boring holes; one of*
                                    the others has meanwhile made the stoppers
                                    and plugged the holes
Brander.   What's foreign we can't always shun,   2270
So far from us must good things often be.
A genuine German can't abide the French, not one,
But of their wines he drinks most cheerfully.
Siebel as Mephistopheles *comes near his place.*
I do not like the sour, I'd have you know;
Give me a glass that's really sweet!   2275
Mephistopheles boring.   You'll see, at once Tokay will flow.
Altmayer.   No, gentlemen, just look me in the face! I see't,
You're only fooling us, it is a jest.
Mephistopheles.   Oh! Oh! With such a noble guest
That were a bit too much to dare!   2280
Be quick about it and declare!
What kind of wine then shall I serve?

Altmayer.   Oh, any! Don't keep asking! I don't care!

                    After all the holes are bored and plugged

Mephistopheles with strange gestures.

           Clustered grapes the vine bears!

           And horns the he-goat wears!   2285

           The wine is juicy, wood the vine;

           The wooden table too can give forth wine.

           A view of nature, deep and clear!

           Only believe! A miracle's here!

    Now draw the stoppers and enjoy your fill!   2290

All while they pull out the stoppers and the wine desired runs into each one's

    glass.   O beauteous fountain flowing at our will!

Mephistopheles.   But watch, I say, that not a drop you spill!

                They drink repeatedly

All sing.

           We're just as happy as cannibals,

           As if we were five hundred swine!

Mephistopheles.   Behold how happy is this folk — it's free!   2295

Faust.   I think now I would like to go away.

Mephistopheles.   But first give heed to a display

    Of glorious bestiality.

Siebel drinks carelessly; the wine is spilt upon the ground and turns into

    flame.   Help! Hell's on fire! It's burning me!

Mephistopheles conjuring the flame.   Be quiet, friendly element!   2300

                To the young man

    This time 'twas but a flame that Purgatory sent.

Siebel.   What's that? Just wait! For that you will pay dear.

    You don't know who we are, that's clear.

Frosch.   Don't try that game a second time, I say!

Altmayer.   I think we'd better bid him gently go away.   2305

Siebel.   What, sir! You venture to provoke us

    And carry on your hocus-pocus?

Mephistopheles.   Silence, old wine-butt!

Siebel.   Broomstick, you!

    Will you insult me to my nose?

Brander.   Just wait a bit, 'twill soon be raining blows!   2310

Altmayer draws a stopper out of the table; fire leaps out at him.

    I burn! I burn!

Siebel.   It's sorcery!

The rogue's an outlaw! Come, thrust home with me!
> *They draw their knives and rush at*
> MEPHISTOPHELES

Mephistopheles with solemn gestures.
> False form and word appear,
> Change place and sense's sphere!
> Be there and here!   2315
> *They stand amazed and look at each other*

Altmayer.   Where am I? What a lovely land!
Frosch.   Vineyards! Do I see right?
Siebel.   Grape clusters close at hand!
Brander.   Here underneath this foliage green,
   See, what a bunch! What grapes are to be seen!
> *He seizes* SIEBEL *by the nose. The others do*
> *the same, one to the other, and raise their knives*

Mephistopheles as before.   Error, loose from their eyes the band!   2320
   And mark you how the Devil's jesting goes.
> *He vanishes with* FAUST. *The fellows start*
> *back from one another*

Siebel.   What's up?
Altmayer.   How's this?
Frosch.   Was that your nose?
Brander *to* SIEBEL.   And yours I'm holding in my hand!
Altmayer.   That was a blow, it staggered me down to my toes!
   I can't stand up, get me a chair!   2325
Frosch.   Out with it, say, what's happened?
Siebel.   Where,
   Oh, where's that rascal? If I find him now,
   He shan't escape alive, I vow.
Altmayer.   With my own eyes I saw him riding through
   The cellar-door — upon a wine-cask too!   2330
   I feel a weight like lead about my feet!
> *Turning toward the table*
   My God! I wonder if the wines still flow?
Siebel.   It was a swindle, lies, 'twas all a cheat.
Frosch.   Yet I drank wine or thought it so.
Brander.   But how about the grapes? What was that anyway?   2335
Altmayer.   One should believe no miracles? Oh, say!

Witch's Kitchen

*A great cauldron stands over the fire on a low hearth. In the
steam which rises from it, various figures become visible. A Female Ape sits by the cauldron and skims the
foam off it, taking care that it does not run over. The
Male Ape, with the Young Apes, sits beside it and
warms himself. Walls and ceiling are decked out
with the strangest articles of witches' furniture*

FAUST   MEPHISTOPHELES

Faust.   I am repelled by this mad sorcery.
    I shall get well, you promise me,
    In this chaotic craziness?
    Shall I demand an old crone's remedy?   2340
    And will the dirty, boiling mess
    Divest my body of some thirty years?
    Woe's me, if there's naught better you can find!
    For now my hope already disappears.
    Has nature not, has not a noble mind,   2345
    Discovered somewhere any balm?
Mephistopheles.   My friend, you talk once more as if you're calm.
    By natural means you can acquire a youthful look,
    But it is in another book
    And is a chapter strange to see.   2350
Faust.   Still I will know it.
Mephistopheles.   Good! To have a remedy
    Without physician, money, sorcery:
    Betake yourself into the fields without delay,
    Begin to dig and hack away,
    Maintain yourself, your thought and feeling,   2355
    Within a circle quite confined and fixed;
    Take nourishment of food that is not mixed;
    Live with the beasts as beast, nor deem it base
    To spread the fields you reap with your own dung.
    Be sure, this method's best in any case,   2360
    Though eighty years of age, still to be young.
Faust.   I am not used to that; I can't submit
    To take the spade in hand and dig and ditch.
    For me a narrow life is quite unfit.

Mephistopheles.   So then there is no help save from the witch.   2365
Faust.   But why the old beldame? What is your notion?
   Can you yourself not brew the potion?
Mephistopheles.   That were a lovely pastime on my part!
   Meanwhile a thousand bridges I could rear.
   We can't depend alone on science or on art,   2370
   The work demands a deal of patience too.
   A quiet spirit's busy many a year,
   For time alone produces potent brew.
   And all that is a part of it
   Is wondrous as one must admit!   2375
   It's true, the Devil taught her how to do it,
   And yet the Devil can not brew it.
Catching sight of THE BEASTS
   How delicate the breed! Just see!
   That is the maid! The man is he!
To THE BEASTS
   It seems the dame is not at home with you.   2380
The Beasts.

To a rollicking crew
Out she flew
By the chimney-flue!

Mephistopheles.   How long is it her wont to roam from here?
The Beasts.   As long as it takes to warm a paw.   2385
Mephistopheles to FAUST.   How do you think the dainty beasts appear?
Faust.   Absurd as anyone I ever saw.
Mephistopheles.   I say, this kind of conversation
   I carry on with greatest delection.
To THE BEASTS
   Accursèd puppets! Come and tell,   2390
   What are you querling in that stuff?
The Beasts.   A beggars' soup that's watered well.
Mephistopheles.   Then you've a public large enough.
The Male Ape sidles up to MEPHISTOPHELES *and fawns on him.*

Oh, do throw the dice,
Make me rich in a trice,   2395
And do let it win me!
It all is so bad,
If money I had,
Good sense would be in me.

[69]

Mephistopheles.   How fortunate the ape would think himself, could he   240○
But also risk some money in a lottery!
                              Meanwhile THE YOUNG APES *have been*
                              playing with a great globe which they now,
                              roll forward

The Male Ape.

                    That is the world!
                    It mounts, now whirled,
                    Its fall will follow,
                    Like glass it rings.   240○
                    Soon break such things!
                    Within it's hollow.
                    Here bright it gleams,
                    Here brighter beams.
                    I am alive!   241○
                    My dear son, strive
                    To keep away!
                    For you must die!
                    'Tis made of clay,
                    In bits 'twill fly.   241○

Mephistopheles.

                    What means the sieve?
The Male Ape takes it down.
                    Came you to thieve,
                    I would know you directly.
                         He runs to THE FEMALE APE *and*
                         makes her look through it
                    Look through the sieve!
                    Know you the thief?   242○
                    Dare not name him exactly?

Mephistopheles going nearer to the fire.
                    And then this pot?

Male Ape and Female Ape.
                    The half-witted sot!
                    He knows not the pot,
                    He knows not the kettle!   2425

Mephistopheles.
                    Unmannerly beast!
                         [70]

The Male Ape.
                Take the brush at least
                And sit on the settle!
                  He makes MEPHISTOPHELES *sit
                  down*

*Faust, who all this time has been standing before a mirror, now going near it,
    now going away from it.*
What do I see? What form divinely fair
Within this magic mirror is revealed?   2430
Oh lend me, Love, thy swiftest wing and bear
Me hence into her wondrous field!
Alas! If from this spot I dare
But stir, or if I venture to go near,
Then dim as through a mist doth she appear!   2435
The fairest image of a woman! Can it be,
Is it possible? Can woman be so fair?
Must I in that recumbent body there
Behold of all the heavens the epitome?
Can one so fair be found on earth?   2440
Mephistopheles.   Well, if a God for six whole days, my friend,
Toils hard and says " Ah, bravo! " at the end,
Then something rather neat must come to birth.
For this time gaze till you are satiate.
I know how I can find you such a treasure   2445
And he who as a bridegroom has the happy fate
To lead her home, is blessed beyond all measure!
             FAUST *continues to look in the mirror*
MEPHISTOPHELES, *stretching himself on the settle and playing with
    the brush, continues to speak.*
I sit here like a king upon his throne;
I hold the sceptre here, I lack the crown alone.
*The Beasts, who meanwhile have been playing all sorts of odd confused
    antics, bring a crown to* MEPHISTOPHELES *with a loud outcry.*
               Oh, please be so good   2450
               With sweat and with blood
               The crown to belime!
                  *They handle the crown awkwardly and shatter
                  it into two pieces with which they jump about*
               It's done for! and we,
               We speak and we see,
               We hear and we rhyme.   2455

Faust facing the mirror.   Woe's me! How nearly crazy do I feel!
Mephistopheles pointing to THE BEASTS.
    Now my head too almost begins to reel.
The Beasts.

          And if we succeed
          And all fits indeed,
          Will thoughts in it be!   2460

Faust as above.   My breast begins to burn in me!
    Let's go away immediately!
Mephistopheles in the same attitude as above.
    Well, now at least one has to say,
    There are some honest poets anyway.

        The cauldron which THE FEMALE APE *has neglected, begins to boil over; a great flame arises which streams up the chimney.* THE WITCH *comes careering down through the flame with horrible cries*

The Witch.

        Ow! Ow! Ow! Ow!   2465
        You damnèd beast! Accursèd sow!
        Neglecting kettle, scorching me now!
        Accursèd beast!

        Espying FAUST *and* MEPHISTOPHELES
        What is that here?
        Who are you here?   2470
        What will you wreak?
        Who is the sneak?
        May pangs of hell
        Burn your bones well!

        She plunges the skimming-ladle into the cauldron and sprinkles flames toward FAUST, MEPHISTOPHELES, *and* THE BEASTS. THE BEASTS *whimper*
Mephistopheles who reverses the brush which he has been holding and strikes among the glasses and pots.
        In two! In two!   2475
        There lies the brew!
        There lies the glass!
        Let the joke pass

As beat, you ass,
To melodies from you!   2480
    As THE WITCH *steps back full of rage and
horror*
Do you know me? You skeleton! You fright!
Do you know me, your lord and master?
What holds me back that I don't smite
And crush you and your ape-sprites with disaster?
Have you no more respect before the doublet red?   2485
Can you not recognize the tall cock's-feather?
Was this my face hid altogether?
My name forsooth I should have said?
The Witch.   My rough salute, sir, pardon me!
But yet no horse's-foot I see.   2490
Your pair of ravens, where are they?
Mephistopheles.   This time I'll pardon you that you were rough,
For it's a long time, sure enough,
Since we have crossed each other's way.
Culture that licks and prinks the world anew,   2495
Has reached out to the Devil too.
The northern phantom now is seen nowhere;
Where do you see the horns, the claws, and tail?
And as concerns the foot which I can't spare,
My credit socially it would impair;   2500
So I, as many young men do, avail
Myself of false calves now for many a year.
The Witch dancing.   I almost lose my senses and my brain — oh, dear! —
To see Squire Satan once more here!
Mephistopheles.   That title, woman, I forbid it me!   2505
The Witch.   Why? Has it done you any injury?
Mephistopheles.   That's been known as a fable many a season;
But men have things no better for that reason.
Free are they from the Evil One; the evil are still here.
Just call me Baron, that will satisfy me.   2510
Like other cavaliers I am a cavalier.
My noble blood you don't deny me;
This is the coat of arms I bear, see here!
    He makes an indecent gesture
The Witch laughs immoderately.
Ha! Ha! That is your very way!
Just as you ever were, you are a rogue today!   2515

[73]

Mephistopheles to F A U S T.   My friend, learn well and understand,
 This is the way to take a witch in hand.
The Witch.   Now, gentlemen, what say you I shall do?
Mephistopheles.   A good glass of the well-known juice,
 Yet I must beg the oldest sort of you.   2520
 A double strength do years produce.
The Witch.   With pleasure! Here I have a bottle
 From which I sometimes wet my throttle,
 Which has no more the slightest stink;
 I'll gladly give a little glass to you.   2525
                         In a low tone
 And yet this man, if unprepared he drink,
 He can not live an hour, as you know too.
Mephistopheles.   He is a friend of mine whom it will profit well;
 I would bestow your kitchen's best on him.
 So draw your circle, speak your spell,   2530
 Give him a cup full to the brim!

>   T H E   W I T C H *with curious gestures draws a
>   circle and places marvellous things in it; mean-
>   while the glasses begin to ring, the cauldron to
>   sound and make music. Lastly, she brings a
>   large book and places the* A P E S *in a circle so
>   as to make them serve as a reading-desk and
>   hold the torch. She beckons* F A U S T *to come
>   near her*

Faust to M E P H I S T O P H E L E S.   What is to come of all this? Say!
 These frantic gestures and this crazy stuff?
 This most insipid, fooling play,
 I've known and hated it enough.   2535
Mephistopheles.   Nonsense! She only wants to joke us;
 I beg you, do not be so stern a man!
 Physician-like, she has to play some hocus-pocus
 So that the juice will do you all the good it can.

>   *He obliges* F A U S T *to step into the circle*

The Witch begins to declaim, with great emphasis, from the book.
>   This you must ken!   2540
>   From one make ten,
>   And two let be,
>   Make even three,
>   Then rich you'll be.
>   Skip o'er the four!   2545

From five and six,
The Witch's tricks,
Make seven and eight,
'Tis finished straight;
And nine is one,   2550
And ten is none,
    That is the witch's one-time-one!

Faust.   I think the old hag's talking in delirium.
Mephistopheles.   Much more of it is still to come.
    I know it well, thus doth the whole book chime;   2555
    I've squandered over it much time,
    For perfect contradictions, in the end,
    Remain mysterious alike for fools and sages.
    The art is old and new, my friend.
    It was the way in all the ages,   2560
    Through Three and One, and One and Three,
    Error instead of truth to scatter.
    Thus do men prate and teach untroubledly.
    With fools who'll bandy wordy chatter?
    Men oft believe, if only they hear wordy pother,   2565
    That there must surely be in it some thought or other.
The Witch goes on.
            The lofty power
            Of Wisdom's dower
            From all the world is hidden!
            Who takes no thought,   2570
            To him it's brought,
            Without a care, unbidden.

Faust.   What nonsense is she chanting here before us?
    My head's near splitting from her shrieking.
    I seem to hear a whole, great chorus,   2575
    A hundred thousand idiots speaking.
Mephistopheles.   Enough, O Sibyl excellent, enough!
    Give us your drink, the precious stuff,
    And fill the goblet quickly to the brim.
    Since he's my friend, the drink will not hurt him.   2580
    A man of numerous degrees, he's quaffed
    Already many a goodly draught.
            THE WITCH *with many ceremonies pours*

the drink into a goblet. As FAUST *lifts it to*
his mouth, a light flame rises

Mephistopheles.   Quick, down with it! And make an end!
    Your heart will be delighted by the drink.
    You are the Devil's bosom friend,   2585
    And yet, afraid of fire, you shrink?

                  THE WITCH *breaks up the circle.* FAUST
                  steps out

Mephistopheles.   Quick, now, away! You must not rest.
The Witch.   May you enjoy the small gulp's savour!
Mephistopheles to THE WITCH.   If I can do you any favour,
    Then on Walpurgis Night make your request.   2590
The Witch.   Here is a song! If sometimes sung, you'll see
    In what a special way it will affect you.
Mephistopheles to FAUST.   Come quickly and let me direct you;
    You must perspire — that needs must be —
    So that the potent juice all through you flow.   2595
    I'll teach you afterward to value noble leisure,
    And soon you'll feel with thrilling pleasure
    How Cupid stirs and leaps and trips it to and fro.
Faust.   Let me but briefly gaze once more into the glass,
    Ah! too fair seemed that woman's-form!   2600
Mephistopheles.   No, no! A model that no woman can surpass,
    You'll see anon alive and warm.
                  In a low tone
    With this drink in your body, soon you'll greet
    A Helena in every girl you meet.

A Street

    FAUST   MARGARET *passing by*

Faust.   My fair young lady, may I make so free   2605
    As to lend you my arm and company?
Margaret.   I'm not a lady, am not fair;
    I can go home without your care.
                She frees herself and exit
Faust.   By heaven, but this child is fair!
    I've never seen her equal anywhere!   2610
    So virtuous, modest, through and through,

Yet with a bit of curtness too.
Her ruby lips, her cheek's clear bloom,
I'll not forget till the day of doom!
And then how she casts down her eyes,   2615
Stamped deeply in my heart it lies!
How curt and short were her replies,
That fills me with sheer ecstasy!

MEPHISTOPHELES appears

Faust.   Hear, you must get that girl for me!
Mephistopheles.   Well, which one, then?
Faust.   She just went by.   2620
Mephistopheles.   That one? She was just coming from her priest,
Absolved from every sin, down to the least.
Hard by the chair I stole quite nigh.
She's innocent in deed and thought
And went to confession all for naught.   2625
Over her I have no power.
Faust.   She's over fourteen years old even so.
Mephistopheles.   My word! You talk like gay Lothario
Who covets for himself each lovely flower
And fancies, puffed up, there's no honour, no,   2630
Nor favour that he may not cull;
But yet that is not always possible.
Faust.   Sir Master Worshipful, I beg you, pause
And leave me in peace with all your laws!
And this I say — few words are best —   2635
Unless that sweet young maiden lays
Her head this night upon my breast,
At midnight we've gone different ways.
Mephistopheles.   Consider well what can and can not be.
I'll need at least some fourteen days   2640
But to scent out an opportunity.
Faust.   Had I but seven hours' rest, no need
Of devil would I have, to lead
A little creature such as this astray.
Mephistopheles.   You're talking almost like a Frenchman. Pray   2645
Don't let yourself be vexed beyond due measure.
What good is it to reap immediate pleasure?
The joy's not near so great, I say,
As if you first prepare the ground
With every sort of idle folly,   2650

[77]

Knead and make ready your pretty dolly,
As many Romance tales expound.
Faust. I've appetite without that too.
Mephistopheles. Now jests aside, no more ado.
With that good, lovely child, indeed, 2655
I tell you once for all, we can't use speed.
There's nothing here to take by storm;
To strategy we must conform.
Faust. Get something that the angel owns for me!
Oh, lead me to her place of rest! 2660
Get me a kerchief from her breast,
A garter to my ecstasy!
Mephistopheles. Now just to prove that I will be
Of helpful service in your agony,
We'll lose no moment in delay. 2665
I'll lead you to her room this very day.
Faust. And shall I see her? have her?
Mephistopheles. No!
For she'll be at a neighbour's for a chat or so.
While she is gone, all by yourself you may
Enjoy her atmosphere till you are sated 2670
And feast on all the hope of joys anticipated.
Faust. Can we go there?
Mephistopheles. It is too early yet.
Faust. Provide a gift for her and don't forget.
Exit
Mephistopheles. Ah, gifts at once? That's good! He'll make a hit!
Full many a lovely place I know 2675
And many a treasure buried long ago.
I must survey the ground a bit.
Exit

Evening

A NEAT LITTLE ROOM

Margaret plaiting and binding up her braids of hair.
I would give something, could I say
Who was that gentleman today!
Right gallant did he seem to be 2680

And of some noble family.
That from his brow I could have told —
Else he would not have been so bold.
Exit

Mephistopheles   Faust

Mephistopheles.   Come! come in! and on tiptoe!
Faust after a silence.   Leave me alone here, I entreat!   2685
Mephistopheles peering about.
    Not every girl keeps things so neat.
Exit
Faust looking up and around.   Welcome, O thou sweet twilight glow
   That through this shrine art stirring to and fro.
   Sweet agony of love, possess this heart of mine,
   Thou who on dews of hope dost live and yet dost pine.   2690
   What sense of quiet breathes around,
   Of order, of contentedness!
   What riches in this poverty abound!
   Within this prison, ah! what blessedness!
       He throws himself on the leather arm-chair by
       the bed
   Oh, welcome me, thou who the world now gone   2695
   Didst once receive in joy and sorrow, open-armed!
   How often, ah! around this fathers'-throne
   A flock of children clinging swarmed!
   And, thankful for the Christmas gift, maybe
   My darling here, her childish cheeks filled out,   2700
   Kissed grandsire's withered hand devotedly.
   I feel, O maid, thy spirit radiate
   Abundance, order, round about,
   That, motherly, instructs thee day by day,
   Bids thee the cloth upon the table neatly lay,   2705
   Even make the sand at thy feet decorate.
   O darling hand! So godlike in thy ministry!
   The hut becomes a realm of Heaven through thee.
   And here!
       He lifts one of the bed curtains
    What bliss and awe lay hold on me!
   Here for whole hours I fain would tarry.   2710
   O Nature! Here didst thou in visions airy

Mould her, an angel in nativity.
Here lay the child; with warm life heaving
The tender bosom filled and grew;
And here, with pure and holy weaving,   2715
The image of the gods was wrought anew!
     And thou, O Faust, what led thee here? I feel
My very inmost being reel!
What wouldst thou here? What weights thy heart so sore?
O wretched Faust! I know thee now no more.   2720
      Does magic play about me, sweet and rare?
Some force impelled me to enjoy without delay,
And now in dreams of love I seem to float away!
Are we the sport of every puff of air?
     And if this very moment she might enter here,   2725
For thy rash conduct how wouldst thou atone!
Thou, great big lout, how small wouldst thou appear!
How, melted at her feet, thou wouldst lie prone!
Mephistopheles enters.   Be quick! I see her coming down the lane.
Faust.   Away! I'll never come back here again!   2730
Mephistopheles.   Here is a casket, of some weight,
    Which I got elsewhere as a bait.
    Here, put it in the press, this minute;
    She'll lose her senses, I swear it to you.
    In fact, I put some trinkets in it,   2735
    Enough another nobler maid to woo;
    But still a child's a child, and play is play.
Faust.   I don't know if I should?
Mephistopheles.   Why ask you, pray?
    Do you perhaps intend to hoard the treasure?
    Then I'd advise you in your lustfulness   2740
    To waste no more sweet hours of leisure
    And spare me further strain and stress.
    I hope that you're not greedy!
    I rub my hands, I scratch my head —
               He puts the casket in the press and turns the
               lock again
    Away and speedy! —   2745
    To turn the sweet young child that she be led
    To satisfy your heart's desire and will;
    And you look around
    As if to a lecture you were bound,

As if before you, living still,   2750
Stood Physics and Metaphysics grey!
But off! away!
                    Exeunt
Margaret with a lamp.   Here is such close, such sultry air!
                    She opens the window
And yet it's really not so warm out there.
I feel so strange — I don't know how —   2755
I wish that Mother came home now.
From head to foot I'm shuddering —
I'm but a foolish, fearsome thing!
                    She begins to sing while she undresses
          There was in Thule olden
          A king true till the grave,   2760
          To whom a beaker golden
          His dying mistress gave.
                Naught prized he more, this lover,
          He drained it at each bout;
          His eyes with tears brimmed over,   2765
          As oft he drank it out.
                And when he came to dying,
          His towns and his lands he told,
          Naught else his heir denying
          Except the beaker of gold.   2770
                Around him knight and vassal,
          At a royal feast sat he
          In his fathers' lofty castle,
          The castle by the sea.
                There the old pleasure-seeker   2775
          Drank, standing, life's last glow,
          Then hurled the sacred beaker
          Into the waves below.
                He saw it plunging, drinking,
          And sinking in the sea,   2780
          And so his eyes were sinking,
          Never one drop more drank he.
                *She opens the press to put away her clothes and
                catches sight of the little jewel-casket*
How came this lovely casket in my press?
Indeed I turned the lock most certainly.
It's very strange! What's in it I can't guess.   2785

Someone has brought it as a pledge maybe,
And on it Mother loaned a bit.
Here on the ribbon hangs a little key,
I really think I'll open it.
What is that? God in Heaven! See!   2790
I've never seen such things as here!
Jewels! A noble lady might appear
With these on any holiday.
This chain — how would it look on me?
Ah, whose can all this splendour be?   2795

> *She adorns herself with it and steps before the mirror*

Were but the earrings mine! I say
One looks at once quite differently.
What good is beauty? blood of youth?
All that is nice and fine, in truth;
However, people pass and let it be.   2800
They praise you — half with pity, though, be sure.
Toward gold throng all,
To gold cling all,
Yes, all! Alas, we poor!

A Promenade

FAUST *walking thoughtfully up and down.* MEPHISTO-
PHELES *joins him*

Mephistopheles.   By every despisèd love! By the red-hot fires of Hell!   2805
   Would I knew something worse, to curse by it as well!
Faust.   What is the matter? What's so badly vexing you?
   I've never seen before a face that looked that way.
Mephistopheles.   Off to the Devil I'd betake myself this day
   If I myself were not a devil too!   2810
Faust.   What has gone wrong? Why thus behave?
   It suits you well to rant and rave!
Mephistopheles.   Just think, the gems for Gretchen that I got,
   A wretched priest has bagged the lot!
   The mother gets to see the stuff   2815
   And starts at once to feel a secret shuddering.
   The woman has a scent that's fine enough,

Forever in her prayer-book she delights to snuff,
And smells it out in every single thing
If it be sacred or profane;   2820
So in those gems she noses till it's plain
That they held little blessing, little good.
"My child," she cried, "to keep unrighteous gain
Perturbs the soul, consumes the blood.
We'll dedicate it to the Mother of our Lord,   2825
With heavenly manna She'll reward!"
Then Gretchen drew her mouth askew;
She thought: "It is a gift-horse, it is true,
And surely godless is not he
Who brought it here so handsomely."   2830
The mother summoned in a priest who came
And when he'd scarce perceived the game,
Got much contentment from the sight.
He said: "So one is minded right!
Who overcometh, winneth a crown.   2835
The Church hath a good stomach ever,
Whole countries hath she gobbled down,
And yet hath over-eaten never;
The Church alone, dear ladies, best
Can all unrighteous goods digest."   2840
Faust.   That is a custom that men oft pursue;
    A Jew and king can do it too.
Mephistopheles.   With that he bagged brooch, chain, and rings,
    As if mere toadstools were the things,
    And thanked them neither less nor more   2845
    Than were it a basketful of nuts he bore.
    He promised them all heavenly pay
    And greatly edified thereby were they.
Faust.   And Gretchen?
Mephistopheles.   Now sits restless. What she would
    She knows not, neither what she should,   2850
    Thinks of the jewels night and day,
    Still more on him who brought them to her.
Faust.   The darling's grief distresses me.
    Quick! get new ornaments to woo her.
    The first ones were not much to see.   2855
Mephistopheles.   Oh yes, Milord thinks all is mere child's-play!
Faust.   Make haste and do things as I like them done.

Into her neighbour's graces win your way!
Devil, don't be like mush and move so slow.
Fetch some new ornaments — up, now, and run! 2860
Mephistopheles.   Yes, gracious sir, with all my heart I'll go.
Exit FAUST
Such an enamoured fool would puff and blow
Sun, moon, and stars into thin air
Just as a pastime for his lady fair.
Exit

The Neighbour's House

Martha alone.   God pardon my dear husband! He 2865
Has truly not done well by me!
Off in the world to go and roam
And leave me on the straw at home!
Sure, I did naught to vex him, truly,
And, God knows, always loved him duly. 2870
She weeps
Perhaps he's even dead! — Oh, cruel fate!
If I but had a death-certificate!
MARGARET enters
Margaret.   Dame Martha!
Martha.   Gretchen dear, what can it be?
Margaret.   My knees almost sink under me!
There in my press I've found again 2875
Just such a casket — and of ebony,
And things! magnificent they are,
Much richer than the first, by far!
Martha.   You must not tell that to your mother;
She would confess it like the other. 2880
Margaret.   Ah, only look! ah, see now, do!
Martha decking her out.   You lucky, lucky creature, you!
Margaret.   Alas, these jewels I can never wear
At church or on the street, I'd never dare!
Martha.   Come often over here to me 2885
And here put on the jewels secretly.
Stroll up and down before the mirror for a season;
We'll have our own sweet joy of it.
[84]

And then there'll be a feast-day or some other reason
When one lets people see them, bit by bit.   2890
A chain at first, a pearl then in your ear; your mother
Scarce will see it, we'll coin some fib or other.
Margaret.   But both the caskets! Who could bring
Them both? Some wrong is in this thing!
                    Someone knocks
Good Heaven! My mother — can that have been?   2895
Martha peeping through the curtain.
It's some strange gentleman! Come in!
                    MEPHISTOPHELES *enters*
Mephistopheles.   I'm very bold to walk in right away;
The pardon of the ladies I must pray.
                    He steps back respectfully in the presence of
                    MARGARET
Dame Martha Schwerdtlein I would like to find!
Martha.   I'm she! What has the gentleman upon his mind?   2900
Mephistopheles aside to her.   I know you now, that is enough for me.
You have a most distinguished guest, I see.
Excuse the liberty I took! If it is not too soon,
I'll come again this afternoon.
Martha aloud.   Imagine, child, of all things on this earth!   2905
The gentleman thinks you of noble birth.
Margaret.   I am a poor, young thing, as you can see.
The gentleman is far too kind to me.
The ornaments and jewels aren't my own.
Mephistopheles.   Ah, it is not the ornaments alone;   2910
You've such a manner, so refined a way!
How glad I am that I may stay!
Martha.   What is your errand? I would like to hear —
Mephistopheles.   I wish my tidings brought more cheer!
I hope you'll not make me repent this meeting: 2915
Your husband's dead and sends a greeting.
Martha.   Is dead? That faithful heart! Oh, woe!
My husband's dead! I'm dying! Oh!
Margaret.   Ah! don't despair, Dame Martha dear!
Mephistopheles.   Prepare the mournful tale to hear!   2920
Margaret.   That's why I would not love while I draw breath;
Such loss as this would make me grieve to death.
Mephistopheles.   Joy must sorrow, sorrow joy must know.
Martha.   Relate the ending of his life to me!

Mephistopheles.   In Padua he's buried, midst a row   2925
   Of graves close to St. Anthony,
   In holy ground that was well blessed,
   Forever cool his bed of rest.
Martha.   Did you bring nothing else beside?
Mephistopheles.   Oh yes, a weighty, great petition: 2930
   Three hundred masses are you to provide!
   My pockets? They have naught. Thus endeth my commission!
Martha.   What? Not a medal? Not a trinket? Such
   As every journeyman deep in his pouch doth hide,
   As a remembrance puts aside,   2935
   And rather hungers, rather begs, than touch?
Mephistopheles.   Madame, that grieves me much, but let me say,
   He truly did not throw his cash away;
   And deeply did he all his faults deplore,
   Yes, and bewailed his ill luck still much more.   2940
Margaret.   Alas, the bad luck men do meet!
   Full many a requiem for him will I pray.
Mephistopheles.   You're fit, I think, to wed this very day;
   You are so lovable and sweet.
Margaret.   That would not do as yet. Ah, no!   2945
Mephistopheles.   If not a husband, be it for the while a beau.
   For, of the greatest gifts of Heaven, it is one
   To have within our arms a lover dear.
Margaret.   That's not the custom of the country here.
Mephistopheles.   Custom or not! At any rate it's done.   2950
Martha.   Tell on, oh, please!
Mephistopheles.   I stood where dying he was laid.
   'Twas not a dung-heap; somewhat better it was made
   Of rotting straw; but as a Christian did he die,
   Thinking he owed far greater penance for his life.
   "How deeply must I hate myself," I heard him cry,   2955
   "To leave my business so, my wife!
   Alas, the recollection's killing me.
   If she could but forgive me in this life!"
Martha weeping.   The good man! I forgave him long since—truthfully!
Mephistopheles.   "But she, God knows, was more to blame than I!"   2960
Martha.   He lies! What! at the grave's brink—so to lie!
Mephistopheles.   He fabled as he breathed his last, be sure,
   If I am only half a connoisseur.
   "I could not gape for pastime," so he said;

"First children, then to get them bread,   2965
And bread in all the broadest sense, I swear;
Yet never could I eat in peace my share."

Martha.   To all my love, fidelity, he gave no thought,
Nor to my drudgery by night and day?

Mephistopheles.   Not so; he thought of it most warmly as he ought.   2970
He said: "From Malta once I sailed away
And ardently for wife and children did I pray.
Then Heaven favoured us in gracious measure
Because our ship a Turkish vessel caught
Which to the mighty Sultan bore a treasure.   2975
Then valour was rewarded as was fit,
And I received moreover, as one ought,
My own well-measured share of it."

Martha.   Oh what? Oh where? Perhaps he buried it?

Mephistopheles.   Who knows where the four winds have carried it?   2980
A pretty miss adopted him as her dear friend
When he, in Naples strange, was circulating;
She gave him love and troth so unabating
That he felt the results until his blessèd end.

Martha.   The scamp! The robber of his children, he!   2985
And all that want and all that misery
Could not prevent the shameful life he led!

Mephistopheles.   Well, he has paid for it and now he's dead.
If I were now in your place here,
I'd mourn for him a well-bred year,   2990
Meanwhile be on the lookout for a sweetheart new.

Martha.   Ah, God! Another like the first I knew,
I'll hardly find on earth again!
There scarce could be a dearer little fool than mine.
Only to roam he was too much inclined, and then   2995
He loved those foreign women, also foreign wine,
And that accursed dice-throwing.

Mephistopheles.   Now, now, things could have gone and still be going,
If he perchance as much in you
Had overlooked on his part too.   3000
I swear, on terms like these, if you'd agree,
I'd ask you to exchange a ring with me.

Martha.   The gentleman is pleased to jest.

Mephistopheles aside.   Now to make off betimes were best!
She'd hold the very Devil to his word.   3005

[87]

To Gretchen

How is your heart? Has it been stirred?

Margaret.   What means the gentleman?

Mephistopheles aside.   You innocent, sweet dear!

Aloud

Ladies, good-by!

Margaret.   Good-by!

Martha.   Oh, quickly let me hear

The evidence I'd like to have and save:

Where, how, and when my darling died and where his grave.   3010

Of order I have always been a friend,

And in our "Weekly" I would like to read his end.

Mephistopheles.   Yes, my good woman, what two witnesses attest

Is always known as truth made manifest,

And with me I've a splendid mate.   3015

I tell you, I'll take him before a magistrate.

I'll bring him here.

Martha.   Oh, do that, do!

Mephistopheles.   And this young lady, will she be here too?

A gallant chap! and travelled far has he

And shows young ladies every courtesy.   3020

Margaret.   Before the gentleman I'd flush with shame.

Mephistopheles.   Before no king this earth could name.

Martha.   Behind my house and in my garden then,

This evening we'll await the gentlemen.

A Street

Faust   Mephistopheles

Faust.   How goes it? Will it work? soon win the game?   3025

Mephistopheles.   Ah, bravo! Do I find you all aflame?

Gretchen will in a brief time be your own.

This evening you will see her all alone

At Neighbour Martha's; that's a woman made

For go-between and gypsy trade.   3030

Faust.   'Tis well!

Mephistopheles.   Yet something's wanted from us too.

Faust.   One service may demand another as its due.

Mephistopheles.   We have in due form only to attest

That her good spouse's outstretched limbs repose

In Padua, in consecrated soil at rest.   3035
Faust.   Most wise! We first must make the journey, I suppose!
Mephistopheles.   *Sancta Simplicitas!* Of that there is no need;
You don't know much, but still depose.
Faust.   If that's your best, I tear your plan asunder.
Mephistopheles.   O saintly man! Then you would be a saint indeed!   3040
Is it the first time in your life
You've borne false witness? Well, I wonder!
Of God, the world, and what therein is rife,
Of man, what stirs within his heart and brain,
Have you no definition given with might and main?   3045
With brazen brow and dauntless breast?
And if you'll only probe things truly,
You knew of them — you must confess it duly —
No more than of this Schwerdtlein's death and place of rest!
Faust.   You are and you remain a liar, sophist too.   3050
Mephistopheles.   Yes, if one did not have a little deeper view.
Will you not presently cajole
Poor Gretchen — in all honour too — and swear
To her the love of all your soul?
Faust.   Aye, swear it from my heart.
Mephistopheles.   Fine, I declare!   3055
Then there'll be talk of love, fidelity eternal,
Of one almighty force supernal —
Will that too issue from your heart alone?
Faust.   Have done! It will! — And when I'm feeling,
When for the feeling, for my senses' reeling,   3060
I seek for names and yet find none,
Then through the world with every sense sweep on,
Toward all the loftiest phrases, grasping, turn,
And this the glow from which I burn,
Endless, eternal, aye, eternal name,   3065
Is that a devilish, lying game?
Mephistopheles.   And yet I'm right!
Faust.   Take heed! Mark this from me,
I beg of you, and spare my lungs:
He who maintains he's right — if his the gift of tongues —
Will have the last word certainly.   3070
So come, this prating rouses my disgust;
I'll say you're right, especially since I must.

[89]

A Garden

MARGARET *on* FAUST's *arm,* MARTHA *and* MEPHISTO-
PHELES, *walking up and down*

Margaret.   I feel the gentleman is only sparing me,
So condescends that I am all confused.
A traveller is so much used   3075
To bear with things good-naturedly.
I know too well, my poor talk hardly can
Amuse you, an experienced man.
Faust.   One glance from you, one word, more entertains
Than all the wisdom that this world contains.   3080
                    He kisses her hand
Margaret.
    Don't incommode yourself! How can my hand be kissed by you?
    It is so ugly and so rough!
    What work is there that I've not had to do?
    My mother's more than strict enough.
                    They pass on
Martha.   And you, sir, are you always on the go?   3085
Mephistopheles.   Alas, that business, duty, drive us so!
    With how much pain one goes from many a place,
    And even so, one simply must not stay.
Martha.   In active years perhaps 'tis well this way,
    Thus freely round and round the world to race;   3090
    But then the evil times come on apace,
    And as a bachelor to drag on to the grave alone,
    That has been good for no one, you must own.
Mephistopheles.   With dread I see it far away.
Martha.   Then, worthy sir, consider while you may!   3095
                    They pass on
Margaret.   Yes, out of sight is out of mind!
    To you so easy is this courtesy;
    But many friends you always find,
    More sensible than I can be.
Faust.   O dear one! Trust me, that which men call sense   3100
    Is oft but vanity and narrowness.
Margaret.   But why? Tell me.
Faust.   Ah, that simplicity, that innocence,

That neither its own sacred value knows!
That lowliness, humility, those gifts supreme
That loving Nature's bounteous hand bestows — 3105
Margaret.   Though you may think of me a moment only,
    I'll have, ah, time enough to think of you and dream.
Faust.   You are then often lonely?
Margaret.   Yes, for our household is but small,
    And yet one has to look to all. 3110
    We have no maid — must cook, sweep, sew, and knit,
    And early run about and late;
    And Mother is in all of it
    So accurate!
    Not that in spending she must feel confined; 3115
    We could branch out far more than many do.
    My father left a pretty property behind,
    A house outside the town, a little garden too.
    Yet now I've pretty quiet days. My brother,
    He is a soldier lad. 3120
    My little sister's dead.
    A deal of trouble with the child did I go through;
    Yet once more would I gladly undertake the bother,
    I loved the child so much.
Faust.   An angel, if like you.
Margaret.   I brought it up and it was fond of me. 3125
    Father had died when it was born;
    We gave our mother up for lost, so worn
    And wretched, lying there, was she.
    And she grew well so slowly, bit by bit,
    She could not think of suckling it 3130
    Herself, the poor babe pitifully wee,
    And so I brought it up, and quite alone,
    With milk and water; so it became my own.
    Upon my arm and in my lap it threw
    Itself about, was friendly too, and grew. 3135
Faust.   You've surely felt the purest happiness.
Margaret.   But also many weary hours, I must confess.
    The wee thing's cradle stood at night
    Beside my bed; it scarcely might
    Just stir; I was awake; 3140
    Sometimes I had to give it drink, sometimes to take
    It in with me, sometimes from bed arise

And dandle up and down the room to hush its cries;
And at the wash-tub stand at daylight's break,
Then to the marketing and to the hearth attend. 3145
Tomorrow too just like today, so without end.
Thus, sir, one's spirits are not always of the best,
But in return one relishes both food and rest.
They pass on
Martha.   Poor women have things hard, it's true;
A bachelor's not easy to convert. 3150
Mephistopheles.   It but depends upon the like of you,
For then my present ways I might desert.
Martha.   Speak out, sir, is there none you've ever met?
Has your heart never bound itself as yet?
Mephistopheles.   One's own good wife and hearth, we're told, 3155
Are worth as much as pearls and gold.
Martha.   I mean, if you have never felt a passion?
Mephistopheles.   I've always been received in very courteous fashion.
Martha.   I mean: has love in earnest never stirred your breast?
Mephistopheles.   With ladies one should never dare to jest. 3160
Martha.   Ah, you don't understand me!
Mephistopheles.   That distresses me!
And yet I understand — most kindly would you be.
They pass on
Faust.   Did you, O little angel, straightway recognize
Me when I came into the garden?
Margaret.   Did you not see that I cast down my eyes? 3165
Faust.   That liberty I took, you'll pardon?
The daring impudence that day
When coming from the church you went your way?
Margaret.   I was confused; to me it never had
Occurred; no one could say of me what's bad. 3170
Ah, thought I, in your manner, then, has he
Seen something bold, unmaidenly?
It seemed to strike him right away
To have some dealings with this girl without delay.
Yet I confess I know not why my heart 3175
Began at once to stir to take your part.
But with myself I was right vexed, it's true,
That I could not become more vexed toward you.
Faust.   Sweet darling!
Margaret.   Wait a bit!

She plucks a star-flower and picks off the petals,
one after the other

Faust.   What's that? A nosegay?

Margaret.   No,
   It's just a game.

Faust.   What?

Margaret.   You will laugh at me, do go!   3180

She pulls off the petals and murmurs

Faust.   What are you murmuring?

Margaret half aloud.   He loves me — loves me not!

Faust.   Sweet, heavenly vision!

Margaret goes on.   Loves me — not — loves me — not —
   He loves me!   *Plucking off the last petal with lovely joy*

Faust.   Yes, my child! and let this blossom's word
   Be oracle of gods to you! He loves you!   3185
   You understand that word and what it means? He loves you!

He seizes both her hands

Margaret.   I'm all a-tremble!

Faust.   Oh, shudder not! But let this look,
   Let this hand-pressure say to you
   What is unspeakable: 3190
   To give one's self up wholly and to feel
   A rapture that must be eternal!
   Eternal! — for its end would be despair.
   No! no end! no end!

           MARGARET *presses his hands, frees herself,*
           and runs away. He stands a moment in thought
           and then follows her

Martha coming.   The night comes on.

Mephistopheles.   Yes, and we must away.   3195

Martha.   I'd ask you make a longer stay;
   But it's a wicked place, here roundabout,
   As if no one had naught to carry through
   And naught to do
   But gape at all the neighbours going in and out.   3200
   One's talked about, do all one may.
   And our dear couple?

Mephistopheles.   Up that walk I saw them whirr,
   The wanton butterflies!

Martha.   He seems to take to her.

Mephistopheles.   And she to him. So runs the world away.

A Garden House

MARGARET *runs in, hides behind the door, holds the tip
of her finger to her lips, and peers through the crevice*

Margaret.　He's coming!

Faust enters.　　　　　Rogue, it's thus you tease!　　　　3205
I've caught you!

He kisses her

Margaret embracing him and returning the kiss.
　　　　　　　Best of men, I love you from my heart!

Mephistopheles knocks

Faust stamping.　Who's there?

Mephistopheles.　　　　　A friend!

Faust.　　　　　　　A beast!

Mephistopheles.　　　　　　　I think it's time to part.

Martha enters.　Yes, sir, it's late.

Faust.　　　　　　　Mayn't I escort you, please?

Margaret.　My mother would — Good-by!

Faust.　　　　　　　Must I go then?
Good-by!

Martha.　Adieu!

Margaret.　　　But soon to meet again!　　　　　3210

FAUST *and* MEPHISTOPHELES *exeunt*

Margaret.　Dear God! The things that such a man
Can think of! Everything! I only can
Stand there before him shamed and quivering
And answer "Yes" to everything.
I am a poor unknowing child, and he —　　　　3215
I do not see what he can find in me.

Exit

Forest and Cavern

Faust alone.　Spirit sublime, thou gav'st me, gav'st me all
For which I prayed. Thou hast not turned in vain
Thy countenance to me in fire and flame.
Thou gav'st me glorious nature as a royal realm,　　3220

The power to feel and to enjoy her. Not
Amazed, cold visits only thou allow'st;
Thou grantest me to look in her deep breast
Even as in the bosom of a friend.
Thou leadest past a series of the living   3225
Before me, teaching me to know my brothers
In silent covert and in air and water.
And when the storm roars screeching through the forest,
When giant fir-tree plunges, sweeping down
And crushing neighbouring branches, neighbouring trunks,   3230
And at its fall the hills, dull, hollow, thunder:
Then leadest thou me to the cavern safe,
Show'st me myself, and my own heart becomes
Aware of deep mysterious miracles.
And when before my gaze the stainless moon   3235
Soothing ascends on high: from rocky walls
And from damp covert float and soar about me
The silvery forms of a departed world
And temper contemplation's austere joy.
　　　Oh, that for man naught perfect ever is,   3240
I now do feel. Together with this rapture
That brings me near and nearer to the gods,
Thou gav'st the comrade whom I now no more
Can do without, though, cold and insolent,
He lowers me in my own sight, transforms   3245
With but a word, a breath, thy gifts to nothing.
Within my breast he fans with busy zeal
A savage fire for that fair, lovely form.
Thus from desire I reel on to enjoyment
And in enjoyment languish for desire.   3250
Mephistopheles appears.   Have you now led this life quite long enough?
　　　How can it long have any charm for you?
　　　'Tis well, indeed, for once to try the stuff,
　　　But then, in turn, away to something new!
Faust.   I wish that you had something else to do   3255
　　　Than on a happy day to plague me like a pest.
Mephistopheles.   Now, now! I'll gladly let you rest!
　　　You do not dare to say this seriously.
　　　A comrade mad, ungracious, cross,
　　　Would truly be a trifling loss.   3260
　　　The livelong day one's hands are full as they can be.

[95]

What he would like for one to do or leave alone,
His lordship's face will never let one see.
Faust.   So! That is just the proper tone:
You now want thanks for boring me.   3265
Mephistopheles.   Without me how would you, Earth's wretched son,
Have kept on living? What would you have done?
Your hodge-podge of imagination — balderdash!
At least I've cured you now and then of all that trash.
In fact, if I had not been here at all,   3270
You'd long since sauntered off this earthly ball.
Why here within the cavern's rocky rent
Thus sit your life away so owl-like and alone?
Why from the sodden moss and dripping stone
Sip, like a toad, your nourishment?   3275
A fine sweet way to pass the time. I'll bet
The Doctor's in your body yet.
Faust.   Can you conceive what new vitality
This walking in the desert works in me?
Yes, could you sense a force like this,   3280
You would be devil enough to grudge my bliss.
Mephistopheles.   It's more than earthly, such delight!
To lie in night and dew on mountain height,
Embracing earth and heaven blissfully,
Puffing one's self and deeming one a deity;   3285
To burrow through earth's marrow, onward pressed
By prescient impulse, feel within one's breast
All six days' work, in haughty power enjoy and know
I can't tell what, soon all creation overflow
In rapturous love, lost to all sight the child of clay,   3290
And then the lofty intuition
                    With a gesture
Ending — I dare not say in what fruition!
Faust.   Shame on you!
Mephistopheles.   That's not to your liking, eh?
You have the moral right to cry out "Shame!"
Before chaste ears one must not name   3295
What chaste hearts can't dispense with, just the same!
In short, I grudge you not the pleasure of evasion,
Of lying to yourself upon occasion;
But you will not stick long to that, it's clear.
Again you are already spent,   3300

And if this goes on longer, you'll be rent
To shreds by madness or by agony and fear.
Enough of this! Your darling sits at home apart
And more and more she's feeling caged and sad.
Your image never leaves her mind and heart,   3305
The all-consuming love she bears you is half mad.
First came your passion like the furious current
Of brooklets swollen high from melted snow.
Into her heart you poured the torrent,
And now again your brooklet's running low.   3310
I think, instead of sitting throned in forests wild
It would become so great a lord
To seek the poor, young, silly child
And give her for her love some due reward.
To her the time grows pitiably long.   3315
She stands beside the window, sees the clouds that stray
Over the old town wall and far away.
"Were I a little bird!" so goes her song,
All day long and half the night long.
She's mostly sad, at times is gay,   3320
At times is quite wept out, and then,
It seems, is calm again,
And is in love alway.
Faust.   Serpent! Serpent!
Mephistopheles aside.   Good! I'll bet
That I will get you yet!   3325
Faust.   Infamous fiend! Off, get you hence!
And do not name that lovely woman!
Nor yet desire for her sweet body summon
Again before my half-distracted sense!
Mephistopheles.
What would you then? She thinks that you have flown,   3330
And half and half you are, as you must own.
Faust.   I'm near to her, however far I were,
I never can forget nor yet lose her;
I envy even the Body of the Lord
Whenever her sweet lips touch the Adored.   3335
Mephistopheles.   Well said, my friend! Oft have I envied you indeed
The twin-pair that among the roses feed.
Faust.   Off, pander!
Mephistopheles.   Fine! You rail and it's a joke to me.

The God who fashioned youth and maid
At once perceived the noblest trade   3340
Was that He make them opportunity.
Be off! That is a cause of woe!
It's to your darling's chamber you're to go,
Not to your death, indeed!

Faust.　　How am I, in her arms, by Heaven blessed?   3345
Though I grow warm upon her breast,
Do I not always feel her need?
Am I not still the fugitive? unhoused and roaming?
The monster without goal or rest
That like a cataract from rock to rock roared foaming   3350
To the abyss, by greed and frenzy headlong pressed?
She at one side, still with her childlike senses furled,
Upon the alpine meadow in the cottage small,
With all her homely joys and cares, her all,
Within that little world;   3355
And I, the God-detested,
Not enough had I
That all the rocks I wrested
And into pieces made them fly!
Her did I have to undermine, her peace!   3360
Thou, Hell, didst have to have this sacrifice!
Help, Devil, make it brief, this time of agony!
What must be done, let it at once be so!
Then may her fate plunge crushing down on me,
And she with me to ruin go!   3365

Mephistopheles.　　How it seethes again and how again it glows!
You fool, go and console your pretty dear!
When such a brain as yours no outlet knows,
It straightway fancies that the end is near.
Long life to him who bravely dares!   3370
At other times you've been of quite a devilish mind.
Naught more absurd in this world can I find
Than is a devil who despairs.

Gretchen's Room

Gretchen at her spinning-wheel, alone.
　　　　　　　　My peace is gone,
　　　　　　　─ My heart is sore ─;   3375

I'll find it, ah, never,
No, nevermore!
    When he is not near,
My grave is here;
My world is all
Turned into gall.   3380
    My poor, poor head
Is all a-craze,
And my poor wits
All in a maze.   3385
    My peace is gone,
— My heart is sore — ;
I'll find it, ah, never,
No, nevermore!
    To see him only   3390
At the window I stay,
To meet him only
From home I stray.
    His noble form,
His bearing so high,   3395
And his lips so smiling,
And the power of his eye,
    His flowing speech's
Magic bliss,
His hands' fond clasp,   3400
And, ah, his kiss!
    My peace is gone,
— My heart is sore — ;
I'll find it, ah, never,
No, nevermore!   3405
    My bosom yearns
Toward him to go.
Ah! might I clasp him
And hold him so,
    And kiss his lips   3410
As fain would I,
Upon his kisses
To swoon and die!

Martha's Garden

MARGARET   FAUST

Margaret.   Promise me, Henry!
Faust.   What I can!
Margaret.   How do you feel about religion? Tell me, pray.   3415
　　You are a dear, good-hearted man,
　　But I believe you've little good of it to say.
Faust.   Hush, hush, my child! You feel my love for you.
　　For those I love, I'd give my blood and body too,
　　Would no one of his feelings or of church bereave.   3420
Margaret.   That's not enough. We must believe!
Faust.   Must we?
Margaret.   Ah, could I but impress you, Henry dear!
　　The Holy Sacraments you also don't revere.
Faust.   I do revere them.
Margaret.   But without desire, alas!
　　It's long since you confessed or went to mass.   3425
　　Do you believe in God?
Faust.   My darling, who dare say:
　　"I believe in God"? You may
　　Ask priest or sage, and you'll receive
　　What only seems to mock and stay
　　The asker.
Margaret.   So you don't believe?   3430
Faust.   Sweet vision, don't misunderstand me now!
　　Who dare name Him?
　　And who avow:
　　"I believe in Him"?
　　Who feels and would   3435
　　Have hardihood
　　To say: "I don't believe in Him"?
　　The All-Enfolder,
　　The All-Upholder,
　　Enfolds, upholds He not   3440
　　You, me, Himself?
　　Do not the heavens over-arch us yonder?
　　Does not the earth lie firm beneath?
　　Do not eternal stars rise friendly
　　Looking down upon us?   3445

[100]

Look I not, eye in eye, on you,
And do not all things throng
Toward your head and heart,
Weaving in mystery eternal,
Invisible, visible, near to you? 3450
Fill up your heart with it, great though it is,
And when you're wholly in the feeling, in its bliss,
Name it then as you will,
Name it Happiness! Heart! Love! God!
I have no name for that! 3455
Feeling is all in all;
Name is but sound and smoke,
Beclouding Heaven's glow.
Margaret.   That's all quite nice and good to know;
Much the same way the preacher talks of it, 3460
Only in words that differ just a bit.
Faust.   Wherever the light of Heaven doth shine,
All hearts repeat it, everywhere, and each
In its own speech;
Then why not I in mine? 3465
Margaret.   To hear it thus, it's passable, and still I doubt it;
In spite of it all there is some hitch about it,
For you have no Christianity.
Faust.   Dear child!
Margaret.   It long has been a grief to me
That I see you in such company. 3470
Faust.   How so?
Margaret.   The man who is with you as your mate,
Deep in my inmost soul I hate.
In all my whole life there's not a thing
That's given my heart so sharp a sting
As that man's hostile face has done. 3475
Faust.   Don't fear him, my precious one!
Margaret.   His presence makes my blood run so chill,
And toward all others I bear good-will;
But although to see you I yearn and long,
With uncanny horror that man makes me shrink. 3480
He is a knave, I really do think!
God forgive me if I'm doing him wrong!
Faust.   Such queer birds there must also be.
Margaret.   I'd not like to live with one like him!

If he but comes inside the door, you see 3485
Him look always so scoffingly
And so half grim.
For nothing has he any real sympathy;
It's written on his forehead, one can see
That in his sight no soul can be dear. 3490
I feel so happy in your arm,
So free, so yielding, and so warm,
And yet my heart grows stifled whenever he is near.

Faust.   O you foreboding angel, you!

Margaret.   It overcomes me so much too, 3495
That when he but only comes our way,
I even think I've no more love for you,
And when he's there, I nevermore could pray;
That eats into my heart; and so you too
Must feel, dear Henry, as I do. 3500

Faust.   You simply have antipathy!

Margaret.   I must go now.

Faust.   Ah, can there never be
Upon your bosom one calm, little hour of rest,
To mingle soul with soul, press breast to breast?

Margaret.   Ah, if I only slept apart! 3505
For you I'd gladly leave the bolt undrawn tonight,
But then my mother's sleep is light;
And were we found by her, dear heart,
I would fall dead upon the spot!

Faust.   No need of that! You angel, fear it not! 3510
Here is a little phial! Only three
Drops in her drink, and pleasantly
Deep slumber will enfold her like a charm!

Margaret.   For your sake what would I not do?
I hope it will not do her harm! 3515

Faust.   If so, my love, would I thus counsel you?

Margaret.   If I but look at you, O best of men,
I know not what compels me to your will.
I've done so much, your wishes to fulfil,
There's almost nothing left for me to do. 3520

Exit

MEPHISTOPHELES *appears*

Mephistopheles.   The little monkey! Is she gone?

Faust.   You've spied again!

Mephistopheles.   I've heard it all and understood,
    The Doctor was put through the catechisms.
    I hope that it will do you good.
    Girls have a great desire to know, it's true,   3525
    If one is sleek and pious, true to ancient isms.
    They think: if there he knuckles, us he'll follow too.
Faust.   You monster, you've not seen
    How this soul true and dear,
    Full of the faith she hath,   3530
    That quite alone must mean
    Eternal bliss to her, torments herself with awful fear
    To think the man she loves is doomed by endless wrath.
Mephistopheles.   You lover super-sensual, sensual too,
    A damsel leads you by the nose.   3535
Faust.   O monstrous progeny of fire and filthy spew!
Mephistopheles.   And physiognomy quite masterly she knows.
    She feels she knows not how when I'm about,
    And in my mask a hidden meaning sees.
    She feels that I'm a daemon, without doubt,   3540
    Perhaps the very Devil, if you please!
    Well now, — tonight?
Faust.   What's that to you?
Mephistopheles.   I have my pleasure in it too!

At the Well

GRETCHEN *and* LISBETH *with jugs*

Lisbeth.   Of our friend Babbie you've not heard?
Gretchen.   I seldom go where people are, — no, not a word.   3545
Lisbeth.   It's true, Sibylla told me so today!
    So after all she's played the fool, I say.
    That comes of all her airs!
Gretchen.   How so?
Lisbeth.   It stinks.
    She's feeding two now when she eats and drinks.
Gretchen.   Ah!   3550
Lisbeth.   So now it's served her right, in truth.
    How long she's hung upon that youth!
    That was a promenading,

To village and to dance parading!
Had ever as the first to shine, 3555
He always courted her with tarts and wine;
She fancied her beauty was something fine,
Was yet so lost to honour she had no shame
To take his presents as they came.
'Twas cuddling and kissing, on and on; 3560
And now, you see, the floweret's gone!

Gretchen. The poor thing!

Lisbeth. What! You pity her? I don't!
When girls like us were spinning, mother's wont
At night was never to let us out,
But she! With her sweet love she'd stand about. 3565
On the door-bench, in the hallway dim,
No hour became too long for her or for him.
Now she can knuckle under in full view
And in a sinner's shift do penance too.

Gretchen. He'll take her of course to be his wife. 3570

Lisbeth. He'd be a fool! A lively lad
Has plenty elbow-room elsewhere.
Besides, he's gone.

Gretchen. That is not fair!

Lisbeth. If she gets him, she'll find her luck is bad.
The boys will dash her wreath on the floor, 3575
And we will strew chaff before her door.

Exit

Gretchen going home. How I could once so stoutly flay
When some poor maiden went astray!
How I could find no words enough
At others' sins to rail and scoff! 3580
Black as it seemed, I made it blacker still,
But never black enough to suit my will;
I blessed myself! So proud I've been!
Now I'm myself laid bare to sin!
Yet — all that drove me, all I would, 3585
God! was so dear! ah, was so good!

The Ramparts

In a niche of the wall a devotional image of the Mater Dolo-
rosa with jugs for flowers in front of it
Gretchen is putting fresh flowers in the jugs.

Oh, bend Thou,
Mother of Sorrows; send Thou
A look of pity on my pain.

Thine heart's blood welling   3590
With pangs past telling,
Thou gazest where Thy Son hangs slain.

Thou, heavenward gazing,
Art deep sighs raising
On high for His and for Thy pain.   3595

Who feeleth
How reeleth
This pain in every bone?
All that makes my poor heart shiver,
Why it yearneth and doth quiver,   3600
Thou dost know and Thou alone!

Wherever I am going,
How woe, woe, woe is growing,
Ah, how my bosom aches!
When lonely watch I'm keeping,   3605
I'm weeping, weeping, weeping,
My heart within me breaks.

The plants before my window
I wet with tears, — ah, me! —
As in the early morning   3610
I plucked these flowers for Thee.

Ah, let my room but borrow
The early sunlight red,
I sit in all my sorrow
Already on my bed.   3615

[105]

Help! rescue me from death and stain!
Oh, bend Thou,
Mother of Sorrows; send Thou
A look of pity on my pain!

Night

The street before GRETCHEN'S *door*

Valentine, a soldier, Gretchen's brother.

When I've sat with a jovial crowd   3620
Where many a man has boasted loud
And fellows then have praised to me
The beauty of maidens noisily
And drowned the praises with full cup,
Upon my elbow well propped up   3625
Secure in my repose I've sat and so
Heard all the braggadocio.
I've stroked my whiskers, smiling, bland,
And grasped the full cup in my hand
And said: "Let each man have his way!   3630
But is there one in all the land
Like my dear Gretchen, who can hold
A candle to my sister? Say!"
Hear! hear! clink-clink! about it went;
Some cried: "He's right! She is of all   3635
Her sex the pride and ornament!"
Then dumb sat all the boasters bold.
And now! — I could tear out my hair
And try to run straight up a wall!
With stinging speeches, nose in air,   3640
Each scurvy knave may taunt and sneer!
I'll sit like one accursed by debt
And at each casual word I'll sweat!
Though I would like to smash and maul them,
Still, liars I could never call them.   3645
    What's coming here? What sneaks in view?
If I mistake not, there are two.
If he is one, swift at his hide I'll drive!
He shall not leave this spot alive!

[106]

FAUST   MEPHISTOPHELES

Faust.   How from the window of yon sacristy   3650
   Upward the glow of that eternal taper shimmers,
   And weak and weaker sideward glimmers,
   And darkness round it presses nigh!
   So in my bosom do night shadows gather.
Mephistopheles.   I'm like a sentimental tom-cat, rather,   3655
   That stealthy sneaks by fire-escapes,
   Along the walls quite softly scrapes.
   I feel quite like myself in this, I must confess:
   A bit of thievish greed, a bit of rammishness.
   So even now, I feel, through every vein   3660
   Is spooking glorious Walpurgis Night.
   Just two days hence it comes again.
   Then why one keeps awake, one knows aright!
Faust.   Meanwhile does not a treasure rise in air
   That I see glimmering back there?   3665
Mephistopheles.   Ere long you can proceed with pleasure
   To raise the kettle and its treasure.
   Not long ago I took a squint,
   Saw splendid lion-dollars in 't.
Faust.   But not a trinket, not a ring,   3670
   To ornament my darling girl?
Mephistopheles.   I saw among them some such thing,
   A kind of necklace made of pearl.
Faust.   So it is well! I do not find it pleasant
   To go to her without a present.   3675
Mephistopheles.   It should not really trouble you
   To have some pleasure gratis too.
   Now since the sky glows with a starry throng,
   A very masterpiece you'll hear.
   I'll sing to her a moral song,   3680
   More surely to beguile her ear.
                    He sings to his guitar
                 What dost before
                 Thy lover's door,
                 Katrin, before
                 The world with light is laden?   3685
                 Let, let it be!
                 He lets in thee

As maid, but he
Will let thee out no maiden.

Maids, heed aright!   3690
Is it done quite?
Ah, then good-night!
Poor things, he will not linger!
For your own sake,
No robber take,   3695
When love he'd make,
Save with the ring on finger!

Valentine steps forth.   Whom lure you here? God's-element!
  O you rat-catcher, cursèd slinger!
  To the Devil first the instrument!   3700
  To the Devil afterwards the singer!
Mephistopheles.   He's broken my guitar! There's no more use in it.
Valentine.   A skull's now going to be split!
Mephistopheles to F A U S T.   Don't give way, Doctor! Quick! Don't tarry!
  Keep close by as I lead the way.   3705
  Out with your duster, out, I say!
  Thrust hard at him and I will parry.
Valentine.   Then parry that!
Mephistopheles.   And why not, pray?
Valentine.   That too!
Mephistopheles.   Sure!
Valentine.   I believe the Devil's in the fray!
  What's this? My hand's already going lame.   3710
Mephistopheles to F A U S T.   Thrust home!
Valentine falls.   O woe!
Mephistopheles.   Now is the lubber tame!
  But quick away! We must at once be gone,
  For even now a murd'rous cry arises.
  With the police quite nicely I get on
  But fare but ill with the assizes.   3715
Martha at a window.   Out, neighbours, out!
Gretchen at a window.   Here, bring a light!
Martha as above.   They rail and scuffle, yell and fight.
People.   Already one is lying there! He's dead!
Martha coming out.   The murderers! Where have they run?
Gretchen coming out.   Who's lying here?

[108]

People.   Your mother's son!   3720

Gretchen.   Almighty One! What misery!

Valentine.   I'm dying! That is quickly said
   And quicker still can be.
   Why, women, stand and howl and wail?
   Come here and listen to my tale!   3725

                They all come around him

   My Gretchen, see! Young are you still
   And shrewd enough by no means quite.
   You manage your affairs but ill.
   In confidence I tell you, what is more,
   Since once for all now you're a whore,   3730
   So be one then outright!

Gretchen.   My brother! God! What words to me!

Valentine.   In this game let our Lord God be!
   Now what is done is done, alas!
   And as things can, so will they come to pass.   3735
   With one you started secretly,
   And more of them there soon will be.
   When a dozen men have had you down,
   You're common then to all the town.

     When Shame at first is given birth,   3740
   She is smuggled in upon this earth,
   And then the veil of night is thrown
   Around her ears and head;
   Yes, one would gladly murder her instead.
   But when both proud and great she's grown,   3745
   By daylight then she goes forth openly,
   And yet has not become more fair to see.
   The loathsomer her face, straightway
   The more she seeks the light of day.

     I see the time already nearing   3750
   When townsfolk, honest and God-fearing,
   As from an infectious body shrinking,
   Past you, you whore, will hurry slinking.
   In heart and body you'll despair
   If they but look you in the face!   3755
   No more a golden chain you'll wear,
   No more beside the altar take your place!
   In fine lace collar to your pleasure
   You'll dance no more a happy measure.

In some dark corner you will hide   ·   3760
Among beggars and cripples, side by side.
Even if God His pardon give,
On earth you shall accursèd live!
Martha.   Commend your soul to God! Can it then be
You'll cap your other sins with blasphemy?   3765
Valentine.   Could I but to your withered body limp,
You shameless woman, coupling pimp!
Then I indeed might hope to win
Forgiveness plenty for each sin.
Gretchen.   My brother! Oh, what agony!   3770
Valentine.   I tell you, let the weeping be!
When you from honour went apart,
You stabbed me to the very heart.
Now through the slumber of the grave
I go to God, a soldier brave.   3775

Dies

Cathedral

Mass, Organ, and Singing
GRETCHEN *among many people*, EVIL SPIRIT *behind*
GRETCHEN

Evil Spirit.   How different, Gretchen, it was with thee,
When thou, still full of innocence,
Here to the altar cam'st,
Out of the well-worn, little book
Didst prattle prayers,   3780
Half childhood's play,
Half God in thy heart!
Gretchen!
Where are thy thoughts?
Within thy heart   3785
What foul misdeed?
Is it for thy mother's soul thou prayest, who
Through thee to long, long torment fell asleep?
Upon thy door-sill, whose the blood?
— Beneath thy heart already   3790
Is there not stirring swelling life
That tortureth itself and thee

[110]

With its foreboding presence?
Gretchen. Woe! Woe!
  Would I were free of thoughts   3795
  That go within me hither and thither
  Against my will!
Choir. Dies irae, dies illa
  Solvet saeclum in favilla.
Sound of the organ
Evil Spirit. Wrath grips thee!   3800
  The last trumpet sounds!
  The graves are trembling!
  And thy heart,
  From rest in ashes
  To flaming torments   3805
  Raised up, re-created,
  Trembling ascends!
Gretchen. Would I were away from here!
  It seems to me as if the organ
  Would stifle my breathing,   3810
  As if my inmost heart
  Were melted by the singing.
Choir. Judex ergo cum sedebit,
  Quidquid latet adparebit,
  Nil inultum remanebit.   3815
Gretchen. I'm stifling here!
  The walls and pillars
  Imprison me!
  The vaulted arches
  Crush me! — Air!   3820
Evil Spirit. Hide thyself! Sin and shame
  Remain not hidden.
  Air? Light?
  Woe's thee!
Choir. Quid sum miser tunc dicturus?   3825
  Quem patronum rogaturus,
  Cum vix justus sit securus?
Evil Spirit. The faces of the Glorified
  Will turn away from thee;
  To thee their hands to offer   3830
  Will the Pure shudder.
  Woe!

[111]

Choir.   *Quid sum miser tunc dicturus?*
Gretchen.   Neighbour! Your smelling-salts!
                    She falls in a swoon

Walpurgis Night

THE HARTZ MOUNTAINS
Region of Schierke and Elend

FAUST   MEPHISTOPHELES

Mephistopheles.   If you'd a broomstick, wouldn't that be fine?   3835
   I wish the sturdiest he-goat were mine.
   Our goal's still far off and this way is rough.
Faust.   As long as I feel fresh afoot, I say
   For me this knotted staff's enough.
   What good is it when one cuts short the way?   3840
   To loiter through the labyrinth of valleys
   And then to mount these cliffs, whence sallies
   The ever bubbling, leaping spring,
   That is the spice that makes such paths worth wandering!
   Already springtime in the birches stirs,   3845
   It's even felt already by the firs;
   Should not our members also feel effect?
Mephistopheles.   Forsooth, no trace of that can I detect!
   I'm feeling wintry in my every limb;
   Upon my path I should like frost and snow.   3850
   How sadly rises, red and incomplete, the dim
   Moon's disc with its belated glow
   Lighting so ill that at each step or so
   One runs against a rock, against a tree!
   Let's ask a will-o'-the-wisp to lend his flicker!   3855
   I see one there just flaming merrily.
   Hey, friend! May I bid you to help us get on quicker?
   Why will you blaze away so uselessly?
   Do be so good and light us up the hill!
Will-o'-the-Wisp.   Out of respect for you I hope I'll find   3860
   A way to curb my nature's flighty will;
   Our course, as heretofore, is zigzag still.
Mephistopheles.   Ho! Ho! You think you'll imitate mankind.

[112]

Go on and in the Devil's name, but straight! Now mind!
Or else I'll blow your flickering light clean out.   3865
Will-o'-the-Wisp.   You are the master of the house, I have no doubt,
And I'll accommodate myself to you with glee.
But do reflect! The mountain's magic-mad today,
And if a will-o'-the-wisp must show the way,
You must not take things all too seriously.   3870
Faust, Mephistopheles, Will-o'-the-Wisp in alternating song.
            Spheres of dream and necromancy,
     We have entered them, we fancy.
     Lead us well, for credit striving,
     That we soon may be arriving
     In the wide and desert spaces.   3875
            I see trees there running races.
     How each, quickly moving, passes,
     And the cliffs that low are bowing,
     And the rocks, long nose-like masses,
     How they're snoring, how they're blowing!   3880
            Over stones and grass are flowing
     Brook and brooklet downward fleeting.
     Hear I murmuring? Hear I singing?
     Hear sweet plaints of love entreating,
     Voices of those blest days ringing?   3885
     What we're loving, hopeful yearning!
     And the echo, like returning
     Tales of olden times, resoundeth!
            Hoo-hoo! Shoo-hoo! Nearer soundeth
     Cry of owlet, jay, and plover!   3890
     Are they all awake remaining?
     Salamanders, through the cover,
     Long-limbed, fat-paunched, are they straining?
     And the roots, like serpents, winding
     Out of rock and sand, unbinding,   3895
     Stretch out fetters strange to scare us,
     To affright us and ensnare us.
     Living, sturdy gnarls uncanny
     Stretch out polypus-antennae
     Toward the wanderer. Mice are teeming   3900
     In a thousand colours, streaming
     Through the moss and through the heather!
     And the glow-worms fly, in swarming

Columns, ever forming
A bewildering escort hither.   3905
    Tell me, do we stay or whether
We are going onward thither?
All, all seems to be gyrating,
Rocks and trees that make grimaces,
Lights that wander, changing places,   3910
Multiplying, self-inflating.

Mephistopheles.   Grab my mantle's hem, hold tightly!
    Here's a midway peak where nightly
    Man, astounded, sees and knows
    How in the mountain Mammon glows.   3915
Faust.   How strangely glimmers through the gorges,
    Like morning's red, a turbid glow!
    Down the abyss itself it forges,
    Cleaving its way through gulfs far, far below.
    Vapour floats yonder, there is steam up-leaping,   3920
    Here shines a glow through mist and haze,
    Then like a slender thread it's creeping,
    Then forth it breaks like fountain-sprays.
    Here for a long way it goes winding
    Along the vale in a hundred veins   3925
    And here — a corner crowding, binding —
    In sudden isolation wanes.
    There sparks are sprinkling like a shower
    Of widely scattered golden sand.
    And see the rocky walls! They tower,   3930
    They kindle and like ramparts stand.
Mephistopheles.   Does not Sir Mammon splendidly
    Light up the palace for his revelry?
    You see all this! What luck you've had!
    But hark! Now come the guests in tumult mad.   3935
Faust.   How through the air the tempest raves!
    It smites my neck, shock after shock!
Mephistopheles.   You must lay hold on these old ribs of rock;
    Else it will hurl you down to these abysses' graves.
    A mist is making night more dark.   3940
    How through the woods it crashes! Hark!
    Scared away, the owls are flying.
    Hearken! Columns split and quiver

[114]

In palaces of green undying.
The branches sigh and breaking shiver!   3945
The tree-trunks' mighty groaning!
The roots are creaking and moaning!
In frightfully entangled fall
They crash together, one and all,
And through the wreck-over-strewn abysses   3950
The tempest howls and hisses.
Voices over us! Do you hear?
Now far off and now more near?
All the mountain-side along
Streams a furious magic song!   3955
Witches in chorus.

> The witches to the Brocken go;
> The grain is green, the stubble aglow.
> There gathers all the mighty host;
> Sir Urian sits uppermost.
> So goes it over stone and stock;   3960
> The witch . . . , and stinks the buck.

A Voice.   Alone old Baubo's coming now;
    She's riding upon a farrow sow.
Chorus.

> So honour to whom honour is due!
> In front, Dame Baubo! Lead the crew!   3965
> A sturdy sow with mother astride,
> All witches follow in a tide.

A Voice.   Which way did you come here?
A Voice.   The Ilsenstein way.
    I peeped in the owl's nest there today.
    She made great eyes at me!
A Voice.   Oh, fare on to Hell!   3970
    Why ride so pell-mell?
A Voice.   Just see how she's flayed me!
    The wounds she has made me!
Witches. Chorus.

> The way is broad, the way is long;
> What is that mad and crazy throng?   3975
> The broomstick pokes, the pitchfork thrusts,
> The infant chokes, the mother busts.

Wizards. Half Chorus.

We steal along, like snails' our pace;
All women beat us in the race.
If toward Hell we set our pace,   3980
By a thousand steps they win the race.

Other Half.

Not so precisely do we take it,
In a thousand steps may woman make it;
Yet though she hastes as ever she can,
In a single leap it's done by man.   3985

A Voice from above.   Come with us from the cliff-bound mere!
A Voice from below.   We'd like to go with you up there.
We wash and we're scoured all bright and clean,
But sterile still as we've always been.

Both Choruses.

The wind is stilled, the stars take flight,   3990
The dismal moon fain hides its light;
In whiz and whirr the magic choir
By thousands sputters out sparks of fire.

A Voice from below.   Halt there! Ho, there! Ho!
A Voice from above.   Who calls out from the cleft below?   3995
A Voice below.   Take me too! Take me too!
I'm climbing now three hundred years
And I can never reach the summit.
I want to be among my peers.

Both Choruses.

The broomstick bears, and bears the stock,   4000
The pitchfork bears, and bears the buck.
Who can not lift himself today,
Is a lost man for aye and aye.

Half-Witch below.   I've tripped behind so many a day,
And now the others are far away!   4005
I've no repose at home, and yet
Here too there's none for me to get.

Chorus of Witches.

Salve puts a heart in every hag,
Good as a sail is any rag;
A good ship every trough is too.   4010
You'll fly not 'less today you flew.

Both Choruses.

   And when we glide the peak around,
   Then sweep along upon the ground;
   Bedeck both far and wide the heather
   With all your witchdom's swarm together.   4015

       They settle down

Mephistopheles.   They crowd and shove, they rush and clatter,
 They hiss and whirl, they pull and chatter,
 They sputter, stink and burn and flare!
 A real witch-element, I swear!
 Keep close or soon we'll be a parted pair.   4020
 Where are you?

Faust at a distance.   Here!

Mephistopheles.   Already snatched up there?
 Then I must exercise my rightful sway.
 Make way! Squire Voland comes! Make way, sweet folk, make way!
 Here, Doctor, hold to me! and now in one quick rush
 Let us get out of all this crush;   4025
 It is too crazy even for the likes of me.
 Hard by there something gleams with a quite peculiar glare;
 A something draws me to that shrubbery.
 Come, come! We'll go and slip in there.

Faust.   Spirit of Contradiction! On! and lead the way!   4030
 It was a very clever notion, I must say;
 We seek the Brocken on Walpurgis Night,
 Yet choose to isolate ourselves when near the height!

Mephistopheles.   What motley flames! Just look along the heather!
 There is a jolly club together.   4035
 In little circles one is not alone.

Faust.   I'd rather be up yonder, I must own.
 Already whirling smoke and glow come into view.
 A host is streaming to the Devil! See them ride!
 Full many a riddle there must be untied.   4040

Mephistopheles.   Yet many a riddle will be tied anew.
 Just let the great world whiz and riot;
 We'll house us meanwhile here in quiet.
 We've known it as a fact of ancient date
 That men make little worlds within the great.   4045
 I see young witches stripped and naked over there
 And old ones wisely veiled, they don't go bare.
 For my sake be a friend to all;

The fun is great, the trouble small.
I hear the sound of instruments arise! 4050
Accursèd din! One must get used to that ado.
Come! Come with me! It can't be otherwise.
I'll step up here; I'll introduce you too,
And thus in debt to me bind you anew.
That is no little space. What say you, friend? 4055
Just look out there! You scarce can see the end.
A hundred fires are burning, tier on tier.
They dance, they cook, they drink, make love, and chat.
Now say, where's something better than all that?
Faust.   In introducing us, will you appear 4060
As devil or magician here?
Mephistopheles.   True, I'm much used to go incognito,
But on a gala day one lets one's orders show.
No garter have I to distinguish me,
But here the horse's foot is honoured and in place. 4065
You see that snail there? See her groping face!
Already, creeping hither steadily,
She's scented something out in me.
Though I should wish it, I can not belie me here.
But come! From fire to fire we'll make a tour, 4070
I'll be the go-between and you the wooer.
                    To some who are sitting around dying embers
You agèd sirs, what are you doing in the rear?
I'd praise you if right nicely in the midst I found you,
With riot, youthful revelry around you.
At home there's solitude enough for everyone. 4075
General.   What trust in nations can one place?
However much for them one may have done.
In peoples' as in women's grace
Youth stands supreme over everyone.
Minister.   Now all too far away from right are men, 4080
I praise the good and old, and duly;
When we were all-in-all, ah, truly,
The real, real golden age was then.
Parvenu.   We too weren't stupid, I'll be bound.
Oft what we did, we shouldn't rightly; 4085
But now the world turns round and round,
And just when we would hold things tightly.
Author.   Who now in any case will read

A book with contents middling clever?
And as for dear young folks, indeed,   4090
They're pert and saucy now as never.
Mephistopheles who all at once appears very old.
    I feel that men are ripe for Judgment Day,
    Since no more up the witches' mount I'll climb;
    And since my cask drains turbidly away,
    So too the world declines in dregs and slime.   4095
Huckster-Witch.   You gentlemen, don't pass by so!
    Let such an opportunity not go!
    Look at my wares attentively;
    Here are all sorts of things to see.
    Yet in my shop, sirs, there is naught —   4100
    Its like on earth you will not find —
    That at some time or other has not wrought
    Dire harm both to the world and to mankind.
    No dagger's here which has not streamed with blood,
    No cup which has not poured a hot, consuming flood   4105
    Of poison into some quite healthy frame,
    No gem that has not brought some lovely maid to shame,
    Nor sword that has not made a truce miscarry
    Or, from behind maybe, has stabbed no adversary.
Mephistopheles.   Dear Coz, you understand but badly times like these: 4110
    What's done is past! What's past is done!
    Provide yourself with novelties!
    By novelties alone can we be won.
Faust.   If I'm not to forget myself, I must watch out!
    That's what I call a fair beyond all doubt.   4115
Mephistopheles.   Upward strives the whirling throng;
    You think you shove, and you are shoved along.
Faust.   Who can that be?
Mephistopheles.   Observe her with great care!
    That's Lilith.
Faust.   Who?
Mephistopheles.   Adam's first wife. Beware
    That lovely hair of hers, those tresses   4120
    Which she incomparably delights to wear!
    The young man whom she lures into their snare
    She will not soon release from her caresses.
Faust.   Yonder sit two, one old and one young thing.
    They have already done some right good capering.   4125

[119]

Mephistopheles. There is no rest today for young or old.
A new dance starts; come now! let us take hold!
Faust dancing with T HE Y OUNG W ITCH.

Once came a lovely dream to me.
I saw therein an apple-tree;
Two lovely apples on it shone,   4130
They charmed me so, I climbed thereon.
The Beauty.

The little apples man entice
Since first they were in Paradise.
I feel myself with pleasure glow
That such within my garden grow.   4135
Mephistopheles with T HE O LD W ITCH.

Once came a wanton dream to me.
I saw therein a riven tree;
It had a . . . ;
'Twas . , yet I was pleased with it.
The Old Witch.

I proffer now my best salute   4140
To you, the knight with horse's foot!
Let him a . . . prepare,
If him . . . does not scare.

Proctophantasmist. Accursèd folk! how dare you then?
Have you not long had proof complete,   4145
A spirit never stands on ordinary feet?
And now you're dancing like us other men!
The Beauty dancing. Why is he at our ball? that fellow there?
Faust dancing. Ha! He is simply everywhere.
He must appraise what others dance.   4150
If over each step he can't make a din,
The step's as good as if it had not been.
It irks him most the moment we advance.
If you'd but turn around in endless repetition
As he is wont to do in his old mill,   4155
That, to be sure, he'd call not ill,
Especially if you asked his permission.
Proctophantasmist. You are still here! This is unheard-of, on my word!
Vanish! We brought enlightenment as you have heard!
This devilish crew cares not for rules or books.   4160
We are so wise, and yet in Tegel there are spooks!

How long I've swept and swept at this conceit absurd
And can't sweep clean — this is unheard-of, on my word!
The Beauty.   Then do stop boring us in such a place!
Proctophantasmist.   I say it, Spirits, to your face,   4165
    This spirit despotism I will not endure;
    My spirit can not act that way.
The dancing goes on

    I see that I have no success today;
    But anyway I'll take along "A Tour"
    And hope still, ere my last step, to subdue   4170
    The devils and the poets too.
Mephistopheles.   He'll straightway in a puddle set him.
    That's how he gets relief, of solace well assured.
    When leeches, feasting on his rump, beset him,
    Of spirits and of spirit he is cured.   4175
To FAUST *who has left the dance*

    Why do you let the pretty maiden go
    Who sang so sweetly as you danced along?
Faust.   Ugh! in the very middle of her song
    A mouse sprang from her lips — 'twas small and red.
Mephistopheles.   That's quite all right. There's naught in that to dread.   4180
    It is enough you did not find the mouse was grey.
    Who in a lover's hour will bother anyway?
Faust.   I saw then —
Mephistopheles.   What?
Faust.   Mephisto, see you there —
    Far off she stands, alone — a girl so pale and fair?
    She drags herself but slowly from that place.   4185
    She seems to move with shackled feet.
    I must confess, I thought it was the face —
    That she looks like my Gretchen sweet.
Mephistopheles.   Do let that be! That is of good to none.
    It is a magic image, lifeless eidolon.   4190
    It is not well to meet that anywhere;
    Man's blood grows frigid from that rigid stare;
    And he is turned almost to stone.
    The story of Medusa you of course have known.
Faust.   In truth, the eyes of one who's dead are those,   4195
    Which there was no fond, loving hand to close;
    That is the breast that Gretchen offered me,
    That is the body sweet that I enjoyed.

[121]

Mephistopheles.   It's sorcery, you fool, you're easily decoyed!
 She seems to each as though his love were she.   4200
Faust.   What rapture! Ah, what misery!
 Yet from this vision I can't turn aside.
 How strange that such a lovely neck
 A single band of crimson must bedeck!
 A knife's edge scarcely seems less wide.   4205
Mephistopheles.   Quite right! I see it likewise, it is true!
 And she can bear her head twixt side and elbow too,
 For Perseus struck it off for her —
 I vow, illusion's still bewitching you!
 Do come on up the little height!   4210
 The Prater is not livelier;
 And if someone has not bewitched me quite,
 I truly see a theatre.
 What's going on?
Servibilis.   They're starting now. The play
 Will be the last of seven, one that's new;   4215
 To give so many is the usual way.
 A dilettante wrote the play
 And dilettanti will enact it too.
 Excuse me, gentlemen, if I must disappear;
 With dilettant delight I raise the curtain.   4220
Mephistopheles.   I find that all is well, to find you here;
 Your proper place is on the Brocken, that is certain.

[122]

Walpurgis Night's Dream

or OBERON AND TITANIA'S GOLDEN WEDDING

INTERMEZZO

Theatre Manager.	Now for once we'll rest today, Valiant sons of Mieding. Misty vale and mountain grey Are all the scene we're needing!	4225
Herald.	Golden wedding can not be Till fifty years have vanished; And yet golden is 't to me When the strife is banished.	4230
Oberon.	Are ye spirits to be seen, Come forth and show it duly! Fairy king and fairy queen, They are united newly.	
Puck.	Now comes Puck and whirls about And slides his foot a-dancing; After come a hundred out, Themselves and him entrancing.	4235
Ariel.	Ariel awakes the song With pure and heavenly measure; Many frights he lures along, And fair ones too, with pleasure.	4240
Oberon.	Spouses who would live in peace, Learn from our example! When a pair would love increase, To separate them's ample.	4245
Titania.	Sulks the husband, carps the wife, Just seize them quickly, harry Her away far to the south And him to far north carry.	4250

Orchestra Tutti
FORTISSIMO.   Snout of fly, mosquito-bill,
With kin of all conditions,
Frog in leaves and crickets shrill,
These are the musicians!

Solo.   See, here comes the bagpipe's sack!   4255
Soapbubble-like, it's blowing.
Hear the snecke-snicke-snack
Through its snub nose flowing!

*A Spirit that is
just taking
form.*   Spider's foot and paunch of toad
And wings the wight doth grow him!   4260
True, a beastie 'twill not be
But yet a little poem.

*A Little
Couple.*   Short step here and high leap there
Through honey-dew and sweetness;
Yet you'll soar not through the air,   4265
With all your tripping fleetness.

*Inquisitive
Traveller.*   Is that not mummers' mocking play?
Shall I trust to my vision?
Fair god Oberon today
Is here on exhibition?   4270

Orthodox.   Claws or tail I do not see
And yet, beyond a cavil,
Just like "The Gods of Greece" is he
Likewise a very devil.

*Northern
Artist.*   What I may grasp today may be   4275
But sketches of this tourney,
Yet I'm betimes preparing me
For my Italian Journey.

Purist.   Woe! bad luck has led me here.
How decency they're mocking!   4280
Of all the witches' host, dear! dear!
But two are powdered! Shocking!

Young Witch.	Powder is like a petticoat, For grey hags hoddy-doddy; So I sit naked on my goat And show a strapping body.	4285
Matron.	We are too well-behaved by far, With you to snarl a lot here; Yet, young and tender as you are, I hope that you will rot here.	4290
Leader of the *Orchestra.*	Snout of fly, mosquito-bill, Don't swarm around the naked! Frog in leaves and cricket shrill, Do mark the time and take it!	
Weather-Vane *turning in one* *direction.*	The comp'ny's all one can wish for, Each one a bride, I swear it! And man by man a bachelor, Most prom'sing, I declare it!	4295
Weather-Vane *turning in the* *other direc-* *tion.*	And will the ground not open out To swallow all who're dancing, Then I will swiftly leave this rout And straight to Hell go prancing.	4300
Xenia.	See us here as insects! Ha! Each one with sharp shears on her, That Lord Satan, our papa, We fittingly may honour.	4305
Hennings.	Just see them all, a crowding throng, Naïvely jesting, playing! That they had kind hearts all along, They'll in the end be saying.	4310
"Leader of *the Muses."*	Amid this witches' host, indeed, One's way one gladly loses; For, sure, I could these sooner lead Than I can lead the Muses.	

The Quondam *" Spirit of the* *Times."*	With proper folk one can all do. Come, cling close, none can pass us! The Blocksberg has a broad top too, Like Germany's Parnassus.	4315
Inquisitive *Traveller.*	What's the name of that stiff man? He goes with haughty paces; He snuffles all he snuffle can. "He scents the Jesuits' traces."	4320
Crane.	If water clear or muddy be, I fish with pleasure, really; That's why this pious man you see With devils mixing freely.	4325
Worldling.	By pious people, I speak true, No vehicle's rejected; Conventicles, more than a few, On Blocksberg are erected.	4330
Dancer.	Another chorus now succeeds! I hear a distant drumming. "Don't be disturbed! It's, in the reeds, The herons' changeless booming."	
Dancing *Master.*	How each his legs kicks up and flings! Somehow gets on, however! The clumsy hops, the crooked springs, And how it looks, ask never!	4335
Fiddler.	They hate each other well, that crew, And they would like to rend them. As Orpheus' lyre the beasts all drew, The bagpipe here will blend them.	4340
Dogmatist.	I'll not let screams lead me to war With doubts and critic-cavils. The Devil must be something, or Else how could there be devils?	4345

[126]

Idealist.   For once, as I see phantasy,
It is far too despotic.
In truth, if I be all I see,
Today I'm idiotic.   4350

Realist.   This riot makes my torture sheer
And greatly irks me surely;
For the first time I'm standing here
On my feet insecurely.

Supernaturalist.   With much delight I join this crew   4355
And share with them their revels;
For that there are good spirits too
I argue from these devils.

Skeptic.   They go to track the flamelets out
And think they're near the treasure.   4360
Devil alliterates with Doubt,
So I am here with pleasure.

*Leader of the
Orchestra.*   Frog in leaves and cricket shrill,
Cursed dilettants! Perdition!
Fly-snout and mosquito-bill,   4365
You're each a fine musician!

The Adroit.   Sans-souci, we call us so,
Gay creatures free from worry;
We afoot no more can go,
So on our heads we hurry.   4370

*The Ne'er-
Do-Wells.*   We once sponged many a bite, 'tis true,
God help us! That is done now!
We've danced our shoes entirely through,
On naked soles we run now.

*Will-o'-the-
Wisps.*   From the marshes we come out,   4375
Where we arose from litter;
Yet here in dancing roundabout
We're gallants all a-glitter.

A Falling Star.	From the heights above plunged I, With star- and fire-light o'er me; Crookèd now in grass I lie, Who'll to my feet restore me?

4380

The Heavy Ones.	Room! more room! All round us too! Thus downward go the grasses. Spirits come and they, it's true, Are clumsy, heavy masses.

4385

Puck.	Bloated, enter not the fray, Like elephant-calves about one! And the clumsiest today Be Puck himself, the stout one!

4390

Ariel.	If kind Nature gave you wings, If them Mind uncloses, Follow my light wanderings To yon hill of roses!

Orchestra

PIANISSIMO. Cloud and mist drift off with speed,
Aloft 'tis brighter growing.
Breeze in leaves and wind in reed,
And all away is blowing.

4395

A Dismal Day   A Field

FAUST   MEPHISTOPHELES

Faust. In misery! Despairing! Long pitiably astray upon the earth and
now imprisoned! That lovely, ill-starred creature locked up in a prison
as a criminal, to suffer horrible tortures. To that has it come! to that! —
Treacherous, contemptible spirit, and that you have concealed from me!
— Stay, then, stay! Roll your devilish eyes ragingly in your head! Stay   5
and defy me with your intolerable presence! Imprisoned! In irrepara-
ble misery! Delivered up to evil spirits and to condemning, feelingless
mankind! And me, meanwhile, you cradle in insipid diversions, hide
from me her increasing wretchedness, and let her, helpless, go to ruin!

Mephistopheles. She's not the first one.   10

Faust. Dog! Detestable monster! Turn him, Thou Spirit Infinite, turn
the worm back into his dog's-form, as at night it often pleased him to trot
along before me, to roll in a heap before the feet of the innocent wanderer, and as he fell, to spring upon his shoulders. Turn him back into
his favourite form, that he may crawl on his belly, before me in the sand,   15
that I may trample him beneath my feet, the outcast! — Not the first one!
— Woe! Woe! that no human soul can grasp it, that more than one creature has sunk down into the depths of this misery, that the first one, in
writhing, deathly agony, did not atone for the guilt of all the others in
the sight of the Eternal Pardoner! The misery of this single one pierces   20
the marrow of my life; and you are calmly grinning at the fate of thousands!

Mephistopheles. Now we are again at our wits' end, there where the reason of you mortals snaps from over-stretching. Why do you enter into
fellowship with us if you can not carry it through? Will you fly and are   25
not safe from dizziness? Did we force ourselves on you, or you on us?

Faust. Bare not so your greedy fangs at me! It fills me with loathing!
Great, glorious Spirit, Thou who didst deign to appear to me, Thou who
knowest my heart and my soul, why fetter me to the infamous comrade
who feeds on mischief and slakes his thirst in destruction?   30

Mephistopheles. Have you ended?

Faust. Save her! or woe to you! The most hideous curses be on you for
thousands of years!

Mephistopheles. I can not loose the bonds of the avenger, nor undo his
bolts. Save her! Who was it that plunged her into ruin? I or you?   35

FAUST *looks around wildly*

Mephistopheles. Will you reach for the thunder? 'Tis well that it was not given to you miserable mortals! To smash to pieces the man who blamelessly answers back, that is the tyrant's way of venting himself when embarrassed.

Faust. Take me to her! She shall be free! 40

Mephistopheles. And the danger to which you will expose yourself? Know that the guilt of blood, from your hand, still lies upon the town. Over the spot where a man was slain, avenging spirits hover and lie in wait for the returning murderer.

Faust. That too from you? The murder and death of a world be upon you, 45 monster! Lead me to her, I say, and set her free!

Mephistopheles. I will lead you, and what I can do, hear! Have I all power in Heaven and on earth? The warder's senses I will becloud; make yourself master of the keys and lead her forth with human hand. I'll watch! The magic horses are ready, I will carry you away. That I 50 can do.

Faust. Up and away!

Night   An Open Field

FAUST *and* MEPHISTOPHELES *storming along on*
black horses

Faust. What weaving are they round the Ravenstone?

Mephistopheles. I know not what they are brewing and doing. 4400

Faust. Hovering up, hovering down, bending low, bowing down.

Mephistopheles. A witches' guild.

Faust. They strew and dedicate.

Mephistopheles. On! On!

A Prison

Faust with a bunch of keys and a lamp, in front of an iron wicket.

A long-unwonted shudder over me falls, 4405
The woe of human lot lays hold on me.
Here then she dwells, within these humid walls,
And all her crime was a fond fantasy.
You hesitate to go to her? You fear

Again to see her near?   4410
On! Your faltering brings death lingering here!
He grasps the lock
Someone is singing inside.
                        My mother, the whore,
                        She has murdered me!
                        My father, the rogue,
                        He has eaten me,   4415
                        My sister, so small,
                        My bones, one and all,
                        In a cool place did lay.
                        A forest bird fair I became that day;
                        Fly away! Fly away!   4420

Faust unlocking the wicket.
    She does not dream her lover listens, near again,
    And hears the rustling straw, the clanking chain.
                        He steps in
Margaret hiding herself on her pallet.
    Woe! Woe! They come! How bitter 'tis to die!
Faust softly.   Hush! Hush! I come to set you free!
Margaret grovelling at his feet.
    If you're a man, then feel my misery!   4425
Faust.   You will wake the warders with your cry!
                        He takes hold of the chains, to unlock them
Margaret on her knees.   Who, headsman, ever had this power
    Over me to give?
    You fetch me at the midnight hour!
    Be merciful and let me live!   4430
    Will it not be soon enough when the matin's rung?
                        She stands up
    Ah! I am still so young, so young!
    And now to die!
    It was my ruin that so fair was I.
    My love was near, now he is far;   4435
    Torn lies the wreath, scattered the flowers are.
    Seize me not thus so violently!
    What have I done to you? Oh, pity me!
    Let me not in vain implore!
    I've never, my life long, seen you before!   4440
Faust.   Can I survive this misery?

Margaret.   You now have power over me.
    Let me but nurse my baby once again.
    I fondled it the livelong night;
    They took it from me, just to give me pain,   4445
    And now they say I murdered it outright.
    I never shall again be glad.
    They're singing songs about me! That is bad
    Of people! An old story ends just so.
    Who bids them tell it of me, though?   4450
Faust throws himself down.
    Here at your feet a lover lies,
    To loose the bondage of these miseries.
Margaret throws herself beside him.
    Oh, let us kneel, call on the saints to hear us!
    See! under these steps near us
    And the threshold's swell,   4455
    Seething all Hell!
    The Devil,
    In fearful brawling,
    Holds awful revel!
Faust loudly.   Gretchen! Gretchen!   4460
Margaret listening attentively.
    That was my lover calling!
                She springs up. The chains fall off
    Where is he? I heard him calling! I am free!
    No one shall hinder me.
    To his neck will I fly,
    On his bosom lie!   4465
    He called "Gretchen!" He stood at the door of my cell.
    Through the midst of the howl and clatter of Hell,
    Through the anger and scorn of the devilish crew,
    The tones of that sweet, loving voice I knew.
Faust.   It's I!
Margaret.   It's you! Oh, say it once again!   4470
                Embracing him
    It's he! It's he! Where's all my misery?
    And where the anguish of the gaol? the chain?
    It's you! You've come to save me!
    And I am saved!
    The very street is here anew   4475
    Where for the first time I saw you,

And the cheerful garden too
Where I and Martha wait for you.
Faust urging her to go.　　Come! Come with me!
Margaret.　　　　　　　　　　　　　　Oh, tarry!
So gladly do I tarry where you tarry!　　　　　　　　4480
　　　　　　　　Caressing him
Faust.　　Hurry!
Unless you hurry,
We must pay for it dearly.
Margaret.　　What? And can you kiss no more! Is this
My love, away from me a short while merely,　　　　4485
And yet forgotten how to kiss?
Why do I cling about your neck so fearfully?
When once but at a glance, a word, from you,
All Heaven swept me through and through,
And you kissed me as if you'd smother me.　　　　　4490
Kiss me! Do!
Or I'll kiss you!
　　　　　　　　She embraces him
Oh, woe! Your dear lips are so cold,
Are still!
Where has your loving　　　　　　　　　　　　4495
Been roving?
Who did me this ill?
　　　　　　　　She turns away from him
Faust.　　Come! follow me, love, have courage, be bold!
I'll press you to my heart with warmth a thousandfold;
I only beg you now to follow me!　　　　　　　　4500
Margaret turning toward him.
And is it you, then? You, quite certainly?
Faust.　　It's I! Come with me!
Margaret.　　　　　　　　You unlock the chain,
You take me in your lap again!
How is it that you do not shrink from me?
And do you know, my love, whom you set free?　　　4505
Faust.　　Come! come! The depths of night already wane.
Margaret.　　My mother I have slain.
My child I've drowned! It's true!
Was it not given to me and you?
To you as well! It's you! I scarce can deem　　　　4510
It real. Give me your hand! It is no dream!
　　　　　　　　[133]

FAUST : THE FIRST PART

Your darling hand! But ah, it's wet!
Quick wipe it off! It seems that even yet
I see blood run.
Ah, God! What have you done? 4515
Oh, put away
The sword, I pray!
Faust. Let what is done and over, over be!
You're killing me.
Margaret. No, you must stay alive, you must indeed! 4520
I'll tell you how the graves must be.
For them you must take heed
Tomorrow morn for me.
The best place give to my mother,
And close beside her my brother, 4525
Me a little to one side,
A space — but not too wide!
And put the little one here on my right breast.
No one else will lie beside me!
Ah, in your arms to nestle and hide me, 4530
That was a sweet, a lovely bliss!
But now, much as I try, it seems to go amiss.
It seems to me as if I must
Force myself on you and you thrust
Me back, and yet it's you, so kind, so good to see. 4535
Faust. If you feel it is I, then come with me!
Margaret. Out there?
Faust. To freedom!
Margaret. If the grave's out there,
Death lurking near, then come with me!
From here to the eternal bed of rest 4540
And no step further — No!
You go away now? Henry! Oh, that I could go!
Faust. You can! Just will it! Open stands the door.
Margaret. I dare not go; for me there's no hope any more.
Why flee? They'll surely lie in wait for me. 4545
It is so wretched to beg one's way
And with an evil conscience too.
It is so wretched, in unknown parts to stray,
And they will seize me anyway.
Faust. I shall remain with you. 4550
Margaret. Quick! Quick! Begone!

[134]

Save your poor child! On! On!
Keep to the way
Along the brook,
Over the bridge   4555
To the wood beyond,
To the left where the plank is
In the pond.
Quick! Seize it! Quick!
It's trying to rise,   4560
It's struggling still!
Save it! Save it!

Faust.   Collect your thoughts! And see,
It's but one step, then you are free!

Margaret.   If we were only past the hill!   4565
There sits my mother upon a stone,
My brain is seized by cold, cold dread!
There sits my mother upon a stone,
And to and fro she wags her head;
She becks not, she nods not, her head's drooping lower,   4570
She has slept long, she'll wake no more.
She slept and then we were so glad.
Those were happy times we had.

Faust.   No prayers help here and naught I say,
So I must venture to bear you away.   4575

Margaret.   Let me alone! No, I'll not suffer force!
Don't pounce so murderously on me!
I have done all for love of you.

Faust.   My darling! See!
The day is dawning! Darling!

Margaret.   Day! Yes, day is dawning! The last day breaks for me! 4580
My wedding-day this was to be!
Tell no one you have been with Gretchen.
My wreath's gone forever!
It is gone and in vain.
We'll see one another again,   4585
But at dances never.
The crowd comes surging, no sound it makes,
The street and square
Can not hold all there.
The death-bell tolls, the white wand breaks.   4590
How they seize me, bind me with lashes!

Away and to the block I'm sped.
Each neck is wincing at the flashes
As swift the keen blade flashes over my head.
Hushed lies the world as the grave.   4595

Faust.   Oh! had I never been born!

Mephistopheles appears outside.   Off! or you're lost and lorn.
What vain delaying, wavering, prating!
My shivering steeds are waiting,
The morning twilight's near.   4600

Margaret.   What rises up from the threshold here?
He! He! Thrust him out!
In this holy place what is he about?
He seeks me!

Faust.   You shall live!

Margaret.   Judgment of God! My all to thee I give!   4605

Mephistopheles to F A U S T.
Come! Come! Along with her I will abandon you.

Margaret.   Thine am I, Father! Rescue me!
Ye angels! Ye heavenly hosts! Appear,
Encamp about and guard me here!
Henry! I shrink from you!   4610

Mephistopheles.   She is judged!

A Voice from above.   She is saved!

Mephistopheles to F A U S T.   Here to me!

                    He disappears with F A U S T

A Voice from within, dying away.   Henry! Henry!

Second Part

OF THE TRAGEDY

❧

Act I

A Pleasing Landscape

TWILIGHT

FAUST, *reclining on flowery turf, weary, restless, try-ing to sleep*

SPIRITS, *charming little figures forming a circle, hover-ing about*

Ariel, song accompanied by Aeolian harps.

When in spring the rain of flowers
Hovering sinketh over all,
When the meadows, bright with showers,   4615
Unto all the earth-born call,
Tiny elves with souls propitious
Haste to help where help they can;
Be he blameless, be he vicious,
They lament the luckless man.   4620

Hovering around this head in circles airy,
Look that ye show the noble law of fairy:
Appease the furious conflict in his heart!
Draw out the burning arrows of remorse,
From suffered horrors cleanse his inmost part!   4625
Four pauses makes the night upon its course:
Hasten to fill them with your kindly art!

[137]

His head upon a cooling pillow lay,
Then bathe him in the dew from Lethe's stream!
His limbs, cramp-stiffened, soon will freely play   4630
When rest has made him strong for morn's new beam.
Perform the fairest elfin rite,
Restore him to the holy light!

Chorus singly, or two or more, alternating and together.

When the breezes, warmth exhaling,
Fill the green-encircled plain,   4635
Twilight sinks its mists enveiling,
Brings sweet fragrance in its train,
Softly whispers peace to mortals,
Rocks the heart to childlike rest,
Closes eyelids, daylight's portals,   4640
Of the weary and oppressed.
    Night already sinks and darkles,
Holy follows star on star,
Light now bright, now fainter sparkles,
Glitters near and gleams afar,   4645
Glitters, in the lake reflecting,
Gleams in night's clear canopy;
Deepest slumber's bliss perfecting,
Reigns the moon's full majesty.
    Now the hours are passed and over,   4650
Pain and bliss have fled away.
Feel it now! Thou wilt recover!
Trust the gleam of new-born day!
Vales grow green and hills are swelling,
Lure to bowers of rest again;   4655
Harvest's coming now foretelling,
Roll the silvery waves of grain.
    If thou every wish wouldst gain thee,
Gaze at yonder glory wide!
Lightly do the bonds restrain thee;   4660
Sleep's a shell, cast it aside!
Be the crowd faint-hearted, quailing,
Falter not, but be thou bold!
All is his who never-failing
Understands and swift lays hold.   4665

*A tremendous tumult announces the approach
of the sun*

[138]

Ariel.

Hark! The storm of hours is nearing!
Sounding loud to spirit-hearing,
Is the new-born day appearing.
Rocky portals grate and shatter,
Phoebus' wheels roll forth and clatter.   4670
What a tumult Light brings near!
Trumpets, trombones, are resounding,
Eyes are blinking, ears astounding;
The unheard ye shall not hear.
Slip into a flowery bell   4675
Deeper, deeper; quiet dwell
Under the leaf, in the cliff,
If it strikes you, ye are deaf.

Faust.   Refreshed anew life's pulses beat and waken
To greet the mild ethereal dawn of morning;   4680
Earth, through this night thou too hast stood unshaken
And breath'st before me in thy new adorning,
Beginst to wrap me round with gladness thrilling,
A vigorous resolve in me forewarning,
Unceasing strife for life supreme instilling. — 4685
Now lies the world revealed in twilight glimmer,
The wood resounds, a thousand voices trilling;
The vales where mist flows in and out lie dimmer,
But in the gorges sinks a light from heaven,
And boughs and twigs, refreshed, lift up their shimmer 4690
From fragrant chasms where they slept at even;
Tint upon tint again emerges, clearing
Where trembling pearls from flower and leaf drip riven:
All round me is a Paradise appearing.
Look up! — The peaks, gigantic and supernal,   4695
Proclaim the hour most solemn now is nearing.
They early may enjoy the light eternal
That later to us here below is wended.
Now on the alpine meadows, sloping, vernal,
A clear and lavish glory has descended   4700
And step by step fulfils its journey's ending.
The sun steps forth! — Alas, already blinded,
I turn away, the pain my vision rending.
Thus is it ever when a hope long yearning

[139]

Has made a wish its own, supreme, transcending, 4705
And finds Fulfilment's portals outward turning;
From those eternal deeps bursts ever higher
Too great a flame, we stand, with wonder burning.
To kindle life's fair torch we did aspire
And seas of flame — and what a flame! — embrace us! 4710
Is it Love? Is it Hate? that twine us with their fire,
In alternating joy and pain enlace us,
So that again toward earth we turn our gazing,
Baffled, to hide in youth's fond veils our faces.
  Behind me therefore let the sun be blazing! 4715
The cataract in gorges deeply riven
I view with rapture growing and amazing.
To plunge on plunge in a thousand streams it's given,
And yet a thousand, downward to the valleys,
While foam and mist high in the air are driven. 4720
Yet how superb above this tumult sallies
The many-coloured rainbow's changeful being;
Now lost in air, now clearly drawn, it dallies,
Shedding sweet coolness round us even when fleeing!
The rainbow mirrors human aims and action. 4725
Think, and more clearly wilt thou grasp it, seeing
Life is but light in many-hued reflection.

The Emperor's Palace

THE THRONE–ROOM

The State Council awaiting the Emperor. *Trumpets.
Courtiers of all kinds enter, splendidly dressed. The
Emperor ascends the throne, at his right hand the
Astrologer*

Emperor. I greet you, faithful friends and dear,
Assembled here from far and wide.
I see the wise man at my side, 4730
But wherefore is the Fool not here?
A Squire. A pace behind your mantle's sweep
There on the stairs he fell in a heap;
They bore away that load of fat,
But dead or drunk? No one knows that. 4735

A Second Squire.   Now at a swift, amazing pace
 Another's pushing to his place.
 He's quaintly primped, in truth, and smart,
 But such a fright that all men start.
 The guards there at the doorway hold   4740
 Their halberds crosswise and athwart —
 But here he is. The Fool is bold!
Mephistopheles kneeling before the throne.
 What is accursed and welcomed ever?
 What's longed for, ever chased away?
 What's always taken into favour?   4745
 What's harshly blamed, accused each day?
 Whom don't you dare to summon here?
 Whose name hears gladly every man?
 What to your throne is drawing near?
 What's placed itself beneath your ban?   4750
Emperor.   Your words you may at present spare!
 The place for riddles is not here;
 They are these gentlemen's affair. —
 Solve them yourself! I'd like to hear.
 My old fool's gone far, far away, I fear me;   4755
 Take you his place and come and stand here near me.
       MEPHISTOPHELES *mounts the steps and*
      stations himself on the left
Murmurs of the Crowd.
   A brand-new fool — new pains begin —
   Whence did he come? — how came he in? —
   The old one fell — he's spent and done —
   A barrel he — a lath this one —   4760

Emperor.   And so, ye faithful whom I love,
 Be welcome here from near and far.
 Ye meet beneath a favouring star;
 Fortune is written for us there above.
 Yet wherefore in these days, oh, say,   4765
 When all our cares we'd thrust away
 And wear the mummer's mask in play
 And gaiety alone enjoy,
 Why should we let state councils us annoy?
 But since the task seems one we may not shun, 4770
 All is arranged, so be it done.

[141]

Chancellor.   The highest virtue like an aureole
Circles the Emperor's head; alone and sole,
He validly can exercise it:
'Tis justice! — All men love and prize it;   4775
'Tis what all wish, scarce do without, and ask;
To grant it to his people is his task.
But ah! what good to mortal mind is sense,
What good to hearts is kindness, hands benevolence,
When through the state a fever runs and revels,   4780
And evil hatches more and more of evils?
Who views the wide realm from this height supreme,
To him all seems like an oppressive dream,
Where in confusion is confusion reigning
And lawlessness by law itself maintaining,   4785
A world of error evermore obtaining.
      This man steals herds, a woman that,
Cross, chalice, candlestick from altar;
For many years his boastings never falter,
His skin intact, his body sound and fat.   4790
Now plaintiffs crowd into the hall,
The judge, encushioned, lords it over all.
Meanwhile in billows, angry, urging,
A growing tumult of revolt is surging.
Great crimes and shame may be the braggart's token,   4795
On worst accomplices he oft depends;
And " Guilty! " is the verdict often spoken
Where Innocence only itself defends.
To pieces is our world now going,
What's fitting loses all its might;   4800
How ever shall that sense be growing
Which, only, leads us to the Right?
At last will men of good intent
To briber, flatterer incline;
A judge who can impose no punishment,   4805
At last with culprits will combine.
I've painted black, and yet a denser screen
I'd rather draw before the scene.
            Pause
Decisions can not be evaded;
When all do harm and none are aided,   4810
Majesty too becomes a prey.

Commander-in-Chief.   In these wild days what riots quicken!
  Each strikes and he in turn is stricken,
  And no command will men obey.
  The citizen behind his wall,   4815
  The knight upon his rocky nest,
  Have sworn to last us out, and all
  Maintain their power with stubborn zest.
  The mercenaries, restless growing,
  Blusteringly demand their pay,   4820
  And if to them no more were owing,
  They would be quick to run away.
  Let one forbid what all men fain expect,
  He's put his hand into a hornets' nest;
  The empire which they should protect   4825
  Lies plundered, desolate, and waste.
  This furious riot no one is restraining,
  Already half the world's undone;
  Outside the realm kings still are reigning,
  But no one thinks it his concern — not one.   4830
Treasurer.   Who will depend upon allies!
  The funds they pledged as subsidies,
  Like leaking pipe-borne water, do not flow.
  Then, Sire, of these wide states — yours by succession —
  Who now has come into possession?   4835
  A new lord rules wherever one may go,
  Insists on living independently;
  How he keeps house, we must look on and see.
  Of rights we've given up so many,
  We're left without a claim to any.   4840
  And as to parties, of whatever name,
  There's been no trust in them of late;
  They may give praise or they may blame,
  Indifferent are their love and hate.
  To rest them well from all their labour   4845
  Lie hidden Ghibelline and Guelph.
  Who is there now who'll help his neighbour?
  Each has enough to help himself.
  Barred are the gates where gold is stored,
  And all men scratch and scrape and hoard,   4850
  And empty all our coffers stay.
Steward.   What ills I too must learn to bear!

We want each day to save and spare,
And more we're needing every day,
And daily do I see new trouble growing. 4855
The cooks lack nothing, they've no woes;
For boars and stags and hares and roes
And fowls, geese, ducks, and turkeys too,
Allowances-in-kind, sure revenue,
They still are not so badly flowing. 4860
The flow of wine? That, to be sure, is slowing.
Where once in cellars cask on cask was nuzzling,
The best of brands and vintages befuzzling,
Our noble lords' eternal guzzling
Is draining every last drop out. 4865
The City Council's store must now be opened up.
A basin, bowl, is seized as drinking-cup
And under the table ends the drinking-bout.
Now I'm to pay, give each his wages.
The Jew will spare me no outrages, 4870
He'll make advances which for ages
Will put our revenues to rout.
The swine are no more fatten fed,
Pawned is the pillow on the bed,
At table we eat bread for which we owe. 4875

Emperor, after some reflection, to MEPHISTOPHELES.
Say, Fool, can you not add a tale of woe?
Mephistopheles. Indeed, not I! I see this ambient splendour,
Yourself and yours! — Should one his trust surrender
Where Majesty holds undisputed sway
And ready might sweeps hostile force away? 4880
Where honest purpose holds command
And wisdom guides the active hand?
What can the powers of evil do, combining
To make a darkness where such stars are shining?
Murmurs.
That is a rogue — full well he knows — 4885
Sneaks in by lying — while it goes —
I know for sure — what lurks behind —
What then? — he has some scheme in mind —

Mephistopheles. Where in this world does not some lack appear?
Here this, there that, but money's lacking here. 4890

[144]

One can not pick it off the floor, that's sure,
But what lies deepest, wisdom can procure.
In veins of mountains, walls far underground,
Gold coined and uncoined can be found;
And do you ask me who'll bring it to light?   4895
A man endowed with Mind's and Nature's might!
Chancellor.   Nature and Mind — don't talk to Christians thus!
Men burn up atheists, fittingly,
Because such speeches are most dangerous.
Nature is sin, and Mind is devil,   4900
They nurture doubt, in doubt they revel,
Their hybrid, monstrous progeny.
That's not for us! — Our Emperor's ancient land
Has seen arise two castes alone
Who worthily uphold his throne: 4905
The saints and knights. Firm do they stand,
Defying every tempest day by day
And taking church and state in pay.
In rabble minds that breed confusion
Revolt arises like a tide.   4910
Heretics, wizards! Imps of delusion!
They ruin town and country-side.
Them will you now with brazen juggle
Into this lofty circle smuggle,
While in a heart depraved you snuggle.   4915
Fools, wizards, heretics are near allied.
Mephistopheles.   I see the learnèd man in what you say!
What you don't touch, for you lies miles away;
What you don't grasp, is wholly lost to you;
What you don't reckon, you believe not true;   4920
What you don't weigh, that has for you no weight;
What you don't coin, you're sure is counterfeit.
Emperor.   That's not the way to help or aught determine.
What do you mean now with this Lenten sermon?
I'm sated of this endless " If " and " How."   4925
There is no money. Well, then, get it now!
Mephistopheles.   I'll furnish what you wish and more. It's true,
It is a light task, yet the light's a burden too.
The gold lies there and yet to win it,
That is the art — who knows how to begin it?   4930
Recall those fearful times when roving bands

[145]

Poured like a deluge drowning men and lands,
How many men, so greatly did they fear,
Concealed their dearest treasure there and here.
So it was of old when mighty Rome held sway,   4935
So it was till yesterday, aye, till today.
It all lies buried in the earth, to save it;
The earth's the Emperor's, and he should have it.
Treasurer.   Now for a fool, his words are noways trite.
That is, in truth, the old Imperial Right.   4940
Chancellor.   Satan is laying you his golden nooses;
We're dealing with no right and pious uses.
Steward.   If he brings welcome gifts to court, I'm sure,
A little wrong with them I can endure.
Commander-in-Chief.   Shrewd fool to promise each what will befit;   4945
Whence it may come, no soldier cares a whit.
Mephistopheles.   Perhaps you think I'm trying to betray you;
Well, here's the astrologer; ask him, I pray you.
Circle on circle, hour and house he knows.
Tell us then what the heavenly aspect shows.   4950
Murmurs.

> Two rogues — each to the other known —
> Dreamer and Fool — so near the throne —
> An ancient ditty — worn and weak —
> The Fool will prompt — the Sage will speak —

Astrologer speaks, MEPHISTOPHELES *prompting him.*
The Sun himself is gold of purest ray,   4955
The herald Mercury serves for love and pay;
Dame Venus has bewitched you all, for she,
In youth and age, looks on you lovingly.
Chaste Luna has her humours whimsical;
The strength of Mars, though striking not, threats all;   4960
And Jupiter is still the fairest star.
Saturn is great, small to our eyes and far;
Him as a metal we don't venerate,
Little in worth but heavy in his weight.
Ah, when with Sol chaste Luna doth unite,   4965
Silver with gold, the world is glad and bright.
It's easy then to get all that one seeks:
Parks, palaces, and breasts and rosy cheeks.
All these procures the highly learnèd man

[146]

Who can perform what one of us never can. 4970
Emperor.   All that he says I hear twice o'er,
And yet I'm not convinced the more.
Murmurs.

What's all this smoke — a worn-out joke —
Astrology — or alchemy —
An oft-heard strain — hope stirred in vain — 4975
If he appear — a rogue is here —

Mephistopheles.   They stand around and gape in wonder;
They won't believe that a great prize is found.
Of mandrakes one appears to maunder,
Another of the sable hound. 4980
What though one's wit make others prickle,
Another cry out: "Sorcery!" —
If still he sometimes feels his sole a-tickle
And his stride is not what it used to be!
You feel the secret operation 4985
Of Nature's endless ruling might,
And from earth's undermost foundation
A living trace steals up to light.
When in your limbs you're feeling twitches,
When something lays uncanny hold, 4990
Be swift to delve, dig up the riches,
There lies the fiddler, lies the gold!
Murmurs.

My foot's like lead, can't move about —
Cramp's in my arm — that's only gout —
A tickle's jerking my big toe — 4995
All down my back it hurts me so —
From signs like these it should be clear
The richest gold-preserve is here.

Emperor.   Make haste! You shan't escape today.
Prove now your scummy, lying phrases 5000
And show at once those noble spaces.
My sword and sceptre I will put away;
If you're not lying, I will lend
My own exalted hands, this work to end,
But if you're lying, I'll send you to hell! 5005
Mephistopheles.   That pathway I could find full well! —

[147]

But I've not words enough to tell
What, ownerless, is waiting everywhere.
The farmer, ploughing furrows with his share,
Turns with the clods a pot of gold;   5010
He seeks saltpetre in a clay wall, and
He finds a golden, golden roll to hold,
Scared and rejoiced, in his own wretched hand.
Who would explore the earth-hid wonder,
What vaultings must he burst asunder,   5015
What dark ways burrow through and under
Near neighbouring on the world below!
In cellars vast, preserved of old,
Plates, dishes, beakers too, of gold
He sees displayed there, row on row.   5020
There goblets, made of rubies, stand,
And if he'll put them to a use,
Beside them is an ancient juice.
Yet — you'll believe my master-hand —
The wooden staves are long since rotten;   5025
A cask of tartar has the wine begotten.
Not only gold and jewels rare,
Proud wines of noble essences are there,
Enveiled in horror and in gloom.
The wise seek here without dismay.   5030
A fool can recognize a thing by day;
In darkness mysteries are at home.
Emperor.   What is the gain of dark? You can have that!
If aught has value, it must come to light.
Who can detect a rogue in dead of night?   5035
All cows are black, and grey is every cat.
The pots down there, heavy with golden freight —
Drive your plough on, unearth them straight.
Mephistopheles.   Take hoe and spade yourself, dig on!
You'll grow great through this peasant-toil.   5040
A herd of golden calves anon
Will wrench their way out of the soil.
Then with delight, without delay,
Yourself you can, you will your love array.
A jewel in which light and colour dance   5045
Both Majesty and Beauty can enhance.
Emperor.   Be quick, be quick! How long are we to wait?

[148]

Astrologer as above.　　Such urgent longing, Sire, pray moderate!
　　Let first the motley, joyous play proceed,
　　To no fair goal can minds distracted lead.　　　　　　　　　5050
　　First, penance in a calm mood doth behoove us,
　　Earn what's beneath us by what is above us.
　　Who wishes good, should first be good,
　　Who wishes joy, should mollify his blood,
　　Who asks for wine, the ripe grape should he press,　　　　5055
　　Who hopes for miracles, more faith possess.
Emperor.　　So let the time in merriment be spent!
　　Ash-Wednesday's coming to our heart's content.
　　Meanwhile we'll celebrate, whate'er befall,
　　All the more merrily mad Carnival.　　　　　　　　　　　5060
　　　　　　　　　　Trumpets, exeunt
Mephistopheles.　　How closely linked are Luck and Merit,
　　Is something fools have never known.
　　Had they the Wise Man's Stone, I swear it,
　　There'd be no Wise Man for the Stone.

A Spacious Hall

with adjoining apartments decorated and adorned for a masquerade

Herald.　　Don't think ye'll here see German revels,　　　　5065
　　A Dance of Death, of Fools and Devils!
　　A cheerful festival awaits you here.
　　Our ruler, when to Rome he went campaigning,
　　His profit and your pleasure gaining,
　　The perils of the Alps disdaining,　　　　　　　　　　　5070
　　Won for himself a realm of cheer.
　　First, at the holy feet bowed down,
　　A grant of power he besought,
　　And when he went to fetch his crown,
　　The fool's-cap too for us he brought.　　　　　　　　　　5075
　　Now we are all new-born in years,
　　And every well-sophisticated man
　　Happily draws it over head and ears.
　　Akin to crazy fools he now appears,
　　Under it acting wisely as he can.　　　　　　　　　　　　5080
　　I see the crowds are coming yonder,

Some pair in love, some swing asunder,
Crowd presses crowd, like youth let out of school.
Come in or out, let naught be daunting!
Now too as ever holds the rule: 5085
A hundred thousand follies vaunting,
The world remains one great, big fool!

Flower Girls, song accompanied by mandolins.

       That ye may approval tender
We're adorned tonight in sport;
Florentines, we joined the splendour   5090
Of this festive German court.
       Flowers in our chestnut tresses
We are wearing gay and bright,
Silken threads and silken jesses
Also play their part tonight;   5095
       For we think we are deserving
All your praises full and clear.
See the flowers we made, preserving
All their bloom throughout the year.
       Scraps of every tint we've taken,   5100
Each with due symmetric form;
Though each may your wit awaken,
See the whole and feel its charm.
       Fair are we in every feature,
Flower maidens gay of heart;   5105
For the ways of women's nature
Are so near akin to art.

Herald.

Let us see your baskets' riches;
Head and arms bear lovely treasure,
Bear gay beauty that bewitches.   5110
Let each choose what gives him pleasure.
Hasten till we see appearing
Gardens in each nook and alley.
Pedlars, wares, such beauty bearing,
Well the throng may round them rally.   5115

Flower Girls.

Barter in these cheery places,
But don't haggle as ye go!
And in brief and pithy phrases,
What he has, let each one know.

[150]

An Olive Branch with Fruits.

Flowery sprays I do not covet,   5120
Strife I shun, I am above it;
To my nature it is strange.
Yet I am the nation's marrow,
Pledge secure 'gainst spear and arrow,
Sign of peace where men may range.   5125
And today I'm hoping, fleetly
To adorn a fair head meetly.

A Wreath of Golden Ears.

To bedeck you, gifts of Ceres
Will be lovely, sweet, and rare;
What for us most wished and dear is   5130
Be for your adornment fair.

A Fancy Wreath.

Mallow-like, these gay-hued flowers,
From the moss, a wondrous bloom!
They are rare, in Nature's bowers,
But Dame Fashion gives them room.   5135

A Fancy Nosegay.

Name me? Theophrastus never
Would a name for me assever!
If to some scarce worth a penny,
Still I hope I may please many
If she'll take whom she possesses,   5140
If she'll twine me in her tresses,
Or the fairest fate deciding,
On her heart grant me abiding.

Rosebuds, a Challenge.

Let fantastic gaudy flowers
Bloom as Fashion oft empowers,   5145
Wondrous-strange and finely moulded,
Such as Nature ne'er unfolded.
Green stalks, gold bells, look entrancing
From rich locks, their charm enhancing! —
But we hide from mortal eyes.   5150
Happy he who us espies!
When anew the summer beameth
And the rosebud, kindling, gleameth,
From such bliss who'd be abstaining?
Sweet the promise and attaining   5155

[151]

Which in Flora's fair domain
Rule over vision, heart, and brain.

Under green, leafy arcades the FLOWER
GIRLS *adorn their waves daintily*

Gardeners, song accompanied by theorbos.

See the flowers sprout unhasting,
Charms around your head they're weaving!
Fruits lead not astray, deceiving;   5160
One enjoys them in the tasting.

Sun-burnt faces offer gladly
Cherries, royal plums, and peaches.
Buy! The tongue, the palate, teaches
That your eye can judge but badly.   5165

Come! The ripest fruit entices,
Eat it, with glad relish smitten;
Over a rose one poetizes,
But an apple must be bitten.

Grant us, prithee, to be mated   5170
With your youth so flowery-fair!
Neighbourly so decorated
Be our plenteous ripe ware.

Under garlands gay that wind them
In adorned and leafy bowers,   5175
All are here for you to find them:
Buds and leaves and fruit and flowers.

Midst alternating songs, accompanied by gui-
tars and theorbos, both choruses continue to
set their wares out attractively in tiers and to
offer them for sale

MOTHER *and* DAUGHTER

Mother.

Maiden, when thou cam'st to light,
Little caps I wove thee:
Body tender, face so bright,   5180
How they made me love thee!
Thought of thee as quickly won,
Wedded to the richest son,
Thought as wife wouldst prove thee.

Ah, already many a year   5185
Hence, unused, has fleeted;
Motley host of wooers here
Swiftly past has speeded.
With the one didst nimbly dance,
Gav'st the other nudge and glance   5190
Which he might have heeded.
        Every fête that we might plan,
Vain it was to match one;
Forfeit games and " Hindmost Man,"
Naught availed to snatch one.   5195
Each fool wears today his cap;
Darling, open now thy lap,
Haply wilt thou catch one.

*Girl playmates, young and fair, join the group;
a confidential chatter is heard. Fishers and
fowlers with nets, fishing-rods, limed twigs, and
other gear enter and mingle with the pretty
girls. Reciprocal attempts to win, catch, escape, and hold fast give opportunity for the
most agreeable dialogues*

Woodcutters enter boisterously and boorishly.

Make room! A clearing!
Spaces for revel!   5200
Trees that we level
Crash in their falling;
And when we're hauling,
We hit what's nearing.
Our praises grudge not,   5205
This truth pray nourish:
Did rough folk drudge not
In every county,
Could fine folk flourish,
Come by their bounty,   5210
However they fretted?
Learn this in season!
For ye'd be freezing,
Had we not sweated.

Pulcinelli awkward, almost silly.

Oh, fools that ye are,   5215
Born bent, and we are

[153]

The really clever,
Loads bearing never.
Our caps and jackets
And rags are packets   5220
Quite light to carry.
And we are merry,
Forever lazy,
In slippers easy,
In them to shuffle   5225
Through market and scuffle,
To gape at the pother,
Croak at each other.
Heeding the racket,
Through crowds that pack it,   5230
Like eels we're slipping,
Together tripping,
All mad together.
We care not whether
Ye blame or praise us,   5235
Nothing can faze us.

Parasites fawningly lustful.

Of you, stout porters,
And your supporters,
The charcoal-burners,
We are not spurners.   5240
For all the bending
And nods assenting,
Phrases too flowing,
And two-ways blowing,
They're warming and chilling   5245
Just as one's feeling,
Yet what the profit?
Heaven might send fire,
Enormous, dire,
But, then, what of it,   5250
Were there no billets
Or coal in barrows
To grill your skillets
Through to their marrows?
There's sizzling, broiling,   5255
There's bubbling, boiling.

True taster, picker,
The platter-licker,
He smells the roasting,
He sniffs the fishes,   5260
With gusto accosting
His patron's dishes.

A Drunken Man maudlin.

'Sdeath today to all my worry!
For I feel so frank and free;
Fresh delight and ditties merry,   5265
These I brought along with me.
So I'm drinking, drink ye, drink ye!
Clink your glasses, clink ye, clink ye!
Ye behind there, now come on!
Clink your glasses, so it's done.   5270
Angrily my wife shrieked loudly,
Sneering at my piebald suit,
And although I swaggered proudly,
"Scarecrow, scarecrow!" did she hoot.
Yet I'm drinking, drink ye, drink ye!   5275
Clink your glasses, clink ye, clink ye!
Clink them, scarecrows, every one!
Clinking, clinking, so it's done.
Say not that my way I'm losing,
I am where my worries fade.   5280
If mine host lend not, refusing,
Hostess lends, or eke the maid.
Still I drink on! Drink ye, drink ye!
Up, ye others! Clink ye, clink ye!
Each to each! Thus on and on!   5285
Now methinks that it is done.
How and where I'm pleasure plying,
Still may it always be at hand.
Let me lie where I am lying,
For I can no longer stand.   5290

Chorus.

Brothers all, now drink ye, drink ye!
Toast ye gaily, clink ye, clink ye!
Sit ye firm on bench and board!
Under the table lies one floored.

THE HERALD

announces various poets, poets by nature, courtly and knightly minstrels, sentimentalists as well as enthusiasts. In the throng of competitors of all kinds no one allows another to begin a speech. One slips past with a few words

Satirist.

Know ye what my soul as poet   5295
Chiefly would delight and cheer?
Sing and say, if I dared do it,
That which none would like to hear.

> *The poets of night and churchyards excuse themselves, because they are just engaged in a most interesting conversation with a newly-arisen vampire, and from it a new school of poetry may perhaps arise;* THE HERALD *is obliged to accept their apologies and meanwhile he calls forth Greek mythology which, in modern masks, loses neither its character nor its charm*

THE GRACES

Aglaia.

Charm we're bringing into living,
So be charming in your giving!   5300

Hegemone.

Charming be ye in receiving!
Lovely is desire's achieving.

Euphrosyne.

And when peacefully ye're living,
Be most charming your thanksgiving!

THE FATES

Atropos.

I, the eldest Fate, from yonder   5305
For the while to spin am bidden.
Much to think of, much to ponder,
In life's tender thread is hidden.

[156]

Finest flax I winnow featly
That your thread be supple, tender;   5310
Fingers shrewd will twirl it neatly,
Make it even, smooth, and slender.
Ye who, warm with dance and pleasure,
All too wanton, snatch a token,
Think that this thread has a measure,   5315
Have a care! It might be broken.

Clotho.

Know ye that the shears were lately
Given to my care to ply;
For our Ancient's conduct greatly
Did, in truth, none edify.   5320
She drags on most useless spinnings
On and on in air and light,
Promise of most glorious winnings
Clips and drags to realms of night.
Yet when I was young and reigning,   5325
I, too, erred oft in those years;
Now I yield to curb restraining,
In their case I keep the shears.
So I gladly wear a bridle,
And this scene with joy survey.   5330
In these hours so gay and idle,
Revel, riot, sport, and play!

Lachesis.

Unto me, alone discerning,
Was the thread's control decreed;
For my reel, forever turning,   5335
Never erred through too great speed.
Threads are coming, threads are reeling,
Each one in its course I guide;
None may slip from spindle wheeling,
Each must in its orbit glide.   5340
Could I once forget in leisure,
For the world I'd fear with pain;
Hours, they count, and years, they measure,
And the Weaver takes the skein.

Herald.   Those coming now, ye'd never recognize them,   5345
However learned ye were in ancient letters.

To look at them — the world's worst ill-abettors —
Ye'd call them welcome guests and prize them.
    They are the Furies, no one will believe us.
Fair are they, well-made, friendly, young moreover;   5350
But if ye lend them ear, ye will discover
How serpent-like such doves can wound and grieve us.
    Malicious are they — true! — and with effront'ry,
But now when each fool boasts his reputation,
They too ask not angelic exaltation;   5355
They know they are the pests of town and country.

THE FURIES

Alecto.   What boots it? For to trust us ye'll not stickle,
For each is young and fair, a coaxing kitten.
If one among you by a girl is smitten,
We shall not cease, his ears to scratch and tickle,   5360
    Until we dare to tell him, to his loathing,
That for this man and that one she is primping,
Crooked in her back, all wit doth lack, and limping,
And if betrothed to him, she's good-for-nothing!
    And the betrothed — we know the way to sting her.   5365
Why scarce a week ago her precious lover
To such-and-such a girl spoke basely of her; —
Though they be reconciled, a sting will linger.
Megaera.   That's but a jest! For when they once are married,
I go to work in every case to fritter   5370
The fairest bliss away with fancies bitter.
The moods of men are varied, hours are varied.
    None holds embraced what his desire has chosen,
But seeks a More-desired with foolish yearning
And from long-wonted, highest blessings turning,   5375
Flees a warm love and tries to warm a frozen.
    I'm skilled in managing such household troubles,
And Asmodeus, comrade true, I summon
To scatter strife betimes twixt man and woman;
Thus I destroy the human race in couples.   5380
Tisiphone.
          Poison, steel, — not words malicious —
      Mix I, whet I, for the traitor.
      Lov'st thou others? Sooner, later,

Overwhelms thee ruin vicious.
      What the sweetest moment offers,   5385
Turns perforce to wormwood galling!
Here no haggling, pulling, hauling;
As one sins, one always suffers.
      None shall sing about forgiving!
To the rocks my cause I'm crying.   5390
Echo, hark! " Revenge! " replying.
For the unstable, death! not living!

Herald.   Now, if it please you, stand aside a pace,
For what comes now is not your kind or race.
Ye see a mountain pressing through the throng,   5395
Its flanks with brilliant housings proudly hung,
A head with long tusks, snake-like snout below.
A mystery! but soon the key I'll show.
A dainty woman on his neck is sitting
And with her wand subjects him to her bidding;   5400
Another stands aloft, sublime to see,
Girt by a radiance dazzling, blinding me.
Beside them chained, two noble women near,
Fearful the one, the other blithe of cheer.
One longs for freedom and one feels she's free.   5405
Let each declare now who she be.
Fear.
      Lamps and lights and torches smoking
Through this turmoil gleam around;
Midst these faces, shamming, joking,
I, alas, in chains am bound.   5410
      Hence, ye throngs absurdly merry!
I mistrust your grins with right;
Every single adversary
Presses nearer in this night.
      Friend turned foe would here bewray me,   5415
But his mask I know well. Stay,
Yonder's one who wished to slay me;
Now revealed, he slinks away.
      Through the wide world I would wander,
Following every path that led,   5420
But destruction threatens yonder,
Holds me fast twixt gloom and dread.

Hope.   Hail, belovèd sisters, hail!
　　Though today and yesterday
　　Ye have loved this maskers' play,　　　　　　5425
　　Yet tomorrow ye'll unveil.
　　This I know of you quite surely.
　　If beneath the torches' flaring
　　We can't find our special pleasure,
　　Yet in days of cheerful leisure,　　　　　　5430
　　As our will doth bid us purely,
　　Now in groups, now singly faring,
　　We'll roam over lovely leas,
　　Resting, doing, as we please,
　　In a life no cares assailing,　　　　　　5435
　　Naught forgoing, never failing.
　　Everywhere as welcome guest
　　Let us enter, calm in mind,
　　Confident that we shall find
　　Somewhere, certainly, the best.　　　　　　5440
Prudence.

　　　　　　Two of man's chief foes, behold them,
　　　　Fear and Hope, in fetters mated;
　　　　From this crowd I'll keep and hold them.
　　　　Room, make room! Ye're liberated.
　　　　　　I conduct the live colossus,　　　　5445
　　　　See the burden that it carries,
　　　　And the steepest pass it crosses,
　　　　Step by step, and never wearies.
　　　　　　But upon the summit of it
　　　　Yonder goddess with her pinions　　　5450
　　　　Broad and agile, seeking profit,
　　　　Turns to spy all man's dominions.
　　　　　　Girt is she by splendour glorious
　　　　Shining far along all courses,
　　　　Victory her name! Victorious　　　　5455
　　　　Goddess of all active forces.

Zoïlo-Thersites.   Ho, ho! Just right I've reached this spot,
　　We're one and all a wretched lot!
　　And yet the goal I've chosen me
　　Is she up there, Dame Victory.　　　　　　5460
　　She with her snowy wings spread out

Thinks she's an eagle, past all doubt,
And wheresoever she may stir,
Thinks men and lands belong to her.
But when some glorious deed is done,   5465
At once I put my armour on.
Up with the low, down with the high,
The crookèd straight, the straight awry —
That, only, makes me feel aglow,
And on this earth I'll have it so.   5470

Herald.   Then take thou that, a master-blow
From my good staff, thou wretched hound,
Then straightway writhe and twist around! —
How swift the two-fold dwarfish clump
Balls up into a loathsome lump! —   5475
But see! lump turns to egg — a wonder!
Puffs itself up and bursts asunder.
Thence comes a pair of twins to earth,
Adder and bat — a wondrous birth!
On in the dust one crawls and creeps,   5480
The black one round the ceiling sweeps,
And where they haste to join again,
To be the third I am not fain.

Murmuring.

    Come! they're dancing now back there! —
    No! I want to flee from here —   5485
    Feel ye not the ghost-like breed
    Creeping, wheeling, round us speed? —
    Something whizzes past my hair —
    My foot felt a something there —
    Still not one of us is harmed —   5490
    But we all have been alarmed —
    Now all ruined is our fun —
    This, the beasts! they wanted done.

Herald.   Since on me, when masquerading,
Herald's duties ye've been lading,   5495
Stern I guard the portal, wary
Lest into your revels merry
Aught may slink of harmful savour;
Neither do I shrink nor waver.
Yet I fear lest spectres erring   5500

Through the windows may be faring;
If black arts and spooks beset you,
From them I could never get you.
Of the dwarf we were suspicious.
Lo! Back there a pageant issues!   5505
As a herald, it's my duty
To explain those forms of beauty,
But what's past all comprehending,
For that I've no explanation.
Help ye, all, my education! —   5510
See what hitherward is tending!
Lo! a four-yoked chariot splendid
Through the crowd its way has wended,
Yet the crowd it does not sunder;
I can see no crushing yonder.   5515
In the distance colours shimmer,
Stars gay-coloured beam and flimmer,
Magic-lantern-like they glimmer.
All storm on as to assault.
Clear the way! I shudder!
A Boy Charioteer.   Halt!   5520
Steeds, let now your wings fall idle,
Feel the well-accustomed bridle;
Master self as you I master;
When I thrill you, on! and faster!
Let us honour now these spaces!   5525
Look around at all the faces;
More and more admirers cluster.
Herald, up! Take wonted muster!
Ere we flee, tell thou our stories,
Name us and describe and show us;   5530
For we all are allegories,
Therefore thou shouldst surely know us.
Herald.   There's no name I could ascribe thee,
But I rather might describe thee.
Boy Charioteer.   Try it then!
Herald.   I must avow,   5535
Firstly, young and fair art thou.
A half-grown boy thou art; but women rather
Would see thee full-grown altogether.
It seems that thou wilt be a fickle wooer,

Right from the start a real undoer. 5540

Boy Charioteer. That's well worth hearing! On with thee,
Discover now the riddle's happy key.

Herald. Thy flashing ebon eyes, locks black and glowing,
More radiant from the jewelled diadem!
And what a graceful robe doth stream 5545
From shoulder down to buskin flowing,
With glittering gaud and purple hem!
Now might we flouting "Maiden!" deem thee,
Yet, good or ill as it might be,
Already maidens would esteem thee. 5550
They'd teach thee soon thine A B C.

Boy Charioteer. And yonder one, in splendour glowing,
Who proudly sits on chariot throne?

Herald. A king he seems, of wealth o'erflowing;
Happy the man who has his favour won! 5555
He has naught more to earn and capture,
He swift espies where aught's amiss,
And has in giving more pure rapture
Than in possessing and in bliss.

Boy Charioteer. To stop with this will not avail; 5560
Thou must describe him in far more detail.

Herald. There's no describing Dignity.
The healthy, full-moon face I see,
The lips so full, the cheeks so blooming
Beneath the turban's beauty looming, 5565
The flowing robe he's richly wearing —
What shall I say of such a bearing?
He seems a ruler known to me.

Boy Charioteer. Plutus, the god of wealth, is he.
Hither he comes in gorgeous trim; 5570
Sorely the Emperor longs for him.

Herald. Now thine own *What* and *How* relate to me!

Boy Charioteer. I am Profusion, I am Poesy!
The poet who's attained his goal
When he's poured out his inmost soul. 5575
I too am rich with untold pelf
And value me the peer of Plutus' self,
Adorn, enliven, make his revels glow;
And what he lacks, that I bestow.

Herald. Bragging becomes thee charmingly, 5580

[163]

But now thine arts, pray, let us see.
Boy Charioteer.   Here see me snap my fingers. Lo!
  Around the chariot gleam and glow!
  And now a necklace of pearls appears!
                    Continuing to snap his fingers in every direction
  Here spangled gold for neck and ears   5585
  And flawless comb and coronet
  And rings with precious jewels set.
  Flamelets I scatter too in turn,
  Waiting to see where they may burn.
Herald.   How the dear mob is snatching, seizing,   5590
  Even the giver almost squeezing!
  Dream-like he's scatt'ring gems where all
  Are snatching in the spacious hall.
  But what is this? A brand-new juggle!
  However busily one snatch and struggle,   5595
  His trouble really does not pay;
  The gifts take wing and fly away.
  The pearls are loosened from their band
  And beetles scrabble in his hand;
  He shakes them off, the poor biped,   5600
  And then they hum around his head.
  Others, instead of solid things,
  Catch butterflies with flimsy wings.
  How much he promises, the knave!
  Glitter of gold was all he gave.   5605
Boy Charioteer.
  Of masks, I note, thou canst proclaim each feature.
  Beneath the shell to fathom out the nature
  Is not the herald's courtly task;
  A keener eye for that we ask.
  But feuds I shun, if only in suggestion;   5610
  To thee, lord, I address my speech and question.
                 Turning to PLUTUS
  Didst thou not give me charge supreme
  Over the four-yoked, whirlwind team?
  Guide I not happily as thou leadest?
  Am I not everywhere thou biddest?   5615
  And on bold pinions did I not for thee
  Bear off the palm of victory?
  However oft for thee as I've contended,

Success was ever my portion; and when now
The laurel decorates thy brow, 5620
Did not my hand and art entwine and blend it?
Plutus. If need be that I testify, then hear it!
I say with joy: Thou art spirit of my spirit!
Thy deeds are ever after my own will;
Rich as I am, thou art richer still. 5625
Thy service to reward in fitting measure,
The laurel more than all my crowns I treasure.
This truth in all men's hearts I would instil:
In thee, dear son, I have much pleasure.
Boy Charioteer to the crowd.
The greatest gifts my hand deals out, 5630
Lo! I have scattered roundabout.
On this head and on that one too
There glows a flamelet that I threw.
From one to other head it skips,
To this one cleaves, from that one slips; 5635
It seldom flares up like a plume,
And swiftly beams in transient bloom.
Ere many its worth recognize,
It burns out mournfully and dies.
Women's Chatter.
There on the chariot sits a man 5640
Who surely is a charlatan,
Hunched up behind, a perfect clown,
By thirst and hunger so worn down
As naught before, and if ye'd pinch,
He has no flesh to feel and flinch. 5645

Starveling. Away from me, ye odious crew!
Welcome, I know, I never am to you.
When hearth and home were women's zone,
As Avaritia I was known.
Then did our household thrive throughout, 5650
For much came in and naught went out!
Zealous was I for chest and bin;
'Twas even said my zeal was sin.
But since in years most recent and depraving
Woman is wont no longer to be saving 5655
And, like each tardy payer, collars

Far more desires than she has dollars,
The husband now has much to bore him;
Wherever he looks, debts loom before him.
Her spinning-money is turned over   5660
To grace her body or her lover;
Better she feasts and drinks still more
With all her wretched lover-corps.
Gold charms me all the more for this:
Male's now my gender, I am Avarice!   5665
Leader of the Women.
With dragons be the dragon avaricious,
It's naught but lies, deceiving stuff!
To stir up men he comes, malicious,
Whereas men now are troublesome enough.
Women en masse.
The scarecrow! Box his ears, the japer!   5670
Why does the wooden cross threat here?
As if his ugly face we'd fear!
Dragons are made of wood and paper.
Have at him, crowd him, scoff and jeer!

Herald.   Peace! By my staff! Peace or begone!   5675
And yet my aid's scarce needed here.
In yonder space so quickly won
See the grim monsters moving on,
Swift to unfold their pinions' double pair.
The dragons shake themselves in ire;   5680
Their scaly jaws spew smoke and fire.
The crowd has fled, the place is clear.
                    PLUTUS *descends from his chariot*
Herald.   He's stepping down, what royal grace!
He becks, the dragons move apace;
Down from the chariot they've borne the chest   5685
With all its gold, and Avarice thereon.
There at his feet it stands at rest;
A marvel how it was ever done.
Plutus to the CHARIOTEER.
Now art thou rid of thy too heavy burden,
Free art thou! Off to thine own sphere and guerdon!   5690
Thy sphere's not here! Here shapes most hideous,
Distorted, motley, wild, press in on us.

[166]

Where thou see'st naught but lovely clarity,
Where thine own vision is enough for thee,
Thither where only Good and Beauty please and wait,   5695
Away to Solitude! there thine own world create!
Boy Charioteer.   Thus I esteem myself a worthy envoy of thee,
And as my nearest kinsman do I love thee.
Where thou art, Plenty is; where I remain,
Each feels himself enriched by glorious gain.   5700
Oft in the clash of life a man doth waver:
Shall he in thee or me seek favour?
Thy followers can idly rest, it's true;
Who follows me always has work to do.
My deeds in darkness never are concealed;   5705
If I but breathe, I am at once revealed.
And so, farewell! My bliss thou grantest me,
But whisper low and I am back with thee.
                    Exit as he came
Plutus.   It's time now to unloose the precious metals.
I strike the padlocks with the herald's rod.   5710
The chest flies open! See in brazen kettles
A boiling, bubbling up of golden blood.
First, ornaments of crowns, chains, rings will follow!
Seething, it threatens all to melt and swallow.
Alternating Cries from the crowd.
                    See here! and there! how treasures brim!   5715
                    The chest is filling to the rim —
                    Vessels of gold are grilling there,
                    And coins in rolls are milling there. —
                    As if just minted, ducats jump,
                    Oh, how my heart begins to thump! —   5720
                    All that I want I see and more!
                    They're rolling there along the floor. —
                    It's yours, they say — appease your itch,
                    Just stoop a bit and rise up rich. —
                    Swift as the lightning, we, the rest,   5725
                    Will take possession of the chest.

Herald.   What does this mean? Ye silly folk!
It's but a masquerading joke.
Naught more can be desired tonight;
Think ye we give you gold outright?   5730

[167]

Verily in this game for such
As ye, yes, vouchers were too much.
Blockheads! A pleasant show, forsooth,
Ye take at once as solid truth.
What's truth to you? — Delusion vain,   5735
Catch where ye can, ye clutch amain.
Plutus, chief mummer, hero of the masque,
Drive from the field this folk, I ask.

Plutus.   Thy staff is apt for it, I see;
Lend it a little while to me. —   5740
I'll dip it swift in seething glare. —
Now, on your guard, ye masks, beware!
Snaps, sparks, and flashes, see it throw!
Thy staff already is aglow.
Whoever crowds too close to me   5745
I'll straightway singe relentlessly. —
And now upon my rounds I'll go.

Cries and Crowding.
               Alas! it's up with us, oh woe! —
               Away, escape! Escape who can! —
               Fall back, fall back, thou hindmost man!   5750
               Hot sparks are flying in my face. —
               I stagger from the glowing mace! —
               Lost are we all, we all are lost! —
               Back, back, ye masquerading host!
               Back, senseless mob, don't come so nigh!   5755
               Had I but wings, away I'd fly! —

Plutus.   Backward the circle round us shrinks,
And no one has been scorched, methinks.
Scattered by fright,
The crowd takes flight. —   5760
Yet, symbol of the reign of law,
A ring invisible I'll draw.

Herald.   A glorious deed hast done tonight.
How can I thank thy sapient might?

Plutus.   My noble friend, be patient yet;   5765
Many a tumult still doth threat.

Avaritia.   Here, if we like, we can look on
And view this circle at our leisure;
To stand in front always gives women pleasure

Where gaping or where nibbling's to be done.   5770
Not yet so wholly rusty are my senses
But that a woman fair is always fair;
And since today it costs me no expenses,
We'll go a-courting with an easy air.
Because, though, in such over-crowded places   5775
Not every ear distinctly hears all phrases,
I'll wisely try — I hope not vainly —
In pantomime to show my meaning plainly.
Hand, foot, and gesture will not now suffice,
So I must use a farcical device.   5780
I'll treat the gold as were it mere wet clay;
This metal I can turn in any way.

Herald.   The skinny fool! What is that he began?
Can he have humour, such a starveling man?
He's kneading all the gold to dough;   5785
Beneath his hands it's soft, yet though
He squeeze it, roll it, as he will,
Misshapen is it even still.
He turns to the women there, and they
All scream and want to get away,   5790
With gestures of disgust and loathing.
The mischievous rogue will stop at nothing.
I fear a joyous man is he
When he's offended decency.
Through silence I'll not lend my backing;   5795
Give me my staff to send him packing.

Plutus.   What threatens from without he does not see.
Let him go on with his tom-fooling;
There'll be no room soon for his drooling;
The Law is mighty, mightier Necessity.   5800

Tumult and Song.
                The wild host comes in all its might,
                From woodland dell and mountain height.
                They stride along — resist who can!
                They celebrate their great god Pan.
                They know indeed what none can guess;   5805
                Into the vacant ring they press.

Plutus.   I know you well, you and your great god Pan!
Together ye've performed a daring plan.

I know right well what is not known to all
And ope the circle duly to their call.   5810
Oh, may good fortune be decreed them!
The strangest thing may now befall,
They know not where their steps may lead them;
They have not looked ahead at all.

Savage Song.

      Ye folk bedight, ye tinsel-stuff!   5815
      They're coming rude, they're coming rough;
      In lofty leap, in speedy chase,
      They come, a stout and sturdy race.

Fauns.   The faun-host flocks
  In merry round,   5820
  The oak-wreath bound
  On curly locks;
  A pair of finely pointed ears
  Out from the curly head appears,
  A stubby nose, face broad and flat.   5825
  With women no one's harmed by that;
  And if the faun his paw advance,
  The fairest will hardly refuse to dance.

A Satyr.   The satyr now comes hopping in
  With foot of goat and withered shin;   5830
  He needs to have them wiry-thin,
  For chamois-like on mountain heights
  To look around him he delights.
  Braced by the air of freedom then,
  He jeers at children, women, and men,   5835
  Who deep in the valley's smoke and stew
  Fondly imagine they're living too,
  While pure and undisturbed and lone
  The world up there is all his own.

Gnomes.   Tripping, a little crowd appears.   5840
  They do not like to go in pairs;
  In mossy garb, with lamplet bright,
  They move commingling, swift and light,
  Where each his task can best perform,
  Like firefly-ants, a crowding swarm.   5845
  They scurry, busy, here and there,
  Bustling and working everywhere.

[170]

Kinship to kind "Good-men" we own,
As surgeons of the rocks are known,
The mountains high, go sapping them,   5850
The swelling veins, go tapping them;
Metals we hurl on pile on pile,
With cheery hail — "Good Luck!" — the while,
A greeting well-meant through and through.
We're friends of all good men and true.   5855
Yet gold we bring and gold reveal
That men may pander and may steal,
That iron fail not his proud hand
Who ever wholesale murder planned.
He whom these three commandments fail to bother   5860
Will pay no heed to any other.
For all that we are not to blame;
As we are patient, so be ye the same!

Giants.   "The Wild Men of the Woods" — their name,
In the Hartz Mountains known to fame.   5865
In nature's nakedness and might
They come, each one of giant height,
A fir-tree's trunk in each right hand,
Around their loins a bulging band,
Apron of twigs and leaves uncouth;   5870
Such guards the Pope has not, in truth.

Nymphs in chorus, surrounding G R E A T   P A N.
He's really here! —
Of this world-sphere
The All we fête
In Pan the Great.   5875
Ye gayest ones, surround him here,
Dance madly, hov'ring round him here,
For since he's solemn and yet kind,
Man's happiness he has in mind.
Even beneath the azure, vaulted roof   5880
He ever kept slumber far aloof;
Yet purling brooks seek him in quest
And soft airs cradle him to rest.
And when he sleeps at mid of day,
No leaflet stirs upon its spray;   5885
Health-giving plants with balsam rare
Pervade the still and silent air.

[171]

Then may the nymph in joy not leap
And where she stood, she falls asleep.
But when at unexpected hour   5890
His voice is heard in all its power,
Like crack of lightning, roar of sea,
Then no one knows which way to flee.
Brave warriors into panic break,
And in the tumult heroes quake.   5895
Hence honour to whom honour's due,
Hail him who led us here to you!

Deputation of Gnomes to GREAT PAN.

When the treasure, rich and shining,
Winds through clefts its thread-like way
And naught but the rod's divining   5900
Can its labyrinths display,
Troglodytes in caverns spacious,
Under vaulted roofs we bide,
While in day's pure air thou, gracious,
All the treasures dost divide.   5905
We discover here quite near us
Treasure rich, a fountain vein,
Aptly promising to bear us
More than one could hope to gain.
This thou mayst achieve at pleasure,   5910
Take it, Sire, into thy care!
In thy hands doth every treasure
Yield the whole world blessings rare.

Plutus to THE HERALD.

We must possess ourselves, serene in spirit,
And come what may must confidently bear it.   5915
Still hast thou shown indeed a valiant soul,
But soon a thing most horrible will try it.
Stoutly men now and later will deny it.
Inscribe it truly in thy protocol.

Herald grasping the staff which PLUTUS *keeps in his hand.*

The dwarfs lead Pan, the great god, nigher,   5920
Quite gently, to the well of fire.
It seethes up from the deepest maw,
Then down again the flames withdraw,
And gloomy gapes the open jaw.

[172]

The foam and flame roll up again.   5925
Complacent doth Great Pan remain,
Rejoicing in the wondrous sight,
While pearls of foam spurt left and right.
How can he in such wizardry confide?
He stoops down low to look inside. —   5930
But now his beard is falling in! —
Whose can it be, that beardless chin?
His hand conceals it from our gaze. —
A great mishap is taking place.
The beard flies backward, all ablaze,   5935
And kindles wreath and head and breast;
Turned into sorrow is the jest. —
To quench the fire they race and run,
But free from flames there is not one,
And as they slap and beat it too,   5940
They only stir up flames anew;
In fiery flames entangled, caught,
A maskers' group is burned to naught.
      But hark! what news is spreading here
From mouth to mouth, from ear to ear!   5945
O evermore ill-fated Night,
How thou hast turned our bliss to blight!
Tomorrow morn will everywhere
Proclaim what no one likes to hear.
Yet everywhere I'll hear the cry: 5950
" The Emperor suffers agony! "
Oh, would that something else were true!
The Emperor burns, his escort too.
Accursed who led him so astray,
Who bound about them resined spray,   5955
Raging around with boisterous song,
Bringing to ruin all the throng.
O Youth, O Youth, and wilt thou never
Keep within proper bounds thy pleasure?
O Highness, Highness, wilt thou never   5960
Use might and reason in due measure?
      The mimic woods are catching fire,
The tongues of flame lick higher, higher,
Where netted rafters interlace;
A fiery doom threats all the place.   5965

Now overflows our cup of woe,
And who shall save us I don't know.
The ashes of a night will be
All that was once rich majesty.
Plutus.   Terror has enough been spread,   5970
Let us now bring help instead! —
Strike, thou hallowed staff, the ground
Till earth quiver and resound!
Fill thyself, O spacious air,
With cool fragrance everywhere.   5975
Hither come, around us streaming,
Mist and clouds with moisture teeming,
Come and veil the rampant flame;
Cloudlets, whirl ye, drizzling, purl ye,
Hither glide ye, softly drenching,   5980
Quelling everywhere and quenching;
Ye, who're moist, allaying, bright'ning,
Change to harmless summer lightning
All this empty fiery game! —
And when spirits threat and lower,   5985
Then let Magic show its power!

Pleasure Garden

MORNING SUN

The EMPEROR   COURTIERS

FAUST *and* MEPHISTOPHELES, *dressed becomingly,*
not conspicuously, according to the mode; both kneel

Faust.   Pardon you, Sire, the flames and wizardry?
Emperor beckoning him to rise.
Many such pleasantries I would like to see. —
Presto! I stood within a glowing zone,
It seemed almost Pluto and I were one.   5990
In coal-black night and yet with fires aglow
Lay an abyss. From many a vent below
Thousands of savage flames were upward whirling,
Into a single vault above me swirling,
Licking their tongues of flame against the dome's far height   5995

Which now appeared and now was lost to sight.
Far, far away, through spiral shafts of flame
Peoples I saw, in moving files they came,
In a wide circle pressing on and on
And paying homage as they've always done.   6000
Courtiers I recognized amid the splendour,
I seemed a prince over many a salamander.
Mephistopheles.   That are you, Sire, since every element
Doth own you absolute to all intent.
Obedient have you now proved fire to be.   6005
Where waves heave wildest, leap into the sea!
The pearl-strewn bottom you will scarcely tread
Ere a glorious billowing dome forms overhead.
You'll see there light-green rolling billows swelling,
Their edges purple, forming the fairest dwelling   6010
Round you, the centre. Wander at your will,
The palaces attend you even still.
The very walls rejoice in life, in teeming,
Arrowy swarming, hither, thither streaming.
Sea-wonders push and dart along to win   6015
The new soft glow but none may enter in.
The dragons, mottled, golden-scaled, are playing;
There gapes the shark but you laugh at his baying.
Though now the court surrounds you in delight,
Still such a throng has never met your sight.   6020
Yet long you're not deprived of forms endearing;
The Nereids come curiously nearing
Your splendid palace in the cool of ocean,
The young with fish-like, shy, and wanton motion,
The old ones prudent. Thetis learns of this,   6025
Gives her new Peleus hand and mouth to kiss. —
The seat, then, on Olympus' wide domain . . .
Emperor.   Over the air I leave to you to reign;
Quite soon enough does one ascend that throne.
Mephistopheles.   Earth, Lord Supreme, already is your own.   6030
Emperor.   What brought you here to ravish us with sights
Directly out of the Arabian Nights?
If like Scheherazade you are inventive,
Be sure of every favour and incentive.
Be near whenever — as is oft the case —   6035
I grutch at this poor world of commonplace.

[175]

Steward enters in haste.   Ah, Most Serene, in all my life I never
    Thought I could give you news of such high favour
    As this which richly blesses me
    And drives me here almost in ecstasy.   6040
    Bill upon bill has now been squared,
    The usurers' talons have been pared.
    From hellish worry I am free!
    In Heaven life can not happier be.
Commander-in-Chief follows in haste.
    Arrears are paid as they were due   6045
    And all the army's pledged anew;
    The soldier feels his blood made over.
    Landlords and wenches are in clover.
Emperor.   How free you breathe, with breasts so lightened!
    Your wrinkled foreheads, how they're brightened!   6050
    How you come in with eager speed!
Treasurer appears.   Inquire of these who did the deed.
Faust.   It's for the Chancellor to tell the story.
Chancellor approaching slowly.
    I'm blessed enough now when I'm old and hoary.
    So hear and see the fateful, solemn leaf   6055
    Which into joy has transformed all our grief.
He reads

    "To all whom it concerns, let it be known:
    Who hath this note, a thousand crowns doth own.
    As certain pledge thereof shall stand
    Vast buried treasure in the Emperor's land.   6060
    Provision has been made that ample treasure,
    Raised straightway, shall redeem the notes at pleasure."
Emperor.   I sense a crime, a monstrous, cheating lure!
    Who dared to forge the Emperor's signature?
    Is still unpunished such a breach of right?   6065
Treasurer.   Remember, Sire, yourself it was last night
    That signed the note. You stood as mighty Pan,
    The Chancellor came and spoke in words that ran:
    "A lofty festal joy do for thyself attain:
    Thy people's weal — a few strokes of the pen!"   6070
    These did you make, then thousand-fold last night
    Conjurors multiplied what you did write;
    And that straightway the good might come to all,
    We stamped at once the series, large and small;

[176]

Tens, twenties, thirties, hundreds, all are there.   6075
You can not think how glad the people were.
Behold your city, once half-dead, decaying,
Now full of life and joy, and swarming, playing!
Although your name has blessed the world of yore,
So gladly was it never seen before.   6080
The alphabet is really now redundant;
In this sign each is saved to bliss abundant.

Emperor.   My people take it for good gold, you say?
In camp, in court, sufficient as full pay?
Although amazed, still I must give assent.   6085

Steward.   The flight of notes we could nowise prevent;
Like lightning notes were scattered on the run.
The changers' shops open wide to everyone;
And there all notes are honoured, high and low,
With gold and silver — at a discount, though.   6090
From there to butcher, baker, tavern hasting,
One-half the world seems thinking but of feasting,
The other in new raiment struts and crows;
The draper cuts the cloth, the tailor sews.
In cellars "Long live the Emperor!" is the toasting;   6095
There platters clatter, there they're boiling, roasting.

Mephistopheles.   Who all alone will down the terrace stray
Perceives the fairest in superb array;
With her proud peacock-fan she hides one eye
And looking for a note goes simpering by;   6100
More swiftly than through eloquence and wit
Love's richest favour can be gained by it.
With purse and scrip one is no longer harried.
A notelet in one's breast is lightly carried;
With billets-doux quite snugly will it nestle.   6105
The priest bears it devoutly in his missal.
The soldier, that he may the faster haste,
Lightens the girdle quickly round his waist.
Pardon, Your Majesty, if I may seem
To mete a lofty work but slight esteem.   6110

Faust.   Treasures in superfluity still sleep
Within your borders, buried deep,
And lie unused. Thought in its widest measure
Gives the most meagre bounds to such a treasure.
Imagination in its highest flight,   6115

[177]

Strain as it may, can't soar to such a height.
Yet spirits, fit to fathom the unsounded,
Have boundless confidence in the unbounded.
Mephistopheles.   Nor gold nor pearls are half as handy as
Such paper. Then a man knows what he has.   6120
There is no need of higgling or exchanging;
In love and wine one can at will be ranging.
If you want metal, changers are at hand;
If lacking there, dig for a while the land.
Goblet and chain are auctioned off and sold;   6125
Paper redeemed without delay in gold
Confounds the doubter who had scoffed and taunted.
This men demand, to metals they are wonted.
Ready at hand the Emperor's realm will hold
Henceforth enough of paper, jewels, gold.   6130
Emperor.   Our realm owes you this great prosperity;
As is the service, the reward should be.
Our empire's soil be trusted to your care,
The worthiest guardians of the treasures there.
You know the vast and well-preservèd hoard,   6135
And when men dig, it's you must give the word.
Become as one, ye masters of our treasure,
Fulfil your stations' dignities with pleasure
Here where in blest accord and unity
The upper and the lower world agree.   6140
Treasurer.   Twixt us no slightest strife shall cause division;
I love to have as colleague the magician.

                    Exit with FAUST

Emperor.   If now I shall endow each man of you,
Let each confess what use he'll put it to.
A Page receiving.   I'll joy to live, be glad and gay.   6145
Another Page likewise.   My love shall have a chain and rings today.
A Chamberlain accepting.
Wine twice as good shall henceforth down me trickle.
Another Chamberlain likewise.   I feel the dice inside my pocket tickle.
A Banneret thoughtfully.   From debt I'll make my lands and castle free.
Another Banneret likewise.   I'll add this treasure to my treasury.   6150
Emperor.   I hoped for joy and heart for new emprise,
But knowing you one can your course surmise.
Well do I see, with all this treasure-store
You still remain just as you were before.

[178]

Fool approaching.   You're scattering favours, grant me some, I pray.   6155
Emperor.   Alive again? You'd soon drink them away.
Fool.   The magic leaves! I don't quite comprehend —
Emperor.   Of course, for you'd put them to some bad end.
Fool.   Still more drop there, I don't know what to do.
Emperor.   Just pick them up, I let them fall for you.   6160

Exit

Fool.   Five thousand crowns are mine? How unexpected!
Mephistopheles.   Two-leggèd wineskin, are you resurrected?
Fool.   That happens oft but like this never yet.
Mephistopheles.   You are so glad you're breaking out in sweat.
Fool.   Is that the same as cash? Look, are you sure?   6165
Mephistopheles.   What throat and belly want it will procure.
Fool.   And cattle can I buy and house and land?
Mephistopheles.   Of course! Just bid and they will be at hand.
Fool.   Castle with wood, chase, fish-brook?
Mephistopheles.   On my word!
    I'd like to see you as a stern Milord!   6170
Fool.   Tonight a landed owner I shall sit!

Exit

Mephistopheles solus.   Who still will have a doubt of our fool's wit?

A Dark Gallery

F A U S T   M E P H I S T O P H E L E S

Mephistopheles.   Why draw me into this dark gallery?
    Is not in there enough of sport,
    Enough of fun and fraud and raillery   6175
    Amid the crowded motley of the court?
Faust.   Don't speak of tricks! Your jests are old and hoary;
    Down to the very soles you've worn that story;
    But now you're going to and fro to flee
    From having any talk with me.   6180
    I am tormented further things to do;
    The Chamberlain is urging and the Steward too.
    The Emperor orders — straightway must it be —
    Both Helena and Paris will he see,
    Of man and woman in their true ideal   6185
    Demands to see the forms distinct and real.
    To work! I gave my word — I must not break it.

Mephistopheles.　　A foolish promise — fool you were to make it.
Faust.　　Whither your powers lead us, friend,
　　You have not well reflected;　　　　　　　　　　　　　　6190
　　We first have made him rich — no end!
　　Now to amuse him we're expected.
Mephistopheles.　　You fancy these things easy to arrange.
　　Here where we stand, the steps are steeper.
　　You grapple with a realm most strange,　　　　　　　6195
　　And wantonly will plunge in debt still deeper.
　　You think that Helena is summoned here
　　As quickly as the paper spectres were.
　　With witches' witchery and ghostly ghost,
　　With changeling dwarfs I'm ready at my post;　　　6200
　　But devils' darlings, though one may not flout them,
　　As heroines no one goes mad about them.
Faust.　　There you go harping on the same old chord!
　　Into uncertainty you always lead us,
　　Sire of all hindrances that can impede us;　　　　　6205
　　For each new help you want a new reward.
　　Mutter a little and the deed is done;
　　She will be here ere I can turn me.
Mephistopheles.　　The heathen-folk do not concern me.
　　They occupy a hell that's all their own.　　　　　　6210
　　But help there is.
Faust.　　　　　　　　Quick! Tell its history!
Mephistopheles.　　Not glad do I reveal a loftier mystery —
　　Enthroned sublime in solitude are goddesses;
　　Around them is no place, a time still less;
　　To speak of them embarrasses.　　　　　　　　　　　6215
　　They are the *Mothers!*
Faust terrified.　　　　　　Mothers!
Mephistopheles.　　　　　　　　Do you fear?
Faust.　　The Mothers! Mothers! Strange the word I hear.
Mephistopheles.　　Strange is it. Goddesses, to men unknown,
　　Whom we are loath to name or own.
　　Deep must you dig to reach their dwelling ever;　　6220
　　You are to blame that now we need their favour.
Faust.　　Whither the way?
Mephistopheles.　　　　　　No way! To the Unexplorable,
　　Never to be explored; to the Unimplorable,
　　Never to be implored. Are in the mood?

There are no locks, no bars are to be riven;   6225
Through solitudes you will be whirled and driven.
Can you imagine wastes and solitude?
Faust.   I think that you might save yourself such chatter;
It savours of the witch's-kitchen patter
After a long, long interlude.   6230
Was I not forced to live with men?
Learn the inane, teach the inane? —
If I spoke wisely, true to my conviction,
Then doubly loud resounded contradiction.
Indeed, from mankind, so perversely given,   6235
To solitude and deserts I was driven;
Till not to be too lone and all-forsaken,
At last to devil's company I've taken.
Mephistopheles.   And had you swum to ocean's farthest verge
And utter boundlessness beheld,   6240
Still yonder you'd have seen surge upon surge;
Although impending doom your fear compelled,
You'd have seen *something.* Dolphins you'd have seen
Cleaving the hushèd ocean's emerald-green,
Have seen the moving clouds, sun, moon, and star.   6245
Naught will you see in that vast Void afar,
Nor hear your footstep when it's pressed,
Nor find firm ground where you can rest.
Faust.   You speak as of all mystagogues the chief,
Whoever brought trustful neophytes to grief;   6250
Only reversed. Into the Void I'm sent,
That art and power I may there augment.
You treat me like the cat's-paw you desire
To snatch the chestnuts for you from the fire.
Come, let us fathom it, whatever may befall.   6255
In this your Naught I hope to find my All.
Mephistopheles.   I praise you, truly, ere you part from me,
Since that you understand the Devil I can see.
Here, take this key.
Faust.   That tiny, little thing!
Mephistopheles.   Seize and esteem it, see what it may bring!   6260
Faust.   It's growing in my hand! It flashes, glows!
Mephistopheles.   Will you see now what blessing it bestows?
The key will scent the right place from all others;
Follow it down, 'twill lead you to the Mothers.

Faust shuddering.   The Mothers! Like a blow it strikes my ear!   6265
  What is that word that I don't like to hear?
Mephistopheles.   So narrow-minded, scared by each new word?
  Will you but hear what you've already heard?
  Let naught disturb you, though it strangely rings,
  You! long since wonted to most wondrous things.   6270
Faust.   And yet in torpor there's no gain for me;
  The thrill of awe is man's best quality.
  Although the world may stifle every sense,
  Enthralled, man deeply senses the Immense.
Mephistopheles.   Descend, then! I might also tell you: Soar!   6275
  It's all the same. Escape from the Existent
  To phantoms' unbound realms far distant!
  Delight in what long since exists no more!
  Like filmy clouds the phantoms glide along.
  Brandish the key, hold off the shadowy throng.   6280
Faust inspired.   Good! Gripping it, I feel new strength arise,
  My breast expands. On, to the great emprise!
Mephistopheles.   When you at last a glowing tripod see,
  Then in the deepest of all realms you'll be.
  You'll see the Mothers in the tripod's glow,   6285
  Some of them sitting, others stand and go,
  As it may chance. Formation, transformation,
  Eternal Mind's eternal re-creation.
  Images of all creatures hover free,
  They will not see you, only wraiths they see.   6290
  So, then, take courage, for the danger's great.
  Go to that tripod, do not hesitate,
  And touch it with the key!
                         F A U S T *assumes a decidedly commanding atti-*
                         tude with the key
Mephistopheles observing him.   So — it is well!
  'Twill come and like a slave obey your spell.
  Calmly you'll rise, upborne by fortune rare,   6295
  And have the tripod here ere they're aware.
  And when you've brought it hither, you can cite
  Hero and heroine from the realms of night,
  The first to face that deed and venture on it.
  It's done and you're the one who will have done it.   6300
  Then must the incense-cloud, by magic hand,
  Turn into gods, as gods before you stand.

Faust.　　And now what?
Mephistopheles.　　　　　　Downward let your being strain!
　　Stamping, sink hence and, stamping, rise again!
　　　　　　　　　　F AUST *stamps and sinks out of sight*
Mephistopheles.　　I only hope he'll profit from the key!　　　　6305
　　Will he come back? I'm curious to see.

Brightly Lighted Halls

E MPEROR *and* P RINCES

The Court moving about

Chamberlain to M EPHISTOPHELES.
　　The spirit-scene you promised still is owing.
　　To work! Impatient is our master growing.
Steward.　　A moment since His Grace inquired of me.
　　Delay not! Don't disgrace His Majesty!　　　　　　　6310
Mephistopheles.　　Upon that errand has my comrade gone;
　　He surely knows what's to be done.
　　He works secludedly and still,
　　And all his powers he perforce engages.
　　Who'd raise that treasure, Beauty, at his will,　　　　　6315
　　Requires the highest art, Magic of Sages!
Steward.　　The kind of arts you need, that is all one;
　　It is the Emperor's will that it be done.
A Blonde to M EPHISTOPHELES.
　　One word, sir! See my face without a spot,
　　But thus in tiresome summer it is not!　　　　　　　6320
　　Then brownish-red there sprout a hundred freckles
　　Which vex my lily skin with ugly speckles.
　　A cure!
Mephistopheles.　　You radiant darling, what a pity,
　　Spotted in May-time like a panther-kitty.
　　Take frog-spawn, toads' tongues, cohobate them,　　　6325
　　And carefully, at full moon, distillate them.
　　When the moon's waning, spread the mixture on,
　　And when the spring has come, the spots are gone.
A Brunette.　　To fawn around you, see the crowd advancing!
　　I beg a remedy! A chilblained foot　　　　　　　　6330

Hinders me much in walking and in dancing
And makes me awkward even when I salute.
Mephistopheles.   Pray let me tread upon it with my foot.
Brunette.   Well, I suppose that happens between lovers.
Mephistopheles.   In my tread, child, a greater meaning hovers.   6335
  Like unto like, whatever pain one undergo!
  Foot healeth foot, so is it with each member.
  Come here! Give heed! Don't *you* tread *me,* remember!
Brunette screaming.   Oh, how that stings! you did tread hard! Oh! Oh!
  'Twas like a horse's hoof.
Mephistopheles.   With this cure you can go.   6340
  Dance to your heart's content, now you are able,
  Or foot it with your sweetheart neath the table.
Lady pressing forward.   Let me go through! Too painful are my sorrows;
  Deep in my heart this anguish burns and burrows.
  Till yesterday his bliss hung on *my* glances   6345
  But now he turns his back; only *her* talk entrances.
Mephistopheles.   That's serious, but listen carefully.
  Press up to him quite softly, take
  This bit of charcoal, and then on him make
  A mark on sleeve or cloak or shoulder as may be;   6350
  Remorse will pierce him to the very core.
  The coal, however, you must straightway swallow,
  Nor let a drop of wine or water follow;
  Tonight you'll have him sighing at your door.
Lady.   It is not poison, is it?
Mephistopheles indignant.   Respect where it is due!   6355
  For such a coal you'd travel many a mile;
  It comes here from a funeral pile
  Such as whose flames we once more fiercely blew.
Page.   I am in love, they do not take me seriously.
Mephistopheles aside.   Whom I am now to listen to, I do not see.   6360
                    To the PAGE
  Let not the youngest maid your fancy fetter;
  Those on in years know how to prize you better.
                    Others crowd up
  Still more and more? It is a brawl, in sooth!
  I'll help myself at last with naked truth,
  The worst of aids! Great is my misery. —   6365
  O Mothers, Mothers! Do let Faust go free!
                    Gazing around him

The lights are burning dimly in the hall,
At once the Court starts forward, one and all.
I see them file according to their grades
Through distant galleries and long arcades.   6370
Now they're assembling in that ample space,
The old Knights' Hall; yet hardly all find place.
The spacious walls with tapestries are rich,
While armour decorates each nook and niche.
Here is no need, methinks, of magic incantation,   6375
Ghosts will come here without an invitation.

Hall of the Knights

Dim illumination. The EMPEROR *and Court have entered*

Herald.   Mine ancient office of announcing plays
    Is marred by spirits' mystic interference;
    In vain one dares in reasonable ways
    To fathom their mysterious appearance.   6380
    The chairs are placed, the seats are ready all;
    The Emperor is seated just before the wall;
    Upon the arras there he may with ease behold
    The glorious battles that men fought of old.
    Now Emperor and Court are seated here;   6385
    The benches crowd together in the rear;
    And lovers in this spirit-hour's uncanny gloom
    Have found beside their loved ones lovely room.
    And so, since all have duly taken places,
    We're ready, let the spirits come and face us!   6390
                    Trumpets
Astrologer.   Now let the drama start without delay.
    Our Sire commands! Ye walls, give way!
    Naught hinders now. Here magic doth conspire;
    The arras rolls away as if by fire.
    The wall is splitting, turning in the gloom,   6395
    A deep stage seems to be appearing,
    A light mysterious to be nearing,
    And I ascend to the proscenium.
Mephistopheles rising to view in the prompter's box.
    I hope for favour here from all and each,
    For promptings are the Devil's art of speech.   6400

[185]

To the ASTROLOGER.   You know the tempo of the stars on high;
    You'll understand my whispering masterly.
Astrologer.   By magic might before us doth appear,
    Massive enough, an ancient temple here.
    Like Atlas who upheld the sky of old,   6405
    Columns enough, in rows, you can behold.
    Well for the weight of stone may they suffice,
    Since two could bear a mighty edifice.
Architect.   So that's antique! I can't say I would praise it;
    Top-heavy, clumsy, is the way to phrase it.   6410
    Rude is called noble, awkward great; far more
    I love slim shafts that boundless soar.
    High pointed arches lift the soul on high,
    Such edifices most do edify.
Astrologer.   Receive with reverent awe star-granted hours.   6415
    By magic's spells enthralled be Reason's powers,
    And in its stead, arising far and free,
    Reign glorious, daring Phantasy!
    What you desired so boldly, be it now perceived;
    It is impossible, therefore to be believed.   6420
                     FAUST *rises to view on the other side of the*
                          proscenium
Astrologer.   In priestly robe and wreathed, a wonder-man!
    Who'll now fulfil what he in faith began,
    A tripod with him from the depths below.
    Now from the bowl the incense-perfumes flow.
    He girds himself, the lofty work to bless;   6425
    Henceforth there can be nothing but success.
Faust in the grand manner.
    In your name, Mothers! ye who have your throne
    In boundless space, eternally alone,
    Yet not alone. Around your heads there waver
    Life's images, astir, yet lifeless ever.   6430
    What once has been, in radiance supernal,
    It's stirring there, for it would be eternal,
    And ye allot it, Powers who all things sway,
    To vaulted night, to canopy of day.
    On some the lovely stream of life lays hold,   6435
    Others are sought by the magician bold;
    Boldly in rich profusion he displays
    The marvel whereon each would like to gaze.

Astrologer.   The glowing key doth scarcely touch the bowl,

    Over the prospect misty vapours roll;   6440

    They creep along, then cloud-like on they fare,

    Spread out, round off, entwine, they part, they pair.

    Now note a mystic masterpiece! For lo!

    The vaporous clouds make music as they go.

    Aerial tones bring forth — what can it be?   6445

    While they proceed, all turns to melody.

    The columned shaft, the very triglyph, rings;

    Yea, I believe that all the temple sings.

    The mist is sinking; from the filmy haze

    A handsome youth steps forth with measured pace.   6450

    Here ends my task, I do not need to name him;

    As gentle Paris who would not proclaim him?

                 PARIS *steps forth*

A Lady.   What glorious, blooming youth and strength I see!

A Second Lady.   Fresh as a peach, as full of juice, is he!

A Third Lady.   The finely chiselled, sweetly swelling lip!   6455

A Fourth Lady.   From such a cup how would you like to sip?

A Fifth Lady.   He's handsome, yes, and yet not quite refined.

A Sixth Lady.   A bit more graceful might he be, I find.

A Knight.   I think I see him when a shepherd boy. He's wearing

    No traces of a prince and naught of courtly bearing.   6460

Another Knight.   Oh, well! Half nude the youth is fair to look upon,

    But we must see him with his armour on.

A Lady.   He seats him gently and with easy grace.

A Knight.   You'd find his lap, perchance, a pleasant place?

Another Lady.   He lays his arm so lightly over his head.   6465

A Chamberlain.   That's not allowed! How thoroughly ill-bred!

A Lady.   You lords can always find some fault to cavil at.

Chamberlain.   Before the very Emperor to stretch himself like that!

A Lady.   He's only playing, thinks he's quite alone.

Chamberlain.   A play too should be courteous near the throne.   6470

A Lady.   Sleep captures now the charming youth completely!

Chamberlain.   And now he'll snore, quite properly and meetly!

A Young Lady enraptured.

    What fragrance with the incense-stream is blending,

    Refreshment to my inmost bosom sending!

An Older Lady.   A zephyr pierces deep into my soul, in truth!   6475

    It comes from him.

A Very Old Lady.   It is the bloom of youth,

Ambrosia-like within the boy distilling
And all the atmosphere around us filling.

HELENA *appears*

Mephistopheles.   So that is she! She'd not disturb my rest;
Pretty indeed, but still I'm not impressed.   6480

Astrologer.   For me right now there's nothing more to do;
I see and honourably confess it true.
The Fair One comes, and had I tongues of fire! —
Always did Beauty many songs inspire.
Who sees her is enrapt! and far too blessed   6485
For human lot the man who her possessed.

Faust.   Have I still eyes? Is Beauty's spring, outpouring,
Revealed most richly to my inmost soul?
My dread path brought me to this loftiest goal!
Void was the world and barred to my exploring!   6490
What is it now since this my priesthood's hour?
Worth wishing for, firm-based, a lasting dower!
Vanish from me my every vital power
If I forsake thee, treacherous to my duty!
The lovely form that once my fancy captured,   6495
That in the magic glass enraptured,
Was but a foam-born phantom of such beauty! —
To thee alone I render up with gladness
The very essence of my passion,
Fancy, desire, love, worship, madness!   6500

Mephistopheles from the prompter's box.
Be calm! Don't drop your role in such a fashion!

An Elderly Lady.   Tall, well-formed, but her head's too small for me.

A Fairly Young Lady.   Just see her foot! How could it clumsier be?

A Diplomat.   I have seen princesses of this same kind!
She's beautiful from head to foot, I find.   6505

A Courtier.   She nears the sleeper, cunningly demure.

A Lady.   How hideous by that form so young and pure!

A Poet.   By her rare beauty he is beamed upon.

A Lady.   A picture! Luna and Endymion!

A Poet.   Quite right! and now the goddess seems to sink,   6510
Bends over him as if his breath to drink.
How enviable! — A kiss! — The cup is full.

A Duenna.   Before the crowd! My word! That is too cool.

Faust.   A fearful favour for the youth!

Mephistopheles.   Be still!

[188]

And let the phantom do all that it will. 6515

A Courtier.   She steals away, light-footed. He awakes.

A Lady.   Just as I thought, another look she takes.

A Courtier.   He is astounded, thinks a wonder doth occur.

A Lady.   But what she sees, no wonder is to her.

A Courtier.   She turns around to him with charming grace. 6520

A Lady.   I see, she'll take him now into her school;
Stupid is every man in such a case.
He thinks, I guess, that he's the first — the fool!

A Knight.   She'll pass with me! A fine, majestic air!

A Lady.   The courtesan! How vulgar, I declare! 6525

A Page.   Where he is now, oh, would that I were there!

A Courtier.   In such a net who would not fain be caught?

A Lady.   Through many hands has gone that jewel rare;
Even the gilding's rather worse for wear.

Another Lady.   From her tenth year she has been good for naught. 6530

A Knight.   Each makes the best his own as chance obtains;
I'd be contented with these fair remains.

A Dryasdust Scholar.   I see her plainly and yet, frankly, I can see
That one may doubt if she the right one be.
What's present always causes obfuscation; 6535
I like to cling to written attestation.
And there I read that, soon as she was sighted,
The Trojan greybeards all were most delighted.
Methinks, that fits the case here perfectly.
I am not young and yet she pleases me. 6540

Astrologer.   A youth no more! A man, heroic, brave,
Embraces her who scarce herself can save.
Strong-armed, he lifts her high in air.
Will he, then, bear her off?

Faust.   Rash fool, beware!
You dare? You hear not? Halt! It is too much! 6545

Mephistopheles.   Why, this mad phantom-play, you've made it such!

Astrologer.   But one word more! From all we've seen today,
I call the piece "The Rape of Helena."

Faust.   What! "Rape"? Fellow, am I for naught here?
This key do I not hold it in my hand, 6550
I whom through stormy solitudes it brought here,
Through waves of horror to this solid land?
Here do I plant my foot! Realities are here,
Here strife with spirits may the spirit dare

[189]

And for itself the great twin-realm prepare.   6555
Though she was far, how can she nearer be?
I'll save her and then doubly mine is she.
I dare! Ye Mothers, Mothers! grant this favour!
Who once has known her can renounce her never!

Astrologer.   What are you doing, Faustus, Faustus! With what might   6560
He seizes her! The form is fading from our sight.
Toward the youth he turns the key, and lo!
He's touching him! — Now! it is done! Ah, woe on woe!

> *Explosion.* F A U S T *lies on the ground. The*
> *phantoms dissolve in vapour*

Mephistopheles taking F A U S T *on his shoulder.*
So there it is! To deal with fools is evil
And in the end it even harms the Devil.   6565

> *Darkness, tumult*

Act II

A High-Vaulted, Narrow, Gothic Chamber

FORMERLY FAUST'S, UNALTERED

Mephistopheles appears from behind a curtain. As he raises the curtain and looks back, F a u s t is seen stretched out on an old-fashioned bed.

Lie there, poor wretch! seduced, unwise,
Scarce to be rescued from Love's chain!
Whom Helena doth paralyze,
His reason he'll not soon regain.

Looking around him

I look around and through the glimmer   6570
Unchanged, uninjured all appears;
Methinks the coloured window-panes are dimmer,
The cobwebs have increased with years.
The ink is dry, the paper brown and sere,
Yet all is in its place, in very fact;   6575
Even the pen's still lying here
Which Faust used when he signed the pact.
Aye, deeper in the pen is lurking still
A trace of blood I lured him on to spill.
To find a relic so unique as this   6580
Would be some great collector's highest bliss.
From its old hook the old fur coat's half falling,
Those merry jests of mine recalling
Which once I taught that lad as truth,
Which still may nourish his ingenuous youth.   6585
Rough, fur-warm cloak, encased in you,
A great desire comes on me truly
To show off as a proud professor newly,
As men think they've a perfect right to do.
The learnèd know how to attain that level;   6590
It is an art long since lost by the Devil.

*He shakes the fur coat which he has taken
down. Crickets, beetles, and moths fly out*

[191]

Chorus of Insects.

Hail! welcome thy coming,
Thou patron of yore!
We're flying and humming
And know thee once more.   6595
All singly, in quiet,
Didst plant us, and lo!
In thousands, O Father,
We dance to and fro.
The rogue in the bosom   6600
Is deeply concealed;
The insects in fur coats
Are sooner revealed.

Mephistopheles.   With what surprising joy this youthful brood I view!
Aye, only sow, you'll harvest when the time is due.   6605
I'll give the old fur coat a second clout;
Still here and there another flutters out.
Up and about, ye darlings, helter-skelter,
And quickly in a thousand nooks seek shelter:
Where ancient pasteboard boxes stand,   6610
In yellowed parchment here at hand,
Where dusty shards of old pots lie,
In yonder death's-head's hollow eye.
Amid such trash and mouldering life
Crickets and crotchets must be rife.   6615

He slips into the fur coat

Come, cloak my shoulders as of yore,
Head of the house as heretofore.
Yet boots it little so to name me;
Where are the people to acclaim me?

He pulls the bell which gives out a shrill, penetrating sound, making the halls tremble and the doors fly open

Famulus tottering down the long, dark corridor.

What a clanging! What a quaking!   6620
Stairs are rocking, walls are shaking!
Through the windows' motley quiver
I see summer lightning shiver.
Over me cracks the ancient flooring,
Down come lime and rubbish pouring;   6625

And the door, securely bolted,
Magic power has open jolted.
There! How terrible! A giant
Stands in Faust's old fur, defiant!
At his look, his beck, his winking, 6630
On my knees I'm near to sinking.
Shall I stay? or shall I flee?
Oh, what will become of me?

Mephistopheles beckoning.
    Come here, my friend! Your name is Nicodemus.

Famulus.   Most worthy sir! That is my name — Oremus. 6635

Mephistopheles.   That we'll omit!

Famulus.   You know me! What a thrill!

Mephistopheles.   I know you well, old and a student still,
    Moss-covered sir! Also a learnèd man
    Still studies on since there's naught else he can.
    A moderate house of cards one builds him so; 6640
    The greatest mind does not complete it, though.
    And yet your master! Great his gifts and fame;
    Who does not know good Doctor Wagner's name?
    First in the learnèd world! 'Tis he alone, they say,
    Who holds the world together; every day 6645
    He proves that he is wisdom's multiplier.
    Hearers and listeners who eagerly aspire
    To universal knowledge, round him flock.
    None from the rostrum can shine meeter;
    He handles keys as doth St. Peter; 6650
    Lower and Upper, both he can unlock.
    Like his — as Wagner glows and sparkles —
    No other's fame can hold its ground.
    The very name of Faustus darkles;
    Wagner alone has sought and found. 6655

Famulus.   Pardon, good sir, for asking your attention
    The while I make an humble intervention:
    With what you've said there can be no dissension,
    But modesty is his allotted part.
    Since that great man's mysterious disappearing 6660
    He knows not where to turn in his despairing;
    For Faust's return he prays with all his heart,
    And thence for weal and solace. None may enter
    The room which Doctor Faustus left. Forlorn,

Untouched, it waits its lord's return.   6665
To enter it I scarcely dare to venture.
What aspect of the stars must now appear?
It seemed to me as if the stout walls quivered,
The door-posts trembled, bolts were shivered,
Else you yourself could not have come in here.   6670
Mephistopheles.   Where has the man gone? Where is he?
Lead me to him! Bring him to me!
Famulus.   Ah, sir! Too strict his orders are a bit,
I know not if I dare to venture it.
Month after month to great work he's been giving,   6675
In stillest stillness he's been living,
The daintiest of men of learning
Looks now as if he had been charcoal-burning,
His face all black from ears to nose,
His eyes all red from flames he blows.   6680
Each moment for the next he longs;
His music is the clang of tongs.
Mephistopheles.   And shall he entrance now deny me?
I'll speed his luck — just let him try me!

> FAMULUS *goes out,* MEPHISTOPHELES
> *sits down gravely*

Scarce am I settled here at rest,   6685
When yonder stirs a well-known guest.
But now most up-to-date is he;
He'll brag and swagger boundlessly.
Bachelor of Arts storming along the corridor.
Gate and door I find are opeing!
Well, at least one can be hoping   6690
That no more in mould unfitting
Men alive, yet dead, are sitting,
Pining, rotting, mortifying,
And of living still be dying.
Here each wall and each partition   6695
Bends down, sinking to perdition.
If we hence don't soon betake us,
Ruin dire will overtake us.
I am bold, no one can match me,
Yet no farther will one catch me.   6700
But today what am I learning!
Many years ago, a yearning

[194]

Freshman, I came hither, fluttering,
Anxious and abashed and stuttering.
Here I trusted long-beards' tattle,   6705
Edified me on their prattle.
  Into heavy, dry tomes reaching,
What they knew they lied in teaching,
Taught without themselves believing,
Me, themselves, of life bereaving.   6710
  What! there in the cell off yonder,
Dimly-lit, one sits asunder!
Stranger still, as I draw nearer,
Sits he there, the brown fur-wearer,
As I left him, piece for piece,   6715
Still in that old shaggy fleece!
Subtle then he seemed to be,
Not yet understood by me,
But today 'twill not avail him.
Up and on now to assail him!   6720

If, ancient sir, your bald head, sidewards bending,
Has into Lethe's dreary waters not been drawn,
Acknowledge now your pupil hither wending
Who academic rods has quite outgrown.
I find you still as then when I began;   6725
But I am here again, another man!
Mephistopheles. I'm glad I brought you with my tinkling.
The other time I valued you quite high;
Even in the worm, the chrysalis, an inkling
Is of the future, gaily-coloured butterfly.   6730
Curls and a fine lace-collar wearing,
You showed a child-like pleasure in your bearing.
I guess you never wore a queue?
I see, today cropped like a Swede are you.
You look quite brave and resolute,   6735
But pray don't go home absolute.
Bachelor of Arts.
Old sir! there on the same old desk you're leaning,
But think how time runs on today
And spare your words of double meaning;
We watch now in a very different way.   6740
Then with an honest stripling you were toying,

Succeeded too, but little art employing.
Today no one will venture that, in sooth.
Mephistopheles.   If, unadulterate, one says to youth
What does not please the callow brood — the truth!   6745
And later after many a tide
They learn it painfully on their own hide,
Each fancies then it came from his own head;
"The Master was a fool!" is what is said.
Bachelor of Arts.
Or rogue perhaps! What teacher has the grace   6750
To tell the truth directly to our face?
To simple children each knows what to say,
Add or subtract, now grave, now wise and gay.
Mephistopheles.   There is, indeed, a time to learn;
You're ready now to teach, as I discern.   6755
For many a moon and now and then a sun
A rich experience you have doubtless won.
Bachelor of Arts.   Experience! Mere foam and fluff!
A peer of mind? No trace of that is showing.
Confess: what men have ever known is stuff   6760
And absolutely not worth knowing . . .
Mephistopheles after a pause.
I long have thought so, but I was a fool;
Now to myself I seem right flat and dull.
Bachelor of Arts.   Good! That has a reasonable sound;
A greybeard talking sense at last is found!   6765
Mephistopheles.   I sought a hidden treasure, one of gold;
'Twas hideous coals when all my search was done.
Bachelor of Arts.   Confess it then! Your skull, now bald and old,
Is worth no more than yonder hollow one.
Mephistopheles good-humouredly.
You're ruder, friend, perhaps than you mean quite.   6770
Bachelor of Arts.   In German people lie when they're polite.
*Mephistopheles moving nearer and nearer toward the proscenium in his
    wheeled-chair, to the spectators.*
Here I'm deprived of light and air. I wonder
Could I find refuge with you people yonder?
Bachelor of Arts.   It is presumption that men old and hoar
Seek to be something when they are no more.   6775
Man's life lives in his blood and where, forsooth,
Does blood so stir as in the veins of youth?

[196]

Ah, that is living blood, with vigour rife,
Creating newer life from its own life.
There all is stirring, there is something done, 6780
The weak fall out, the capable press on.
While half the world we've brought beneath our sway,
What have you done? Thought, nodded, dreamed away,
Considered plan on plan — and nothing won.
It's certain! Age is but an ague cold, 6785
Chill with its fancies of distress and dread.
Once a man's thirty, he's already old,
He is indeed as good as dead.
'Twere best to kill him right away.
Mephistopheles. The Devil, here, has nothing more to say. 6790
Bachelor of Arts. Unless I will it, no devil can there be.
Mephistopheles aside. The Devil, though, will trip you presently.
Bachelor of Arts. This is youth's noblest message and most fit!
The world was not till I created it.
'Twas I that led the sun up from the sea; 6795
The moon began its changeful course with me.
The day put on rich garments, me to meet;
The earth grew green and blossomed, me to greet.
At my behest in that primeval night
The stars unveiled their splendour to my sight. 6800
Who, if not I, your own deliverance wrought
From fetters of Philistine, cramping thought?
I, as my spirit bids me, with delight
I follow onward mine own inner light.
Swift I proceed with mine own raptured mind, 6805
Glory before me, darkness far behind.

Exit

Mephistopheles. Original, in all your glory take your way!
How would true insight make you grieve!
What wise or stupid thing can man conceive
That was not thought in ages passed away? 6810
Danger from him will cause us little bother,
He will be changed when a few years have passed;
Though must within the cask may raise a pother,
It turns to wine no less at last.

To the younger portion of the audience who do
not applaud

I see my words have left you cold; 6815

[197]

Good children, I'll not take it evil.
Remember that the Devil's old;
Grow old, to understand the Devil.

Laboratory

In the style of the Middle Ages; scattered, clumsy apparatus
for fantastic purposes

Wagner at the furnace.   The bell resounds with fearful clangour,
The sooty walls thrill its vibration.   6820
No longer can remain uncertain
My great, most earnest expectation.
Darkness is lifting like a curtain.
Within the phial's inmost chamber
It's glowing like a living ember,   6825
Yea, like a glorious carbuncle, gleaming
And flashing, through the darkness streaming.
A clear white light comes into view!
Oh, may it not escape once more! —
Ah, God! what's rattling at the door?   6830

Mephistopheles entering.   Welcome! I mean it well with you.
Wagner anxiously.   Welcome in this auspicious hour!
                     Softly
Don't speak or even breathe, though, I implore!
Achieved is soon a glorious undertaking.

Mephistopheles more softly.   What is it, then?
Wagner more softly.   A man is in the making!   6835
Mephistopheles.   A man? And, pray, what lovesick pair
Have you shut in the chimney-flue?

Wagner.   May God forbid! Begetting, as men used to do,
Both vain and senseless we declare.
The tender point whence life used to begin,   6840
The gracious outward urgence from within,
To take and give, to have its likeness known,
Near and remote alike to make its own —
All that has lost its former dignity.
Whereas delighted with it still the beast may be,   6845
A man with his great gifts must henceforth win
A higher, ever higher origin.
                     Turning toward the furnace

[198]

It flashes, see! Now truly we may hold
That if from substances a hundredfold,
Through mixture — for on mixture all depends —   6850
Man's substance gently be consolidated,
In an alembic sealed and segregated,
And properly be cohobated,
In quiet and success the labour ends.
                    Turning toward the furnace again
'Twill be! The mass is working clearer,   6855
Conviction gathers, truer, nearer.
What men as Nature's mysteries would hold,
All that to test by reason we make bold,
And what she once was wont to organize,
That we bid now to crystallize.   6860
Mephistopheles.   Whoever lives long learns full many things;
By naught in this world can he ever be surprised.
I've seen already in my wanderings
Many a mortal who was crystallized.
Wagner hitherto constantly attentive to the phial.
It rises, flashes, gathers on;   6865
A moment, and the deed is done.
A great design at first seems mad; but we
Henceforth will laugh at chance in procreation,
And such a brain that is to think transcendently
Will be a thinker's own creation.   6870
                    Looking at the phial rapturously
The glass resounds with lovely might;
It dims, it clears; life *must* begin to be.
A dainty figure greets my sight;
A pretty manikin I see.
What more do we or does the world want now?   6875
The mystery's within our reach.
Come, hearken to this sound, and listen how
It turns to voice, it turns to speech.
Homunculus in the phial, to WAGNER.
Well, Daddy! how are you? It was no jest.
Come, press me tenderly upon your breast,   6880
But not too hard, for fear the glass might shatter.
That is the property of matter:
For what is natural the All has place;
What's artificial needs restricted space.

To MEPHISTOPHELES

How now, Sir Cousin, rogue, are you here too?   6885
And at the proper moment? Many thanks to you!
You've been led here by some good destiny.
The while I'm living, active must I be.
Fain would I gird me for the work straightway;
You are adroit and can curtail my way.   6890

Wagner.   But one word more! I'm shamed that answers fail me,
When with their problems young and old assail me.
For instance: no one's grasped how, each with either,
Body and soul can fit so well together,
Hold fast as if not to be separated,   6895
Yet each by other daily vexed and hated.
And then —

Mephistopheles.   Stop! I would rather ask if he
Can say why man and wife so ill agree?
This point, my friend, will nevermore be clear.
The little chap wants work to do and it is here.   6900

Homunculus.   What's to be done?

Mephistopheles pointing to a side door.

                            Your talents here you're to employ!

Wagner looking steadfastly into the phial.

In truth you are the very loveliest boy!

                 The side door opens and FAUST *is seen*
                 stretched out on the couch

Homunculus astonished.

Significant!

                 The phial slips out of WAGNER'S *hands,*
                 hovers above FAUST *and illumines him*

           With beauty girt! — Clear waters moving
In a dense grove and women who undress;
Fairest of forms! — The picture is improving.   6905
But one outshines the rest in loveliness,
From noblest heroes, nay, from gods, descended.
In the translucent pool her foot she laves;
The living flame of her sweet form is blended
With th' cooling, clinging crystal of the waves.   6910
But what a noise of pinions swiftly dashing,
And in the pool what swishing, splashing!
The maidens flee abashed, but she, the queen,
With calm composure gazes on the scene.

With pleasure proud and womanly she sees   6915
The swan-prince nestle fondly at her knees,
Importunate, yet tame. He grows more daring.
But swiftly upward floats a vapour pale
And covers with its closely woven veil
A scene most lovely and beyond comparing.   6920
Mephistopheles.   How many tales you can relate!
Small as you are, in fancies you are great.
I can see naught —
Homunculus.   Of course. You from the North,
In ages dark and drear brought forth,
In all the murk of knighthood and of papistry,   6925
How could your vision, then, be clear and free?
Only in gloom are you at home.
                         Looking around
Bemouldered stone-work, dingy, horrid,
With pointed arches low and florid!
If this man wakes, there'll be new things to dread;   6930
At once upon the spot he will lie dead.
Prophetic dreams of woodland springs beguile him,
Of swans and naked beauties. Here,
In such a place, how could he reconcile him,
Which I, the most adaptable, scarce bear?   6935
Now off with him!
Mephistopheles.   Whither I'll hear with pleasure.
Homunculus.   Command the warrior to the fight,
Lead forth the maid to tread a measure;
Then all is fitting, all is right.
Just now — my memory brings to light —   6940
Is Classical Walpurgis Night.
For him could be no happier event
Than to be taken to his element.
Mephistopheles.   Of that I've never chanced to hear.
Homunculus.   How would it come, pray, to your ear?   6945
Only romantic ghosts are known to you;
A ghost that's genuine must be classic too.
Mephistopheles.   But whither, then, are we to travel? Tell me!
Your antique cronies now repel me.
Homunculus.   Satan, northwest is where you're wont to play,   6950
But to the southeast we will sail today.
Along a great plain is Peneus flowing free,

[201]

Its silent bays shadowed by bush and tree.
To mountain gorges sweeps the level view,
Above it stands Pharsalus old and new.   6955

Mephistopheles.   Alack! have done! and call not old dissension
Twixt tyranny and slavery to my attention.
It wearies me, no sooner is it done
When once more is the same old fight begun.
And no one notes that he is but the game   6960
Of Asmodeus who still fans the flame.
They're fighters, so they say, for freedom's rights;
More closely scanned, it's slave with slave that fights.

Homunculus.   Oh, leave to men their fractious being.
Each must defend himself as best he can,   6965
From boyhood up; thus he becomes a man.
To this man's cure we must be seeing.
Come, prove it here if you've a remedy;
If you have not, then leave the cure to me.

Mephistopheles.   Many a Brocken-game I might essay,   6970
But heathen bolts, I'll find, will block my way.
The Greeks were never worth much, it is true,
Yet their free play of senses dazzles you,
The heart of man to happy vices winning.
Gloomy will always seem our ways of sinning.   6975
What now?

Homunculus.   I know you're free of squeamish twitches!
And if I touch upon Thessalian witches,
I think I have not talked for naught.

Mephistopheles lustfully.   Thessalian witches! They are persons — well,
For them I long have asked and sought.   6980
Night after night with them to dwell
Is not, I'd say, a pleasant thought;
Let's spy them, try them, though —

Homunculus.   The mantle there!
Come, wrap it straightway round the knight!
As heretofore the rag will bear   6985
You both upon your novel flight.
I'll light the way.

Wagner anxiously.   And I?

Homunculus.   Well, you
Will stay at home, most weighty work to do.
Open the parchment-sheets, collect

[202]

Life-elements as the recipes direct,   6990
With caution fitting each to other. Ponder
The *What* — to solve the *How* still harder try,
While through a little piece of world I wander
To find the dot to put upon the *i.*
Accomplished then will the great purpose be.   6995
Striving earns high requital: wealth,
Honour and fame, long life and perfect health,
Knowledge and virtue too — well, possibly.
Farewell!
Wagner sorrowfully.   Farewell! My heart is wrung with **pain.**
I fear that I will see you never again.   7000
Mephistopheles.   Now to Peneus, quick, descend!
Sir Coz shall not be meanly rated.
                    To the spectators
It's true, at last we all depend
On creatures we ourselves created.

Classical Walpurgis Night

PHARSALIAN FIELDS

Darkness

Erichtho.   To this night's awful festival, as oft before,   7005
I stride in view, Erichtho, I the gloomy one,
Not so atrocious as the tiresome poet-crew
Calumniate me to excess . . . They never end
In praise and censure . . . Even now the vale appears
Far, over-whitened with the billows of gray tents,   7010
Spectres of that most dire and most appalling night.
How oft it has recurred already! Evermore
It will recur forever . . . No one grants the realm
Unto another, none to him who through his might
Has won and rules it. For each one who knows not how   7015
To rule his own, his inborn self, is all too fain
To rule his neighbour's will, as prompts his own proud mind . . .
Here was a great example fought even to the end:
How violence opposes greater violence,
How freedom's lovely, thousand-blossomed wreath is rent,   7020
And the stiff laurel bends around the ruler's head.

Here of an early budding greatness Pompey dreamed,
There Caesar by the wavering balance watchful lay!
Strength will they measure. And the world knows now who won.
   The watch-fires glow and flash, diffusing ruddy flames;   7025
The ground where blood was shed exhales reflected light;
And by the night's most rare and wondrous splendour lured,
The legion of Hellenic myths assembles here.
Round all the watch-fires fabled forms of ancient days
Hover uncertain to and fro or sit at ease . . .   7030
In truth, not fully orbed, yet radiant bright, the moon
Is rising, spreading gentle splendour everywhere;
The tents' illusion vanishes, the lights burn blue.
   But lo! above my head what sudden meteor!
It beams and it illumines a corporeal ball.   7035
'Tis life I scent. Becoming is it not for me
That I approach the living, doing harm to them.
That brings me evil fame and benefits me not.
Already it sinks down. Discreetly I withdraw.
     Moves away
    The A E R O N A U T S *overhead*

Homunculus.

    Once again around I hover,   7040
    Flames and horrors dire I follow;
    Spectral all that I discover
    In the vale and in the hollow.

Mephistopheles.

    As through my old window looking
    Midst far northern waste and gloom,   7045
    Ghosts revolting I see spooking,
    Here as there I am at home.

Homunculus.

    See! a woman tall is stalking
    In long strides before us there.

Mephistopheles.

    As if scared, it seems, she's walking,   7050
    Saw us coming through the air.

Homunculus.

    Let her stalk! Set down the burden
    Of your knight, for near at hand
    Are the new life and the guerdon
    That he seeks in fable-land.   7055

Faust touching the soil.   Where is she?
Homunculus.   That's a question over-tasking,
    But here you'll learn, I think, by asking.
    Make ready, go ere it is day;
    From flame to flame inquiring wander.
    Who to the Mothers dared the way,   7060
    Has nothing more to fear or ponder.
Mephistopheles.   Here I too claim a part to play,
    Yet for our weal naught better can I say
    Than that each one amid the fires
    Should seek his own adventures and desires.   7065
    Then as a sign to reunite us,
    Let, little friend, your lantern sound and light us.
Homunculus.   Thus shall it ring and light display.
                    The glass resounds and emits a powerful light
    Now to new wonders, quick, away!
                    Exit
Faust alone.   Where is she? — now no further question make . . .   7070
    Though it be not the soil on which she stepped,
    Nor this the wave that to her coming leapt,
    Yet 'tis the air that speaks the tongue she spake.
    Here by a wonder! Here in Grecian land!
    I felt at once the earth on which I stand.   7075
    As, while I slept, new strength my limbs was steeling,
    I rise renewed, Antaeus in my feeling.
    And while the strangest things assembled here I find,
    I'll search this labyrinth of flames with serious mind.
                    Goes away

By the Upper Peneus

Mephistopheles peering around.
    As mid these little fires I wander aimless,   7080
    I find myself quite strange and disconcerted.
    Naked are almost all, some few are shirted;
    The griffins impudent, the sphinxes shameless,
    Winged, curly things — who'll ever dare to name them?
    Seen fore and aft, they're crude enough to shame them . . .   7085
    It's true, indecency is our ideal,

But the antique is too alive and real.
By modern taste the nude should be controlled
And overlaid in fashions manifold . . .
A loathsome folk! yet so I must not treat them;   7090
As new-come guest I should politely greet them . . .
Hail, ye wise grizzlies, hail, ye ladies fair!
A Griffin snarling.   Not grizzlies! Griffins! No one likes to hear
Himself called grizzly. In each word there rings
An echo of the source from which it springs.   7095
Graves, growling, grumpy, gruesome, grim, and grey,
All of one sort in etymology are they,
And put us out of sorts.
Mephistopheles.   Yet — not to leave this thesis —
The *gri* in your proud title *Griffin* pleases.
Griffin as above and continuously so.
Of course! The kinship has been proved to hold.   7100
'Tis true, it's oft rebuked but oftener extolled.
Let one but *grip* at maidens, crowns, and gold;
Fortune is mostly gracious to the *Gripper* bold.
Ants of the colossal kind.
You speak of gold! In great heaps did we hoard it,
In rocky caverns secretly we stored it;   7105
The Arimaspians have nosed it out,
They bore it off so far they laugh and shout.
Griffin.   We'll bring them to confess their deed.
Arimaspians.   But not in this free night of jubilee.
Ere morning all will squandered be;   7110
This time we'll probably succeed.
Mephistopheles who has seated himself between the SPHINXES.
How pleasantly I grow familiar here;
I understand them one and all.
A Sphinx.   We breathe our spirit-tones into your ear,
And then you render them material.   7115
Until we know you better, tell your name.
Mephistopheles.   Men think that many a title I may claim.
Are Britons here? Such travellers are they;
Cascades and battlefields they love to trace,
Ruins and many a musty classic place;   7120
A worthy goal they would find here today.
They testified that in the old stage-play
I was seen there as "Old Iniquity."

A Sphinx.   How did they hit on that?

Mephistopheles.   It puzzles even me.

A Sphinx.   Perhaps! — Do you know planets and their power?   7125
    What say you to the aspect of the hour?

Mephistopheles looking upward.
    Star courses star, I see the clipped moon glide
    And feel quite happy at your cosy side;
    I'll warm myself against your lion's-hide.
    'Twould hurt to soar up, I'd but go astray.   7130
    Propound some riddles or charades to play.

A Sphinx.   Express yourself; that too will be a riddle.
    See if your inmost essence you can rede:
    "What both the pious and the wicked need:
    For those a breastplate for ascetic fencing,   7135
    For these a comrade, crazy pranks advancing,
    Both but the joy of Zeus enhancing."

First Griffin snarling.   I don't like him.

Second Griffin snarling more loudly.   What is it he wants here?

Both.   The nasty wretch belongs not in our sphere!

Mephistopheles brutally.
    You think perhaps the guest's nails do not scratch   7140
    And with your sharp claws can not match?
    Just try it!

A Sphinx gently.   Here you might forever stay,
    But from our midst you'll drive yourself away.
    At home you think to do just as you please,
    But if I err not, here you're ill at ease.   7145

Mephistopheles.   Right appetizing are you upward from the bosom,
    But further down your beastly part is gruesome.

A Sphinx.   These words, you hypocrite, you'll surely rue,
    Because our paws are sound; but I can see
    That with that shrunken horse's-foot you do   7150
    Not feel at ease in our society.

SIRENS prelude overhead

Mephistopheles.   What birds are they who're cradled yonder
    On boughs beside the poplared river?

A Sphinx.   Beware! The best of men have ever
    Been led by that singsong to wander.   7155

Sirens.
        Ah, why mar thy taste completely,
        Mid these hideous wonders dwelling?

Hear our notes accordant swelling,
See our hosts come singing sweetly
As becometh sirens meetly.   7160

Sphinxes mocking them in the same melody.

Force them down! And so reveal them!
Mid the branches they conceal them;
Nasty falcon-claws they're wearing
And will fall on thee, unsparing,
If thou lendest willing ear.   7165

Sirens.

Hence with hate, let envy perish!
We the purest pleasures cherish
Strewn beneath the sky's blue sphere!
On the earth and on the ocean
Let him see in every motion   7170
Sign of welcome and of cheer.

Mephistopheles.   What novelties and how assuring
When both from string and voice alluring
The tones about each other twine.
But lost on me is all the trilling,   7175
Tickling my ears but never thrilling
Down in its depths this heart of mine.
Sphinxes.   Speak not of heart! Vain so to call it!
A shrivelled-up, old leathern wallet
Would better with your face combine.   7180
Faust approaching.   How strangely satisfying are these creatures!
Repulsive, yet what big, compelling features!
I feel now the approach of some good chance;
Whither is hailing me that earnest glance?
                    Referring to the SPHINXES
Before such Oedipus once stood his ground;   7185
                    Referring to the SIRENS
Before such did Ulysses writhe, in hemp fast bound;
                    Referring to the ANTS
By such was noblest treasure once amassed;
                    Referring to the GRIFFINS
By these 'twas kept inviolate to the last.
New spirit thrills me when I see all these;
Great are the figures, great the memories.   7190
Mephistopheles.   In former times such creatures you'd have scouted

Which now it seems that you approve;
Aye, when one seeks his lady-love,
Monsters themselves are welcome and not flouted.

Faust to the S P H I N X E S.   Ye forms like women, answer me and say: 7195
Has anyone of you seen Helena?

Sphinxes.   We did not last till Helena's generation;
Hercules slew the last ones of our nation.
From Chiron you might get the information.
This ghostly night he's galloping around;   7200
If he will stop for you, you've gained much ground.

Sirens.

        With us too thou wouldst not miss it! . . .
        When Ulysses, with us whiling,
        Sped not past us, unreviling,
        Much he told made bright his visit;   7205
        All his tales we'd tell to thee
        If thou camest to renew thee
        To our meadows by the sea.

A Sphinx.   Sir, hark not to trickery!
Whereas Ulysses to the mast,   7210
Let us now with good counsel bind thee.
If lofty Chiron thou canst find thee,
What I have sworn, thou wilt learn at last.

                F A U S T *goes away*

Mephistopheles vexed.   What croaks on pinions rushing by?
So fast that they elude the eye?   7215
Swiftly in single file they fly.
A hunter tires of such as these.

A Sphinx.   Like to the storm that winter harrows,
Reached scarcely by Alcides' arrows,
They are the swift Stymphalides.   7220
They mean well with their croak-salute,
Their vulture's-beak, their goose's-foot.
Here in our midst they'd like to be
And prove they're of our pedigree.

Mephistopheles as if intimidated.
Some other things are hissing shrill.   7225

A Sphinx.   For fear of these you need not quake;
They are the heads of the Lernaean snake;
Cut from the trunk, they think they're something still.

But say, what's wrong? why so distressful?
Why this behaviour so unrestful?   7230
Where would you go? Be off, good-by! —
I see, that chorus twists your neck awry.
Don't force yourself to stay! Go, leave this place,
Greet yonder many a charming face.
The Lamiae, wanton wenches, you'll find there,   7235
Their foreheads brazen, faces smiling,
As when the satyrs they're beguiling.
There all things may a goat's-foot dare.
Mephistopheles.   You'll stay here and I'll find you here again?
Sphinxes.   Yes! Go and mingle with the airy train.   7240
We long ago are wont, from Egypt coming here,
To sit enthronèd to the thousandth year.
Respect to our position you must pay.
Thus rule we lunar, rule we solar day.

      At the pyramids our station,   7245
      We look on the doom of races,
      War and peace and inundation,
      With eternal changeless faces.

By the Lower Peneus

PENEUS *surrounded by waters and nymphs*

Peneus.   Wake and stir, ye whispering bushes,
Softly breathe, ye reeds and rushes,   7250
Rustle, willows by the river,
Lisp, ye poplar sprays a-quiver,
To my interrupted dream! . . .
Fearful, stirring breezes wake me
And mysterious tremors shake me   7255
From my rippling, restful stream.
Faust stepping to the edge of the river.
If I dare such fancies harbour,
Deep within the tangled arbour
Of these twigs and bushes noises
Sounded as of human voices.   7260
Wave doth seem a very chatter,
Zephyr sounds a jesting patter.

Nymphs to FAUST.

> Ah, best were it for thee
> To lie here, reviving
> In coolness thy members   7265
> Worn out by their striving,
> The rest thus enjoying
> That from thee doth flee;
> We'll rustle, we'll murmur,
> We'll whisper to thee.   7270

Faust.   I am awake! Oh, let them stay me,
Those peerless forms, and let them sway me
As mine eye sees them in its quest.
What thrills run through my every member!
Do I but dream? Do I remember?   7275
Ah, once before was I so blessed.
A cooling stream is softly gliding,
Amid the trembling copse half hiding;
It scarcely murmurs in its flow.
From every side, clear and delighting,   7280
A hundred streamlets are uniting
To fill a bath-like pool below.
The fair young limbs of women trouble
The liquid mirror, showing double,
And double so the eye's delight!   7285
Bathing with joy, each other aiding,
Now boldly swimming, shyly wading,
Ending in screams and water-fight.
These should content me, here with pleasure
My sight should be restored at leisure;   7290
Yet toward yonder leafy screen
My vision ever further presses;
The verdant wealth of those recesses
Surely enveils the lofty queen.
Strange and marvellous! Swans are swimming   7295
From the inlets, hither skimming
In their stately majesty,
Calmly floating, sweetly loving,
Heads and beaks uplifted moving
In proud self-complacency.   7300
But among them one seems peerless,

In his self-love proud and fearless;
Through the throng he sails apace,
Swells his plumage like a pillow,
He, a billow breasting billow,   7305
Speeds on to the sacred place . . .
The others to and fro, together,
Swim with unruffled, radiant feather,
Or soon in stirring, splendid fray
Seek to divert each timid beauty   7310
Away from any thought of duty
To save herself if save she may.

Nymphs.

        Sisters, hearken, lend a hearing
        At the river's verdant shore;
        If I err not, more and more   7315
        Sounds of horse's hoofs are nearing.
        Would I knew who in swift flight
        Brings a message to this night!

Faust.   I believe the earth's resounding
To a steed that's hither bounding.   7320

        Turn there, my glance!
        A most auspicious chance,
        Can it be hither faring?
        O marvel past comparing!

A rider's trotting on toward me.   7325
Spirited, strong, he seems to be;
Borne on a snow-white steed he's nearing . . .
I do not err, I know him now,
The famous son of Philyra! —
Halt, Chiron, halt! and give me hearing!   7330

Chiron.   What now? What is it?
Faust.   Check your pace and stay!
Chiron.   I do not rest.
Faust.   Take me along, I pray!
Chiron.   Then, mount! and I can question you at leisure:
Whither your way? You're standing on the shore
And I will bear you through the stream with pleasure.   7335
Faust mounting.   Whither you will, I'll thank you evermore . . .
The noble pedagogue, so great in name,

Who reared full many a hero, to his fame,
The troop of Argonauts, renowned in story,
And all who built the poets' world of glory.   7340
Chiron.   Let us not talk of that. As mentor, none,
Not Pallas' self, is venerated.
For, after all, in their own way men carry on
As if they never had been educated.
Faust.   The doctor who can name each plant, who knows   7345
All roots, even that which deepest grows,
Who soothes the wounded, makes the sick man whole,
You I embrace with all my might and soul.
Chiron.   If at my side a hero felt the smart,
I knew the aid and counsel to be tendered!   7350
But in the end all of my art
To parsons and herb-women was surrendered.
Faust.   Upon a true, great man I gaze!
Who will not hear a word of praise,
Modestly strives to shut his ears   7355
And acts as had he many peers.
Chiron.   You are well-skilled, I see, in idle patter,
Princes and common folk alike to flatter.
Faust.   At least confess that you have seen
The greatest men that in your time have been.   7360
You've with the noblest vied in earnest strife
And like a demigod have lived your life.
Of all the figures of heroic mould
Whom as the ablest did you hold?
Chiron.   Among the Argonauts, superb procession!   7365
Each one was worthy after his own fashion,
And by the special power that he possessed,
Could do what lay beyond the rest.
Castor and Pollux ever did prevail
Where youthful bloom and beauty turned the scale.   7370
In swift resolve and act for others' good
The sons of Boreas proved their hardihood.
Reflective, strong and shrewd, in council wise,
Thus Jason ruled, a joy to women's eyes.
Then Orpheus, gentle, still, and contemplating,   7375
But, when he smote the lyre, all subjugating;
Keen-sighted Lynceus who by day and dark
Past reef and shallow steered the sacred bark.

Danger is tested best by banded brothers:
When one achieves, then praise him all the others.　　7380
Faust.　I beg, of Hercules I would be learning!
Chiron.　Oh, woe! Awaken not my yearning! . . .
Phoebus I ne'er had seen, nor yet
Seen Ares, Hermes, as they're called, in fine,
When my enraptured vision met　　7385
A form that all men call divine.
A king by birth as was no other,
A youth most glorious to view,
A subject to his elder brother
And to the loveliest women too.　　7390
His like will Gaea bring forth never
Nor Hebe lead to Heaven again;
Songs struggle in a vain endeavour,
Men torture marble all in vain.
Faust.　Though men may strive in stone and story,　　7395
Never has he appeared in all his glory.
You now have spoken of the fairest man;
Tell of the fairest woman all you can!
Chiron.　What! Woman's beauty? That is not worth telling,
Too oft a rigid image do we see;　　7400
I praise alone a being welling
With love of life and gaiety.
Self-blest is beauty, cold and listless,
'Tis winsomeness that makes resistless,
Like that of Helena whom once I bore.　　7405
Faust.　You bore her?
Chiron.　　　　　Aye, upon this back.
Faust.　Was I not crazed enough before?
And here to sit! Such bliss I do not lack!
Chiron.　She also grasped me by the hair,
Seizing it just as you are doing now.　　7410
Faust.　I'm losing all my senses! Tell me how,
Whence, whither? Ah, you really did her bear?
She only is my whole desire!
Chiron.　Easy it is to tell what you require.
Castor and Pollux had at that time freed　　7415
Their darling sister from base robbers' greed.
The robbers, wonted not to be subdued,
Took heart and in a storm of rage pursued.

Brothers and sister, speeding on their way,
Were checked by swamps that near Eleusis lay;   7420
The brothers waded, but I splashed, swam over;
Then off she sprang, she stroked and pressed me
On my wet mane, thanked and caressed me
Sweetly self-conscious, affectionate and sage.
How charming was she! young, the joy of age!   7425

Faust.   Just ten years old!

Chiron.   The doctors of philology
Have fooled you like themselves, I see.
Peculiar is it with a mythologic dame;
The poet brings her, as he needs, to fame;
She never grows adult and never old,   7430
Always of appetizing mould,
Ravished when young, still wooed long past her prime.
Enough, the poet is not bound by time.

Faust.   Then, here too, be no law of time thrown round her!
On Pherae's isle indeed Achilles found her   7435
Beyond the pale of time. A happiness, how rare!
In spite of fate itself love triumphed there.
Is it beyond my yearning passion's power
To bring to life the earth's most perfect flower?
That deathless being, peer of gods above,   7440
Tender as great; sublime, yet made for love!
You saw her once, *today* I've seen her too,
Charming as fair, desired as fair to view.
My captured soul and being yearn to gain her;
I will not live unless I can attain her.   7445

Chiron.   Strange person! As a man you feel an ecstasy,
But to us spirits you seem mad to be.
Now, as it haps, good fortune meets you here,
Since for some moments every year
I'm wont to Manto to repair   7450
Who, Aesculapius' child, in silent prayer
Implores her father, for his honour's gain,
To throw some light in the physicians' brain
That from rash slaughter may their hands refrain . . .
I love her most of all the guild of sybils,   7455
Gentle and kind, nor prone to shifty quibbles.
If but a while you stay, her art secure
By powerful roots will work your perfect cure.

[215]

Faust.   I'm sound in mind. A cure is not my aim;
    Else, like to others, I'd be base and tame.   7460
Chiron.   The noble fountain's cure, neglect it not!
    Be quick, dismount! We've reached the spot.
Faust.   Say, whither have you in this gruesome night
    Borne me through pebbly waters in our flight?
Chiron.   Here Rome and Greece each bearded each in fight,   7465
    Olympus on the left, Peneus on the right.
    The greatest realm that ever was lost in sand;
    The monarch flees, the conquering burghers stand.
    Look up! Here stands, significantly near,
    The eternal temple in the moonlight clear.   7470
Manto dreaming within.

            From horse-hoofs bounding
            The sacred stairs are resounding;
            Demigods are drawing near.
Chiron.

            Quite right!
            Raise your eyes; behold who's here!   7475
Manto awakening.   Welcome! I see you do not fail to come.
Chiron.   Likewise for you still stands your temple-home.
Manto.   Are you still roaming, never weary?
Chiron.   Well, you abide in stillness eerie,
    The while I circle joyously.   7480
Manto.   I wait here, time encircles me.
    And this man?
Chiron.   Him hath this ill-fated night
    Caught in its whirl and brought here to your sight.
    Helena, go his wits a-spinning,
    Helena he has dreams of winning,   7485
    But knows no way to make beginning,
    Most worthy, Aesculapian cure to prove.
Manto.   Who yearns for the impossible I love.
               Chiron *is already far away*
Manto.   Enter, audacious one, glad shall you be;
    The gloomy way leads to Persephone.   7490
    Within Olympus' cavern foot
    She lists in secret for prescribed salute.
    Here did I smuggle Orpheus in of old.
    Use your turn better! Quick! Be bold!
             They descend

By the Upper Peneus

Sirens by the upper Peneus as before.

7495

Plunge ye in Peneus' flood!
Meetly splashing, swimming, fording,
Linking songs in tones according,
For these ill-starred people's good.
Without water weal is none!
If our goodly bands were faring   7500
To the Aegean, swift repairing,
Every joy would then be won.

Earthquake

Sirens.

Back the foaming wave is going,
Down its bed no longer flowing;
Quakes the ground, the waters choke,   7505
Shores and pebbles crack and smoke.
Let us flee! Come, all! Come on!
For this marvel profits none.
Hence! Ye noble guests and merry,
To the ocean revel hurry,   7510
Glittering where the waves are twinkling,
Heaving gently, shores besprinkling,
There where Luna twofold gloweth,
Holy dew on us bestoweth.
There a life astir and cheerful,   7515
Here an earthquake dire and fearful.
Hence, ye prudent, haste away!
For this place strikes with dismay.

Seismos growling and blustering in the depths.

Shove again with shoulders straining,
Stoutly all your strength arraigning!   7520
Upper regions we'll be gaining,
Where to us must all give way.

Sphinxes.

What a most unpleasant quivering,
What a hideous, fearsome shivering!
What a wavering, what a shocking,   7525
Surging to and fro and rocking!
An unbearable affray!

[217]

But we shall not change our places,
Though all hell bursts in our faces.

Now a dome — behold the wonder! —   7530
Is arising. Ah, 'tis yonder
Very Ancient, long since hoar,
Who built Delos' isle of yore,
Drove it upward from the billow
For a travailing woman's pillow.   7535
He, with straining, pressing, rending,
Rigid arms and shoulders bending,
Like an Atlas in his gesture,
Heaves up earth and all its vesture,
Loam and stone and sand and gravel,   7540
Quiet shores and calm beds' level.
Thus the valley's placid bosom
Rends he with a power gruesome,
Still most strenuous, never sated,
A colossal caryatid,   7545
Bears an awful weight of boulders,
Buried still up to his shoulders.
But 'twill not come near these spaces;
Sphinxes now are in their places.

Seismos.   I, only, wrought this little matter   7550
As men will finally declare;
But for my batter and my clatter
How would this world be now so fair?
How would your mountains stand above there
In clear and splendid ether-blue,   7555
If them I had not worked to shove there?
A picturesque, entrancing view!
Whenas (the primal sires surveying,
Chaos and Night) I saw my honour lost,
I, with the Titans joined in playing,   7560
Hurled Ossa, Pelion too, as balls are tossed.
Thus we raged on in youthful passion
Till vexed and weary at the last
Both mountains we, in wanton fashion,
Like twin peaks on Parnassus cast . . .   7565
Apollo gladly lingers yonder

[218]

There in the muses' blest retreat.
For Jove himself and for his bolts of thunder
I heaved on high his lofty seat.
Thus I, by strainings superhuman,   7570
Pushed from the depths to upper air,
And dwellers glad I loudly summon
New life henceforth with me to share.

Sphinxes.   Surely one would call primeval
What so burg-like looms today,   7575
But we saw the earth give way
To the straining, vast upheaval.
A bushy wood is spreading up the side,
While rocks on rocks still roll on like a tide.
A sphinx will never let such things perturb her,   7580
Nor in her sacred seat will aught disturb her.

Griffins.   Gold a-spangle, gold a-flitter,
Through the chinks I see it glitter.
Let none rob you of the prize:
Up and claw it, emmets! Rise!   7585

Chorus of Ants.

Whereas the giant ones
Upward could shove it,
Ye nimble, pliant ones,
Swift speed above it!
Scurry ye out and in!   7590
In each cranny
Is every crumb ye win
Wealth for the canny.
Ye must discover it,
The slightest treasure,   7595
Swiftly uncover it
In every fissure.
Toil like the busy bees,
Ye swarms, retrieve it.
Gold only shall ye seize!   7600
What's oreless, leave it!

Griffins.   Come, come! Bring in a heap of gold!
Beneath our claws fast will we hold.
They're bolts none others can excel,
They guard the greatest treasure well.   7605

[219]

Pygmies.   We are in our places truly,
    Know not how it did befall.
    Whence we came, don't ask unduly,
    For we're here now once for all.
    As a joyous place to settle,   7610
    Suitable is every land;
    If a rocky rift shows metal,
    Straightway is the dwarf at hand.
    Male and female, busy, ready,
    Exemplary is each pair;   7615
    We know not if once already
    This the case in Eden were.
    Our lot gratefully we treasure,
    For we find things here are best;
    Mother Earth brings forth with pleasure   7620
    In the east as in the west.
Dactyls.
                Hath in a night the Earth
                The little ones brought to birth,
                The smallest she will create too,
                They will find each his mate too.   7625
Eldest Pygmies.
                Hasten, in spaces
                Pleasant take places!
                Haste, the work heeding,
                Not strong but speeding!
                Peace is still with ye,   7630
                Build ye the smithy
                For troops to shapen
                Armour and weapon.

                All ye ants, cluster,
                Busily fluster,   7635
                Metals to muster!
                Dactyls conforming,
                Tiny but swarming,
                Our orders hear ye
                And firewood bear ye!   7640
                Heap in a pyre
                Smothering fire!
                Charcoal prepare ye!

Generalissimo.

With bow and arrow
Foes will we harrow! 7645
Herons that wander
By that pond yonder,
Numberless nesting there,
Haughtily breasting there,
Shoot them straightway, 7650
All them together,
In helm and feather
Us to array.

Ants and Dactyls.

Who now will save us!
Iron we're bringing, 7655
Chains to enslave us.
Chains we're not springing,
Not yet's the hour;
Heed, then, their power!

The Cranes of Ibycus.

Cries of murder, moan of dying! 7660
Fearful pinions fluttering, flying!
What a groan and moan and fright
Pierces upward to our height!
All have fallen in the slaughter,
Reddened with their blood the water. 7665
Greedy lust, misshapen, cruel,
Steals the heron's noble jewel.
On the helmet now it waves,
Oh, these fat-paunched, bow-legged knaves!
Comrades with our host in motion, 7670
Serried wanderers of the ocean,
Summon we, for vengeance mated,
In a case so near related.
Let none spare his strength or blood!
Hate eternal to this brood! 7675

They disperse in the air, croaking

Mephistopheles on the plain.

The northern witches I command, but these,
Spirits so alien, make me ill at ease.
The Blocksberg's a convenient place to roam;
Wherever you are, you find yourself at home.

[221]

Dame Ilsa watches for us on her Stone, 7680
Wakeful is Henry on his lofty Throne;
The Snorers snort, in truth, in Elend's ears,
But all remains unchanged a thousand years.
But who knows here, if, where he stand or go,
The ground will not heave upward from below? . . . 7685
I wander through a level dale quite happily,
And then behind me rises suddenly
A mountain — scarce a mountain, yet in height
Enough to block the sphinxes from my sight.
Here, down the valley, many a fire is glaring, 7690
Its light on these strange scenes and figures flaring . . .
Still, knavishly confusing, lo! the amorous crew
Flutter and dance before me, flee and woo.
But softly now! Though used to many savours,
Wherever they be, one still seeks novel flavours. 7695

Lamiae drawing MEPHISTOPHELES *after them.*

Quicker and quicker!
And never tarry!
Then hesitating,
Chatting and prating.
It is so merry, 7700
The ancient tricker
To lure behind us
To penance dreary.
Foot-stiff and weary,
On he comes hobbling, 7705
After us wobbling;
He drags his foot,
Hasting to find us.
Vain is his suit.

Mephistopheles standing still.

Cursed fate! Men are but women's fools! 7710
From Adam down, becozened tools!
Older we grow but who grows wise and steady?
Were you not fooled enough already?
We know that wholly worthless is this race
With pinched-in waist and painted face; 7715
Naught's wholesome in a folk so misbegotten;
Grasp where you will, in every limb they're rotten.

[222]

We know it, see it, we can feel it,
And still we dance if but the vile jades reel it!

Lamiae pausing.   Halt! See him ponder, hesitate, delay!   7720
Turn back to meet him lest he slip away!

Mephistopheles striding forward.   Go on! nor in the web of doubt
Let yourself be entangled foolishly;
For if no witches were about,
Why, who the devil would a devil be!   7725

Lamiae most winsomely.   Round this hero circle we;
Surely soon within his breast
Love for one is manifest.

Mephistopheles.   True, in this uncertain gleam,
Pretty wenches do you seem,   7730
And you'll hear no slurs from me.

An Empusa intruding.   Nor slur me! A maiden too,
Let me join your retinue.

Lamiae.   In our group she'll never fit,
And our sport? she ruins it.   7735

Empusa to MEPHISTOPHELES.   From ass-foot Coz Empusa, greeting!
The trusty one whom now you're meeting.
You only have a horse's foot;
Still, take, Sir Coz, my best salute!

Mephistopheles.   Strangers alone were here my expectations,   7740
But now, alas! I'm finding near relations.
Indeed, an ancient book doth tell us:
Everywhere cousins from the Hartz to Hellas.

Empusa.   I'm swift in acting with decision,
In many forms could meet your vision;   7745
But honour due you I would pay
And so the ass's head I've donned today.

Mephistopheles.   I note, with people of this sort
Kinship is stuff of great import;
But come what may, it's all the same,   7750
The ass's head I'd fain disclaim.

Lamiae.   Avoid this hag! She doth but scare
Whatever lovely seems and fair;
What fair and lovely was before,
She comes, and see! it is no more!   7755

Mephistopheles.   These cousins too, slim and delicious,
Of one and all I am suspicious;
Behind such darling cheeks of roses

[223]

I have a fear of metamorphoses.

Lamiae.   Just try it, do! We are not few.   7760
   Lay hold! and if the game's luck favours you,
   Grab for yourself the first, great prize.
   What means this lustful, droning tune?
   What sort of way is this to spoon?
   You strut along and act so wise!   7765
   Into our group now see him stride!
   Lay one by one your masks aside
   And show your nature to his eyes.

Mephistopheles.   The fairest I have chosen me . . .
                Clasping her
   Oh, woe! A withered broomstick, she!   7770
                Seizing another
   And this one? . . . Hideous face! Oh, what a lot!

Lamiae.   Do you deserve things better? Think it not!

Mephistopheles.   The little one I'd like to clasp . . .
   A lizard's slipping from my grasp!
   And snake-like is her slippery braid.   7775
   Well, then, a tall one I will catch . . .
   And now a thyrsus-pole I snatch!
   Only a pine-cone as its head.
   Where will this end? . . . Let's try a fat one.
   Perhaps I'll find delight in that one.   7780
   A last attempt! Then it will do!
   So flabby, fubby, worth a treasure
   As Orientals such things measure . . .
   But ah, the puff-ball bursts in two!

Lamiae.   Scatter asunder, flicker around him,   7785
   Like lightning, in black flight surround him.
   The interloping witch's son!
   Ye bats, in horrid, changeful reeling,
   Whirl ye, on noiseless pinions wheeling!
   He'll get off cheap when all is done.   7790

Mephistopheles shaking himself.
   I have not grown much wiser, that seems clear.
   The North's absurd, absurd it's also here;
   Ghosts here and there are a confounded crew,
   Tasteless the people and the poets too.
   A masquerade is here, I swear,   7795
   A sensual dance as everywhere.

At lovely rows of masks I grasped
And shuddered at the things I clasped . . .
I gladly lend myself to cheating
But ask to have it not so fleeting.   7800

Losing himself among the rocks

Where am I? Where does this lead out?
There was a path, now stone-heaps roundabout.
I came along on level ways,
And rubble-stuff now meets my gaze;
I clamber up and down in vain.   7805
My sphinxes — where find them again?
I'd not have dreamed so mad a sight,
Aye, such a mountain in one night!
"A witch-ride" would not name it wrong;
They bring their own Blocksberg along.   7810

Oread from a natural rock.   Come up to me! My mount is old
And still has its primeval mould.
Revere these cliff-paths steep ascending
And Pindus' last spur far extending!
Unshaken, thus I reared my head   7815
When over my shoulders Pompey fled.
Beside me here this phantom rock
Will vanish at the crow of cock.
Such fairy-tales I often see arise
And perish in like sudden wise.   7820

Mephistopheles.   Honour to thee, thou honoured head!
With mighty oaks engarlanded.
Moonbeams, however clear and bright,
Never can pierce thy sable night. —
But by the bushes there I see   7825
A light that's glowing modestly.
How strange that all must happen thus!
In truth, it is Homunculus.
Whence do you come, you little rover?

Homunculus.   From place to place I flit and hover   7830
And wish that in the best sense I might *be*.
My glass I long impatiently to shatter;
Only from what I've seen and see,
I do not like to venture on this matter.
But I'll tell you quite confidentially: 7835
I've tracked two sages whom I've overheard

[225]

Say "Nature!" "Nature!" — 'twas their only word.
I will not part me from them, seeing
That they must know this earthly be-ing;
And in the end I'll doubtless learn   7840
Whither most wisely I'm to turn.
Mephistopheles.   Accomplish that in your own way.
Wherever ghosts may be appearing,
The sage finds welcome and a hearing;
And that his art and favour may elate,   7845
A dozen new ghosts he'll at once create.
You'll not gain sense, except you err and stray!
You'll come to birth? Do it in your own way!
Homunculus.   Good counsel, though, a man should never scout.
Mephistopheles.   Proceed, then, and we'll see how things turn out.   7850
                    They separate
Anaxagoras to THALES.   You will not let your rigid mind be bent.
Is aught more needed to make you assent?
Thales.   To every wind the wave bows fain enough,
But from the rugged rock it holds aloof.
Anaxagoras.   Through flaming gas arose this rock we're seeing.   7855
Thales.   In moisture came organic life to being.
Homunculus between the two.
Ah, by your side to go, pray, suffer me!
I'm yearning to begin to be.
Anaxagoras.   Have you, O Thales, even in one night
Brought such a mountain out of slime to light?   7860
Thales.   Nature with all her living, flowing powers
Was never bound by day and night and hours.
By rule she fashions every form, and hence
In great things too there is no violence.
Anaxagoras.   But here there was! Plutonic, savage fire,   7865
Aeolian vapours' force, explosive, dire,
Broke through the ancient crust of level earth
And a new mountain straightway came to birth.
Thales.   The hill is there; so much at least is gained.
But what is thereby furthered and attained?   7870
Both time and leisure in such strife one poses
And only leads the patient rabble by their noses.
Anaxagoras.   Quickly with Myrmidons the hill is teeming,
They occupy the clefts; and now come streaming
Pygmies and ants and fingerlings   7875

[226]

And other active little things.
To HOMUNCULUS
After the great you never have aspired
But hermit-like have lived retired;
If you can wont yourself to sovereignty,
Then crowned as king I'll have you be. 7880
Homunculus.　　What says my Thales?
Thales.　　　　　　　　That I won't advise.
With little people little deeds arise;
Among the great, the little man grows great.
See there! The cranes, the swarthy cloud,
They menace the excited crowd 7885
And they would menace thus the king.
With beaks sharp-pointed, talons fierce,
The little ones they tear and pierce;
Already doom comes thundering.
Herons had suffered impious slaughter, 7890
Standing about the tranquil water.
But from that rain of murd'rous engines
Has sprung a blessèd, bloody vengeance;
It stirs the rage of brotherhood
And lust for pygmies' impious blood. 7895
Shield, helmet, spear — how profit these?
What use to dwarfs the heron-feather?
How ant and dactyl hide together!
The host now wavers, breaks, and flees.
Anaxagoras after a pause, solemnly.
If till now subterranean I praised, 7900
In this case be my prayer to Heaven raised . . .
O Thou on high, the same eternally,
In name and form threefold supernally,
By all my people's woe I cry to Thee,
Diana, Luna, Hecate! 7905
Thou breast-expanding One, most deeply pensive One,
Thou peaceful seeming One, mighty intensive One,
Break from the glooms of Thy dark chasm clear,
And without magic let Thine ancient might appear!
Pause
Am I too quickly heard? 7910
Hath my prayer
To yonder sphere

The ordered course of Nature stirred?
And greater, ever greater, draweth near
The goddess' throne, her full-orbed sphere — 7915
To gaze upon, appalling, dire!
And ruddier, redder glows its fire . . .
No nearer! threatening orb, I pray,
Lest Thou wilt sweep us, land, and sea away!
    Thessalian witches? Can it then be true 7920
That Thee once from Thy proper path they drew,
By spells of impious magic sung,
And fatal gifts from Thee so wrenched and wrung? . . .
The brilliant shield, behold, it darkles!
And now it splits and flares and sparkles! 7925
What clattering! What hissing yonder!
And midst it what wild hurricane and thunder!
Humbly I kneel here at Thy throne!
Forgive! I have invoked it, I alone!

               He throws himself on his face

Thales.   What has this man not seen and heard! 7930
I know not rightly what occurred;
Nor yet like him have I experienced it.
They're crazy hours, let us admit.
And Luna's swaying comfortably
In her old place as formerly. 7935
Homunculus.   Look at the pygmies' seat! I vow,
The hill was round, it's pointed now.
I seemed to feel an awful shock;
Down from the moon had plunged a rock;
At once, without a question, too, 7940
Both friend and foe it squashed and slew.
High arts like these I have to praise,
Which, by some great creative might,
Working above, below, could raise
This mountain-pile in but one night. 7945
Thales.   Be calm! 'Twas but like thought in rapid flight.
Let them be gone, the nasty brood!
That you were not their king is good.
Now to the sea's glad fête let us repair.
They hope and honour rare guests there. 7950

               Exeunt

Mephistopheles climbing up on the opposite side.

[228]

Up steep rock stairways I am forced to fag me,
Through stubborn roots of ancient oak-trees drag me!
Up in my Hartz there is a resinous savour
With hints of pitch, and that enjoys my favour
Almost like brimstone . . . In this Grecian place, 7955
Of scents like these there's scarcely any trace.
I'm curious to know and would inquire
Wherewith they feed hell's torments and hell's fire.

A Dryad. At home be wise as it befits you there;
Abroad you have no cleverness to spare. 7960
Homeward you should not turn your thoughts while here;
You should the sacred oaks' high worth revere.

Mephistopheles. We think of what behind us lies;
What we were used to seems a Paradise.
But say: What cowers in the cavern there, 7965
Threefold in form and dimly lighted?

A Dryad. The Phorkyads! Approach them if you dare
And speak to them if you are not affrighted.

Mephistopheles. Why not? — I see a something and I wonder.
I must confess although it hurts my pride: 7970
The like of them I've never yet espied.
Why, worse than mandrakes, they look yonder . . .
How can the Deadly Sins then ever be
Considered ugly in the least degree
If one has seen this monstrous trinity? 7975
We would not suffer it to dwell
Upon the threshold of our grimmest hell.
Here in the land of beauty it is rooted,
The classic, antique land reputed . . .
They seem to scent me now and stir and chitter; 7980
Like vampire bats they peep and twitter.

A Phorkyad. Give me the eye, my sisters, to espy
Who to our temple dares to come so nigh.

Mephistopheles. Most honoured! I approach you, with your leave,
That I your threefold blessing may receive. 7985
I come, though as a stranger, be it stated,
Yet, if I err not, distantly related.
Gods ancient and revered I've seen ere now,
To Ops and Rhea made my deepest bow.
The Fates, your sisters too, whom Chaos bore, 7990
I saw them yesterday — or else the day before.

[229]

But others like yourselves I've never sighted,
And I stand mute, amazed, delighted!
The Phorkyads.   Intelligent this spirit seems to be.
Mephistopheles.   That no bard sings your praise amazes me.   7995
And say! How came it, how could it have been?
Your likeness, worthy ones, I've never seen!
On you the chisel should try out its art,
And not on Juno, Pallas, Venus, and that sort.
The Phorkyads.   Immersed in stillest night and solitude,   8000
We Three have never felt that thought intrude.
Mephistopheles.   How should it? Since withdrawn from earthly view,
Here you see none, nor anyone sees you.
But choose in other places to reside
Where art and splendour equally preside,   8005
Where daily in quick time from marble blocks
Heroes leap into life in flocks,
Where —
The Phorkyads.   Silence! Stir in us no longings new!
What would it profit if we better knew?
We, born in night, akin to night alone,   8010
Are almost to ourselves, to others quite, unknown.
Mephistopheles.   In such a case there is not much to say.
To others, though, one can one's self convey.
One eye, one tooth, suffices for you three,
So it would tally with mythology   8015
If into two the being of you three were blended
And your third form to me were lended
For a brief time.
One Phorkyad.   What think you? Should we try?
The Other Phorkyads.   Let's try it! But without the tooth or eye.
Mephistopheles.   Take these away? The essence then you'll take,   8020
For it's the perfect image that they make.
One Phorkyad.   Press one eye to — quite easily it's done —
And of your tusks show only one;
At once you will attain our profile meetly
And sisterly resemble us completely.   8025
Mephistopheles.   Much honour! Be it so!
The Phorkyads.   So be it!
Mephistopheles in profile like a PHORKYAD.   Done!
Here stand I, Chaos' well-belovèd son!
The Phorkyads.   Daughters of Chaos we, by undisputed right!

Mephistopheles.　　Oh, shame! They'll call me now hermaphrodite!
The Phorkyads.　　What beauty in the sisters' triad new!　　　　8030
　　We have two eyes, our teeth are two.
Mephistopheles.　　From all eyes I must hide this visage well
　　To fright the devils in the pool of Hell.
Exit

Rocky Coves of the Aegean Sea

Moon tarrying in the zenith

Sirens couched around on the cliffs, fluting and singing.

　　　　If of yore, by spells nocturnal,
　　　　Did Thessalian hags infernal　　　　　　　　　8035
　　　　Draw thee down, a crime intending,
　　　　Gaze thou where night's arch is bending
　　　　Down with calmness never-ending
　　　　On the billowy, twinkling ocean,
　　　　And illumine the commotion　　　　　　　　　8040
　　　　Rising from the billowing sea!
　　　　To thy service vowed are we,
　　　　Lovely Luna, gracious be!

Nereids and Tritons as wonders of the sea.

　　　　With a louder, shriller singing,
　　　　Through the breadth of ocean ringing,　　　　8045
　　　　Summon here the deep's gay throng!
　　　　From the cruel tempest's riot
　　　　Fled we to the deepest quiet,
　　　　Hither lured by lovely song.

　　　　Here behold us decorated　　　　　　　　　8050
　　　　With gold chains and high elated;
　　　　Crowns and jewels do ye capture,
　　　　Brooches, girdles that enrapture.
　　　　All this harvest is your prey.
　　　　To us here these shipwrecked treasures　　　8055
　　　　Ye have brought with your sweet measures,
　　　　Ye, the magnets of our bay.

Sirens.

　　　　Well we know, in cool seas biding,
　　　　How the fishes, smoothly gliding,

[231]

Joy in life, from trouble far;   8060
Yet, ye festive hosts quick moving,
We today would see you proving
That ye more than fishes are.

Nereids and Tritons.

We, before we hither wandered,
Thought of that and deeply pondered.   8065
Sisters, brothers, swiftly fare!
Needs today but little travel
Proof to show past any cavil
That we more than fishes are.

They disappear

Sirens.

Away they speed and race   8070
Straight toward Samothrace;
With kindly wind gone are they far.
What mean they to do in the eerie
Domain of the Mighty Cabiri?
They're gods, and stranger were never;   8075
They beget their like ever and ever
And never know what they are.

Linger thou on thy height,
Lovely Luna, stay thy light,
That the night may not vanish   8080
Nor the day may us banish.

Thales on the shore, to HOMUNCULUS.

To ancient Nereus I would lead the way;
We're not far distant from his cave today,
But hard and stubborn is his pate,
Contrary, sour, old reprobate.   8085
Nothing of mortal humankind
Is ever to that grumbler's mind.
The future, though, is known to him,
Wherefore men hold him in esteem
And honour him where he holds sway.   8090
Kind has he been to many a one.

Homunculus.   Let's try it then and see. Come on!
My glass and flame 'twill not cost me straightway.

Nereus.   Are they men's voices that my ear has heard?
How quick with wrath my inmost heart is stirred!   8095

[232]

These creatures would be gods by sheer endeavour,
Yet damned to be like their own selves forever.
In days of old I could divinely rest,
Yet I was oft impelled to aid the Best,
But when at last I saw what they had done, 8100
'Twas quite as if I had not counselled one.

Thales. Yet people trust you, greybeard, ocean seer;
You are the Sage; oh, drive us not from here!
Gaze on this flame, like to a man, indeed;
Your counsel only will it hear and heed. 8105

Nereus. Counsel! With men has counsel once availed?
Vain are shrewd warnings to a fast-closed ear.
Oft as their deeds proved, men have grimly failed;
Self-willed are they still as they always were.
How I warned Paris with a father's trust 8110
Before another's wife ensnared his lust!
Upon the Grecian shore he stood up bold,
And what I saw in spirit I foretold:
The reeking air above, a ruddy glow,
Rafters ablaze, murder and death below: 8115
Troy's Judgment Day, held fast in noble rhyme,
A horror famous to the end of time.
Reckless he laughed at all that I could tell;
He followed his own lust and Ilion fell —
A giant corpse, stark when its torments ceased, 8120
To Pindus' eagles a right welcome feast.
Ulysses too! Told I not him erewhiles
Of Cyclops' horrors and of Circe's wiles?
His dallying, his comrades' thoughtless vein,
And what not all — but did it bring him gain? 8125
Till, late enough, a favouring billow bore
The long-tossed wanderer to a friendly shore.

Thales. Of course such action gives a wise man pain;
Still, if he's kind, he'll try it once again.
An ounce of thanks will in its bliss outweigh, 8130
Yes, tons of thanklessness for many a day.
And nothing trifling to implore have we:
The boy here wisely wants to come to be.

Nereus. Don't spoil my rarest mood, I pray!
Far other things await me here today: 8135
My daughters all I've summoned here to me,

The Dorides, the Graces of the Sea.
Olympus not, nor yet your soil, can bear
A form that is so dainty and so fair.
From dragons of the sea, all in most winsome motion,   8140
They leap on Neptune's coursers; in the ocean,
Their element, so tenderly at home
They seem to float upon the very foam.

      On Venus' radiant, pearly chariot drawn,
Comes Galatea, lovely as the dawn.   8145
Since Cypris turned from us her face,
She reigns in Paphos in the goddess' place.
And so, long since, the gracious one doth own,
As heiress, templed town and chariot-throne.
Away! It spoils a father's hour of pleasure,   8150
Harshness of tongue or hate of heart to treasure.
Away to Proteus! Ask that wondrous elf:
How one can come to be and change one's self.
                  He goes off toward the sea

Thales.   We have gained nothing by this stay.
Though one finds Proteus, straight he melts away;   8155
And if he stops for you, he'll say at last
Things that confuse you, make you stand aghast.
But, after all, such counsel do you need;
Let's try it and pursue our path with speed.
                  They go away

Sirens above on the rocks.
        What's that far off, half hiding,   8160
        Through ocean's billows gliding?
        As if, to breezes bending,
        White sails were hither wending.
        Bright beam they over waters,
        Transfigured ocean's daughters!   8165
        Let us climb down! They're singing!
        List to the voices ringing!

Nereids and Tritons.
        What we escort and carry
        Shall make you glad and merry.
        Chelone's shield gigantic   8170
        Gleams with stern figures antic;
        They're gods whom we are bringing.
        High songs must ye be singing.

Sirens.

> Little in height,
> Potent in might   8175
> Who shipwrecked men deliver,
> Gods old and honoured ever.

Nereids and Tritons.

> We're bringing the Cabiri
> To the peaceful pageant cheery,
> For where they rule auspicious   8180
> Neptune will be propitious.

Sirens.

> We give way to you:
> With resistless power
> Ye save the perishing crew
> In dire shipwreck's hour.   8185

Nereids and Tritons.

> We have brought three only,
> The fourth one tarried lonely;
> He said he must stay yonder
> Since he for all must ponder.

Sirens.

> One god the other god   8190
> Can jeer and prod.
> Their good deeds revere ye!
> All their ill ones fear ye!

Nereids and Tritons.

> To seven ye should be praying.

Sirens.

> Where are the three delaying?   8195

Nereids and Tritons.

> For that we've no suggestion,
> But on Olympus question;
> Haply the eighth's there biding,
> Not thought-of yet, and hiding.
> In favours to us steady,   8200
> Yet are they all not ready.
>
> Peerless, unexplainable,
> Always further yearning,

[235]

>   With desire and hunger burning
>   For the unattainable.   8205

Sirens.

>   Such our ways:
>   Where power most sways,
>   Worship we raise,
>   Sunward, moonward: it pays!

Nereids and Tritons.

>   How brightly shines our fame! behold!   8210
>   Leading this pageant cheery!

Sirens.

>   The heroes of olden time
>   To such fame don't climb,
>   Where and how it unfold,
>   Although they've won the Fleece of Gold,   8215
>   Ye've won the Cabiri!
>   *Repeated in full chorus*
>   Although they've won the Fleece of Gold,
>   We! Ye! the Cabiri!
>   NEREIDS *and* TRITONS *move past*

Homunculus.   These shapeless forms I look upon,
>   As poor clay-pots I take them;   8220
>   Their hard heads wise men often run
>   Against them and there break them.

Thales.   That's just the thing that men desire;
>   The rusty coin is valued higher.

Proteus unperceived.   This pleases me, an ancient fabler!   8225
>   The odder 'tis, the respectabler.

Thales.   Where are you, Proteus?

Proteus ventriloquizing, now near, now far.   Here! and here!

Thales.   I pardon you that ancient jeer;
>   But with a friend such idle words forgo!
>   You speak from some false place, I know.   8230

Proteus as if from a distance.   Farewell!

Thales softly to HOMUNCULUS.   He is quite near. Shine brilliantly!
>   As curious as a fish is he;
>   Assume what form and place he may, be sure,
>   Flames are for him unfailing lure.

Homunculus.   At once a flood of light I'll scatter,   8235
>   Discreetly, though, for fear the glass might shatter.

Proteus in the form of a giant tortoise.

What beams so winsome, fair, and dear?

Thales concealing HOMUNCULUS.

Good! If you wish, you can observe it near.
Don't let the little effort worry you,
Appear on two feet just as humans do.   8240
It's with our will and by our courtesy
That what we now conceal, who wills may see.

Proteus in a noble form.

In clever, worldly pranks you still have skill.

Thales.   You change your form with pleasure still.

            He has uncovered HOMUNCULUS

Proteus astonished.   A radiant dwarflet! Such I never did see!   8245

Thales.   He asks advice and fain would come to be.
He has, he told me, come to earth
But half-way formed, a quite peculiar birth.
He has no lack of qualities ideal
But lacks too much the tangible and real.   8250
Till now the glass alone has given him weight;
He'd like forthwith to be incorporate.

Proteus.   You are a virgin's son, yea, verily:
You are before you ought to be!

Thales softly.   And from another angle things seem critical;   8255
He is, methinks, hermaphroditical.

Proteus.   Success must come the sooner in that case;
As soon as he arrives, all will fit into place.
But here there is not much to ponder:
Your start must be in that wide ocean yonder!   8260
There on a small scale one begins,
The smallest things is glad to swallow,
Till step by step more strength he wins
And forms himself for greater things to follow.

Homunculus.   Here stirs a soft and tender air,   8265
What fragrant freshness and what perfume rare!

Proteus.   Dearest of urchins! I believe your story.
Farther away, it grows more ravishing;
The air upon that narrow promontory
Is more ineffable, more lavishing;   8270
There, near enough, the host we'll see
Now floating hither over the sea.
Come with me there!

Thales.   I'll come along. Proceed!

Homunculus.   A threefold spirit striding — strange, indeed!

TELCHINES OF RHODES on hippocampi
and sea dragons, wielding Neptune's trident

Chorus.   The trident of Neptune we've forged which assuages   8275
   The wildest of billows when old Ocean rages.
   When in the dense cloud-banks the Thund'rer is grumbling,
   It's Neptune opposes the horrible rumbling;
   However forked lightning may flash and may glow,
   Still wave upon wave dashes up from below,   8280
   And all that between them in anguish has wallowed,
   Long hurled to and fro, by the depths all is swallowed;
   Wherefore he has lent us his sceptre today.
   Now float we contented and lightly and gay.

Sirens.

        You, to Helios dedicated,   8285
        You, to bright day consecrated,
        Greet we in this stirring hour
        When all worship Luna's power!

Telchines.   O loveliest goddess in night's dome appearing!
   The praise of thy brother with rapture art hearing.   8290
   To Rhodes ever blessèd an ear thou dost lend,
   For there doth a paean eternal ascend.
   He begins the day's course, with keen, radiant gaze,
   When finished the journey, our troop he surveys.
   The mountains, the cities, the wave, and the shore   8295
   Are lovely and bright to the god we adore.
   No mist hovers round us, and if one appear,
   A beam and a zephyr — the island is clear!
   Phoebus there sees his image in forms hundredfold,
   As giant, as youth, as the Gentle, the Bold.   8300
   We first, it was we who first nobly began
   To shape the high gods in the image of man.

Proteus.

        Oh, leave them to their boasting, singing!
        To sunbeams, holy and life-bringing,
        Dead works are but an idle jest.   8305
        They melt and mould in tireless rapture,
        And when in bronze a god they capture,
        They deem it great and swell their breast.
        What end comes to these haughty men?

[238]

Their forms of gods, so great and true, 8310
Long since an earthquake overthrew,
And they were melted down again.

All life on earth, whatever it be,
Is never aught but drudgery;
In water life has far more gain. 8315
I'll bear you to the endless main,
I, Proteus-Dolphin.
                    He transforms himself
                       Now it's done!
There where the happiest fates are leading
I'll take you on my back and speeding
I'll wed you to the ocean. On! 8320

Thales.   Yield to the worthy aspiration
    And at its source begin creation,
    Ready for life's effective plan!
    There you will move by norms unchanging;
    Through forms a thousand, myriad, ranging, 8325
    You will, in time, become a man.
                    HOMUNCULUS *mounts upon* PROTEUS-
                       DOLPHIN
Proteus.   Come, spirit, seek the realm of ocean;
    At once, unfettered every motion,
    Live here and move as you would do.
    But let not higher orders lure you, 8330
    For once a man, I can assure you,
    Then all is at an end with you.
Thales.   That's as may be; yet it's not ill
    A man's role in one's time to fill.
Proteus to THALES.   Well, one of your kind, to be sure! 8335
    For quite a while they do endure;
    For midst your pallid phantom-peers
    I've seen you now for many hundred years.
Sirens on the rocks.
                    See yon cloudlets, how they mingle
                    Round the moon, how fair a ring! 8340
                    Doves they are, with love a-tingle,
                    White as light is every wing.
                    Paphos sent them as her greeting,

[239]

Ardent, radiant, they appear,
Thus our festival completing,   8345
Fraught with rapture full and clear!

Nereus approaching THALES.
  Though night-wanderer make a pother,
  Call yon ring an apparition,
  Still we spirits take another,
  Take the only right position.   8350
  They are doves that are attending
  On my daughter's pearly car;
  Taught long since, in times afar,
  Wondrously they're hither wending.
Thales.   Since it gives a real man pleasure,   8355
  I too hold that as the best
  When a sacred, living treasure
  Finds in him a still, warm nest.
Psylli and Marsi on sea-bulls, sea-calves, and sea-rams.
  In Cyprus' rugged vaults cavernal
  By sea-god never battered,   8360
  By Seismos never shattered,
  Fanned by the zephyrs eternal,
  And, as in days long departed,
  In conscious quiet glad-hearted,
  The chariot of Cypris we've guarded,   8365
  Through murmuring night's soft vibration,
  Over waves and their lovely pulsation,
  Unseen by the new generation,
  The loveliest daughter we lead.
  Our duty we're quietly plying,   8370
  From no Eagle nor Wingèd Lion flying,
  Nor from Cross nor Moon,
  As each dwells upon its throne,
  Now swaying, now essaying,
  Driving forth and now slaying,   8375
  Harvest and towns in ashes laying.
  Thus on, with speed,
  Hither the loveliest mistress we lead.
Sirens.
        Lightly moving, hasting never,
        Round the chariot, line on line,   8380

[240]

Now ring twines with ring, to waver
In a series serpentine.
Come, ye vigorous Nereides,
Sturdy women, pleasing, wild,
Bring, ye delicate Dorides,   8385
Galatea, her mother's child:
Earnest, like the gods, a woman
Meet for immortality,
Yet like women gently human,
Of alluring charm is she.   8390

Dorides in a chorus, all mounted on dolphins, passing by NEREUS.
Light and shadow, Luna, lend us,
On this flower of youth shine clear!
To our father we present us,
Pleading bring we bridegrooms dear.
                    To NEREUS
They are boys we saved from dreaded   8395
Gnashing of the angry main;
On the reeds and mosses bedded,
Warmed we them to light again.
Here, with kisses warm and tender,
Loyal thanks must they now render;   8400
May the Good thy favour gain!

Nereus.   Great is the gain to win a twofold treasure:
    Pity to show and in the show take pleasure.
Dorides.
Father, laudst thou our endeavour,
Grant us joy deserved, in truth;   8405
Let us hold them fast forever
To the deathless breast of youth.

Nereus.   You may delight in your fair capture.
    Fashion to men the youthful crew;
Not mine to lend an endless rapture,   8410
That only Zeus can grant to you.
The wave that surges and that rocks you,
Allows to love no constant stand,
And when this fancy fades and mocks you,
Then set them quietly on land.   8415

[241]

Dorides.

> Your love, sweet boys, doth us inspire,
> Yet sadly we needs must sever;
> Eternal the troth that we desire,
> But gods will suffer it never.

The Youths.

> We're sailor-boys of gallant mood,   8420
> Pray further kindly tend us!
> We've never had a life so good,
> Nor can fate better send us.

GALATEA *approaches in her shell chariot*

Nereus.   It is you, my darling!

Galatea.   O Sire, the delight!

> Linger, ye dolphins! Entrancing the sight!   8425

Nereus.   They're gone already, they draw us apart,

> Wider and wider the circles sweep.
> What do they care for the pain of my heart?
> Would they but take me out over the deep!
> Yet only one glance is so dear   8430
> That it pays for the whole long year.

Thales.   Hail! Hail again!

> How blooms my joy amain!
> By Truth and Beauty I'm penetrated . . .
> From water first was all created!   8435
> And water is the all-sustaining!
> Ocean, continue forever thy reigning.
> If thou the clouds wert sending not,
> Wert swelling brooks expending not,
> Here and there rivers wert bending not,   8440
> And streams beginning, ending not,
> Where then were the world, the mountains, and plain?
> 'Tis thou who the freshest of life dost maintain.

Echo, chorus of all the circles.

> 'Tis thou from whom freshest of life wells again.

Nereus.   Wheeling afar, they turn apace,   8445

> No more meet us face to face;
> In lengthened chains extended,
> In circles festively blended,
> In countless companies they career.
> But Galatea's sea-shell throne   8450
> I see ever and anon.

It shines like a star
The crowd among!
My loved one beams through all the throng,
However far,   8455
Shimmers bright and clear,
Ever true and near.

Homunculus.
          In this dear water brightens
          All that my lamplet lightens,
          All wondrous fair to see.   8460

Proteus.
          This living water brightens
          Where first thy lamplet lightens
          With glorious harmony.

Nereus.   What mystery new to our wondering eyes
Do I see in the midst of these bevies arise?   8465
What flames round the sea-shell, at Galatea's feet?
Now mighty it flares up, now lovely, now sweet,
As if with love's pulsing 'twere touched and arrayed.

Thales.   Homunculus is it, by Proteus swayed. . . .
The symptoms are those of a masterful yearning,   8470
Prophetic of agonized throbbing and burning.
He'll shatter himself on the glittering throne.
See it flame, now it flashes, pours forth — it is done!

Sirens.   What marvel of fire in the billows is flashing
That sparkling against one another are crashing?   8475
It beams and hitherward wavers, and bright
All forms are aglow on the pathway of night,
And roundabout all is by fire overrun.
Now Eros be ruler who all hath begun!

          Hail, ye waves! Hail, sea unbounded,   8480
          By the holy fire surrounded!
          Water, hail! Hail, fire's glare!
          Hail to this adventure rare!

All Together.
          Hail, thou gently blowing breeze!
          Hail, earth rich in mysteries!   8485
          Hail, fire, sea, whom we adore,
          Hail, ye elements all four!

Act III

Before the Palace of Menelaus in Sparta

HELENA   PANTHALIS, *leader of the* CHORUS

HELENA *enters with a* CHORUS *of captive Trojan women*

Helena.   I, much admired and much upbraided Helena,
Come from the strand where we but now have disembarked,
Still giddy from the restless rocking of the waves   8490
Which with Poseidon's favour and the strength of Eurus bore
Us on their high reluctant backs from Phrygia's plain
Returning to our native bays and fatherland.
There on the shore with all his bravest warriors
King Menelaus knows the joy of safe return.   8495
But thou, O lofty dwelling, bid me welcome now,
Thou whom, when he came home again from Pallas' hill,
My father Tyndareus built near the slope and then
Adorned supremely, more than all of Sparta's homes,
The while, as sisters do, with Clytemnestra I —   8500
With Castor, Pollux too — grew up in happy play.
And ye, wings of the brazen portal, you I hail!
Yet wider once ye opened to greet a welcome guest
When Menelaus, one from many singled out,
Shone as a radiant bridegroom there before my gaze.   8505
Open thy wings again that I the king's behest
May faithfully fulfil as doth become the wife.
Let me go in and everything remain behind
That hitherto hath stormed about me, threatening doom.
For since, by care untroubled, I departed hence   8510
For Cytherea's fane, as sacred duty bade,
And there a robber seized me, he, the Phrygian,
Since then has happened much that mankind far and wide
So fain relate but not so fain is heard by him
Of whom the waxing legend hath a fable spun.   8515

Chorus.

        O lady glorious, do not disdain
        Honoured possession of highest estate!
        For to thee alone is the greatest boon given:
        The fame of beauty transcending all else.
        The hero's name resounds ere he comes,   ·   8520
        Hence proudly he strides,
        Yet bows at once the stubbornest man
        At the throne of Beauty, the all-conquering.

Helena.   Enough! I've sailed together with my consort here
    And now before him to his city am I sent;   8525
    But what intent he harbours, that I can not guess.
    Do I come here as wife? do I come here as queen?
    Come I as victim for the prince's bitter pain
    And for the adverse fate the Greeks endured so long?
    Conquered I am but whether captive I know not!   8530
    For truly the immortal gods ambiguously
    Ordained my fame and fate, attendants dubious
    For Beauty's person; and on this very threshold now
    They stand in gloomy threatening presence at my side.
    For rarely did my husband cast a glance at me   8535
    There in the hollow ship, nor spake he heartening word.
    As if he brooded mischief, facing me he sat.
    But now when drawing near Eurotas' deep-bayed shore
    The foremost ships scarce touched their beaks against the land
    In greeting, he spake as if by Zeus himself inspired: 8540
    "Here will my warriors in due order disembark;
    I'll muster them drawn up along the ocean-strand,
    But thou, proceed, go up Eurotas' holy stream
    Along its fruit-abounding shore, and ever on,
    Guiding the coursers on the moist, bejewelled mead,   8545
    Until what time thou comest to the beauteous plain
    Where Lacedaemon, once a wide and fruitful field,
    By solemn mountains close-engirdled, has been built.
    Then enter in the lofty-towered, princely house
    And muster me the maids whom there I left behind,   8550
    And with them summon too the wise old stewardess.
    Let her display before thee all the treasure-hoard,
    Just as my father left it and what I myself
    Since then have added to the pile in war and peace.

All wilt thou find there in due order standing, for 8555
It is the prince's privilege on coming home
That he find all in faithful keeping in his house
And each thing in its place just as he left it there.
For of himself the slave has power to alter naught."
Chorus.

> Now quicken with the glorious wealth, 8560
> The ever-increased, thine eyes and thy breast;
> For the grace of chain, the glory of crown,
> Rest in their pride and hold themselves rare;
> But enter in and challenge them all.
> They quickly will arm. 8565
> I joy in the conflict when beauty vies
> With gold and with pearls and with jewels of price.

Helena.   Thereafter followed further mandate from my lord:
"Now when thou hast reviewed in order everything,
Then take as many tripods as thou thinkst to need 8570
And vessels manifold which for the sacrifice
The priest desires when he performs the sacred rite,
The cauldrons and the bowls, the round and shallow plate;
The purest water from the holy fountain be
At hand in ewers high, and ready keep dry wood 8575
As well, that rapidly accepts and feeds the flame;
And be not wanting finally a sharpened knife.
But to thy care alone I now resign the rest."
So spake he, urging me be gone, but not a thing
That breathes with life did he, the orderer, appoint 8580
Which he, to honour the Olympians, wishes slain.
Dubious it is, but further worry I dismiss,
And let all be committed to the lofty gods
Who evermore fulfil as seemeth good to them;
Men may esteem it evil or esteem it good, 8585
But we who are but mortals must accept and bear.
Ere now full oft the sacrificing priest has raised
The heavy axe to consecrate the earth-bowed beast
And yet he could not finish it, for he was checked
By nearing foes or by an intervening god. 8590
Chorus.

> Thou canst not imagine what will come next;
> Queen, we beg, enter and be

[246]

Of good cheer.
Evil and good still come
Unexpected to mortals;   8595
Though foretold, we credit it not.
Truly, did Troy burn; truly, we saw
Death before us, shamefullest death;
And are we not here
Joined with thee, serving gladly,   8600
Seeing the dazzling sun in the heavens,
Also thee, the earth's fairest,
Gracious to us happy ones?

Helena.   Be it as it may! What may impend, me it beseems
That I at once ascend into the royal house,   8605
The long-renounced, much yearned-for, well-nigh forfeited,
Which stands again before mine eyes, I know not how.
My feet do not with so much spirit bear me up
The high steps I sped over lightly as a child.
                              Exit

Chorus.   Cast now, O sisters, ye   8610
              Captives who mourn your fate,
              All your sorrows far from you;
              Share in our mistress' joy,
              Share ye in Helena's joy,
              Who to her father's hearth and house   8615
              — True, with tardily homeward-turned
              But with so much the firmer foot —
              Draweth joyfully nearer.
                      Praise ye the ever holy,
              Happy establishing   8620
              And home-bringing Immortals!
              How the unfettered one
              Soars as on eagle-wings
              Over the roughest! while in vain
              Doth the sad captive yearningly   8625
              Over the prison's high parapets
              Spread his arms abroad and pine.
                      But a god laid hold on her,
              Her the exile,
              And from Ilion's ruins   8630
              Hither he bore her again

                         [247]

To the ancient, the newly adornèd
Father-house,
From unspeakable
Raptures and torments,   8635
Days of early youth
New-refreshed to remember.

Panthalis as leader of the CHORUS.
But now forsake ye the joy-encompassed path of song
And turn your gaze toward the portal's open wings.
Sisters, what do I see? Does not the Queen return   8640
Again to us here with swift and agitated step?
What is it, O great Queen, that here within the halls
Of this thy house, instead of greeting from thine own,
Could meet and shake thee thus? Conceal it thou canst not;
For on that brow of thine I see aversion writ,   8645
A noble anger that is battling with surprise.
Helena who has left the wings of the door open, agitated.
A vulgar fear beseemeth not the child of Zeus,
No lightly fleeting hand of terror touches her;
But that grim Fright, that from the womb of ancient Night
Rose at the first beginning and still multiform,   8650
Like glowing clouds out of the mountain's fiery throat,
Rolls upward, might make even heroes' breasts to quake.
In such appalling wise today the Stygians
Have marked my entrance to the house that I am fain
To leave this threshold often trod and wished-for long,   8655
Turning my steps away as of a guest dismissed.
But no! I have retreated hither to the light
And ye'll not drive me further, Powers, be who ye may!
I'll plan some consecration and then, purified,
May glowing hearth bid lord and mistress welcome home.   8660
Leader of the CHORUS.   Disclose, O noble lady, to thy serving-maids,
To us who aid and honour thee, what has occurred.
Helena.   What I have seen, ye too with your own eyes shall see
Unless old Night indeed has forthwith swallowed up
Her creature in the fearful depths of her dark womb.   8665
But yet that ye may know, I'll tell it you in words.
When through the sombre courtyard of the royal house
I stepped with reverence, my nearest task in mind,
I marvelled at the drear and silent corridors.

[248]

No sound of busy going to and fro fell on 8670
Mine ear, no diligent swift hasting met my gaze.
Before me there appeared no maid, no stewardess,
They who are wont to greet each stranger as a friend,
But when I now drew near to the bosom of the hearth,
Beside the tepid glimmering embers there I saw 8675
What huge, veiled form! a woman seated on the ground,
Not like to one asleep but one far lost in thought.
With sharp, commanding words I summon her to work,
Supposing her the stewardess whom there perhaps
My husband prudently had stationed ere he left; 8680
But in her mantle's folds she still sits motionless;
And only at my threat her right arm doth she move,
As if from hearth and hall she'd motion me away.
Angry I turn from her and forthwith hasten on
Toward the steps on which aloft the thalamos 8685
Rises adorned, the treasure-chamber near thereto;
But swiftly now the monster starts up from the floor,
Imperiously it bars the way to me and shows
Its haggard height, its hollow eyes bedimmed with blood,
A form so strange, such as confuses eye and mind. 8690
Yet to the winds I speak, for all in vain do words
Essay to build up forms as if they could create.
There see herself! She even ventures forth to light!
Here we are master till the lord and monarch comes.
The grisly births of night doth Phoebus, Beauty's friend, 8695
Drive far away to caverns or he binds them fast.

PHORKYAS *appears on the sill between the*
door-posts

Chorus.

Much have I lived through, although my tresses
In youthful fashion flow round my temples!
Many the horrors that I have witnessed,
Woe of dire warfare, Ilion's night 8700
When it fell.
Through the beclouded, dust-raising tumult,
Warriors crowding, I heard th' Immortals
Terribly shouting, I heard the brazen
Accents of Strife that clanged through the field 8705
Rampart-ward.
Ah, still standing were Ilion's

Ramparts then, but the glowing flames
Soon from neighbour to neighbour ran,
Hence and thence spreading out   8710
With the gust itself had made
Over the city in darkness.
      Fleeing I saw through smoke and glow
And the fluttering tongues of flame
Ghastly presences, wrathful gods,   8715
Wondrous forms, great as giants,
Striding on through sinister
Vapours illumined by fire.
      Saw I this or was it my
Mind that, anguish-torn, bodied forth   8720
Such mad confusion? I'll never say
That it was, but yet that I
See with mine eyes this horrid thing,
Certainly this I do know;
I could indeed lay hold on it,   8725
But that fear is restraining me,
From the perilous keeps me.
      Which one of Phorkys'
Daughters, then, art thou?
For to that family   8730
Thee would I liken.
Art thou perchance of those born hoary,
With but one eye and but one tooth,
Sharing them alternately,
Art thou one of the Graiae?   8735
      Darest thou, monster,
Here beside beauty
Under the eye of great
Phoebus to show thee?
Come, only step forth, notwithstanding,   8740
For the hideous sees he not,
As his holy eye has not
Yet alighted on shadow.
      But a sorrowful adverse fate
Us poor mortals doth force, alas!   8745
To the unspeakable pain of eyes
Which the detestable, ever accursed, on
Beauty's lovers doth still inflict.

Yea, then hearken, if thou darest
Meet and defy us, hear the curse, 8750
Hear the menace of each rebuke,
Out of the cursing mouths of the happy ones
Formed and fashioned by very gods.

Phorkyas.   Old is the word, yet high and true remains the sense,
That Modesty and Beauty never, hand in hand, 8755
Pursue their way along the verdant paths of earth.
Deep-rooted dwells in both of them an ancient hate,
That wheresoever on the way they chance to meet,
Each on the other turns her back in enmity.
Then each one hastens on with greater vehemence, 8760
Modesty sad but Beauty insolent of mood,
Till Orcus' hollow night at last envelops them,
Unless old age has fettered them before that time.
You find I now, ye wantons, here from foreign lands,
Your insolence outpouring, like a flight of cranes 8765
Proceeding high overhead with hoarse and shrilling screams,
A drawn-out cloud that earthward sends its croaking tones,
Which lure the quiet wanderer to lift his gaze
And look at them; but they fly onward on their way,
He goes on his, and so with us too will it be. 8770
        Who are ye then, that round the high house of the king
Like Maenads wild or like Bacchantes dare to rave?
Who are ye then to meet the house's stewardess
With howling as a pack of dogs howls at the moon?
Dream ye 'tis hidden from me of what race ye are, 8775
Thou callow, war-begotten, slaughter-nurtured brood?
Man-crazy, thou, seducing as thou art seduced,
Wasting the strength of warrior and of burgher too.
To see you in your crowd, a swarm of locusts seems
To have swooped down, hiding the verdant harvest-field. 8780
Devourers, ye, of others' toil! Ye parasites,
Destroyers, in the bud, of all prosperity,
Thou ravished merchandise, bartered and marketed!
Helena.   Who in the presence of the mistress chides the maids,
Doth boldly overstep the mistress' household right; 8785
For her alone 'tis meet to praise the laudable
As it is hers to punish what there is to blame.
And I am well contented with the service that

They rendered when the lofty power of Ilion
Beleaguered stood and fell and lay, and not the less   8790
When on our erring course the grievous, changeful woe
We bore, where commonly each thinks but of himself.
Here also I expect the like from this blithe throng;
Not what the slave is, asks the lord, but how he serves.
Therefore be silent, grin and jeer at them no more.   8795
Hast thou the palace of the king kept well till now,
In place of mistress, to thy credit shall it stand;
But now that she has come in person, step thou back
Lest punishment be thine, not merited reward.

Phorkyas.   To threaten her domestics doth remain the right   8800
The which the heaven-blest ruler's lofty consort earned
Indeed through many a year of prudent governance.
Since thou, now recognized, dost tread thine ancient place
Anew and once again as mistress and as Queen,
Lay hold upon the reins long-slackened, govern now,   8805
Take in thy keep the treasure, all of us thereto.
But first of all protect me now, the older one,
Against this crowd that by thy swan-like beauty are
Only a meanly-wingèd lot of cackling geese.

Leader of the CHORUS.   How ugly, near to beauty, ugliness appears!   8810
Phorkyas.   How senseless, near to wisdom, seems the want of sense!

> *From here on, members of the* CHORUS *respond in turn, stepping forth singly from the* CHORUS

The First Chorister.   Of Father Erebus tell us, tell us of Mother Night!
Phorkyas.   Then speak of Scylla, thine own flesh's kith and kin!
The Second Chorister.
There's many a monstrous shoot on thine ancestral tree.
Phorkyas.   Away to Orcus! There seek out thy kindred tribe!   8815
The Third Chorister.
They who dwell there, in sooth, are far too young for thee.
Phorkyas.   Go to Tiresias the Old, make love to him!
The Fourth Chorister.
Great-great-granddaughter to thee was Orion's nurse.
Phorkyas.   Harpies, I fancy, fed thee up on filthiness.
The Fifth Chorister.
With what dost nourish thou such cherished meagreness?   8820
Phorkyas.   'Tis not with blood for which thou all too lustful art!
The Sixth Chorister.   Greedy for corpses, thou, a loathsome corpse thyself!

Phorkyas. The teeth of vampires glitter in thy shameless maw.
Leader of the CHORUS. That maw of thine I'll stop if I say who thou art.
Phorkyas. First do thou name thyself! The riddle then is solved. 8825
Helena. Not angry but in sorrow I step in between,
Forbidding all such turbulent alternate strife!
For naught more harmful can befall the ruling lord
Than faithful servants' secret festering dispute.
The echo of his commands returneth then no more 8830
To him in swift accomplished deed accordingly.
No! roaring wilfully around him raves the storm
While he, himself bewildered, chides, but all in vain.
Not this alone! Ye have in wrath unmannerly
Evoked the dreadful figures of unhallowed forms 8835
Which crowd around me till I feel me torn away
To Orcus in despite of these my native fields.
Is it memory? Was it delusion seized on me?
Was I all that? and am? shall I in future be
The phantom horrible of town-destroying men? 8840
The maidens shudder, but the eldest, thou, I see,
Dost stand unmoved. Speak to me then some word of sense!
Phorkyas. Who many years of fortune manifold recalls,
To him divinest favour seems at last a dream.
But thou, so highly favoured, past all bound and aim, 8845
Sawst midst the living only men inflamed by love,
Quick kindled to each kind of boldest enterprise.
Thus Theseus, roused by greed, laid hands upon thee first,
A man of glorious form, as strong as Heracles.
Helena. He bore me off, a ten-year-old and slender roe, 8850
And shut me in Aphidnus' tower in Attica.
Phorkyas. But then by Castor and by Pollux soon released,
Thou wert engirt by chosen heroes courting thee.
Helena. Yet most my secret favour — as I own with joy —
Patroclus won; he was Pelides' counterpart. 8855
Phorkyas. Thy father wedded thee to Menelaus, though,
The bold sea-rover and sustainer of his house.
Helena. To him he gave his daughter, gave the kingdom's sway,
And from our marriage union sprang Hermione.
Phorkyas. But whilst afar he wrested heritage in Crete, 8860
To thee, left solitary, came too fair a guest.
Helena. Wherefore recall that time of semi-widowhood?
And hideous ruin that sprang out of it for me?

Phorkyas.   That voyage for me too, a free-born maid of Crete,
   Brought hateful capture, brought me lasting slavery.   8865
Helena.   At once he did install thee here as stewardess,
   Entrusting much, castle and treasure boldly won.
Phorkyas.   Which thou forsookst, turning to Ilion's tower-girt town,
   Lured by the joys of love, the inexhaustible.
Helena.   Remind me not of joyance! An infinity   8870
   Of all too bitter woe perfused my breast and brain.
Phorkyas.   Yet men say thou appeardst a phantom duplicate,
   In Ilion beheld, in Egypt too wert seen.
Helena.   Confuse not wholly my distraught and clouded mind.
   Here even, who I am indeed, I do not know.   8875
Phorkyas.   And, then, they say: from out the hollow realm of shades
   Achilles, fired by passion, joined himself to thee!
   Who earlier loved thee spite of all decrees of fate.
Helena.   To him the phantom I a phantom bound myself.
   It was a dream, indeed the words themselves say so.   8880
   I vanish hence, become a phantom to myself.
                    Sinks into the arms of half of the CHORUS
Chorus.
         Silence, silence!
      False seeing one, false speaking one, thou!
      From such horrible, single-toothed mouth,
      What will breathe forth from it,   8885
      Such a fearful and loathsome gorge?
            For the malignant, benevolent appearing,
      Wolfish wrath under sheep's woolly fleece,
      To me is more terrible far than Hell's
      Three-headed monster's gullet.   8890
      Anxious, watching, we stand here,
      When, how, where will it break forth,
      Lurking monster,
      Lurking deeply with malice so great?
            Well, then, instead of word freighted with comfort,   8895
      Lethe-sprinkling, most mild, friendly and fair,
      Stirrest thou up more of the past's worst ills
      Than of the good we suffered,
      And thou darken'st at once
      Both the present moment's sheen   8900
      And the future's
      Kindly glimmering light of hope.

[254]

      Silence, silence!
That the soul of our lady,
Even now ready to flee,   8905
Still may hold fast, hold firmly
Loveliest form, the form of all forms,
On which the sunlight ever has shone.

                  HELENA *has revived and again stands in the*
                  centre

Phorkyas.
   From the floating clouds move forward now, high sun of this bright day,
   When veiled, thou didst us enrapture; blinding now in splendour reign!   8910
   As the world looks bright before thee, dost thou look with lovely gaze.
   Though as ugly they revile me, well I know the beautiful.

Helena.   Tottering from out the void which in my swoon engirdled me,
   Gladly would I rest again, for so weary are my limbs;
   But for queens it is becoming — yea, all men it doth become —   8915
   To compose one's self, take courage, whatsoever threat astound.

Phorkyas.   Standing in thy greatness, in thy beauty here and now,
   If thy glance says thou commandest, what dost thou command? Declare!

Helena.
   For your strife's neglect disgraceful be prepared to make amends;
   Haste a sacrifice to order as the king commanded me.   8920

Phorkyas.   In the house is all now ready: bowl and tripod, sharpened axe,
   For the sprinkling, for the incense; show the destined sacrifice.

Helena.   That the king did not determine.

Phorkyas.   Spake it not? Oh, word of woe!

Helena.   What the woe that overcomes thee?

Phorkyas.   Queen, it is thyself art meant.

Helena.   I?

Phorkyas.   And these.

Chorus.   Oh, woe and sorrow!

Phorkyas.   Thou wilt fall beneath the axe.   8925

Helena.   Frightful! yet foreboded! Ah, me!

Phorkyas.   Unavoidable it seems.

Chorus.   Ah! and us? What will befall us?

Phorkyas.   She will die a noble death;
   But within from lofty rafters which support the gabled roof,
   Like the thrushes in a bird-trap, ye shall dangle in a row.

                  HELENA *and the* CHORUS *stand, astounded*
                  and frightened, in a significant, well-arranged
                  group

Phorkyas.

Phantoms! . . . Like forms grown rigid are ye standing there,   8930
Fearing to quit the life to which ye have no claim.
Men likewise — all of them are phantoms just as ye —
Renounce not willingly the glorious shining sun.
Yet no one begs them free or saves them from the end.
All know it well, and nevertheless it pleases few.   8935
Enough, ye all are lost! So quickly to the work!

> PHORKYAS *claps her hands; thereupon*
> *masked dwarfish figures appear at the door who*
> *execute at once and with alacrity the commands*
> *which* PHORKYAS *utters*

Hither, thou swarthy, roly-poly, goblin throng,
Trundle along, there's harm to do here as one will.
The altar, golden-horned, bring forth and give it place,
And let the glittering axe lie on the silver rim;   8940
Fill all the water-jugs that one can wash away
The black gore's horrible, polluting blemishment.
Spread out the carpet sumptuously here in the dust
That so the victim may kneel down in royal wise
And in it wrapped at once, although with severed head,   8945
May still be sepulchred with fitting dignity.

Leader of the CHORUS.

The Queen, absorbed in thought, is standing at one side,
The maidens wither like to new-mown meadow grass;
Methinks that I, the eldest, by sacred duty bound,
Should speak a word with thee, thou primal eldest one.   8950
Thou art experienced, wise, seem'st well disposed to us,
Although this brainless troop, misjudging, struck at thee.
Say, then, what rescue thou mayst know as possible.

Phorkyas.   'Tis easy said! Upon the queen alone it rests
If she will save herself, you adjuncts too with her.   8955
Determination's needful and the speediest.

Chorus.   Most revered of all the Parcae, wisest of the sibyls, thou,
Hold the golden shears wide open, then proclaim us life and health;
For we feel our precious limbs already swinging, swaying, dangling
Undelightfully, for they in dancing rather would delight them,   8960
Resting then on lover's breast.

Helena.   Let these be anxious! Pain I feel but naught of fear;
But if thou know'st of rescue, grateful be 't received.
For to the wise, far-seeing, oft in very truth

[256]

Impossible still seems possible. Then speak, say on!   8965
Chorus.   Speak and tell us, tell us quickly: how we may escape the awful,
Odious nooses that so threaten as the very vilest necklace,
Drawing round our throats. Now in advance we feel it, we poor victims,
Feel the choking, stifling, unless thou, O Rhea, lofty mother
Of all gods, hast pity on us.   8970
Phorkyas.   Have ye the patience silently to hear my whole,
Long-drawn-out discourse? It involves tales manifold.
Chorus.   Patience enough! The while we listen we still live.
Phorkyas.   If one remains at home and noble treasure guards
And knows how to cement the lofty dwelling's walls   8975
And to secure the roof against the pressing rain,
It will go well with him all his long days of life;
But he who over his threshold's sacred limits steps
With light and fleeting foot in buoyant wantonness,
Will find indeed on his return the ancient place   8980
But all things changed about, if they're not quite destroyed.
Helena.   Whereto the like of such familiar sayings here?
Thou wouldst narrate, so stir not up what gives offence!
Phorkyas.   It is historical, by no means a reproach.
A corsair, Menelaus steered from bay to bay;   8985
The shores and islands all he skirted as a foe,
Returning with the spoils that in his house abound.
Besieging Ilion, he then passed ten long years;
How many on the voyage home I do not know.
But how stand matters here with the exalted house   8990
Of Tyndareus? How stand they roundabout the realm?
Helena.   So thoroughly incarnate in thee is abuse
That not a lip of thine can stir without rebuke?
Phorkyas.   Full many years forsaken stood the valleyed hills
Which northward back of Sparta rise into the sky,   8995
Taygetus in the rear whence as a merry brook
Eurotas tumbles down and then along our vale
By reed-beds broadly flowing nourishes your swans.
Remote and still in mountain-vale a valiant race
Has settled, pressing hither from Cimmerian night,   9000
And piled a towering stronghold insurmountable.
From there they pester land and people as they please.
Helena.   Could they accomplish this? It seems impossible.
Phorkyas.   They had the time, perhaps 'twas nearly twenty years.
Helena.   Is one the lord? and are they many robbers? leagued?   9005

[257]

Phorkyas.   They are not robbers and yet one of them is lord.
I blame him not and though he persecuted me.
Well could he all have taken but contented him
With few things which he called not tribute but free gifts.
Helena.   How does he look?
Phorkyas.   Not ill! I like his looks full well.   9010
He is a man who's cheery, bold, of well-built form,
A man of sense such as are few among the Greeks.
Men brand these people as barbarians, yet methinks
Not one so cruel, not so like a cannibal
As many a hero proved himself at Ilion.   9015
His greatness I respect, I'd trust myself to him.
His castle too! With your own eyes ye should see that!
It is quite different from the clumsy masonry
Which your forefathers loosely piled up heedlessly,
Cyclopean like the Cyclops, hurling undressed stone,   9020
One on the other. There, contrariwise, ah, there!
The work is level, plumb, according to a rule.
Gaze at it from outside! It strives aloft toward heaven,
All rigid, all well-joined, and mirror-smooth like steel!
To climb there — why, the very thought slides down!   9025
And inside are great courts and roomy spaces girt
By structures roundabout of every kind and use.
There ye see arches, archlets, pillars, pillarets,
Balconies, galleries for gazing out and in,
And scutcheons.
Chorus.   What are scutcheons?
Phorkyas.   Ajax used to bear   9030
A coiling serpent on his shield, as ye have seen.
The Seven against Thebes, each one upon his shield,
A pictured emblem bore, rich in significance.
One saw there moon and stars in heaven's nocturnal field,
A goddess, hero, ladder, swords, and torches too,   9035
And all that fiercely threats good towns with violence.
Such emblems are borne also by our hero-band,
Aglow with colour, heritage from primal sires.
There ye see lions, eagles, also claw and beak,
Then horns of buffaloes, wings, roses, peacocks' tails,   9040
Bars also, gold and black and silver, blue and red.
The like of these hangs there in halls, row after row,
In long, unending halls, wide as the world is wide.

[258]

There ye can dance!

Chorus.   Oh, say, are dancers also there?

Phorkyas.   The best! a blooming troop of boys with golden locks,   9045
Fragrant with youth, so fragrant only Paris was
When he approached too near the Queen.

Helena.   Thou fallest quite
Outside thy role! Come, tell me now the final word!

Phorkyas.   Speak thou that word, say plainly and in earnest: "Yes!"
Then with that castle I'll encompass thee at once.   9050

Chorus.   Oh, speak that little word and save thyself with us!

Helena.   What? Must I fear King Menelaus will transgress
In ways so horrible and do me so much wrong?

Phorkyas.   Hast thou forgot how thy Deïphobus he maimed,
Brother of war-slain Paris? In unheard-of ways   9055
He maimed him who for thee, when a widow, stubborn fought
And happily won as mistress. Nose and ears he lopped
And mangled him still worse: a horror to behold.

Helena.   That did he unto him; for my sake did he that.

Phorkyas.   And he will do the same to thee because of him.   9060
Beauty can not be shared; who has possessed it quite,
Destroys it rather, cursing all part ownership.

            Trumpets at a distance; the Chorus
               shudders

Just as shrill trumpets' blare lays hold with rending might
On ears and bowels, jealousy doth clinch its claws
Within the bosom of a man forgetting not   9065
What once he has owned and now has lost and owns no more.

Chorus.

Hear'st thou not the horn resounding? Dost not see the weapons flash?

Phorkyas.   Be thou welcome, lord and monarch, gladly give I reckoning.

Chorus.   Ah, but we?

Phorkyas.   Ye know it well, before your eyes ye'll see her death.
Mark, your own will be within there. No, there is no help for you.   9070

            Pause

Helena.   I have thought out what first I dare to venture on.
Thou art a hostile daemon, this I feel full well
And fear that into evil thou wilt turn the good.
But first to yonder castle I will follow thee.
The rest I know; but what thereby in her deep breast   9075
The Queen mysteriously may hide, be that for each
A secret inaccessible. On, Ancient, lead!

Chorus.

Oh, how glad do we go hence,
Hast'ning our footsteps,
Death in our rear, 9080
And before us again
A towering stronghold's
Inaccessible ramparts.
Grant they may shelter as well
As once did Ilion's walls, 9085
Which fell down at last
Through contemptible craft alone!
    Mists spread out, veil the background and now
    the foreground at pleasure
How is this? How?
Sisters, gaze around!
Was not serene sunlight here? 9090
Drifts of cloud are swaying aloft
From Eurotas' sacred stream;
Vanished has the beautiful
Reed-engarlanded shore from our sight,
And the swans gliding on 9095
Freely, gracefully, proudly,
Swimming glad together,
Ah, I see them no more!
    Still, though, yes, still
Crying I hear them, 9100
Crying afar their hoarse cry!
Death presaging, so mortals say;
Ah, that only to us too,
Instead of promised salvation's weal,
Doom at last it proclaim not to us, 9105
Doom to us swan-like maids,
Fair, white-throated ones, and ah!
To her, our swan-begotten!
Woe to us, woe! woe!
    All is covered and hid 9110
Roundabout in the mist.
We can see each other no more!
What befalls? Do we move?
Float we only,
Footing uncertainly on the ground? 9115

See'st thou naught? Wings not haply e'en
Hermes ahead? Gleams not his golden wand
Waving, commanding us backward again
To the unenjoyable, grey-glimmering,
With impalpable phantoms teeming,   9120
Over-crowded, ever empty Hades?

Yes, 'tis growing darker swiftly; lifts the mist but leaves no sunlight,
Darkly-greyish, brown as walls are. Walls encounter our free vision,
Standing stark against our seeing. Is it a court? Is it a dungeon?
Horrible in any case! Sisters, alas, we are imprisoned,   9125
Prisoned as we ever were.

The Inner Court of the Castle

surrounded by rich, fantastic buildings of the Middle Ages

Leader of the CHORUS.   Impetuous and foolish, perfect woman-type!
　　Dependent on the moment, sport of every breeze
　　Of good and evil fortune, neither this nor that
　　Can ye with calmness bear. One always contradicts   9130
　　The other fiercely, and crosswise the others her;
　　In joy and pain alone ye howl and laugh alike.
　　Now hush! and waiting hearken what the mistress may,
　　High-spirited, resolve both for herself and us.
Helena.   Where art thou, Pythoness? Whatever be thy name,   9135
　　Come from the vaulted chambers of this gloomy keep.
　　If haply thou art gone to the wondrous hero-lord,
　　Announcing me, preparing fit reception thus,
　　Then take my thanks and lead me speedily to him;
　　I wish an end of wandering. Rest alone I wish.   9140
Leader of the CHORUS.
　　In vain, O Queen, thou lookst around on every side;
　　That sorry form has vanished, has remained perhaps
　　There in the mist from out whose bosom hitherward
　　We came, I know not how, but swift and treading not.
　　Perhaps she too in doubt strays in this labyrinth   9145
　　Of many castles strangely mingled into one,
　　Seeking the lord that he may princely welcome thee.
　　But see up there a crowd of servants stirring now

In corridors, past windows, and in wide doorways,
Hast'ning in ready service, swiftly, to and fro: 9150
A portent of distinguished welcome for a guest.

Chorus.

    My heart is exalted! See, oh, see there
    How so modestly downward with lingering step
    The fairest of youths becomingly move
    In appointed procession. At whose command   9155
    Can appear, so well-taught and so fitly arrayed,
    Of youthful squires this glorious troop?
    What most do I admire? The delicate gait,
    Perhaps the curling hair round the dazzling white brow,
    Perhaps the pair of cheeks like the red of the peach   9160
    And clad like the peach with soft, fleecy down?
    I gladly would bite them but shudder in fear,
    For in similar case was the mouth all filled up —
    Oh, horrible tale! — with ashes.

        And now the fairest   9165
        Are coming along;
        What is it they bear?
        Steps for a throne,
        Carpet and seat,
        Hangings and tent —   9170
        Similar gear;
        Now it rolls over,
        Wreathing cloud-like festoons
        Round the head of our Queen,
        Who now, invited,   9175
        Has climbed to the glorious couch.
        Forward advance,
        Step upon step, stand
        Gravely aligned.
        Worthy, oh, worthy, threefold worthy   9180
        Of her may such a welcome be blessed!

            All that the CHORUS *describes occurs by*
            degrees

FAUST

After the boys and squires have descended in a
long procession, FAUST *appears above on the*

[262]

staircase in the knightly court costume of the Middle Ages; he descends slowly and with dignity

Leader of the CHORUS *observing him attentively.*

If to this man the gods have not, as oft they do,
Lent only for a brief time admirable form,
His amiable presence, his exalted mien,
All transitory, then will he ever succeed   9185
In what he undertakes, be it in fights with men
Or in the little war with fairest women waged.
Indeed to many others he may be preferred,
Others whom high-esteemed I've seen with mine own eyes.
With slowly solemn step restrained by reverence   9190
I see the prince approaching. Turn and see, O Queen!

Faust approaching with a fettered man at his side.

In lieu of solemn greeting, as were fitting,
In lieu of reverent welcome, I bring thee
This servant fettered fast in manacles,
Whose slight of duty made me slight mine own.   9195
Before this noble lady kneel thou down,
To make confession and avow thy guilt.
Exalted mistress, here thou seest the man
Of vision rare who on the lofty tower
Was placed to gaze around, there to survey   9200
Keenly the firmament and earth's expanse,
If here and there perchance aught may appear,
Descending by the hill-encircled vale
To our firm castle, be it billowing herds,
Perhaps a marching host; those we protect,   9205
Meet these in fight. Today, what negligence!
Thou comest, he reports it not, we fail
To greet most duly and most honourably
So great a guest. His life he wantonly
Has forfeited, should lie now in the blood   9210
Of well-deservèd death; but thou alone
Mayst punish or mayst pardon, as thou wilt.

Helena.   High is the honour that thou grantest me,
As judge, as ruler, and although it were
To test me merely, as I may suspect,   9215
Still, now the judge's foremost duty I
Will do, to give the accused a hearing. Speak!

[263]

Lynceus, the warder of the tower.

> Let me kneel and gaze upon her,
> Let me live or let me perish,
> Since my all I only cherish   9220
> For this god-sent lady's honour.
>   Waiting for the bliss of morning,
> Spying eastward its first glows,
> Lo! the sun, without a warning,
> Wondrous in the south arose.   9225
>   Thither did it draw my glances
> Off from gorge and mountain-cone,
> Off from earth's and heaven's expanses,
> Her to see, the Only One.
>   Piercing sight to me is given   9230
> As to lynx on highest tree,
> Yet I had to struggle, even
> As from dream's obscurity.
>   Could I the delusion banish?
> Ramparts? tower? or bolted gate?   9235
> Vapours rise and vapours vanish,
> Such a goddess comes in state!
>   Eye and bosom I turned to her,
> Drinking in her gentle light;
> Beauty, blinding all that view her,   9240
> Blinded my poor senses quite.
>   I forgot the warder's duty
> And the horn I swore to wind.
> Threaten to destroy me! Beauty
> Doth all anger ever bind.   9245

Helena.   The ill that I occasioned I dare not
> To punish. Woe is me! That fate austere
> Pursues me, everywhere the breasts of men
> So to infatuate that they themselves
> Spare not nor aught else worthy. Ravishing,   9250
> Seducing, fighting, harrying hither, thither,
> Demigods, heroes, gods, aye, demons also,
> To and fro they led me ever wandering.
> My first estate confused the world, my second
> The more, my third and fourth bring woe on woe.   9255
> Remove this good man, let him now go free;

Let no disgrace befall the god-befooled!
Faust.   Astonished, I behold alike, O Queen,
The unerring archer and the stricken one;
I see the bow which hath the arrow sped   9260
That wounded him. Arrows on arrows fly,
Me do they smite. Criss-cross through keep and court
I feel their feathered whirring everywhere.
What am I now? The faithfulest thou mak'st
At once rebellious to me, insecure   9265
My walls. And so my army, I fear now,
Obeys the conquering, unconquered Queen.
What else remains save that I give to thee
Myself and all that I have fancied mine?
Freely and truly let me at thy feet   9270
Acknowledge thee as Queen who by her coming
Acquired at once possession and a throne.
Lynceus with a chest and men who carry chests after him.
              O Queen, thou see'st me back again!
        The rich man begs one glance's gain;
        Poor as a beggar feeleth he   9275
        And princely rich when he sees thee.
              What was I erst? and what now too?
        What is to wish for? what to do?
        What use is sharpest flash of eyes!
        Back from thy throne it bounding flies.   9280
              Out of the East we hither pressed
        And all was over with the West;
        A people far and wide were massed,
        The foremost knew not of the last.
              The first man fell, the second stood,   9285
        The third man's lance was prompt and good;
        Each one was backed a hundredfold,
        Thousands, unmarked, lay slain and cold.
              We crowded on, stormed on apace,
        Masters were we from place to place;   9290
        Where for the day I held control
        Tomorrow another robbed and stole.
              We looked — and hurried was the look;
        The fairest woman one man took,
        And one the steer both firm and strong,   9295
        And every horse must come along,

[265]

But I delighted to espy
The things most rare to human eye,
And what another man possessed,
For me was dried-up grass at best.   9300
    Upon the trail of treasures bright,
I followed only my keen sight;
At every pocket I peeped in,
Transparent was each box and bin.
    And heaps of gold I made my own,   9305
And many a lordly precious stone.
Now on thy breast the emerald green
Alone is worthy to be seen.
    Now swaying twixt thy lip and ear
Let ocean's oval pearl appear;   9310
Rubies would all their radiance lose
Beside thy glowing cheek's bright hues.
    The treasure greatest and most rare
Before thy presence I lay here;
And to thy feet is brought today   9315
The fruit of many a bloody fray.
    As many chests as here I bore,
Of iron chests I have yet more;
Admit me to thy train, I will
Thy vaults with every treasure fill.   9320
    For scarce dost thou the throne ascend,
Ere now they bow, ere now they bend,
Intelligence and wealth and power,
Before thy peerless form and flower.
    Firmly I held all this as mine,   9325
But now it's free and it is thine;
'Twas precious, sterling, vast, I thought,
But now I see that it was naught.
    Vanished is what I once possessed.
A mown and withered grass at best;   9330
Oh, with one happy glance but deign
To give it all its worth again!

Faust.   Quickly remove the burden boldly won,
    Indeed not censured but without reward.
    Already all is hers that in its depths   9335

[266]

The castle hides; to offer her aught special
Is useless. Go, pile treasure upon treasure
In order fit. Set up the stately show
Of splendour yet unseen! And let the vaults
Glitter like new-born firmaments, prepare   9340
New paradises filled with lifeless life.
Hastening before her steps let flowered rug
On rug unroll; thus may her every tread
Meet kindly footing, may her gaze alight
On splendour blinding all but the divine.   9345

Lynceus.

        Easy are the lord's commands,
        Child's-play to the servant's hands:
        Beauty in such fair excess
        Rules all wealth, rules blood no less.
        All the army now is tame,   9350
        All the swords are blunt and lame.
        By this glorious form, behold!
        Even the sun seems faint and cold.
        By this wealth of loveliness
        All is empty nothingness.   9355

             Exit

Helena to FAUST.   I wish to speak to thee; up to my side
   Hither I bid thee come! The empty place
   Calls to its lord and thus makes mine secure.
Faust.   First kneeling, let my true devotion gain
   Thy favour, lofty lady; let me kiss   9360
   The gracious hand that lifts me to thy side.
   Confirm me as co-regent of thy realm
   Whose bounds are limitless; win for thyself
   Adorer, servant, guardian, all in one.
Helena.   Manifold marvels do I see and hear.   9365
   Amazement strikes me, I would fain ask much,
   But first I'd ask to know why that man's speech
   Sounded so new and strange, strange and yet friendly.
   It seems that one tone makes way for another,
   And hath a word grown friendly to the ear,   9370
   Another woos caressingly the first.
Faust.   If thou art pleased with this our people's speech,
   Oh, surely then its song will ravish thee,

[267]

Fill ears and mind alike with deep content.
But best it were to practise it straightway,   9375
Alternate speech allures it, calls it forth.
Helena.   Then tell me how to learn such lovely speech.
Faust.   It's easy, quite, if from the heart it come.
And when the breast with longing overflow,
One looks around and asks —
Helena.   Who shares the glow.   9380
Faust.   The soul looks not ahead in hours like this,
Nor back; the present only —
Helena.   Is our bliss.
Faust.   It is a pledge, great gain, possession grand;
What confirmation has it?
Helena.   This, my hand.
Chorus.

      Who would think to blame our princess   9385
If she grants the castle's lord
Friendly show of favour?
For confess, we all of us are
Captives, aye, as oft already
Since the infamous overthrow   9390
Of Ilion and the agonizing
Labyrinthian woeful journey.
      Women, used to men's affection,
Are not choosers, yet they are
Well-informed and knowing,   9395
And to golden-haired shepherds
Or else to fauns with black bristles,
As occasion may bring about,
Over their fair rounded members
Fully grant they an equal right.   9400
      Near and nearer they're sitting now,
Leaning one on the other,
Shoulder to shoulder, knee to knee,
Hand in hand, cradle they them
Over the throne's   9405
Richly cushioned magnificence.
Now no scruples has majesty
In its revealing
All its intimate pleasures
Thus before all the eyes of the people.   9410

Helena.   I feel so far away and yet so near
    And all too glad I say: Here am I! Here!
Faust.   I scarcely breathe, words tremble, check their pace;
    It is a dream, vanished are time and place.
Helena.   I feel I'm lived-out sheer, and yet so new,   9415
    Blent with thee here, to thee, the unknown, true.
Faust.   Probe not the dower of this rare destiny;
    Though life's but an hour, our duty's still to *be.*
Phorkyas entering hastily.

                Spell love's primer through, enjoying
                Lovesick brewing, cooing, toying;   9420
                Brew and coo on, idle, cloying,
                Yet for that 'tis not the day.
                Feel ye not a dull storm growing?
                Hearken to the trumpet's blowing!
                Ruin is not far away.   9425
                Menelaus hither urges
                All his host in mighty surges.
                Arm ye for a bitter fray!
                By the victor's host entangled,
                As Deïphobus was mangled,   9430
                For this gallantry thou'lt pay.
                When this trash hangs on a halter,
                Straight she'll die upon the altar,
                To the sharpened axe a prey.

Faust.   Bold interruption! Odious it presses in;   9435
    In danger itself I can't stand senseless violence.
    Ill-message uglifies the fairest messenger;
    Only bad messages bringst, ugliest, thou with joy.
    But this time thou shalt not succeed. With empty breath
    Go, shatter thou the air. There is no danger here,   9440
    And even danger itself would seem an idle threat.
                Signals, explosions from the towers, trumpets
                and cornets. Martial music, a powerful armed
                force marches past
Faust.

                No, heroes heart-united ever
                Forthwith assembled thou shalt see;
                He only merits women's favour
                Who can protect them valiantly.   9445

To the leaders of the army who detach them-
selves from their columns and step forward

With bated, silent fury's power,
Sure pledge of victory to come,
Ye, of the North the budding flower,
Ye, of the East the mighty bloom,
  In steel encased, light round them breaking,   9450
Hosts that crushed realm on realm at will,
They come, the very earth is shaking,
They stride along, it thunders still.
  We came to Pylos, there we landed,
The agèd Nestor is no more,   9455
And all the kinglets thither banded
Our free hosts routed on the shore.
  Back from these walls with voice of thunder
Drive Menelaus to the sea;
There let him rove, waylay, and plunder;   9460
It was his wish and destiny.
  I hail you dukes as forth ye sally,
Such the command of Sparta's Queen;
Now at her feet lay hill and valley,
And yours be all the realm ye win.   9465
  Thine, German! be to stand defending
At wall and rampart Corinth's bay.
Achaea's hundred vales unending
I bid thee, Goth, to hold and sway.
  Toward Elis, march, ye Frankish legions,   9470
Messenia be the Saxons' gain,
Ye Normans, clear the ocean's regions
And great make Argolis again.
  Then each, within his walls abiding,
Will be prepared the foe to meet;   9475
Sparta, over you all presiding,
Shall be the Queen's ancestral seat.
  She'll see you one and all retrieving
The land whose weal no want can blight,
Ye at her feet, assured, receiving   9480
Authority and law and light.

> F A U S T *descends, the princes form a circle*
> *around him in order to hear better his com-*
> *mands and instructions*

[270]

Chorus.

Who the fairest one coveteth,
Be before all things able
And let him weapons prudently seek.
Flattering he may win indeed   9485
What all the earth holds highest;
But in peace possesseth he not.
Crafty rogues will entice her from him,
Robbers boldly will snatch her from him;
This to prevent let him be on his guard.   9490
Therefore do I praise our prince,
Prize him higher than others,
That he, so wise and brave, drew allies
And the mighty, obeying, stand
Waiting his every signal.   9495
Faithfully they fulfil his hest,
Each for himself, for his own gain
And the ruler's enguerdoning thanks,
Both winning thus the supreme meed of fame.
For who will now ravish her   9500
From the mighty possessor?
His is she, to him granted be she,
Granted twofold by us whom he
Gathered to her, safe within sheltering walls,
Guarded without by a mighty host.   9505

Faust.

Gifts have I granted, great and glorious,
To each of these a goodly land,
Let them march on, through war victorious,
Here in the midst we take our stand.
And they in rivalry protect thee,   9510
Half-island, lapped by dancing main,
While slender, fair, green hills connect thee
With the last link of Europe's mountain-chain.
This land, the land of lands, forever
May it be blessed to every race,   9515
Won for my Queen's enduring favour.
It early gazed upon her face,
When from the shell she burst and gleaming
Rose mid Eurotas' reedy sighs,
On mother, brother, sister beaming   9520

[271]

With light that overcame the eyes.
  This land presents its choicest flower
To thee, it turns to thee alone;
From all the world which owns thy power,
Oh, choose thy fatherland, thine own!   9525
  And even if the jaggèd peak uprearing
Doth on its back the sun's cold arrow bear,
We see a green tinge on the rock appearing;
The wild goat nibbling crops his scanty fare.
  Springs leap and plunging brooks unite in revel;   9530
Already gorges, slopes, and meads are green.
Upon a hundred hillsides' broken level
The moving, fleecy herds spread out are seen.
  With measured step, divided, steady,
Horned beasts draw near the dizzy ledge's fall,   9535
But shelter for them all is ever ready
In hundred caves arched in the rocky wall.
  Pan shields them there, enlivening nymphs are dwelling
In bosky chasms' moist, refreshened lee,
And, yearningly toward higher regions swelling,   9540
Aloft crowds branch-abounding tree on tree.
  Primeval woods! The mighty oak is standing
With branch on branch crooked wilfully and bowed;
The gentle maple, with sweet juice expanding,
Shoots cleanly upward, playing with its load.   9545
  And in that silent realm of shadows
Warm mother's milk for child and lambkin wells;
Fruit is not far, the ripe food of the meadows,
And honey from the hollowed tree distils.
  Here comfort is the birthright of a nation,   9550
Both cheek and lips express serenity,
Each is immortal in his age and station,
Healthy they live and happily.
  And thus the lovely child develops, gaining
The father's strength as bright day follows day.   9555
We marvel, in our minds a doubt remaining
If they are gods, if men are they.
  Thus was Apollo shepherd-like in feature,
Only the fairest was as fair as he;
For where in a pure orbit ruleth Nature,   9560
All worlds unite and blend in harmony.

Taking his seat beside HELENA
Thus hath success both thee and me attended,
Now let the past be past, behind us flung;
Oh, feel thyself from highest god descended,
Thou of the primal world whence thou art sprung!   9565
Thee shall no fortress keep in hiding!
Still in eternal youth, stands, as it stood,
A wide domain for us, for blissful biding,
Arcadia in Sparta's neighbourhood!
Enticed to dwelling in this blessed harbour,   9570
Hast fled into the brightest destiny!
Now let our thrones become an arbour,
Arcadian be our bliss and free!

The Scene Changes Altogether

*Closed arbours lean against a series of rocky caverns. A shady
grove extends to the surrounding cliff-walls.* FAUST
and HELENA *are not visible. The* CHORUS *lies
sleeping, scattered here and there*

Phorkyas.   How long these maidens may have slept I can not tell.
If they allowed themselves to dream that which mine eyes   9575
Saw bright and clear, that likewise is unknown to me,
And so I'll wake them. This young crowd should be amazed,
Ye long-beards too, who sit and wait down there below
To see at length how wonders credible turn out.
Awake! arise! and quickly shake your curly hair,   9580
Sleep from your eyes! And blink not so, but list to me!
Chorus.
Speak and tell us, tell whatever marvellous events have happened;
Most of all we like to hear of what surpasses our believing,
For we're bored, and greatly bored, from looking only on these rocks.
Phorkyas.
With your eyes rubbed open scarcely, children, are ye bored so soon?   9585
Hearken then! Here in these caverns, in these grottoes, in these arbours,
Shield and shelter have been given, as are given to pairs idyllic,
To our lord and to our lady.
Chorus.   How? Within there?

Phorkyas.   Separated
From the world, they summoned me, me only, to their quiet service.
Highly honoured I stood near them, yet, as doth beseem the trusted,   9590
Looked around for something else. So I turned me hither, thither,
Seeking roots and barks and mosses, skilled in all things efficacious,
And so they remained alone.
Chorus.
Truly thou dost speak as if within there were vast world-wide spaces,
Forest, lakes and brooks and meadow; what a fairy tale dost spin!   9595
Phorkyas.
To be sure, ye inexperienced! Those are depths no one hath fathomed:
Hall on hall and court on court which musingly I followed through.
But there echoes all at once a laughter through the spacious caverns;
I look thither, lo! a boy who from the woman's lap is leaping
To the man, and from the father to the mother; the caressing,   9600
Dandling, pranks of foolish fondness, cries of fun, and shouts of pleasure
Deafen me alternately.
Naked, without wings, a genius, faun-like but with nothing bestial,
On the firm ground he is leaping, yet the ground, in turn reacting,
Speeds him up to airy heights, and in the second or the third leap   9605
Doth he touch the lofty arch.
Anxious calls the mother: "Leap! and leap again, and at thy pleasure,
But beware of flying: flight unfettered is denied to thee."
And thus warns the faithful father: "In the earth lies power elastic
That impels thee upward, only with your toe-tips touch the surface   9610
And at once thou wilt be strengthened like Antaeus, son of earth."
And so on these rocky masses he goes skipping from one cornice
To the other and around, as leaps a ball when it is struck.
     All at once, though, in the crevice of a rugged gorge he's vanished,
And he now seems lost to us. The mother wails, the father comforts,   9615
Anxiously I shrug my shoulders. But again now what a vision!
Are there treasures lying hid there? Garments striped with broidered
He has donned becomingly.   [blossoms
     From his arms are tassels waving, round his bosom flutter ribbons,
In his hands the golden lyre; completely like a little Phoebus,   9620
He steps boldly to the brink, then to the precipice. We marvel
And the parents in their rapture clasp each other, heart to heart,
For around his head what splendour! It is hard to say what glitters,
Is it gold-work or the flame of some transcendent spirit-power?
And he moves and gestures, even now though but a boy, proclaiming   9625
Him the future master of all beauty, through whose every member

Melodies eternal stir; and thus ye too will hearken to him,
And will see him thus, with wonder ye have never felt before.
Chorus.

Call'st thou a wonder this,
Thou Crete-begotten?
Hast to poetical speech
Pregnant with thought not listened?
Never yet hast heard Ionia's,
Never hast listened to Hellas'
Vast store of tales ancestral
Celebrating gods and heroes?
   All that may happen now
While we are living
Reëchoes gloomily
Grandeur of days ancestral;
Nor can thy narration equal
That which a lovely fiction,
More credible than truth is,
Sang of him, the son of Maia.
   Him a delicate babe but strong,
Nurseling, scarce more than born yet,
Straight has the nurses' chattering flock,
Full of unreasoning fancy,
Wrapped in the purest swaddling-fleece,
Bound fast in fine, costly wrappings,
But now the strong, though dainty rogue
Draws forth his delicate limbs,
Firm, elastic, and supple,
Craftily thence, the purple shell,
Which so grievously bound him,
Leaving quietly in its place,
Like the perfected butterfly
Which from the cramping chrysalis
Deftly slips with unfolding wings,
Through the sunlit, radiant ether
Boldly, wantonly fluttering.
   So too did he, the agilest,
That to thieves and to tricksters
And all seekers of gain he'd be
Ever a favouring genius.
This straightway he makes manifest

9630

9635

9640

9645

9650

9655

9660

9665

[275]

Through most clever devices.
Swift the trident of ocean's lord
Steals he, and slyly from Ares' self
Steals the sword from the scabbard,   9670
Arrow and bow from Phoebus too,
Also the tongs from Hephaestus,
Even from Zeus the father's bolt
Would have had, but was frightened by fire.
Eros too he overcomes ,   9675
In a leg-tripping wrestling match,
And when Cypris caresses him, steals
From her bosom the girdle.

> *A charming, purely melodious music of stringed instruments resounds from the cave. All become attentive and soon seem to be deeply stirred. Henceforth to the pause indicated, there is a full musical accompaniment*

Phorkyas.

Hear the loveliest chords resounding,
Quick, be free from myths long gone,   9680
And your gods, of old abounding,
Let them go! Their day is done.
None will understand your singing,
We demand a higher mart;
From the heart it must come springing,   9685
If it hopes to touch the heart.
> *She retires toward the rocks*

Chorus.

If these witching tones, dire creature,
Find a welcome in thine ears,
We feel healed, of a new nature,
Softened to the joy of tears.   9690
Let the sun's bright splendour perish
If a dawn within us rise,
If in our own hearts we cherish
What the whole wide world denies.
> HELENA, FAUST, EUPHORION *in the costume described for him*

Euphorion.

Hear ye children carols singing,
Ye at once in sport take part;   9695

When ye see my rhythmic springing,
As a parent's leaps your heart.

Helena.

Love, in human wise to bless us,
Makes Two One in sympathy, 9700
But us godlike joy possesses
When Love forms a precious Three.

Faust.

All is found, our love's requited,
I am thine, and mine art thou;
And so stand we here united, 9705
Were it always thus as now!

Chorus.

Many years of purest pleasure
In the mild light of the boy
Crown this pair in plenteous measure.
How their union stirs my joy! 9710

Euphorion.

Let me be skipping,
Let me be springing!
In all the breezes
Through ether winging
Is now my passion; 9715
It hath me won.

Faust.

But gently! gently!
Don't be rash! Check thee
That plunge and death may
Not overtake thee, 9720
That we may not perish
Through our dear son.

Euphorion.

I will no longer
Stand earthly stresses;
Let go my hands, 9725
Let go my tresses,
Let go my garments,
They are all mine.

Helena.

Oh, think — believe us —
To whom thou belongest! 9730

[277]

How it would grieve us,
And how thou wrongest
The fair fortune won,
Mine, his, and thine!

Chorus.

The bond, I fear me,   9735
Soon is undone!

Helena and Faust.

Curb, thou tempestuous!
For us who love thee,
Over-impetuous
Forces that move thee!   9740
In rural leisure
Grace thou the plain.

Euphorion.

But for your pleasure
I will refrain.
    Winding among the Chorus *and drawing*
      them forth to dance
Round this gay company   9745
Hover I light;
Now is the melody,
Now is the movement right?

Helena.

Yes, that is neatly done!
Lead all the beauties on,   9750
Artfully dance!

Faust.

Oh, that an end might be!
Ne'er can this roguery
My joy enhance.
    Euphorion *and the* Chorus, *dancing*
      and singing, move about in interlocking dance

Chorus.

When thy twin arms so fair   9755
Charming thou raisest,
Radiant thy curly hair
Shaking displacest,
When thou with foot so light
Skimmest the earth in flight,   9760
Hither and off again,

[278]

Dancing a linkèd chain,
Thou hast thy goal attained,
Thou lovely child;
All of our hearts beguiled,   9765
All hast thou gained.
  Pause

Euphorion.

O all ye lithesome
Roes never staying,
Quickly and blithesome,
On, to new playing!   9770
I am the hunter,
Ye are the game.

Chorus.

Wilt thou us capture,
Be not unruly
For we, in rapture,   9775
Only would truly
Closely embrace thee,
Thy beauty claim!

Euphorion.

Through groves and rubble,
Over stock and stubble!   9780
Lightly attainable,
That I detest;
Hardly obtainable
Pleases me best.

Helena and Faust.

Oh what madness! Oh what daring!   9785
There's no hope of moderation.
Hark! It sounds like trumpets' blaring
Over vale and woods resounding;
What a tumult! What a brawl!

Chorus entering singly and quickly.

He ran past us, left us lagging,   9790
Scorned and mocked us, onward bounding;
See how hither he is dragging
Now the wildest one of all.

Euphorion bearing a young maiden.

Here I drag the sturdy maiden
Hither to enforced enjoyment;   9795

For my rapture, for my zest,
I press her resisting breast,
Kiss her lips reluctant still,
Showing thus my strength and will.

Maiden.

Loose me! In this form and cover   9800
Spirit-strength and courage stay,
And our will, like thine moreover,
Is not lightly swept away.
In a strait dost think me truly?
For thine arm great strength dost claim!   9805
Hold me fast, fool, and I'll duly
Scorch thee well, a merry game.
                    She turns to flame and flashes up in the air
To the buoyant breezes follow,
To the caverns' dreary hollow,
Come the vanished prize to claim.   9810

Euphorion shaking off the last flames.

Rocks all around me here,
Thickets and woods among,
Why should they bound me here?
Still am I fresh and young.
Wild winds are dashing there,   9815
Billows are crashing there,
Both far away I hear,
Would I were near!
                    He leaps higher and higher up the rocks

Helena, Faust, and the Chorus.

Like a chamois wouldst aspire?
Dreadful fall we fear for thee.   9820

Euphorion.

Higher must I climb and higher,
Ever farther must I see.
Now I know where I stand,
Midst of great Pelops' land,
Midst of an isle are we,   9825
Kin to the earth and sea!

Chorus.

Wilt not mid wood and hill
Linger contented?
Soon we shall seek at will

Grapes in rows planted, 9830
Grapes on the hillsides fanned,
Figs and gold apples rare.
Ah, stay in this fair land,
Stay thou so fair!

Euphorion.

Dream ye of days of peace? 9835
Dream on whom dreams may please!
"War!" is the signal cry,
Echoed by "Victory!"

Chorus.

Who in peace ever
Wishes war back again, 9840
Himself doth sever
From hope's rich gain.

Euphorion.

They whom this land hath led
Out of dread into dread,
Free, of undaunted mood, 9845
Not sparing of their blood:
To their unbreakable,
Consecrate chain,
Fighters unshakeable,
May it bring gain! 9850

Chorus.

Look aloft! How high he's mounting!
Yet to us not small he seems,
As if armed, on triumph counting,
As of bronze and steel he gleams.

Euphorion.

Not on walls or moats enduring, 9855
On his own strength each must rest;
Fortress firm and all-securing
Is a man's own iron breast.
Would ye live unconquered freemen,
Arm, and off to combat wild! 9860
Amazons will be your women,
And a hero every child.

Chorus.

Hallowèd Poesy,
Soar aloft heavenly,

[281]

Shine on, thou fairest star,   9865
Farther and still more far,
Yet dost thou reach us still,
Yet do we hear and thrill,
Joyous we are.

Euphorion.

No, not a child am I appearing,   9870
A youth in armour I come on,
Who, joined with strong men, free and daring,
Great deeds in spirit now has done.
Away!
No stay,   9875
On to the path where fame is won.

Helena and Faust.

Scarcely thou to life art given,
Scarcely knowing day's glad beam,
Yearning dizzily art driven
To the field where sorrows teem.   9880
Are then we
Naught to thee?
Is the lovely bond a dream?

Euphorion.

Hear ye the thundering on the ocean?
How thunder back the vale and wood?   9885
In dust and foam, in fierce commotion,
Host charges host in weltering blood,
And for all
"Death!"'s the call,
That of course is understood.   9890

Helena, Faust, and the Chorus.

How we shudder! How we quiver!
Does death summon thee to fall?

Euphorion.

From afar look on? No, never!
Worry, need — I'll share it all.

The Above.

Danger his rashness brings,   9895
Fatally bold!

Euphorion.

Still must I! — See the wings
That now unfold!

[282]

Thither! I must! I must!
Grudge not the flight!   9900

> *He casts himself into the air, his garments bear
> him up for a moment, his head is irradiated, a
> trail of light follows him*

Chorus.

Icarus! Icarus!
Piteous plight!

> *A beautiful youth falls at his parents' feet. We
> think we recognize a familiar form in the dead
> body; but the corporeal vanishes at once, the
> aureole rises like a comet toward heaven. The
> robe, mantle, and lyre remain lying on the
> ground*

Helena and Faust.

Quick on joy followeth
Dire pain and moan.

Euphorion's Voice from the depths.

Leave me in realms of death,   9905
Mother, not all alone!

> *Pause*

Chorus, a Dirge.

Not alone! — where'er thou bidest,
For we think that well we know thee;
Ah! and if from life thou hidest,
Never will a heart forgo thee.   9910
For thee scarcely know we sadness,
Enviously we sing thy fate,
For thou hadst in pain and gladness
Songs and courage high and great.

Born with earthly bliss thy dower,   9915
Great thy strength, proud thy descent,
Soon lost to thyself, the flower
Of thy youth was from thee rent.
Keen thy sight, the world discerning,
Feeling for each heart-throb known,   9920
For fair women's passion yearning,
And a song thy very own.

But thy tamelessness engaged thee
In a net without a flaw,

And in headlong strife enraged thee   9925
Against custom, against law;
But at last an aim transcendent
Gave thy noble courage weight,
Thou wouldst win a fame resplendent —
But success was not thy fate.   9930

Who succeeds? — A dismal query,
Shunned by Fate who gives no heed,
When, on days ill-starred and dreary,
Silently the people bleed.
But new songs afresh create them,   9935
Deeply bowed lament no more:
Earth again will generate them
As it ever did of yore.

Complete pause. The music ceases

Helena to FAUST.   Alas, an ancient truth is verified in me:
That bliss and beauty never lastingly unite.   9940
The bond of life is rent no less than that of love;
Bewailing both, I say with sorrow: Fare thee well!
And cast myself once more, once only, in thine arms.
Receive, Persephone, receive the boy and me.

She embraces FAUST, *she herself vanishes,*
robe and veil remain in his arms

Phorkyas to FAUST.   Hold fast what now alone is left to thee!   9945
Let not the garment go. Already demons
Are twitching at its skirts and they would like
To snatch it to the lower world. Hold fast!
It is no more the goddess whom thou lost,
But godlike is it. Make use of the high   9950
And priceless boon, and rising soar aloft.
Swift over all things common will it bear thee
Away through ether while thou canst endure.
We'll meet again, far, far away from here.

HELENA's *garments dissolve into clouds, sur-*
round FAUST, *lift him in the air, and move*
away with him

Phorkyas picks up EUPHORION's *robe, mantle, and lyre from the ground,*
steps forward to the proscenium, lifts up the mementoes, and says.

A lucky find, although belated!   9955
The flame, in truth, is dissipated,

[284]

Yet for the world I've no distress.
Here is enough to start the poet
And swell his tribe with jealousness;
And talent? Though I can't bestow it,   9960
I can at least bestow the dress.

She sits down in the proscenium at the foot of a
column

Panthalis.   Now hasten, maidens! From the sorcery we're free,
From the mad tyranny of the Thessalian hag,
Freed from the wildering, jangling tones that dazed us all,
The ear confounding and still worse the inner sense.   9965
Hence, down to Hades! where our Queen has hastened on,
With solemn steps descending. Let her footsteps be
Directly followed by the steps of faithful maids.
Her shall we find beside the throne of the Inscrutable.
Chorus.

Everywhere indeed do queens ever like to be,   9970
And in Hades too do they stand supreme;
Proudly with their peers are they allied,
With Persephone most intimate.
We, however, in the background
Of deep, asphodelian meadows,   9975
With far-reaching poplars
And unfruitful willows joined,
What diversion shall we have there?
Bat-like to squeak and twitter
In whispers undelighting, spectral.   9980

Panthalis.   Who hath not won a name nor wills a noble deed,
Belongs but to the elements, so fare thy way!
Hotly I wish to join my Queen. Not merit alone,
Faithfulness too preserves our personality.

Exit

All.

Back to the light of day are we now restored,   9985
Truly persons no more.
We feel it, we know it too,
But to Hades we go back never;
For ever-living Nature lays
Claim to us spirits,   9990
We to her lay claim that is valid.

[285]

A Part of the Chorus.

    In these thousand branches' quivering whisper, in their murmuring sway-

    Toying gently, we'll entice up from the roots the vital currents   [ing,

    To the twigs; and now with leafage, now with blooms in great profusion

    We'll adorn the fluttering tresses freely for an airy growth.   9995

    Falls the fruit, at once will gather life-enjoying herds and people,

    Quickly coming, briskly crowding, for the picking, for the tasting;

    They will all bow down around us as before primeval gods.

Another Part.

    In the smooth, far-gleaming mirror by these rocky walls we'll nestle,

    Moving in the gentle wavelets to and fro, caressingly.   10000

    To each sound we'll hearken, list to songs of birds and reedy fluting.

    Be it Pan's own fearful voice, a ready answer is at hand.

    Doth it murmur, we too murmur; thunders it, we roll our thunders

    Overwhelming, doubly crashing, threefold, tenfold echoing back.

A Third Part.

    Sisters, we more nimble, we will hasten with the brooklets onward,   10005

    For those yonder distant, richly-mantled mountain ranges charm us.

    Ever downward, ever deeper, while meandering we'll water

    Now the meadow, now the pasture, then the garden round the house;

    It is marked by slender cypress tree-tops soaring into ether

    Over landscape, winding shore-line, and the mirror of the stream.   10010

A Fourth Part.

    Roam ye others where it please you; we'll engirdle, we will ripple,

    Round the thickly planted hillside where the trellised vines grow green;

    There the grower of the vine in anguish ponders hour- and day-long

    How uncertain is the promise of devoted industry.

    Now with hoe and now with shovel, now with hilling, pruning, tying,   10015

    Unto all the gods he prayeth, to the sun-god best of all.

    Pampered Bacchus frets himself but little for his faithful servant,

    Rests in bowers, lolls in caverns, prattling with the youngest faun.

    What he ever needed for his half-intoxicated dreaming,

    He has always near at hand in wineskins, pitchers, divers vessels,   10020

    Right and left in cool recesses for eternal ages stored.

    But if all the gods together, Helios the most important,   [plenty,

    Fanning, moistening, warming, glowing, filled with grape-vine's horn of

    Where the quiet vintner laboured, there new life will soon be stirring,

    With a rustling in each trellis and a rush from stock to stock.   10025

    Baskets creak and buckets clatter, tubs groan on the bearer's back;

    To the great vat all are going, to the treaders' vigorous dance;

    And thus is the sacred plenty of the pure-born, juicy berries

Rudely trodden, foaming, spurting, crushed to an unsightly mass.
Now the ear is pierced by brazen clash of cymbals and of timbrels, 10030
For the veil of mystery hath Dionysus cast aside;
He comes forth with goat-foot satyrs, whirling goat-foot satyresses;
And amid them brays, untamed and shrill, Silenus' long-eared beast.
Naught is spared! For cloven hoofs are trampling down all decent custom;
For the senses whirling stagger, horribly the ear is stunned. 10035
For the cup the drunken fumble, over-full are heads and bellies.
Careful still is this and that one, but he heightens thus the tumult,
For to garner this year's juices, they drain swiftly the old skin.

> *The curtain falls,* PHORKYAS *in the proscenium rises to a gigantic height, descends from the cothurni, casts aside mask and veil, and appears as* MEPHISTOPHELES *in order, as far as may be necessary, to comment on the piece by way of epilogue*

Act IV

A High Mountain Range

Bold jagged rocky peaks. A cloud approaches, pauses as it touches a peak, and sinks down on a projecting ledge. It divides

Faust steps forth.　Looking to deepest solitudes beneath my feet
I walk in thoughtfulness along this summit's verge,　　　　　　10040
Relinquishing my chariot of clouds that bore
Me gently over land and sea through smiling days.
Slowly, not scattering, it drifts away from me.
Off to the east the mass strains, rolling on and on;
The eye strains after it, admiring and amazed.　　　　　　　　10045
It breaks while moving, billow-like and changefully,
Yet seems re-shaping. — Yes, my eyes deceive me not!
On sun-illumined pillows gloriously reclines —
Of giant size, in truth — a godlike woman's form.
I see it! Like to Juno, Leda, Helena,　　　　　　　　　　　10050
It floats in lovely majesty before my sight.
Alas! It's shifting! Formless, broad, and towering,
It resteth in the east like distant ice-clad peaks,
And, dazzling, mirrors swift days' great significance.

　　　　Yet round me floats a light and tender misty wreath,　　10055
Around my breast and brow, cheering, caressing, cool.
Now it mounts high and higher, lightly, lingering.
It draws together. — Doth a rapturing form deceive
Mine eyes, youth's first, long-unenjoyed and highest bliss?
The earliest, deepest treasures of my heart break forth;　　　10060
The dawn of love, so light of wing, it typifies,
The swiftly-felt, the first, scarce comprehended glance,
Outshining every other treasure, if held fast.
Like beauty of the soul the lovely form becomes
More fair, dissolving not, but through the ether soars　　　　10065
And draws the best of all my being on and on.

[288]

A seven-league boot comes thumping forward.
Another soon follows. MEPHISTOPHELES
steps out of them. The boots stride on hastily

Mephistopheles.　　That I call striding briskly ended!
　　But say, what kind of whim is this?
　　Why midst such horrors here descended,
　　By ghastly yawning precipice?　　　　　　　　　　　　10070
　　I know them well but not in this high station,
　　For such things really were Hell's own foundation.
Faust.　　Of foolish tales you've always had a store
　　And now begin to deal them out once more.
Mephistopheles seriously.
　　When God the Lord — I know well the occasion —　　10075
　　Banned us from air into the deeps profound,
　　Where, glowing from earth's centre all around,
　　Eternal fire waxed hottest past all bound,
　　We found us midst too great illumination
　　In a most crowded, irksome situation.　　　　　　　10080
　　The devils, every one, began a coughing,
　　Above, below, at every vent-hole puffing;
　　Hell was with sulphur-fumes so much inflated
　　And such a gas therefrom was generated,
　　That very soon the earth's flat crust — no wonder! —　10085
　　Thick as it was, was forced to burst asunder.
　　So now we have a different situation;
　　What's now a peak was once a deep foundation.
　　On this men base the doctrines that they boast,
　　Turning the lowest into uppermost.　　　　　　　　10090
　　Thus from that slavish hot cave did we fare
　　To an excessive lording in free air,
　　An open secret but one well concealed
　　And to the common crowd but late revealed. (*Ephes. VI, 12*)
Faust.　　To me a mountain-mass stays nobly dumb,　　10095
　　I ask not wherefore nor from whence it come.
　　When Nature in herself her own self founded,
　　The globe of earth she formed and neatly rounded,
　　In summits and in gorges took delight,
　　Ranged rock on rock and mountain height on height;　10100
　　The hills in easy slopes she downward moulded,
　　Till gently into valleys they unfolded.
　　There all is verdant growth and for her gladness

[289]

She has no need of such convulsive madness.
Mephistopheles.   That's what you say! To you it seems quite clear   10105
   But he knows better who beheld it near.
   I was at hand when still below was surging
   The deep abyss, when streamed a fiery tide,
   When Moloch's hammer rock on rock was forging
   And scattering mountain-ruins far and wide.   10110
   Earth still abounds in ponderous strange masses.
   Such power in hurling who can well explain?
   As wise men know, their reason it surpasses.
   The rock lies evermore where it has lain.
   We've racked our brains, to our disgrace, in vain. —   10115
   Only the faithful common people know
   And let none shake them in their story:
   (Their wisdom ripened long ago)
   It is a miracle, and Satan gets the glory.
   My pilgrim on his crutch of faith limps on   10120
   To Devil's Bridge, to Devil's Stone.
Faust.   There is indeed remarkable attraction
   In seeing a devil's view of Nature's action.
Mephistopheles.   Be Nature what she will! What do I care?
   Honour's at stake! Satan himself was there!   10125
   We are real people, great things we attain.
   Violence, tumult, nonsense! See, the sign is plain! —
   But — to say something now that's wholly clear —
   Has nothing pleased you in our upper sphere?
   You have surveyed a boundless territory,   10130
   The kingdoms of the world and all their glory; (*Matt. IV*)
   Still — with that discontented air —
   Did you not lust for something anywhere?
Faust.   I did! A great work lured me on.
   Divine it!
Mephistopheles.   That can soon be done.   10135
   I'd seek some city, at its heart
   A horrid city victuals-mart,
   Tortuous alleys, pointed gables,
   Beets, kale, and onions on the tables;
   Meat-stalls where blue flies take life easy,   10140
   Feasting on roasts well-done and greasy;
   There you will always surely find
   Stench and activity combined.

Then ample squares, broad streets between,
Where one can stalk with lordly mien, 10145
And lastly, where no town-gates bar,
The suburbs boundless, stretching far.
There I'd enjoy the coaches' rolling,
The noisy hither and thither bowling,
Eternal running hither and thither 10150
Of scattered ants that swarm together.
And whether driving, whether riding,
The centre of them all abiding,
Honoured by thousands would be I.

Faust. With that I can not be contented! 10155
One likes to see the people multiply
And in their way live comfortably,
Even develop, learn thereby —
And yet, in fine, rebels are thus augmented.

Mephistopheles. Then, swelling with self-conscious pride I'd raise 10160
A pleasure-castle in a pleasant place.
Hill, level, meadow, field, and forest glade
Into a splendid garden I'd have made,
Before green walls of verdure, velvet meadows,
And measured paths and art-directed shadows, 10165
Cascading falls among the rocks designed,
And fountain-sprays of every kind,
One rising proud and stately in the middle,
While at the sides a thousand spraylets spurt and piddle.
And then I'd build, for loveliest women meet, 10170
Snug villas, each an intimate retreat.
I'd pass there endless time in joyous mood,
Blessed by the dearest social solitude.
"Women," I say, for here, as everywhere,
I think in plurals of the ladies fair. 10175

Faust. Sardanapalus! Vile and new, I swear!

Mephistopheles. Who could divine toward what you would aspire?
It must have been sublimely bold, in truth,
Toward the moon you'd soar and ever nigher;
Did your mad quest allure you *there* forsooth? 10180

Faust. By no means! For this earthly sphere
Affords a place for great deeds ever.
Astounding things shall happen here,
I feel the strength for bold endeavour.

Mephistopheles.   So you'd earn glory? One can see   10185
    You've been in heroines' company.
Faust.   Lordship, possession, are my aim and thought!
    The deed is everything, the glory naught.
Mephistopheles.   Yet poets will come forward all the same
    To blazon to the later world your fame,   10190
    Through folly more fools to inflame.
Faust.   Of all this naught is known to you.
    How should you know what men will woo?
    Your bitter, sharp, and hostile mood,
    How does it know what men count good?   10195
Mephistopheles.   So be it with you then as best it pleases!
    Confide to me the range of your caprices.
Faust.   Mine eye was drawn out toward the open ocean
    That swelled aloft, self-towering and vaulting,
    And then drew back its billows in commotion,   10200
    The broad expanse of level shore assaulting.
    And that irked me, as always insolence
    Irks the free soul who prizes every right,
    Whose blood, stirred up to passionate vehemence,
    Is fired with feelings of a harsh despite.   10205
    I thought it chance and gazed more sharply at the main.
    The billows paused and then rolled back again,
    Withdrawing from the goal so proudly won.
    The hour returns, again the game's begun.
Mephistopheles to the spectators.
    There's nothing new in that for me to know;   10210
    I knew it a hundred thousand years ago.
Faust continuing passionately.
    It steals along, in countless channels flowing,
    Fruitless itself and fruitlessness bestowing;
    It swells and grows and rolls and spreads its reign
    Over the loathsome, desolate domain.   10215
    Strong with a mighty will there wave on wave rolls on,
    Reigns for a while, retires, and naught is done.
    Even to despair it could harass me, truly,
    The aimless force of elements unruly!
    Here dares my soul above itself to soar;   10220
    Here would I fight, of this be conqueror.
    And it is possible! For though the tide
    May rise, it fawns along each hillock's side.

It may bestir itself and bluster oh! so loudly,
A little height will meet and daunt it proudly,   10225
A little depth will draw it on amain.
So plan on plan flashed swiftly through my brain:
"Win for thyself great joy, a costly store:
Push back the lordly ocean from the shore;
Limit the bounds of that vast, watery deep   10230
And force it, far away, within itself to keep."
Thus step by step I knew I could explain it.
This is my wish, now dare to help me gain it!

Drums and martial music at the rear of the
spectators, at a distance, on the right hand

Mephistopheles.   How easy! Do you hear the drums afar?
Faust.   What, war again? The wise man likes not war.   10235
Mephistopheles.   Be it war or peace! From every circumstance
    The wise man tries to draw himself some profit.
    One watches, notes each favouring chance.
    Now is the moment, Faustus, make use of it!
Faust.   Spare me such riddle-mongering, my friend!   10240
    Be brief, explain, what is it you intend?
Mephistopheles.   As I came here, it was not hid from me,
    Our Emperor suffers great anxiety;
    You know him well. The while that we amused him
    And with illusive show of wealth abused him,   10245
    He thought the whole world could be had for pay.
    For when a youth, the throne fell to his sway
    And wrongly he concluded at his leisure
    Two things one could quite well combine —
    Which would be most desirable and fine —   10250
    To rule and also take one's pleasure.
Faust.   A great mistake. Whoever would command,
    Must in commanding feel his greatest blessing.
    A lofty purpose must his breast expand,
    But what he wills must be beyond all guessing.   10255
    What he to his most faithful whispereth:
    It's done! Amazed, all subjects hold their breath.
    Thus always will he have the most exalted place,
    The worthiest, he! Enjoyment doth debase.
Mephistopheles.   Not such is he! Enjoy? how didn't he?   10260
    Meanwhile the realm was rent by anarchy,
    Where great and small warred criss-cross with each other

And brother drove from home or slaughtered brother,
Castle with castle, town with town in feud,
Guild against noble, all in fiercest mood.   10265
Chapters and flocks against their bishops rose.
If men but saw each other, they were foes.
In churches murder, homicide; outside each gate
Each merchant, traveller, waits the self-same fate.
Boldness in all grew to no mean extent.   10270
To live meant self-defence! — Well, now, that went.
Faust.   It went, it staggered, fell, and up it jumped,
    Fell over itself, and in a heap it plumped.
Mephistopheles.   And such conditions no one dared to blame;
    Some standing each could, each would, claim.   10275
    As peer of any has the least man passed,
    But for the best, things grew too mad at last.
    The capable arose then in their might
    And said: "Who gives us peace is lord by right;
    The Emperor can not, will not — let us choose   10280
    A new one, one who will infuse
    New life into the realm he safeguards duly,
    Where peace and justice govern truly
    The world he strengthens and renews."
Faust.   That sounds like priestcraft.
Mephistopheles.   Priests they were, be sure.   10285
    Their own well-nourished paunch they made secure.
    More than all others were they implicated.
    The riot grew, riot was consecrated.
    Our Emperor, to whom we gave delight,
    Is drawing near, perhaps for his last fight.   10290
Faust.   I pity him, so kind and frank was he.
Mephistopheles.   While there is life, there's hope. Come, let us see.
    Let's liberate him from this narrow vale!
    A single rescue doth a thousand times avail.
    Who knows how yet the dice may fall?   10295
    Grant him good luck, vassals he'll have withal.
            They climb over the middle range of mountains
            and survey the disposition of the host in the val-
            ley. Drums and martial music resound from
            below
Mephistopheles.   They've taken their position well, I see;
    We'll join them and complete the victory.

Faust.   What is there to expect, I'd like to know?
    Fraud! Dazzling magic! Hollow show!   10300
Mephistopheles.   Nay, stratagem to win the fight!
    Just fix your gaze upon a lofty height
    And only think of your high aim.
    If we preserve the Emperor's throne and land,
    Then you can kneel and justly claim   10305
    In feudal right a boundless strand.
Faust.   Much have you ere now carried through;
    Come then and win a battle too.
Mephistopheles.   No, you will win it! For, in brief,
    You'll be the General-in-Chief.   10310
Faust.   A really lofty post for me, commanding
    In places of which I've no understanding!
Mephistopheles.   You let the General Staff provide
    And the Field Marshal's safe whate'er betide.
    Lack of war-counsel I have long since traced,   10315
    Hence a war-council I have straightway based
    On primal mountains' primal human might;
    Blest he who can its elements unite.
Faust.   What do I see there bearing arms?
    Have you stirred mountain-folk with your alarms?   10320
Mephistopheles.   No! I have called, like Peter Quince,
    Of all the lot the quintessence.

                The THREE MIGHTY MEN *appear (2 Sam.*
                XXIII, 8)

Mephistopheles.   You see my fellows coming there!
    Of different ages are they, surely,
    In different garb and outfit they appear;   10325
    With them, I know, you'll not fare poorly.
                To the spectators
    Now every child delights to see
    A knight's bright collar and his armour;
    And allegoric though the rascals be,
    Each is but all the more a charmer.   10330
Fight-hard, young, lightly armed, in motley dress.
    If anyone should look me in the eyes,
    Straight at his jaw my fist shall fare,
    And if a coward from me flies,
    I'll catch him by his streaming hair.
Get-quick, manly, well armed, richly clad.

Such empty brawls are farces dreary, 10335
We lose what such occasion brings;
Only in taking be not weary,
Look afterward to other things.
Hold-fast, along in years, strongly armed, without attire.
Not much is thus accumulated;
Great riches are soon dissipated, 10340
Adown life's stream they rush as swift as thought.
To take is good, better to keep when taken;
Let the old greybeard rule unshaken
And none shall plunder you of aught.

They descend together

On the Headland

EMPEROR   GENERALISSIMO   BODYGUARDS

Drums and martial music from below. The EMPEROR'S
tent is being pitched

Generalissimo.   The project still seems well deliberated, 10345
That back in this convenient vale
Our army all be drawn and concentrated;
I trust this disposition will avail.
Emperor.   How things will go now we must soon be seeing;
But I dislike this giving way, this semi-fleeing. 10350
Generalissimo.   Look here, my prince, at our right flank's position.
In war such ground's a longed-for acquisition:
Not steep the hills, yet not for easy faring,
To us propitious, to the foe ensnaring.
Half hidden on the billowy field are we; 10355
They will not venture here with cavalry.
Emperor.   I can but praise, and hope the best;
Now arm and heart can meet the test.
Generalissimo.   There where the level ground stretches away,
You see the phalanx eager for the fray. 10360
Through morning's fragrant mist in sunshine rare
The lances glint and sparkle in the air.
How dark the mighty square is surging to and fro!
For great achievements all the thousands glow.
The mass's power you thus can comprehend; 10365

The enemy's power I trust them now to rend.

Emperor.   For the first time I have so fair a view.
   An army such as this can count as two.

Generalissimo.   Of our left flank I've nothing to report.
   Stout heroes guard that beetling rocky fort.   10370
   The stony cliffs, lit by the weapons' sheen,
   Protect the vital pass to the ravine.
   Here I foresee, what little they expect.
   Our foes will in the bloody brawl be wrecked.

Emperor.   Yonder they come, false kinsmen, one and other,   10375
   Even as they styled me Uncle, Cousin, Brother,
   Who've more and more presumed, all ties have sundered,
   The sceptre of its might, the throne's respect have plundered,
   Then, in their feuds, the realm have devastated
   And now rebel against me, federated.   10380
   The rabble wavers in uncertain spirit,
   Then streams along wherever the stream may bear it.

Generalissimo.   A trusty scout, for tidings sent in quest,
   Hastes down the rocks. May he have been well blessed!

First Scout.

   Fortune fair on us has waited.   10385
   Through our bold and crafty skill
   Here and there we penetrated;
   But the news we bring is ill.
   Many are pure homage swearing,
   They and many a soldier true;   10390
   But they plead, for not appearing,
   Inner ferment, danger too.

Emperor.   Through selfishness one learns self-preservation,
   Not honour, thanks, affection, obligation.
   Do you not think, when your accounts fall due,   10395
   Your neighbour's burning house will burn up you?

Generalissimo.   The second comes, but slowly down he clambers;
   The weary man trembles in all his members.

Second Scout.

   Wild confusion we detected
   First of all, were highly cheered;   10400
   Then at once and unexpected,
   A new emperor appeared.
   And in fore-determined manner

Through the plain the rabble sweep;
His perfidious unfurled banner   10405
They all follow — they are sheep.

Emperor.   A rival emperor I esteem a gain,
Now know myself an emperor not in vain.
As soldier only did I armour don,
Now for a higher aim is it put on.   10410
At every feast, though brilliant it might be
And naught seemed lacking, danger lacked to *me.*
When ring-sports you advised — whatever your intent —
My heart beat high, I breathed the tournament.
And had you not from war dissuaded me,   10415
Renowned for bright heroic deeds I'd be.
What self-reliance did I feel, what fortitude!
When mirrored in that realm of fire I stood!
The element leapt toward me, infuriate,
'Twas only semblance, yet a semblance great.   10420
I dreamed confusedly of victory and fame,
Now I'll retrieve my fault and expiate my shame.

> *The heralds are despatched to challenge the
> rival emperor to single combat*
> F A U S T *in armour, with half-closed visor. The*
> T H R E E   M I G H T Y   M E N *armed and clothed
> as above*

Faust.   We come and hope that we are welcome here;
Foresight avails even when no need is near.
You know the mountain-people think and pore,   10425
Well-studied in all rocks' and nature's lore.
The spirits, long since vanished from the plain,
Of rocky heights are more than ever fain.
Silent they work through devious crevasses
In rich metallic fumes of noble gases.   10430
On sundering, testing, blending, they are bent,
Their only impulse, something to invent.
With the light touch of spiritual power
They build transparent figures, hour by hour;
The crystal then in its eternal silence glasses   10435
What in the upper world above them passes.
Emperor.   I've heard it and believe that it may be;
Yet, gallant man, say: what is that to me?

Faust.   The Norcian necromant, of Sabine race,
      Your faithful, worthy servant, sends me in his place.   10440
      What fate once threatened him, so monstrous, dire!
      The fagots crackled, leapt the tongues of fire;
      Dry billets, lattice-like, were round about him fixed,
      With pitch and bars of sulphur intermixed.
      Rescue through devil, man, or god was vain.   10445
      Your Majesty it was who burst the fiery chain!
      It was in Rome. Still of most grateful mood,
      He pays heed to your path with deep solicitude.
      He has forgotten self from that dread moment on;
      He questions stars and depths for you alone.   10450
      He charged us, as our task the most immediate,
      To stand by you. The mountain's powers are great;
      Here Nature works omnipotently free.
      The priests' dull wits chide it as sorcery.
Emperor.   On festal days when guest on guest we're greeting,   10455
      Who come for joy and hope for joyous meeting,
      We like to see them shoving, pushing, one and all,
      So many men as make the rooms seem small.
      But still most highly welcome must the good man be
      If to our aid he comes with energy   10460
      Some morning hour when many dangers wait,
      And doubtful hang the balances of Fate.
      But here at this hour's critical demand
      Take not the willing sword in your strong hand;
      Honour the hour when many thousands stride   10465
      To fight against me or upon my side.
      Self is the man! Who asks a throne and crown
      Must in himself be worthy such renown.
      The spectre who against us has arisen,
      Himself as Emperor, Lord of our lands, doth christen,   10470
      Our army's Duke, our nobles' feudal Lord, he must
      With mine own hand into the realm of death be thrust!
Faust.   Though it be done to end the noble undertaking,
      You do not well, your head thus to be staking.
      Is not your helm with plume and crest bedecked?   10475
      The head which fires our zeal it doth protect.
      Without the head what could the limbs avail?
      For if it's drowsy, all droop down and fail;
      If it is hurt, at once all have a wound,

Arise afresh, if quickly it grows sound. 10480
To give its laws effect, swift is the arm,
It lifts the shield to guard the skull from harm.
Instantly doth the sword its duty know,
Parries with vigour and returns the blow.
The active foot shares in the other's weal 10485
As on the slain man's neck it plants its heel.

Emperor.   Such is my wrath, him thus I fain would treat,
Make his proud head a footstool for my feet.

Heralds come back.

Little honour, little glory
Met us yonder at our coming; 10490
At our noble, valiant story
Laughed they as a vapid mumming:
"Vanished is your Emperor yonder,
But an echo through the vale;
If on him we are to ponder, 10495
'There was once'— so runs the tale."

Faust.   As your best men have wished, it doth betide;
Both staunch and true they're standing at your side.
There comes the foe, your troops impatient wait.
Order attack, the hour is fortunate. 10500

Emperor.   Here I surrender the supreme command.
                              To the GENERALISSIMO
So be your duty, Prince, in your own hand.

Generalissimo.   Then let our right wing march on to the field!
The enemy's left wing, that just now is ascending,
Ere they complete their final step, shall yield 10505
Before the tested constancy of our defending.

Faust.   I beg you then to let this hero gay
Be added to your ranks without delay,
Be fully in your ranks incorporated;
His sturdy strength will much avail, so mated. 10510
                              He points to the right

Fight-hard steps forward.   Who shows his face to me turns not away
Till both his cheek- and jawbones get a mangling;
Who turns his back, limp on his nape straightway
Are neck and head and scalp right grimly dangling.
And if your men then strike and lunge 10515
With sword and mace as I go raging round,

Man after man, the foe will plunge
And in their own hot blood be drowned.

Exit

Generalissimo.   Let now our centre phalanx follow slow,
    With caution but in full force meet the foe.   10520
    See, on the right, now fiercely overtaken,
    Their schemes our force has desperately shaken.
Faust pointing to the man in the middle.
    Then let this hero too your hest obey.
    He's quick and in a rush sweeps all away.
Get-quick steps forth.   The imperial host's heroic spirit   10525
    Will rise with hope for booty near it;
    The goal, set up for all, shall be
    The rival emperor's rich marquee.
    Upon his seat he will not swagger long,
    I'll take my place and lead the phalanx strong.   10530
Speed-booty, sutler-woman, fawning on him.
    Although his wife I may not be,
    My dearest lover still is he.
    For us a harvest rare is ripe.
    Women are fierce to grab and gripe,
    In robbing ruthless and uncowed.   10535
    Forward in conquest! — All is allowed.

Exeunt both

Generalissimo.   Against our left, as was to be expected,
    Their right flank has been vigorously directed.
    The narrow, rocky pass they seek to gain;
    To thwart the furious onset ours will strain.   10540
Faust beckons to the left.   I beg you, Sire, also to note this one:
    When strength adds to its strength, no harm is done.
Hold-fast steps forward.   For your left wing dismiss all care!
    For where I am, safe is possession there;
    Thus age asserts itself, we're told;   10545
    No lightning shatters what I hold.

Exit

Mephistopheles coming down from above.
    Look at the background, see how surges
    Out of the jagged, rocky gorges
    A host of armed men — how they pour,
    Crowding the narrow pathways ever more —   10550
    With helmet, armour, sword, and spear

To build a rampart at our rear,
Waiting the signal to strike home.
Aside to the knowing ones
You must not ask from whence they come.
Industriously I've quite cleared out   10555
The halls of armour roundabout.
There were they all, on foot or mounted,
As if lords of the earth they still were counted;
Knight, emperor, king, they were of yore,
Now empty snail-shells, nothing more;   10560
Full many a ghost is thus adorned for strife,
Bringing the Middle Ages back to life.
Whatever devilkin is thus bedecked,
They'll now create a rare effect.
Aloud
Hark how in anger now they chatter,   10565
With clank of tin each other batter!
And torn old flags on standards flutter free,
That waited stirring breezes restlessly.
Reflect, an ancient folk stands ready there
And in this modern conflict fain would share.   10570
*Fearful resounding of trumpets from above, a
perceptible wavering in the enemy's army*

Faust.   Already the horizon darkles,
Yet meaningful anon there sparkles
A crimson-red, portentous light;
And now the weapons glitter bloody,
The air, the woods, and cliffs are ruddy;   10575
The whole sky mingles in the fight.
Mephistopheles.   The right flank stoutly holds its station;
But towering midst them, self-reliant,
I see Jack Fight-hard, nimble giant,
Busy and swift in his own fashion.   10580
Emperor.   At first I saw one arm engaging,
But now I see a dozen raging;
No law of Nature's working here.
Faust.   Have you not heard of mists that over
Sicilian sea-coasts sweep and hover?   10585
There, in the daylight, swaying, clear,
Uplifted into mid-air spaces
And mirrored in especial hazes,

One sees a vision strange appear:
There cities hover backward, onward,   10590
There gardens waver up- and downward,
As form on form breaks through the air.
Emperor.   Yet how suspicious! For I see the tall
Spear-heads flash lightning, one and all;
Behold our phalanx' shining lances!   10595
On each a nimble flamelet dances.
Too spectral seems to me this sight.
Faust.   Oh, pardon, Sire, those are the traces
Of spiritual natures, vanished races,
Pollux' and Castor's reflex, the great pair   10600
By whom all sailors used to swear;
They gather here their final might.
Emperor.   But say: to whom are we indebted
That Nature hath us so abetted
As here her rarest powers to unite?   10605
Mephistopheles.   To whom except that lofty Master
Who bears your fate within his breast?
Your foe's strong menace of disaster
Has stirred his soul to deep unrest.
You would he thank and save and cherish   10610
Though he himself should thereby perish.
Emperor.   They joyed to lead me round, with pomp invested;
I felt my power and wished to test it;
Fitting it seemed — though I was scarce aware —
To give to that white beard the cooling air.   10615
I spoiled a pastime that the clergy savour
And truly thus did not acquire their favour.
Now shall I, when so many years have passed,
Reap the returns of that glad deed at last?
Faust.   Rich is the interest of a generous deed.   10620
Look upwards! For he soon will send us,
If I err not, a sign portentous.
It will reveal itself at once, give heed!
Emperor.   An eagle soaring high in heaven I see,
A griffin wild pursues him threateningly.   10625
Faust.   Give heed: auspicious seems the sign.
The griffin is of fabled line;
Can he forget his foe is regal?
How dare he fight a genuine eagle?

[303]

Emperor.   And now in circles far extending   10630
  They wheel around, and in a flash
  They straight upon each other dash,
  Each other's throat and bosom rending.
Faust.   Mark how the sorry griffin, torn
  And ruffled sore, finds naught but injuries   10635
  And with his drooping lion's tail, forlorn,
  Plunging in tree-tops, vanishes.
Emperor.   Even as the sign, be the event!
  I accept it all with wonderment.
Mephistopheles toward the right.   Under crushing blows repeated   10640
  Has the foe perforce retreated;
  Fighting in uncertain fashion,
  They crowd toward their right wing's station,
  Leave their left wing undirected,
  In confusion, unprotected.   10645
  Now our phalanx, firmly tight'ning,
  Moves to right and like the lightning
  At the foe's weak spot it flashes. —
  Now, like waves the tempest dashes
  Spuming, equal powers are raging,   10650
  Twofold conflict wildly waging;
  Never was aught planned more glorious,
  In this battle we're victorious!
Emperor on the left to F a u s t.   Look! In jeopardy is our position,
  If I'm right in my suspicion.   10655
  Not a stone do I see flying.
  Mounted are the rocks low-lying,
  But the upper stand deserted.
  Now! — To one huge mass converted,
  Press the enemy on and on,   10660
  Now perhaps the pass have won.
  Toil unholy thus ends fruitless!
  And your arts have all proved bootless.
      Pause
Mephistopheles.   Here come my pair of ravens winging,
  What may the message be they're bringing?   10665
  I fear we're in an evil plight.
Emperor.   What are these doleful birds portending?
  Hither their sable sails they're bending
  From the hot combat on the height.

Mephistopheles to the ravens.   Perch near my ears. Lost is he never   10670
 To whom you grant your guardian favour,
 For your advice is sound and right.
Faust to the EMPEROR.   You've surely heard of pigeons flying
 Back to their food and nestlings, hieing
 From farthest lands to their own coast.   10675
 We find a difference here obtaining:
 Pigeon-post serves while peace is reigning,
 But war demands the raven-post.
Mephistopheles.   A fate's reported that distresses.
 See yonder how the enemy presses   10680
 Around our heroes' rocky wall.
 The nearest heights have been surmounted
 And if the pass be theirs accounted,
 We'll find it hard to stand at all.
Emperor.   So then deception was played on me!   10685
 Into these meshes you have drawn me;
 I shudder in this tangling net.
Mephistopheles.   Courage! All has not failed as yet.
 Have patience, craft, for the last knot.
 The usual end is fierce and hot.   10690
 My trusty messengers I have at hand;
 Command that I may give command.
Generalissimo who has arrived meanwhile.
 These men with whom you are confederated
 Have all the time made me feel irritated.
 No stable luck doth magic earn.   10695
 As for this conflict, I can't mend it;
 'Twas they began it, let them end it.
 My staff of office I return.
Emperor.   Keep it until a better hour
 Which luck perchance has in its grip.   10700
 Before this ugly chap I cower,
 Him and his raven-fellowship.

To MEPHISTOPHELES

 I can not grant the staff to you;
 You do not seem the proper man.
 Command! and seek to make us free anew,   10705
 Then happen all that happen can.

Exit into the tent with the GENERALISSIMO

Mephistopheles.   The blunted staff — may he have safety of it!

[305]

Us others it could little profit,
There was a kind of cross thereon.
Faust.   What's to be done?
Mephistopheles.   It is already done! —   10710
Now haste, black kin, in service fleeting
To the great mountain-lake! The undines greeting,
Beg them their torrents' semblance to prepare.
Through women's arts, beyond our seeing,
They can part semblance from real being,   10715
And that it is real being, each will swear.
                    Pause
Faust.   Those water-maidens, look! them must our ravens
Have quite enveigled from their havens,
For yonder is a trickling you can see.
From many a barren, dry place in the mountain   10720
Arises now a full, swift-flowing fountain.
It's over with our enemy's victory.
Mephistopheles.   To such strange greeting they're not used.
The boldest climbers are confused.
Faust.   With might now brook to brook is downward rushing;   10725
From many a gorge redoubled they come gushing.
One cascades in an arch adown the trail,
Soon spreading outward on a rocky level,
Foaming and rushing to and fro in revel,
Leaping down step by step into the vale.   10730
What boots heroic, brave resistance?
The mighty flood sweeps them past all assistance.
Before so fierce a surge I too must quail.
Mephistopheles.   Naught do I see of water and illusion;
Men's eyes alone are subject to confusion.   10735
In this odd case I take a great delight.
The crowds rush on, are fain to leap and bound.
The fools! they think that they'll be drowned,
And, as if swimming, drolly thrash around,
Panting and snorting on the solid ground.   10740
Confusion now is at its height.
                    The ravens have returned
I'll praise you to the lofty Master duly.
Now if you'll prove that you are masters truly,
Hasten ye to the glowing smithy
Where tireless dwarf-folk on their stithy   10745

Strike sparks from metal and from stone.
Ask, while at length you prate and flatter,
For fires that beam and flash and scatter,
Such as to their deep minds are known.
It's true, sheet lightning in the distance dancing   10750
And fall of stars from height of heaven glancing
May happen any summer night;
Sheet lightning, though, amid entangled bushes
And stars that hiss among the quenching rushes:
Not often seen is such a sight.   10755
Don't worry much, but be, with understanding,
At first entreating, then commanding.

Exeunt the ravens. All takes place as prescribed

Mephistopheles.   Before the foe there falls a thick, dark curtain!
Their step and tread become uncertain!
Everywhere flitting scintillations,   10760
Sudden and blinding illuminations.
That's fine, methinks, and has succeeded.
But now a sound of terror's needed.

Faust.   The hollow armour from the vaulted chambers
Revives in open air in all its members;   10765
There it's been rattling, clattering all around,
A wondrous-strange, discordant sound.

Mephistopheles.   Quite right! They're now past all restraining.
Hark to the sound of blows those knights are raining
As in the dear old times of yore.   10770
Brassards and cuisses, charging, rearing,
As Guelph and Ghibelline appearing,
Renew the everlasting strife once more.
Their enmity still unabated,
Firm in the hate their fathers hated,   10775
Both far and wide resounds the wild uproar.
Hate between parties is the devil's
Best helper still in all his revels,
Till the last horror ends it all;
Abhorrent sounds of panic panic,   10780
From time to time sharp, shrill, satanic,
Through all the valley rise and fall.

*Warlike tumult in the orchestra, finally passing
over into lively martial airs*

The Rival Emperor's Tent

THRONE, RICH SURROUNDINGS

Get-quick   Speed-booty

Speed-booty.

So we're the first ones here, I see!

Get-quick.

No raven flies as fast as we.

Speed-booty.

Oh, what a store lies here heaped up!   10785
Where shall I start? Where shall I stop?

Get-quick.

How full indeed the whole place stands;
I don't know where to lay my hands.

Speed-booty.

This rug is just the thing I need;
My couch is oft too hard indeed.   10790

Get-quick.

Here hangs a club with many a spike;
I long have wished to have its like.

Speed-booty.

The scarlet mantle, golden-hemmed,
Of such a one I've often dreamt.

Get-quick taking the weapon.

With this the job is quickly done;   10795
One strikes his man dead and goes on.
You've piled so much now on your back
But nothing worth while's in your sack.
That rubbish, leave it where it lay,
Take one of these small chests away!   10800
The army's destined pay they hold,
In this one's belly naught but gold.

Speed-booty.

This thing's a killing weight, I swear it;
I can not lift it, can not bear it.

Get-quick.

Quick! Duck down! Stoop! and I will pack   10805
The booty on your sturdy back.

[308]

Speed-booty.

    Oh, woe! Oh, woe! I'm done for! Whew!
    That load will break my back in two.
             The chest falls and springs open

Get-quick.

    There lies in heaps the ruddy gold;
    Quick, rake it up, fall to, lay hold!   10810

Speed-booty crouches down.

    Quick to the work, fill up my lap!
    'Twill be enough for any hap.

Get-quick.

    And so enough! Make haste and go!
             She stands up
    Your apron has a hole! Oh, woe!
    Go where you will or stand, I see   10815
    You sowing treasures all too free.

Bodyguards of our EMPEROR.

    This spot is sacred! What are you up to?
    Rifling the Emperor's treasure? Shame on you!

Get-quick.

    We risked our limbs for little pay
    And fetch our portion of the prey.   10820
    In enemies' tents it's custom so,
    And we, we're soldiers too, you know.

Bodyguards.

    In our profession that won't do.
    A carrion-thief and soldier too!
    Who nears our Emperor must be   10825
    A soldier used to honesty.

Get-quick.

    Yes, honesty — we know that same
    And "Contribution" is its name.
    All of you lie under one same cover:
    The password of your trade's "Fork over!"   10830
          To SPEED-BOOTY
    Away and drag off what you've got,
    Since welcome guests here we are not.
           Exeunt

First Bodyguard.

    Say, why did you not straightway slap
    His cheek? the dirty, saucy chap!

Second.

I don't know, strength had gone from me,   10835
So spectre-like they seemed to be.

Third.

Things all went bad before my sight;
They flickered, I could not see right.

Fourth.

How to express it I know not;
The whole day long it was so hot,   10840
Fearsome, oppressive, close as well.
While one man stood, another fell.
We groped and struck both high and low;
A foeman fell at every blow.
Before us swayed a kind of mist,   10845
And something hummed and roared and hissed.
Thus it went on — here are we now!
It happened but we don't know how.

> *The* EMPEROR *enters accompanied by four*
> PRINCES. *The* BODYGUARDS *retire*

Emperor.   Now be it as it may! The battle's won! And shattered,
Over the level plain the fleeing foes are scattered.   10850
Here stands the empty throne; with tapestry hung round,
The traitor's store of treasure blocks up all the ground.
With our own bodyguards in honour due protecting,
The people's envoys we're imperially expecting;
Glad messages are coming in from every side,   10855
In happy loyalty the realm is pacified.
Though in our fight, in truth, we've been by magic aided,
For our own selves alone we fought — so be it stated.
To combatants, we know, chance often works some good:
From heaven falls a stone, upon the foe rains blood,   10860
From caves may echo strains, great wonders radiating,
Lifting our hearts on high, the foeman's palpitating.
Doomed to eternal scorn, the vanquished bit the sod;
The victor, while he boasts, exalts the favouring God.
Without command, this thanks all men unite in bringing: 10865
"We praise Thee, God our Lord," a million throats are singing.
It rarely happed before, but now in highest praise
On my own grateful breast I turn my pious gaze.
A young and merry prince may give his days to pleasure,
But he will learn in time the moment's fitting measure.   10870

Wherefore I choose for counsel wholly to consort
With you four worthy men in realm and house and court.

To the FIRST PRINCE

You, Prince, achieved the host's well-ordered disposition,
Then, when the crisis came, moved it with bold precision.
Be active now in peace, just as the times suggest;   10875
Arch-Marshal you I dub and with the sword invest.

Arch-Marshal.   Your army, tasked till now to keep the civil order,
When it has made your throne secure along the border,
Then at your festive throngs we'll ask it as our care
In wide ancestral halls the banquet to prepare.   10880
The bright sword I will bear before you, hold beside you,
Your Majesty Supreme, ever to guard and guide you.   [grace,

Emperor to the SECOND.   Who as a gallant man doth show a pleasing
Shall be Arch-Chamberlain, no easy task and place.
The master you shall be of those of household station,   10885
Whose quarrels make their service oft a sore vexation.
You as a model to be honoured I install
To show how one can please the lord and court and all.

Arch-Chamberlain.

To further what his lord intends brings one to favour:
To help the best men on, to harm even bad ones never,   10890
Be frank and free from guile, reserved without deceit!
If you, Sire, read my heart, then is my joy complete.
But may my fancy now on to the banquet hasten?
When you go to the board, I'll hand the golden basin;
I'll hold your rings for you that so on gala days   10895
Your hands may be refreshed as I am by your gaze.

Emperor.   To think about a feast, too grave I'm feeling, truly;
Yet be it! Festal moods promote glad actions duly.

To the THIRD

I choose you as Arch-Steward. Henceforth you shall guard
The game-preserves, the manor-farm, and poultry-yard.   10900
Give me a choice of favourite foods at every season
As each month brings them forth, prepared with care and reason.

Arch-Steward.   Strict fasting be my highest duty, dearest wish,
Until I've placed before you some delighting dish.
The kitchen servants all shall be with me united;   10905
What's far will be brought near, the season expedited.
True, far-fetched early things with which the board is graced,
Do not attract you. Plain and hearty fare you'd taste.

[311]

Emperor to the FOURTH.   Since here to feasts the talk is evermore di-
    As cupbearer to me, young hero, be converted.   [verted,
    Arch-Cupbearer, take care that every cave of mine   10911
    Be stored most plentifully with the best of wine.
    Be temperate yourself, let not a gay occasion
    Lead you to yield yourself to happy chance's suasion.
Arch-Cupbearer.
    The young themselves, my prince, when trust in them is shown,   10915
    Before one is aware, stand forth as men full-grown.
    So I at that high feast shall duly take my station
    And to your sideboard's pomp add noblest decoration,
    Rare, gorgeous vessels, gold and silver, all set up.
    Beforehand, though, I'll choose for you the loveliest cup: 10920
    Of clear Venetian glass wherein delight lies waiting,
    Enhancing wine's good taste but never inebriating.
    On such a wondrous prize men oft too much depend,
    But you, most noble Sire, your temperance doth defend.
Emperor.   What I've designed for you in this most solemn hour,   10925
    You've heard with confidence because I speak with power.
    The Emperor's word is great and makes each gift secure,
    Yet needs his noble script to make the matter sure;
    It needs his signature. And in due form to make it,
    Here comes the fitting man this fitting hour to take it.   10930

                 The ARCHBISHOP-ARCH-CHANCELLOR
                      enters

Emperor.   If in the keystone doth a vaulted arch confide,
    Then is it built securely against time and tide.
    You see the princes four! We have but just now noted
    How next the state of house and court might be promoted.
    Now what the realm contains, in all its breadth enclosed,   10935
    Shall be with weight and power upon you five imposed.
    In lands you shall outshine all other men and orders,
    So of your property I'll now extend the borders
    Out of the lands once left to that disloyal band.
    To you who're true I grant full many a lovely land,   10940
    With this the lofty right to widen these possessions,
    As chance occurs, by barter, purchases, successions,
    To practise undisturbed — be this secured to you —
    Whatever sovereign rights, as landlords, are your due.
    As judges it's for you to make the last decisions,   10945
    And these shall suffer no appeals and no revisions.

Then imposts, interest, tributes, rents, safe-conduct, toll,
Dues from the mines, salt-works, and mints, yours is the whole,
For that my gratitude be fully demonstrated,
Nearest to Majesty you have I elevated.   10950
Archbishop.   In deepest gratitude to you we all unite,
You make us strong and firm and strengthen your own might.
Emperor.   Yet honour to you five I'll give in fuller measure.
I still live for my realm, to live is still my pleasure;
Ancestral chains, however, draw men's gaze from hours   10955
Of swift endeavour to the doom that always lowers.
In time I too shall part from all whom I hold dear;
Then you must choose the man who shall succeed me here.
Crown him and on the holy altar lift him high;
May then peace end what now began so stormily.   10960
Arch-Chancellor.   With pride at heart, yet humbly, as each mien convinces,
Here stand, before you bowed, the first of earthly princes.
As long as loyal blood through our full veins doth thrill,
We are the body which obeys your lightest will.
Emperor.   So, to conclude: what we've ordained and manifested,   10965
For all the years to come be it written and attested.
As lords, in truth, you've your possessions wholly free,
But on condition that they never parcelled be.
What you receive from us, however you expand it,
Shall to the eldest son be undivided handed.   10970
Arch-Chancellor.   At once I'll put on parchment in most joyous mood
This statute weighty for the realm's and for our good;
Engrossment, seal — thus shall the chancery invest it,
Your sacred signature, the lord's, will then attest it.
Emperor.   Thus I dismiss you so that each of you now may   10975
With tranquil mind reflect upon the glorious day.
                        The secular PRINCES *withdraw*
The Ecclesiastic remains and speaks with feeling.
The Chancellor went away, the Bishop stays before you;
A warning spirit bids him straightway to implore you.
With deep concern for you his father's-heart doth quake.
Emperor.   In this glad hour what makes you apprehensive? Speak!   10980
Archbishop.   With what a bitter pang I find that in this hour
Your consecrated head's in league with Satan's power.
True — as it seems — you're on the throne, secured by right,
But woe! in the Lord God's, in Father Pope's despite.
Which when the Pontiff learns, swift judgment he'll deliver,   10985

[313]

His holy bolt will crush your sinful realm forever.
He has not yet forgot — the day that you were crowned,
A solemn time — you had the sorcerer unbound.
And from your crown, where Christian honour hung suspended,
The ray of pardon first on that damned head descended. 10990
But smite your breast, and straightway from your wicked gain
Give back a moderate mite unto the holy fane;
That broad and hilly space where your tent stood erected,
Where by an evil spirits'-league you were protected,
Where to the Prince of Lies you lent attentive ear, 10995
Devote the land to holy use in pious fear,
With hill and forest dense, as far as they're extending,
With heights all clad in green, rich luscious pasture lending,
Clear lakes alive with fish, uncounted brooks that flow
Swiftly and serpent-like and plunging as they go, 11000
Then the broad vale itself with mead and lea and hollow.
Thus is remorse expressed, and pardon soon will follow.

Emperor.   My horror of this grievous fault is so profound
The borders of the land yourself shall measure round.

Archbishop.   First, where one so has sinned, the spot, so desecrated, 11005
Be to the Most High's service straightway dedicated.
My spirit sees the massive walls mount swiftly higher;
The morning sun's first rays already light the choir;
The growing edifice a cross's form is taking;
The nave grows long and high, believers' joy awaking; 11010
Through solemn portals they stream in with ardent zeal,
While over hill and dale resounds the bell's first peal.
It sounds from lofty towers aspiring up to Heaven.
Now comes the penitent to whom new life is given.
The consecration day — oh, may it soon be sent! — 11015
Your presence then will be the highest ornament.

Emperor.   Let this great work be done, a pious proclamation
That God the Lord I praise and seek my expiation.
Enough! I feel my soul already mounting high.

Archbishop.   As Chancellor I'll conclude the last formality. 11020

Emperor.   Produce a formal deed to show that I resign it
To Holy Mother Church, and I will gladly sign it.

Archbishop has taken his leave but turns back as he is about to go out.
Then to the work as it proceeds you'll not refuse
All tribute, interest, tithes — the land's whole revenues —
Forever. 'Twill need much for worthy sustentation 11025

And heavy are the costs of wise administration.
That we may build it fast on such a desert spot,
Some gold from all your booty surely you'll allot.
Besides, one has to have — I needs must seem insistent —
Wood, lime, and slate, and other things from places distant.   11030
The people will haul these, thus from the pulpit taught;
The Church doth bless a man who serving her has wrought.

Exit

Emperor.   Great is the sin and heavy that I've loaded on me;
These tiresome sorcerers — sore damage have they done me.

Archbishop returning again, with a very low obeisance.

Pardon, O Sire, you gave that most notorious man   11035
The empire's coast; but he'll be smitten by the ban
Unless due penance to the Holy Church you tender
And there tithe, interest, gifts, and revenues surrender.

Emperor vexed.   The land is not yet there; far out at sea it lies.

Archbishop.   A man who's right and patient sees his day arise.   11040
May your word in its strength forever be our stay!

Emperor alone.   I might as well cede my whole realm this very day.

Act V

Open Country

Wanderer.   Yes, the lindens stand there gloomy,
  Stand there yet in sturdy age,
  Now again appearing to me   11045
  After my long pilgrimage!
  It's the old place, and still standing
  Is the hut that sheltered me
  When the storm-tossed billow, stranding,
  Hurled me duneward from the sea!   11050
  And my hosts? I fain would greet them,
  Helpful folk, a valiant pair,
  But today I'll scarcely meet them;
  Agèd in those days they were.
  Pious they, in God believing!   11055
  Shall I knock or raise my voice?
  Hail! if you, a guest receiving,
  Still in kindly deeds rejoice.
Baucis, a little woman, very old.
  Stranger dear! Hush, hush! You're breaking
  My good husband's peaceful rest.   11060
  Sleeping long gives the brief waking
  Of an old man active zest.
Wanderer.   Tell me, mother, is it you really,
  Here to take the thanks of one
  Whose young life you saved so freely,   11065
  You and your good spouse alone?
  Are you Baucis who devoutly
  My half-dying lips restored?
                           The husband enters
  You Philemon who so stoutly
  Wrested from the wave my hoard?   11070
  'Twas your hurried flames ascending,
  'Twas your silver-chiming bell,

[316]

Brought to me a happy ending
Of adventure dread and fell.
Let me step forth that I may there   11075
Gaze upon the boundless sea;
Let me kneel and let me pray there,
Sore my heart oppresses me.

He strides forward on the dune

Philemon to BAUCIS.   Hasten, pray, and set the table
Where the garden blooms serene.   11080
Let him run, be dazed, unable
To believe what he'll have seen.

Standing beside the WANDERER

Where fierce billows did maltreat you,
Where waves, wildly foaming, rolled,
There a garden now doth greet you,   11085
Fair as Paradise of old.
Older grown, I was not able
To give help as once of yore;
As my limbs grew more unstable,
Far the waves drew from the shore.   11090
Wise lords' menials, bold and daring,
Dug the trenches, dammed the sea,
Ocean's ancient rights not sparing,
Lords, instead of it, to be.
See green meadows far extending,   11095
Garden, woodland, field, and town. —
Come, enjoy the meal attending,
For the sun will soon go down. —
Sails are gliding far out yonder,
Nightly to safe ports they fare.   11100
To their nests the sea-birds wander,
For the harbour now is there.
Far away, you scarce can see it,
Lies the blue sea and its strand;
Right and left, though far may be it,   11105
Spreads a thickly-peopled land.

The Three at table in the little garden

Baucis.   Silent still? and is there going
To your starved lips not a bit?
Philemon.   Fain the wonder he'd be knowing;
Fond of talking, tell him it.   11110

Baucis. 'Twas a wonder if there's any!
      Even today it troubles me;
      For the whole thing was uncanny,
      It was not as things should be.
Philemon. Can the Emperor be called sinning   11115
      Who bestowed on him the strand?
      Did a herald-trumpet's dinning
      Not proclaim it through the land?
      From our dunes a little distance
      First they set foot as we've seen: 11120
      Tents and huts! — Soon to existence
      Springs a palace midst the green.
Baucis. Vainly slaves by day were storming,
      Pick and shovel, stroke on stroke;
      Where by night the flames were swarming,   11125
      Stood a dike when we awoke.
      Wails of human victims bleeding
      Nightly to our ears were borne;
      Torches toward the ocean leading,
      A canal was there at morn.   11130
      Godless is the man; our labour,
      Grove, and cottage covets he,
      Such an overlording neighbour,
      Master of us will he be.
Philemon. Be it so, he's offered to us   11135
      Fair estate in his new land!
Baucis. Little good will marsh-land do us;
      On your own height keep your stand!
Philemon. To the chapel let's awaying,
      There the sun's last rays behold,   11140
      Ring the bell and kneeling, praying,
      Trust us to the God of old.

Palace

Spacious, ornamental garden; broad, straight canal. **FAUST,**
      in extreme old age, walking about, reflecting

Lynceus, the warder, through a speaking-trumpet.
      The sun is setting, ships are nearing

The safe home-port with song and cheer.
A mighty barge is just appearing   11145
On the canal; 'twill soon be here.
Their motley flags the breeze caressing,
The rigid masts stand up to view;
In you the seaman finds his blessing,
And Fortune at your prime greets you.   11150
        The little bell rings on the dune
Faust starting up.   Accursèd bell! Base clangour sending,
It wounds like spiteful shot from slings;
Before mine eyes my realm's unending,
Yet at my back vexation stings.
The envious bell is aye recalling: 11155
From blemish is my realm not free!
The lindens, brown hut, church half-falling,
Not one of these belongs to me.
And if I'd seek rest, there repairing,
I'll shudder as with alien fear,   11160
A thorn to feet and eyes, unsparing!
Oh, would that I were far from here!
Warder as above.   How blithely doth the gay bark glide
Before the breeze of eventide!
How tower, as it swiftly sails,   11165
The chests and boxes, sacks and bales!
      A splendid bark, richly and variously laden with
      products of foreign countries

MEPHISTOPHELES   THE THREE MIGHTY COMRADES
Chorus.
      Here do we land,
      Come from on board.
      Hail to our patron,
      Hail, our Lord!   11170
      They disembark; the goods are brought ashore
Mephistopheles.   We've proved ourselves as it behooves,
Pleased if our patron but approves.
With but two ships we sailed away,
With twenty we're in port today.
The great things we have done — how great,   11175
That can be seen well from our freight.
      [319]

The free sea sets the spirit free.
Who'll stop to think when he's at sea!
What helps is suddenness of grip.
You catch a fish, you catch a ship,   11180
And when you're once the lord of three,
You hook the fourth one easily;
Then is the fifth in sorry plight,
You have the Power and so the Right.
You ask not *How* but *What* it be.   11185
I know not how the sea is charted
If war and trade and piracy
Are not triune and can't be parted.

The Three Mighty Comrades.

He doesn't greet!
He doesn't thank!   11190
As if we brought
Our lord what stank.
See what a
Wry face he has got,
The royal wealth   11195
Doth please him not.

Mephistopheles.

Do not await here
Further pay;
You took indeed
Your share away.   11200

The Comrades.

That took we but
As pastime fair;
We all demand
An equal share.

Mephistopheles.

First range in order,   11205
Hall on hall,
The costly objects,
One and all.
When this rich sight
He comes to see   11210
And reckons all
More narrowly,
A niggard he'll

[320]

Not be at least;
He'll give the fleet   11215
Feast after feast.
Tomorrow come the gay birds here;
For them I shall provide good cheer.
The cargo is taken away

Mephistopheles to FAUST.
With gloomy gaze, with brow austere,
Of your supreme good luck you hear.   11220
High wisdom has been crowned. 'Tis done,
The shore and ocean are at one.
Now from the shore, for their swift trips,
The willing ocean takes the ships.
So say what's true: from this high place   11225
Your arm doth all the world embrace.
Here it began: here once there stood
The first rude shanty made of wood.
A little ditch was dug away
Where busy oars now toss their spray.   11230
Your will, your people's industry,
Have won the prize of earth and sea.
From here—

Faust.   Oh, that accursèd *here!*
That is the burden hard to bear.
Wise one, to you I must declare it.   11235
It gives my heart sting after sting;
It is impossible to bear it,
And yet I'm shamed to say the thing.
The old folks there should make concession,
I'd have the lindens for my throne;   11240
The few trees there, not my possession,
Spoil me the world I call my own.
There I would fain, for world-wide gazing
From branch to branch a scaffold raising,
Open to view the course I've run,   11245
That I might see all I have done,
View at one glance, before me brought,
The masterpiece of human thought,
Which made a fact shrewd wisdom's plan
And won broad dwelling-place for man.   11250
    Thus suffer we the sorest rack,

Midst riches feeling what we lack.
The chime, the scent of linden-bloom,
Close round me as with church and tomb.
The power of my all-conquered will   11255
Breaks down before that sandy hill.
How shall I ever free my spirit?
The bell rings and I rage to hear it!
Mephistopheles.   Of course! Some paramount distress
Must gall your life to bitterness.   11260
Who doubts it? To each noble ear
That jangle seems a hostile fleer.
And that accursèd bim-bam-booming,
The cheerful evening sky be-glooming,
Mingles in each event that passes,   11265
From the first bath to burial-masses,
As if all mortal life should seem,
Twixt *bim* and *bam,* a vanished dream.
Faust.   Their opposition, stubbornness,
Spoil the most glorious success,   11270
Till in deep, angry pain one must
At last grow tired of being just.
Mephistopheles.   Why are you troubling? temporizing?
Aren't you long used to colonizing?
Faust.   Then go and shift them to one side! —   11275
You know the farm — it's small but fair —
I've chosen for the agèd pair.
Mephistopheles.   We'll bear them off and on new ground
They'll stand before one looks around.
For violence that's past and done   11280
A pretty dwelling will atone.
                    He whistles shrilly. THE THREE *enter*
Mephistopheles.   Come! Do the lord's command — 'tis meet! —
Tomorrow he will feast the fleet.
The Three.   The old lord gave us naught but slights;
A feast that's fleet is ours by rights.   11285
                    Exeunt
Mephistopheles to the spectators.   Here haps a hap of long ago;
With Naboth's vineyard it happed so. (*1 Kings XXI*)

Deep Night

Lynceus the warder singing on the watch-tower of the castle.

Keen vision my dower,
Placed here for my sight,
And sworn to the tower,   11290
In the world I delight.
I gaze at the far,
I look at the near,
The moon and the star,
The wood and the deer.   11295
In all things around me
Is grace without end,
And as they astound me,
Myself I commend.
Thou fortunate vision,   11300
Thou mayest have seen
Whatever there may be,
Yet fair hath it been.
                    Pause
          But not only to delight me
Am I stationed here on high;   11305
What a gruesome sight, to fright me,
Threatens from the dark world nigh!
Flashing sparkles I see gushing
Through the lindens' twofold night;
Ever stronger rages, rushing,   11310
Fanned by draughts, a glowing light.
Ah! inside the cabin's flaming,
Though moss-grown and damp it stand;
Speedy succour is it claiming
And no rescue is at hand.   11315
Ah, those good old folk whom duty
Once made careful of the fire,
Now of smoke become the booty!
What a misadventure dire!
Flames are flaring, now they wave them   11320
Through the black, moss-covered shell;
Could the good folk only save them

[323]

From that furious burning hell!
Brilliant tongues of flame are flashing,
Through the leaves and branches lashing;   11325
Withered boughs that flare up, burning,
Swiftly glow, plunge from the tree.
Must ye eyes — such things discerning —
Must I, so far-sighted be?
Down the little chapel crashes,   11330
Burdened under branches' fall.
Winding upward, pointed flashes
Seize upon the tree-tops tall.
To their roots the trunks, ignited,
Hollow, purple-red, glow on.   11335

Long pause. Song

Gone what once the eye delighted,
With the centuries is gone.

Faust on the balcony, facing the dunes.

What song hear I of lamentation?
Too late, the word or tone to heed.
My warder wails, and deep vexation   11340
Stirs me for this impulsive deed.
Yet though the lindens, grown so thickly,
Now half-charred trunks, defile the place,
An outlook-point is builded quickly,
Where I can gaze through endless space.   11345
Thence too I'll see the new-made dwelling
Which for that agèd pair I'll raise,
Who, of my kind forbearance telling,
Will there enjoy their latter days.

Mephistopheles and THE THREE *below.*

Here we're coming at full trot,   11350
But pardon us! well went it not.
We rapped on it, we chapped on it,
And still not opened was a slit;
We rattled on, we pounded more,
Till down there lay the rotten door.   11355
We called, a loud and threatening call,
But found no hearing there at all.
As in such case has oft occurred,
They would not, so they had not heard.
We tarried not long thereabout;   11360

Swift, as you bade, we cleared them out.
The couple suffered scarce a jot;
From fright they fell dead on the spot.
A stranger, hid there, made a show
Of fight but he was soon laid low. 11365
But in the brief and furious fray,
From embers that around us lay,
The straw caught fire. It's blazing free,
A funeral pyre for all the three.
Faust. To my commands then deaf were ye? 11370
Exchange I meant, not robbery.
This unconsidered, savage blow,
I curse it! Share the curse and go!
Chorus. The old saw says — it echoes still —
To violence submit thy will! 11375
If bold and steadfast, stake thy pelf,
Thy house and home and — thine own self.

Exeunt

Faust on the balcony.
The stars conceal their light and glow,
The fire is sinking, flickering low;
A cool wind fans it with its wings. 11380
Vapour and smoke it hither brings.
Rash the command, too quick obeyed! —
What hovers hither like a shade?

Midnight

Four grey women enter

First. My name, it is Want.
Second. And my name is Guilt.
Third. My name, it is Worry.
Fourth. And mine is Distress. 11385
Three Together. The door is locked fast, we can not get in:
A rich man dwells there, we may not go in.
Want. Here I turn to shadow.
Guilt. Here I cease to be.
Distress. The pampered ones turn their faces from me.

[325]

Worry.   Ye sisters, ye can not, may not go within   11390
    But even at the keyhole will Worry slip in.
Worry vanishes

Want.   Grey sisters, away! Ye must vanish from here!
Guilt.   I'll bind me beside thee and keep me quite near.
Distress.   Distress keepeth pace with you, still as a breath.
The Three.   Fast gather the clouds, they blot out each star!   11395
    Behind there! behind! From afar, from afar,
    There cometh our brother, there cometh he . . . Death.
Exeunt

Faust in the palace.   Four saw I come and only three go hence;
    Of what they said I could not grasp the sense.
    "Distress" one seemed to say — 'twas like a breath —   11400
    A gloomy word then followed — "Death."
    Hollow the sound, with spectral message fraught.
    My way to freedom I have not yet fought.
    Could I all magic from my pathway banish,
    Could quite unlearn its spells and bid it vanish,   11405
    Nature, could I face thee, in thy great plan,
    Then were it worth the pain to be a man.
      Such was I once ere I the gloom explored
    And cursed me and the world with impious word.
    The air so teems with many a ghostly shape,   11410
    No way appears whereby one may escape.
    If one day, bright with reason, on us beams,
    The night entangles us in webs of dreams.
    From young green fields we homeward turn, elate;
    A bird croaks, and his croaking tells — ill-fate.   11415
    Thus superstitions all our hours entwine,
    With happening, with warning, or with sign.
    And thus abashed, we find ourselves alone.
    The portal creaks, and no one enters — none!
Agitated

    Is someone here?
Worry.   The question claims an "Aye!"   11420
Faust.   And thou, who art thou then?
Worry.   Enough! — 'Tis I.
Faust.   Away! Begone!
Worry.   I am where I should be.
Faust first furious, then appeased, to himself.
    Take care and say no word of sorcery.

[326]

Worry.

Though the ear hear not my droning,
Yet the heart doth feel it, moaning.   11425
In a variable guise
Cruel force I exercise.
On the pathway, on the billow,
Ever-agonizing fellow,
Always found though never sought,   11430
Flattered, cursed, in word and thought.
Is Worry still to thee unknown?

Faust.   Through the world I have but flown.
Whatever I craved, I seized it by the hair,
Whatever sufficed not, I let fare.   11435
Whatever escaped, I let it go.
I've but desired and but achieved, each hour,
And then again have wished, and so with power
Stormed through my life; at first with power and greatness;
But now life moves with cautious, wise sedateness.   11440
Well do I know the sphere of earth and men.
The view beyond is barred to mortal ken;
A fool! who thither turns his blinking eyes
And dreams he'll find his like above the skies.
Let him stand fast and look around on earth;   11445
Not mute is this world to a man of worth.
Why need he range through all eternity?
Here he can seize all that he knows to be.
Thus let him wander down his earthly day;
When spirits spook, let him pursue his way;   11450
Let him find pain and bliss as on he stride,
He! every moment still unsatisfied.

Worry.

Whom I once possess will ever
Find the world not worth endeavour;
Endless gloom around him being,   11455
Rise nor set of sun he's seeing.
Be each outer sense excelling,
Still is darkness in him dwelling;
He can not through any measures
Make him lord of any treasures.   11460
All luck turns into caprices;
Him midst plenty hunger seizes.

[327]

Be it joy or be it sorrow,
He postpones it till the morrow,
Waiting for the future ever   11465
And therefore achieving never.

Faust.   Be still! Not so wilt thou get hold of me!
I do not care to hear such drivel.
Begone! That wretched litany
Could even befool the wisest man to evil.   11470
Worry.
                Go or come? How shall he guide him?
                All decision is denied him;
                Though with but a smooth road coping,
                He takes half-steps, wavering, groping,
                Wandering as if bemisted,   11475
                Everything he sees as twisted;
                Burdening himself and others,
                Breathing deeply, still he smothers,
                Though not smothered, lifeless faring,
                Not resigned and not despairing.   11480
                Rolling on without remission,
                Painful quitting, loath submission,
                Freedom now, now subjugation,
                Semi-sleep, poor recreation,
                Bind him fast within his cell   11485
                And prepare the wretch for Hell!

Faust.   Ill-omened spectres, ye! Thus mangle ye still
The human race on thousands of occasions;
Indifferent days themselves entangle ye still
In a vile web of mingled tribulations.   11490
It's hard, I know, from spirits to get free;
The strenuous spirit-tie we can not sever.
Still, Worry, though it great and stealthy be,
Thy power I shall not acknowledge ever.
Worry.
                Then learn it now. My parting curse thou'lt find   11495
                Swift and forever thee attending.
                Throughout their lives are mortals blind;
                So, Faustus, be thou too at thy life's ending!
                         She breathes on him and goes

[328]

Faust blinded.   Night presses round me, deep and deeper still.
And yet within me beams a radiant light;   11500
What I have planned, I hasten to fulfil;
Only the master's word has weight and might.
Up from your couches, vassals, every man!
Bring happily to sight my daring plan.
Seize shovel, spade! With all your tools lay on!   11505
The work staked out must with all speed be done.
Strict order and swift diligence
Result in fairest recompense.
To consummate the greatest enterprises
One spirit for a thousand hands suffices.   11510

Great Outer Court of the Palace

Torches

Mephistopheles as overseer, leading the way.
    This way, this way! Come on, come on,
    Lemurs, ye shambling creatures,
    Of tendons, sinews, and of bones
    Ye patched-up semi-natures.

Lemurs in chorus.
    We come at once, are at your hand,   11515
    And it's our half-impression
    The call concerns a spacious land
    Where we shall have possession.
    The pointed stakes, here are they all,
    Long chains with which to measure;   11520
    But we've forgotten why the call
    Came to disturb our leisure.

Mephistopheles.   An artist's zeal would here be wrong;
You need no measure but your brothers'.
Let him who's longest lay his length along,   11525
And you, lift up the turf round here, you others.
As for our fathers it was done,
Dig out a square, a longish one!
Out of the palace to the narrow home,
So stupidly at last the end doth come.   11530

Lemurs digging with mocking gestures.

When I was young and lived and loved,
Methought it very sweet,
When joy rang out and all was gay,
Then merrily went my feet.

But now Old Age with his stealthy steps   11535
Hath clawed me with his crutch;
Over a grave's door stumbled I,
Why yawned the door so much?

Faust coming out of the palace, gropes his way by the door-posts.

The click of spades — ah, how it heartens me!
It is my crowd that toils the while,   11540
Earth with itself to reconcile,
To set fixed limits to the sea
And gird it with a rigid zone.

Mephistopheles aside.   And yet you work for us alone
While you for dikes and pens are caring,   11545
Since now for Neptune you're preparing —
That Devil of the Sea — a great repast.
In every way you're lost and lorn;
To aid us every element is sworn,
And ruin is the end at last.   11550

Faust.   Overseer!

Mephistopheles.   Here!

Faust.   Be it done as it may,
Bring crowd on crowd of workmen here!
Spur them with rigour and good cheer,
Entice, coerce, give ample pay!
I wish each day fresh news of what's been done,   11555
How the groove lengthens that we have begun.

Mephistopheles half aloud.   The talk was — when the news they gave —
Not of a groove but of a grave.

Faust.   A marsh extends along the mountain-chain
That poisons what so far I've been achieving;   11560
Were I that noisome pool to drain,
'Twould be the highest, last achieving.
Thus space to many millions I will give
Where, though not safe, yet free and active they may live.
Green fertile fields where straightway from their birth   11565
Both men and beast live happy on the newest earth,
Settled forthwith along the mighty hill

[330]

Raised by a daring, busy people's will.
Within, a land like Paradise; outside,
Up to the brink may rage the mighty tide,   11570
And where it gnaws and would burst through or sap,
A common impulse hastes to close the gap.
Yes! to this thought I hold unswerving,
To wisdom's final fruit, profoundly true:
Of freedom and of life he only is deserving   11575
Who every day must conquer them anew.
Thus here, by danger girt, the active day
Of childhood, manhood, age will pass away.
Aye! such a throng I fain would see,
Stand on free soil among a people free.   11580
Then might I say, that moment seeing:
"Ah, linger on, thou art so fair!"
The traces of my earthly being
Can perish not in aeons — they are there!
That lofty moment I now feel in this: 11585
I now enjoy the highest moment's bliss.

> FAUST *sinks back, the* LEMURS *take him up*
> *and lay him on the ground*

Mephistopheles.   Him could no pleasure sate, suffice no bliss,
So wooed he ever changeful phantoms' favour.
The last vile, empty moment — this! —
The poor wretch wished to hold it fast forever.   11590
Him who against me stoutly held his stand,
Time conquers — here the old man lies in sand.
The clock stands still —
Chorus.   Stands still! No sound is heard.
The clock's hand falls.
Mephistopheles.   It falls, 'tis finished.
Chorus.   'Tis past.
Mephistopheles.   "Past" — 'tis a stupid word.   11595
Past — why?
Past and pure Naught, sheer Uniformity!
Of what avail's perpetual creation
If later swept off to annihilation?
"So it is past!" You see what that must mean?   11600
It is the same as had it never been,
And yet whirls on as if it weren't destroyed.
I should prefer the Everlasting Void.

[331]

Burial

Lemur Solo.

           Who hath so badly built the house
           With shovel and with spade?   11605

Lemurs Chorus.

           For thee, dull guest, in hempen vest,
           It all too well was made.

Lemur Solo.

           Who hath so badly decked the hall?
           Not chairs, not table, any!

Lemurs Chorus.

           'Twas loaned for a short interval;   11610
           The creditors are so many.

Mephistopheles.   The body lies, and ere the spirit flee,
    I'll quickly show the blood-writ scroll; —
    But they've so many means — alas for me! —
    To cheat the Devil out of many a soul.   11615
    If one pursues the old way, one's resisted,
    And to the new we do not feel commended;
    I could of old have done it unattended,
    But now I have to be assisted.
        In all things, wretched is our plight!   11620
    Transmitted custom, ancient right —
    Naught's to be trusted now as in the past.
    The soul once with its last breath left its house;
    I watched my prey, and like the swiftest mouse,
    Snap! in my firm-shut claws I held it fast.   11625
    Now it delays, won't quit the dismal place,
    The wretched corpse's house so nauseating;
    The elements, each other hating,
    Will finally expel it in disgrace.
    And though for days I fret till I am weary,   11630
    When? how? and *where?* that is the tiresome query.
    In power swift and strong Old Death's played out;
    Even the *whether* long has been in doubt.
    With lust I've often watched the rigid members —
    'Twas but a sham; they moved: life stirred the embers.   11635

              Gestures of conjuration like those of a fantastic
              fugleman

Lords of the straight, lords of the crookèd horn,
Come quick! in double time! and show your fettle,
You of old diabolic cut and metal,
And with you let the maw of Hell be borne.
True, many maws hath Hell, in short,   11640
To use as due to rank and dignity;
But henceforth in this final sport
Not so particular shall we be.

The horrible maw of Hell opens up on the left

Tusks yawn; and from the vaulted gorge profound
The furious, fiery torrents flow,   11645
And at the rear, in seething vapours wound,
I see the flaming city in eternal glow.
Up to the very teeth the crimson billow dashes,
The damned, in hope of help, swim into view;
But now the huge hyena bites and gnashes,   11650
And their hot course the agonized renew.
Much more is left to spy in corners there,
In narrowest space horrors supreme!
You do well, sinners to affright and scare,
But they'll think it a lie and sham and dream.   11655

To the fat devils with short, straight horns

You fat-paunched rogues with cheeks like hell-fire burning,
You glow so fattened by Hell's sulphur and its steam;
What necks, so thick-set, short, and never turning!
Watch here below for phosphorescent gleam:
That's the wee soul, Psyche with fluttering wing;   11660
Don't pluck the wings, 'twere else a nasty worm.
I'll stamp my seal upon the beastly thing,
Then off with it in whirling-fiery-storm.
These lower regions, watch them duly,
You bladders — that's the duty you've to show;   11665
If it was pleased to live there, truly,
That we do not so accurately know.
It feels at home in navels, there's no doubt;
So heed my words, for there it may pop out.

To the lean devils with long, crookèd horns

You clowns, huge fuglemen, bashaws,   11670
Clutch at the air — no respite take or give;
Stretch out your arms, show your sharp claws,
That you may catch the fluttering fugitive.

[333]

In its old home bad surely is its plight;
Genius is quick to soar, so too will be this sprite.   11675
Glory, from above, on the right

A Heavenly Host.

           Heavenly kindred,
           Envoys unhind'red,
           Follow in flight:
           Sinners forgiving,
           Making dust living!   11680
           Bring while ye're swaying,
           Lingering, staying,
           To all things living
           A trace of delight.

Mephistopheles.   Discords I hear, a most disgusting humming   11685
That with unwelcome light comes from above;
It is that boyish-girlish bungling strumming
That sanctimonious tastes are prone to love.
You know how we in deep depravèd hours
Planned the destruction of the human race;   11690
The shamefullest we planned with all our powers
In their devotion finds a perfect place.
    The canting tribe, they come in foppish fettle!
Many they've snatched away before our eyes;
With our own weapons are they giving battle;   11695
They're devils too, though in disguise.
If you lose here, in endless shame you'll sink;
On to the grave and hold fast by the brink!

Chorus of Angels strewing roses.

           Roses, ye glowing ones,
           Balsam-bestowing ones,   11700
           Fluttering and soaring,
           Sweet life restoring,
           Branchlets revealing,
           Fresh buds unsealing,
           Blooming be seen!   11705

           Springtime, awake him
           In purple and green;
           Paradise take him,
           The sleeper serene.

Mephistopheles to the Satans.
    Why duck and jerk? Is that Hell's wonted rule?   11710
    Do stand your ground and let them scatter.
    Back to his place, each gawky fool!
    They think perhaps that with such flowery matter
    They'll snow hot devils in and make them cool.
    Your breath will melt and shrivel it. — Now puff,   11715
    You puffers! — Hold! It is enough, enough!
    Your foul breath bleaches all the fluttering stuff. —
    Be not so violent! Shut your jaws and noses!
    You've blown indeed too strongly at the roses.
    Oh, that the proper measure you would ever learn!   11720
    They shrivel — yes, they scorch, they char, they burn!
    With poisonous bright flames they're floating hither.
    Stand fast against them and press close together!
    Your strength dies out, your courage is all spent!
    A strange, voluptuous glow the devils scent.   11725
Chorus of Angels.
              Blossoms ethereal,
              Flamelets empyreal,
              Love now are bearing they,
              Bliss are preparing they,
              All hearts they sway.   11730
              Words of true charity,
              In ether's clarity,
              Bring hosts in verity
              Infinite day.

Mephistopheles.   Oh, curses, shame on such an idiot band!   11735
    Upon their heads the Satans stand.
    Head over heels fat ones are curving,
    Plunging in Hell ass-uppermost.
    So be your bath as hot as you're deserving!
    But I'll remain here at my post.   11740
             Fighting the hovering roses
    Off, will-o'-the-wisp! However bright your flake,
    When caught, you're but a sticky, filthy cake.
    Why flutter thus? Away with you and quick! —
    Like pitch and sulphur they cling to my neck.
Chorus of Angels.   What ye've no title to,   11745
              Ye may not share it;

What bringeth pain to you,
Ye must forbear it.
If we'll press in with might,
Valiantly must we fight.   11750
Only the loving
Does Love lead to light.

Mephistopheles.   My head burns, heart and liver too. I scent
A more than devilish element,
Sharper by far than Hell's own fire! —   11755
And hence your wailing, monstrous, dire,
You haplessly enamoured! who, when spurned,
Toward your darlings keep your faces turned.
    I too! What draws my head in that direction?
Am I not sworn to its complete rejection?   11760
To see it I was once so bitterly averse!
Has something alien pierced me through and through?
Now these most charming youths I love to view.
What holds me back that I can't curse? —
And if I let myself be fooled and baited,   11765
Who henceforth fool-in-chief will be?
The stunning rascals whom I've always hated,
Charming beyond words do they seem to me! —
    Tell me, sweet children, that I may not miss you!
Aren't you too of the race of Lucifer?   11770
You are so fair I'd truly like to kiss you;
To say you come just right, I scarcely err.
I feel so much at home, so natural,
As though we'd met a thousand times before;
So stealthy, kitten-like, desirable,   11775
At every glance your beauty charms me more.
Oh, do draw near! Grant me one glance, I pray!
Angels.   We're coming now, why do you shrink away?
We're drawing near, remain now if you can.
                    The ANGELS *hover around and occupy the*
                        whole space
Mephistopheles crowded into the proscenium.
You call us damnèd spirits! You,   11780
You are yourselves the wizards true,
For you seduce both maid and man.
Oh, what a damnable event!

Is this indeed love's element?
A raging fire fills all my frame, 11785
My neck scarce feels the scorching flame. —
You hover to and fro — come down, I say,
Bestir your lovely limbs in a more worldly way;
In truth, it suits you well, that serious style,
But just for once I'd like to see you smile; 11790
'Twould be for me eternally entrancing.
I mean like lovers at each other glancing,
A flicker round the mouth, done easily.
You tall boy, you would I possess most gladly;
That priestly mien befits you very badly, 11795
Do look at me a little lustfully!
More nude, yet decently, could you appear,
That flowing shirt is over-moralizing —
They turn around — To see them from the rear!
The little rogues are quite too appetizing. 11800
Chorus of Angels.

> Flames, love revealing,
> Grow ever clearer;
> To damned through error
> May truth bring healing,
> That they from evil 11805
> Find glad retrieval,
> In the All-Unity
> Blessèd to be.

Mephistopheles recovering his self-possession.
What's happ'ning to me! — Like Job I've boil on boil
From head to foot so that I shrink to view me, 11810
Yet triumph still when I search through and through me
And place my trust in my own self and kin.
My noble parts are saved despite the broil;
The love-spell works no deeper than the skin.
Now are the damned flames burned out past recall, 11815
And as is right, I curse you one and all!
Chorus of Angels.

> Ardours of Heaven!
> Round whom they brood,
> In life is given
> Bliss with the Good. 11820

Laud ye together,
Rise to your goal;
Cleansed is the ether,
Breathe thou, O Soul!

They rise aloft, bearing away FAUST'S *immortal part*

Mephistopheles looking around.

How's this? — Where have they gone, I wonder?   11825
You have surprised me, young folk though you be,
And flown away to Heaven with the plunder.
Hence played they round this grave so wantonly!
A treasure great, unique, they've confiscated.
The lofty soul, to me hypothecated,   11830
Out of my hands they've smuggled craftily.
      To whom now shall my sad case be presented?
Who'll get for me my well-earned right?
In your old age you have been circumvented,
But you deserved it, wretched is your plight.   11835
I have mismanaged in disgraceful fashion;
Great outlay shamefully I've thrown away.
A vulgar lust, an absurd, lovesick passion,
Led the well-seasoned Devil far astray.
Since with this childish, silly folderol   11840
I — shrewd and would-be wise — obsessed me,
In very truth the folly is not small
That in conclusion has possessed me.

Mountain Gorges

FOREST, ROCKS, DESERT

Holy anchorites scattered up the mountain-side, dwelling among the clefts

Chorus and Echo.

Forests are swaying here,
Rocks weight them downward sheer,   11845
Roots clutching rocks appear,
Trunk close by trunk is near.
Wave dashes after wave,

[338]

Shelter hath deepest cave.
Lions, soft-footed, dumb,   11850
Friendly around us come,
Honouring the sacred place,
Refuge of love and grace.

Pater Ecstaticus hovering up and down.

Endless ecstatic fire,
Glow of pure love's desire,   11855
Pangs of the yearning breast,
Rapture in God to rest.
Arrows, pierce through me here,
Lances, subdue me here,
Bludgeons, come, batter me,   11860
Lightnings, come, shatter me,
That my mortality
Flee from reality,
Endless star shine above,
Core of eternal love.   11865

Pater Profundus, Lower Region.

As chasms at my feet descending
Burden the chasms more profound,
As a thousand radiant streams are wending
To foaming cataracts' awesome bound,
As, by its own strong impulse driven,   11870
The tree mounts upward, straight and tall,
So to Almighty Love 'tis given
To fashion all, to cherish all.
All round me is a savage roaring
As if swayed wood and rocky steep;   11875
Yet plunges, lovely in its pouring,
The wealth of water to the deep,
Summoned below, the vale to brighten,
The bolt that fell with sudden flare,
The atmosphere to cleanse and lighten   11880
Which in its bosom poison bare,
Heralds of love are they, proclaiming
Creative powers that us enfold.
May they, my inner self inflaming,
Quicken my soul confused and cold,   11885

[339]

Its blunted senses galled unceasing,
Bound fast in chains that cramp and smart.
O God! these thoughts of mine appeasing,
Illumine Thou my needy heart!

Pater Seraphicus, Middle Region.

What a morning cloudlet hovers   11890
Through the pine-trees' tossing hair!
Do I guess what life it covers?
They are spirits young and fair.

Chorus of Blessèd Boys.

Tell us, father, whither go we?
Tell us, kind one, who are we?   11895
Happy are we all, that know we;
Sweet, oh, sweet it is to be.

Pater Seraphicus.

Boys! At midnight born, with only
Halfway opened sense and brain,
Straightway lost to parents lonely,   11900
For the angels sweetest gain.
If ye feel that in this place is
One who loves, then hither fare;
But of earth's rude ways no traces
Do ye happy spirits bear.   11905
In mine eyes descend, pray choose them,
Organs meet for earthly sphere;
As your own eyes ye can use them,
Gaze upon this landscape here.

He receives them into himself

Those are trees, and cliffs are yonder,   11910
There a stream that downward leaps,
Rolling with the voice of thunder
Down its short way to the deeps.

Blessèd Boys from within.

Grand the scene to which we're waking,
But too full of gloom and woe;   11915
We're from fright and terror quaking,
Noble, kind one, let us go!

Pater Seraphicus.

On to higher spheres ascending,
Unawares grow endlessly,
As in fashion pure, unending,   11920

God's high presence strengthens thee.
That is spirits' sustentation,
In free ether all effecting,
Endless loving's revelation,
To beatitude perfecting.   11925

Chorus of Blessèd Boys circling round the highest peaks.
                    Hand in hand clinging,
                    In a glad ring unite,
                    Soaring and singing,
                    Feeling a pure delight.
                    Godlike the yearning,   11930
                    Confident be;
                    For whom ye're yearning,
                    Him shall ye see.

Angels soaring in the higher atmosphere, bearing FAUST'S *immortal part.*
                    Lo! rescued is this noble one
                    From evil machination;   11935
                    "Who e'er aspiring, struggles on,
                    For him there is salvation."
                    And if to him Celestial Love
                    Its favouring grace has given,
                    The Blessèd Host comes from Above   11940
                    And welcomes him to Heaven.
The Younger Angels.
                    Roses sainted women spended,
                    Penitent through mercy glorious,
                    Helped to make the fight victorious,
                    That the lofty work be ended,   11945
                    That be won this spirit-treasure.
                    Demons shrank in sore displeasure,
                    Devils fled the roses' flinging.
                    Not with wonted hell-pangs stinging,
                    Love-pangs brought them to disaster.   11950
                    Even the old Satan-Master
                    By sharp pain was penetrated.
                    Shout with joy! It's consummated!
The More Perfected Angels.
                    Still earthly rests remain
                    Which have oppressed us;   11955

[341]

They'd not be pure of stain,
Though of asbestos.
When every element
Strong spirit-forces
Have borne away and blent,   11960
No angel divorces
The natures two in one,
So close they weave them;
Eternal Love alone
Can ever cleave them.   11965

The Younger Angels.

Mist-like round yonder height,
I'm just discovering
Where in approaching flight
Spirit-life's hovering.
The clouds are growing clear,   11970
I see a host draw near
Of Blessèd Boys,
Freed from the stress of earth,
Circling, united!
They taste the joys   11975
Of spring in their new birth,
Therein delighted.
Let him at once begin
Perfected joy to win,
With these united!   11980

The Blessèd Boys.

Glad we're receiving now
Him as a chrysalis,
Thereby achieving now
Pledge of angelic bliss.
Loosen all earthly flakes   11985
That cling around him;
Fair and great now he wakes,
Divine life has crowned him.

Doctor Marianus in the highest, purest cell.

Here is the outlook free,
The soul uplifting.   11990
Women I yonder see,
Heavenward drifting,

[342]

And glorious, midway seen,
Star-crowned, yet tender,
Heaven's own lofty Queen!   11995
It is Her splendour.

Enraptured

Highest mistress of the world,
Let me, of Thy pleasure,
See Thy mystery unfurled
In the vaulted azure.   12000
Look with grace on what doth move
Human hearts to greet Thee
And with holy bliss of love
Bears them up to meet Thee.

All invincible we feel   12005
When supreme Thou willest,
Swiftly tempered is our zeal
When its glow Thou stillest.
Virgin, pure in fairest sense,
Mother sweet, supernal,   12010
Chosen Queen of our defence,
Peer of gods eternal!

Little clouds circle
Around Her splendour:
Penitent women,   12015
Of natures tender,
Ether respiring,
At Her knees pleading,
Her mercy needing.

O Thou of immaculate ray,   12020
From Thee 'tis not taken
That those lightly led astray
Come with trust unshaken.

Rapt away, to weakness prone,
It is hard to save them.   12025
Who by their own strength alone
Rend the lusts that slave them?
Whose foot does not slip awhile
On steep, slippery places?
Whom befool not glance and smile,   12030
Flattery's breath and phrases?

The Mater Gloriosa soars into view

Chorus of Penitent Women.

To heights art soaring
Of realms eternal,
Hear our imploring,
Matchless, Maternal,   12035
Of grace supernal!

Magna Peccatrix (*St. Luke VII, 36*).

By the love that ever glowing
For Thy Son, the Heaven-born,
Shed warm tears to balsam flowing
Spite of Pharisaic scorn;   12040
By the box whose ointment precious
Dropped its perfume rare and sweet;
By the locks whose gentle meshes
Dried the Saviour's holy feet —

Mulier Samaritana (*St. John IV*).

By the well to which were driven   12045
Abram's herds in days of yore;
By the pitcher once 'twas given
Our dear Saviour to restore;
By the spring, rich and supernal,
Whence flow waters far and wide,   12050
Overflowing, bright, eternal,
Pouring through the worlds their tide —

Maria Aegyptiaca (*Acta Sanctorum*).

By the sacred place where mortals
Our dear Master's body laid;
By the arm which at the portals   12055
Warningly my entrance stayed;
By the forty years' repentance
Truly passed in desert-land;
By the blessèd farewell sentence
That I wrote upon the sand —   12060

All Three.

Thou who women greatly sinning
Grantest to come nigh to Thee,
By sincere repentance winning
Bliss through all eternity,
Grant to this good soul Thy blessing,   12065
Who but once herself forgot,

[344]

Who knew not she was transgressing,
Pardon meet refuse Thou not!
Una Poenitentium, formerly named G R E T C H E N, *drawing closer.*
Bend, oh bend now,
Matchless, attend Thou,   12070
Thy radiance spend now,
Look on my bliss in charity.
My early lover,
His troubles over,
Comes back to me.   12075
Blessèd Boys hovering in a circle.
Mighty of limb, he towers
Already above us;
Soon for this care of ours
Richly he'll love us.
Early were we removed,   12080
Life did not reach us;
But he has learned and loved
And he will teach us.

The One Penitent formerly named G R E T C H E N.
Girt by the noble choir of Heaven,
Himself the new-come scarcely knows,   12085
Scarce feels the fresh life newly given
Ere like the holy throng he grows;
See! how each earthly bond he's riven,
From that old vesture freed at length,
Now in ethereal garb of Heaven   12090
Appears his pristine, youthful strength,
Oh, grant that I may now instruct him,
Since blinds him still the new-born day.
Mater Gloriosa.   Come, rise to higher spheres! Conduct him!
If he feels thee, he'll go thy way.   12095
Doctor Marianus prostrate, adoring.
Penitents, look up, elate,
Where ye see salvation;
Grateful, to your blessèd fate
Grow through re-creation.
May each better sense be keen   12100
In Thy service precious;

[345]

O Thou Virgin, Mother, Queen,
Goddess, be Thou gracious!

Chorus Mysticus.

All earth comprises
Is symbol alone;   12105
What there ne'er suffices
As fact here is known;
All past the humanly
Wrought here in love;
The Eternal-Womanly   12110
Draws us above.

FINIS

Notes

to Goethe's "Faust"

PREFATORY: The following Notes are not intended for professors of German literature nor for anyone else who can read German editions of *Faust* with their commentaries. These Notes are intended for men and women who have no knowledge of the German language and no prospect of learning it but who may desire explanation or elucidation of passages in the play which are not immediately clear to a reader. Further, learnèd professors may smile at the multiplicity of these Notes, but wherever the question of the inclusion or exclusion of a Note has arisen, the Note has been included, wisely or not, and it is hoped that the less sophisticated will accept and read the Notes with indulgence if not with appreciation and gratitude.

In the compilation of the Notes highly valuable assistance has been derived from many commentaries but most of all from the editions of *Faust* by Ernst Beutler (Leipsic. 1939) and Georg Witkowski (9th edition. Leiden. 1936) who have contributed numerous ideas and interprctations that are here incorporated, occasionally verbatim. In effect, be it said at once, the reader as well as the compiler of these Notes is deeply indebted to Beutler and Witkowski and to other commentators.

Although Goethe calls *Faust* a "tragedy," the play is not a tragedy in any usual sense. The play is a tragedy in its presentation of the limitations of human existence, of man's vain longing for unrealizable perception and knowledge, of the struggle for the unattainable. But, on the other hand, the play does offer a solution of the problem of living: salvation through acceptance of the limitations of life on earth united with glad, aspiring activity within those limitations.

It has been said that Goethe's *Faust* is "the most faulty of the world's great poems." The author of this dictum doubtless had several phases of *Faust* in mind. There are indeed striking anachronisms in the play (not specified in the following Notes) such as the assumption that newspapers and paper money were in circulation in the time of the historical Faust; but Goethe knew too much not to be aware of his anachronisms and he employed them freely in order to achieve his poetic-dramatic purpose, since "the poet is not bound by time," cf. 7426–33. Far more importantly, numerous instances or occasions stand out in the course of *Faust* when the intelligent, thoughtful reader or spectator may wish, often justifiably, to know much more than Goethe tells, for example, how much time has elapsed between two scenes, why the background or setting has been changed and why the whither of the shifting scene, also how characters have learned this or that. The simplest, most reasonable, and truest explanation is that Goethe was careless about details and he was far more interested in leading up to, or preparing for, a situation and in presenting the result of the situation than he was in the depiction of the situation itself. Hence, many shortcomings or faults arose in the construction of *Faust* and became a part of the finished play, but whatever, or however many, shortcomings may be in the play, we may take Goethe's *Faust* as it is and be infinitely grateful for it.

Notes

TO THE FIRST PART
OF THE TRAGEDY

DEDICATION
(1–32)

Goethe wrote the " Dedication " in the summer of 1797 at a time when
the " forms " of Faust and Gretchen and other characters in the play had
long been " wavering " before his mental vision. He now expresses to his
readers his fears that it is an " illusion " that he will ever complete the play
but nevertheless he girds himself to the undertaking. He uses a form of
verse which he often employed in expressing personal experiences with an
elegiac background.

9–26. These lines suggest many incidents, people, and experiences in
Goethe's early life: his first love-affairs, the " labyrinthine, erring course " of
his young manhood, his sister and various friends who now were dead, and
friends who were no longer a part of his life. Goethe is known to have read
scenes from *Faust* to friends in Frankfort and Weimar more than twenty
years before he wrote the " Dedication."

PRELUDE ON THE STAGE
(33–242)

This scene presents the function of the playwright more or less ironically
from three points of view, each of which was familiar to Goethe as he, a
creative poet, directed the Weimar Theatre from 1791 to 1817 and wrote
several humorous farces and satirical plays. The scene pretends that a
company of strolling players has arrived in a German city and set up an
improvised stage. The three men most concerned discuss what shall be the
content of the play that is still not composed though the audience has already assembled. A " Dramatic Poet " was, in Goethe's time, often a regular
member of the staff of high-class theatrical troupes; his office was to re-
mould plays for production, to write prologues and epilogues, and to contribute original plays. Goethe wrote the " Prelude " perhaps in the summer
of 1797, possibly not until 1802, under the influence of Kalidasa's *Cakuntala*
which he had greatly admired in Forster's translation (1791); in the Hindu
drama the Director and an actress discuss a curtain-raiser that is to be presented.

35. " German nation ": that is, one of the practically autonomous states
which made up " The Holy Roman Empire of the German Nation " and
which were often referred to as " the Germanies."

52. Cf. Matt. VII, 14: strait is the gate, and narrow is the way.

53. The performances at Weimar have always begun and still begin
at different hours according to the length of the play or opera to be given,
sometimes as early as four p.m.

99–103. "Don't bother about writing an artistic, unified drama; in any case each spectator will pick out what pleases him most."

122. "You surely don't think that a full house is attracted by your art alone?"

133. The Poet has perhaps looked toward Heaven in despair.

136. The "Right of Man" means here the power or capacity of man as compared with that of beasts. Beasts can perceive and comprehend single facts of life only singly and unrelatedly. Man is aware of a lofty, cosmic harmony which the Poet proceeds to describe and elucidate.

140–9. In the eyes of the Poet Nature winds her threads upon the spindle, indifferent to disharmonies; the Poet takes up into himself the discordant facts of Nature, measures or weighs them, animates them, and gives them forth in rhyme. He conceives the cosmos as a great symphony to which each single element is called to contribute in building up "noble harmonies."

150–1. The storm and the sunset are, to the Poet, symbolic reflections of human moods.

154. That is, a laurel wreath would be "unmeaning" without the glory bestowed on a hero in a poet's ballad or epic.

156. "Who makes us sure of the existence of Heaven and lets us see divine harmony?"

181. The poet's "flight" of imagination and the drama's "illusion" of life.

198–213. That is, youth enjoys an advantage in the realm of physical playfulness whereas age finds us childlike in understanding playfulness.

235. The sun and the moon. In later lines of *Faust* the reader will find many references to stars and water and fire and beasts and birds.

242. Heaven and Earth and Hell are all to appear in the play, it seems, if the Manager is to have his will, but neither he nor Goethe means that the play is to end in Hell. However, Goethe said to Eckermann (May 6, 1827) that the action of the play was to proceed "from Heaven through the world to Hell," and among Goethe's notes on this portion of the First Part of *Faust* stands the notation "Epilogue in Chaos on the way to Hell," suggesting that the play was to end with an epilogue, but such an epilogue was never written as far as we know.

PROLOGUE IN HEAVEN
(243–353)

The exact year in which Goethe wrote the "Prologue" is uncertain; he wrote it possibly in 1797 but probably in 1800–1. The scene prepares the reader for the subsequent, everlasting conflict between the forces of Heaven and Hell and forms with the very last scene of the whole play the fulcrum on which Faust's life and salvation depend. The Lord appears but only as a voice; He is rarely, if ever, represented in person in the productions of *Faust* on the stage.

Mephistopheles stands out as the representative of the principle of evil. The Lord speaks of him (337–9) as one of a host of spirits of negation, but Mephistopheles appears as the one old Devil (353), acting independently throughout the play, and at the end summoning many devils to his assistance.

He is called " Squire Satan " (2504) and " Squire Voland " (another name for the Devil, 4023). Nevertheless he disclaims any lofty rank among beings of his kind (1335–6, 1641). Goethe evidently had different conceptions of Mephistopheles at different times and he carried no conception through consistently, though that of an independent hellish spirit predominates.

Goethe wrote to a friend: " Whence the name ' Mephistopheles ' I can not say directly." Nor can anyone else, unless it be that the oldest form of the name " Mephostophiles " goes back to " Mephostophiel," a Hebrew name for a demon of Hell. In this case the name probably means " destroyer of good " but other guesses have been hazarded that the name signifies " not a lover of light," " destroyer-liar," " forger of lies," " no friend of Faust," " Hephaestus's (devil's) friend " in antithesis to Theophilus, " God's friend."

Goethe drew the basic idea of the " Prologue " from Job I, 6–12: Now there was a day when the sons of God came to present themselves before the Lord, and Satan came also among them. And the Lord said unto Satan, Whence comest thou? Then Satan answered the Lord, and said, From going to and fro in the earth, and from walking up and down in it. And the Lord said unto Satan, Hast thou considered my servant Job, that there is none like him in the earth, a perfect and an upright man, one that feareth God and escheweth evil? Then Satan answered the Lord, and said, Doth Job fear God for nought? Hast thou not made an hedge about him, and about his house, and about all that he hath on every side? Thou hast blessed the work of his hand, and his substance is increased in the land: But put forth thine hand now, and touch all that he hath, and he will curse thee to thy face. And the Lord said unto Satan, Behold, all that he hath is in thy power; only upon himself put not forth thine hand. So Satan went forth from the presence of the Lord. Cf. Shelley's translation of the " Prologue."

243–6. Perhaps an allusion to the harmony of the spheres and the pre-ordained divine plan of the universe.

247–8. The angels can not " solve " (understand) the sun as a natural phenomenon, but their contemplation of it inspires them constantly with new awe and strength. To them the sun is " a manifestation of the Supreme Being," forever giving forth, creative, reproducing, sustaining and evolving. In German the word for " sun " is feminine.

249. " beyond us ": beyond our comprehension.

265–6. Natural phenomena excite awe, but the angels revere most profoundly the evolutionary, " gentle progress " of nature.

277. " pathos ": real feeling, perhaps, emotional eulogy.

299. The Lord implies that he sees in Faust another higher being than the average man Mephistopheles has just described; Faust is God's " servant " because he serves God in his aspiring and striving.

302. The " ferment " of Faust's soul.

308–9. The " now " may mean life on earth where but little is clear, and the " soon " may mean the life beyond. But the Lord sees service to Himself in activity, wherever it may appear, whether activity appears in nature or in man and though activity may not be directed by clear-sighted vision of a goal. Clarity — that is, absolute perception or perfect understanding — is God's alone.

[353]

312 ff. The attentive reader will perceive that the Lord does not enter into a bet with Mephistopheles. In His omniscience the Lord knows now of course how Faust's life will proceed and end, and Goethe does not have the Lord bet on a certainty even with the Devil. The Lord merely gives Mephistopheles His " permission " to " lay hold " on Faust if he can, and He promises that Mephistopheles shall meet with no " prohibition " in his choice and use of means for Faust's seduction. Mephistopheles, on the other hand, can — out of countless experiences and successes with men — feel confident that he can win Faust because he knows the " ferment " that is going on in Faust's soul. He never realizes, now or later, that he, a destructive spirit of negation, can not comprehend the aspiring, upward striving spirit of Faust.

317. Error does not attend a man who does not strive, a stagnant man; hence, the fact that a man errs may be in his favour since it may prove that he is at least not stagnant but striving.

328–9: " good ": good for something, capable, aspiring; such a man has faith that there is " one right way," whatever difficulty he may have in finding the way or in knowing the origin or goal of his faith.

334–5. Cf. the words of God to the serpent, Gen. III, 14: Dust shalt thou eat all the days of thy life. Mephistopheles means to satisfy Faust with sensual enjoyments. The snake, the first seducer of mankind, is conceived as a " near relation " of the Devil in character, so too in 2049.

336. " In that too ": just as you will now be free in your attempts upon Faust, so, if you can triumph later, " in that too " will you be unhampered, that is, in celebrating your triumph.

340–3. That is, it is good for men to be stirred to counter-activity by one who through his nature must be active; though destructive in intent he may ultimately be productive indirectly in effect.

344–9. At the beginning of the " Prologue in Heaven " the archangels have glorified nature. The Lord now urges them to gaze in rapture on all evolutionary progress (which, in a sense, is God Himself), also to express their rapture, and thus to make all the transitory, phenomenal manifestations of God " enduring."

NIGHT
(354–807)

A large part of this scene (354–597 and 602–5) was written when Goethe was young but most creative and productive, that is, between 1771 and 1775; the remainder of the scene was composed by a mature, finished artist as the reader can see in the style and imagery employed, and it was in fact written just before the end of the eighteenth century. The title and the " narrow Gothic chamber " suggest the semi-darkness and the limitations of Faust's life and thinking, but night was chosen for the scene, more especially, as the time for evoking spirits. The varying number of stressed and unstressed syllables in 354–85 aptly conveys the restlessness of Faust's spirit.

354–6. Faust names the four faculties which European universities comprise. " Philosophy " includes all university subjects not taught by one of the other three faculties. Cf. Mephistopheles's discussion of the four faculties in his talk with the student in 1908–2036. In addition to the degree of

[354]

Bachelor of Arts Faust has also acquired the degrees of Master of Arts and Doctor. In German universities, however, " Master " (" Magister ") was also a title of teachers of lower rank, whereas " Doctor " was in effect a title of a so-called full professor.

361. How old is Faust? Since Faust says that he has been teaching " nearly ten years," not a very long time, he might now be between thirty and thirty-five years old, but he has studied the four faculties " all through and through," and such prolonged study could hardly have taken less than twenty years. It may therefore be assumed that Faust is now between fifty and fifty-five years old, cf. the note to 2342.

383–4. " inmost folds ": a free translation, equivalent of " what holds the world together at its innermost part." The " seeds " of the alchemists were primordial substances corresponding roughly to the " elements " of the chemists.

420. The French astrologer and physician, Michel de Nôtredame (1503–66), a contemporary of the historical Faust, wrote prophecies with startling success. Goethe ascribes to him here a book containing magic symbols which a man might gaze upon and thus become enabled to evoke corresponding spirits.

422. The ideas developed in the following lines are attributed by implication to Nôtredame, but it is now established that Goethe drew them from Swedenborg. Faust could not very well be made to attribute them to the Swedish spiritist, however, because Swedenborg was not born until 1688.

429+. " Macrocosm ": this " great world " was, according to the conception of the Middle Ages, the whole universe imagined as consisting harmoniously of many interacting parts. Faust is supposed to gain through some kind of geometrical figure a vision of the harmony of the universe.

442. The " sage " has not been identified.

446. The dawn symbolizes a Most High, Most Holy, an exaltation to the Inexpressible, a daily re-creation of the world out of darkness.

447–53. Faust sees the interweaving, interacting, of all the elements of the universe; heavenly powers, conceived as angels who soar up and down on wings exhaling blessings, inspire the All with sublime harmony. These heavenly powers, drawing their inspiration from the great heavenly Source, pass the containing " golden vessels " on and on. Goethe may have been thinking of Jacob's ladder and its ascending and descending angels portrayed in Bibles in Goethe's father's library. Cf. Gen. XXVIII, 12: And he (Jacob) dreamed, and, behold, a ladder set up on the earth, and the top of it reached to heaven: and, behold, the angels of God ascending and descending on it.

454–9. Faust turns abruptly from mere contemplation to the thought of living, active nature and voices his yearning for personal nourishment.

459+. The Earth-Spirit represents not only animate and inanimate nature; it embodies also all human activity. To this Spirit Faust feels himself nearer. He is inspired by the sight of the " sign " of the Earth-Spirit to a feeling of great potentiality and to a sense of the presence of the Spirit. He utters the symbol and the Spirit appears.

468–74. Goethe expresses intense feeling by discarding rhyme in several passages, cf. 3440–58 and 3776–834.

481+. Goethe once drew a sketch of Faust cringing away from an apparition (the Earth-Spirit) which was visible in superhuman form down to the breast and beardless and which had rays of light about the head.

501–9. The Earth-Spirit is water and storm, birth and death; all of these are manifestations of it. Visible nature, the product of the Earth-Spirit's activity, weaves the garment in which the Deity manifests itself.

518. "famulus": a student who acted as secretary and general factotum to a professor who in return gave him free tuition or some other emolument. Wagner is not an old man, though he is sometimes made up and impersonated as such, and though he may appear as a pedantic dry-as-dust. He rarely, if ever, fully understands Faust.

528. That is, if a preacher is hypocritically only acting a part and is not sincere in what he says and does. Note the great emphasis that Faust lays on purity and sincerity of heart and feeling, 534–45.

538–41. Pedants who have nothing to say may make up books of unacknowledged quotations from their predecessors and pose as creators; they may, like cooks of no imagination, concoct stews out of left-overs; or, having no fire within themselves, they may try to blow a semblance of flame out of a heap of cold ashes.

555. "Speakers often take shreds of thoughts (bits of paper) and twist them into forms that attract men but are really mere rhetoric."

560. Wagner refers to critical examination of old documents and ideas.

562. The "means" comprise costly old books as well as knowledge (for example, of languages) necessary to a scholar's investigations.

576. "book of seven seals," cf. Revelations V, 1.

580–5. "Presentations of the past are a wretched mockery of truth, and with the shallow moralizings common in them they are no better than a catch-all or a melodrama."

589. "the child": the truth about "the mind and heart of men" (586).

593. The poet is thinking of Christ, John Huss, Giordano Bruno, and perhaps of others.

617. "the earthly son": mortality.

618. "more than cherub": because cherubs are passive attendants of the Deity whereas Faust has exulted in his impulse to activity.

631–3. "Shall I no longer seek the aid of magic?" Since the Earth-Spirit has rebuffed him, Faust can not seek that way again as a path of escape, and as yet he knows no other way.

635–7. Faust means the material things of life which drag the spirit down from a lofty plane of ideas or aspirations. When we attain to the "good," we are apt to call it "good enough."

644 ff. Worry embodies paralyzing, futile brooding and uneasiness as to what may happen. Faust can not become fully obsessed by worry at this moment because urgent energy and striving can not be checked by worry. Cf. the appearance of Worry as "a grey woman" in the scene 11384–510.

664–9. We may imagine a skull lying on the desk or a bookshelf and various, odd-looking medieval instruments lying or standing near.

[356]

671. The " ward " of a key revolves in the lock and usually draws back or raises up the bolt.

682–3. These lines constitute one of Goethe's fundamental ideas: that if anything we have is to be of any value to us, we must earn the right, and learn the way, to use it; thus we may possess it and not merely have it.

685. That is, that hour is useful and profitable that produces something.

692. Faust means the knowledge and skill which concocted the opiate in the phial, a long-necked, glass bottle.

696–8. Faust grows calm as he gazes on a means of escape from life.

705. Faust anticipates the other world as one of " pure " activity, freed from any sense of limitation, thus justifying to himself his determination to commit suicide.

720. The " goblet " is obviously one adorned with figures more or less enigmatical. On a festive occasion such a goblet would be filled and passed and " pledged " to somebody who would be called upon to explain the figures in impromptu rhymes or to drain the goblet at one draught.

736. " morn ": in the sense of " tomorrow " or the new day that Faust foresees. Cf. note to 446.

736+. The choruses are conceived as sung in a near-by church in celebration of Easter Sunday. The bells are those of the various churches of the town.

737–41. A literal translation of the German is: " Christ has arisen, joy to mortal man whom destructive, insidious, hereditary (human) shortcomings entwined."

748. The news of His resurrection assures believers that the promises of Christ, and with them the new covenant of which He is the mediator, have been fulfilled.

749–54. Goethe holds closely to medieval tradition but, in doing so, he deviates slightly from the Biblical account of the burial of Christ. Women bought and brought spices and were near when Joseph of Arimathea (or Joseph and Nicodemus) prepared the body for burial but they took no part in the ceremony. Cf. John XIX, 40; Mark XVI, 1; and Luke XXIII, 56. The German of 749–61 says literally: " We had tended Him with spices; we, His faithful, had laid Him away; cloths and bands, spotless, we wound about Him; ah! and we find Christ no longer here. Christ is arisen! Blessed the loving one (that is, a man) who has endured the troubling, healing, and improving test."

766. People of faith gladly believe in miracles and thus, in a sense, faith begets miracles, but happenings which are called " miracles " often implant faith in people.

785–807. The German may be translated literally: " Although He who was buried has already risen gloriously On High, living and exalted; although in the joy of a new life He is near to the joy of creating; ah! to our sorrow we are here on the breast of earth. Us, His own, He left pining here behind. Ah, Master, we bemoan Thy happiness! Christ is arisen from the womb of decay. Tear yourselves joyously free from your bonds! If ye praise Him in your actions, if ye show love, feed your brothers, travel and preach Him, promise His bliss, the Master will be near to you, He will be here with you!" The altruism inherent in these last lines should be noted. Cf. the emphasis on Faust's own altruism as indicated in the note to 998–1005.

789. That is, in the bliss of birth into a new life.

799–807. These lines are addressed to the mourning disciples, assuring them that *if* they preach Christ and live Christ in their deeds, He will always be near to them.

OUTSIDE THE GATE OF THE TOWN
(808–1177)

When sketching the background of this scene, between 1797 and 1800, Goethe had in mind the country outside of Frankfort-on-the-Main, his native city; places mentioned can be identified with resorts near Frankfort, some of which are still in existence; but such places are common in the vicinity of almost every German town, and we need not locate those of the play exactly. Faust's home is not specifically thought of as Frankfort, since a university was not established there until 1914. The beginning of the scene (through 902) is assumed to take place just outside of the town at some cross-road where people scatter in different directions.

824. German peasants often dance on a platform that is laid down for dancing under the trees or in the open either in or near German villages. Cf. 948+.

856. The beggar is turning the crank of some sort of stringed instrument more or less like a guitar.

878. St. Andrew's Night, between November 29th and November 30th, was the favourite time for such fortune-telling, because unmarried people regarded St. Andrew as their patron saint.

880. People often looked into a piece of crystal, frequently spherical in form, and saw in its dim reflections what they hoped to see.

903–1010. Faust and Wagner approach and linger near a village.

940. Faust does not hear the people saying this; he is only interpreting sounds of them as expressing their joy in a free life in the midst of nature.

998–1005. According to semi-historical accounts Faust's father was a peasant, but Goethe makes him a physician, perhaps thinking of the scholar Paracelsus (1493–1541) whose father acquired much fame as a physician. The Old Peasant gratefully emphasizes Faust's altruistic feeling for his fellow-man, a fundamental, very significant trait in Faust's character as will appear later in the play and in these Notes.

1011–141. Faust and Wagner proceed to some stone, fairly near, where they sit and talk.

1020–1. That is, as devout Roman Catholics do when the holy wafer is borne past them.

1037. "wayward zeal": zeal without a logical method.

1038. Experts in alchemy were called "adepts" because they were supposed to "have found" (*adipiscor*) a cure-all or panacea.

1039. "black kitchen": a laboratory of "black art," a term associated with the medieval interpretation of *nigromantia*, "black-divining."

1040. "receipts" or "recipes."

1041. Faust means substances chemically " contrary," or opposed, to each other.

1042–7. These lines contain a very free use of alchemistic jargon describing the union of two substances (perhaps gold, or mercury, and silver) which are fancifully named and conceived as male and female. From this union which is brought about first in tepid water and then in a retort over a free flame, there arises an offspring, " the youthful queen," which passes over into another retort as a precipitate which was supposed to be " the philosophers' stone." This precipitate was the cure-all, the " medicine," which in the ignorance of the alchemists could easily be poison. It is possible that the precipitate was so-called " powder of Algaroth," that is, antimony oxychloride, a white, fairly insoluble powder which was formerly used as a very efficient purgative and which is still used occasionally by people addicted to old-fashioned remedies. Algarotti was a physician of Verona.

1053. In his present pessimistic mood Faust is ready to say that the cure-all *was* poison.

1076–88. Faust imagines himself flying after the sun and delighting in the calm radiance of the sun as it is setting. To him the sun is a symbol of the divine, a " god."

1079. The reflection of light at the time of sunset makes a small stream look " silvery " but when the stream flows into or becomes a broad river, it looks " golden."

1083. The shallow water of bays remains warm for a long time as compared with the water of the sea.

1117. " high ancestral spheres ": the higher other-world which popular imagination peopled with ancestral heroes.

1126–33. Wagner thinks that Faust means weather-spirits and so he proceeds to talk superstitiously about the bite of the north wind and about the east wind which in Germany is usually dry and harmful to the lungs.

1136. Wagner thinks the west wind malicious because refreshing coolness preceding it is apt to be followed by a drenching rain.

1142. Faust and Wagner now rise from the stone where they have been sitting and start back toward the town.

1147–59. Faust senses the supernatural nature or character of the poodle.

1173. " spirit ": in the twofold sense of " supernatural being " and " intelligence."

STUDY
(1178–1529)

Goethe wrote different parts of this and the following scene at different times, some lines in the early seventies, some in the late eighties, and the rest around 1800. Faust has returned to his study in a much calmer mood after his communion with nature. His religious feeling has been deeply stirred. The better of his " two souls " (1112) has been awakened.

1185. Faust means a selfless, undesiring " love of God," a reflection of a saying of Spinoza's that made a deep impression on Goethe in his young manhood and influenced him throughout his life. Cf. Spinoza's " Ethics," V, 19: " He who loves God can not strive to have God love him in return."

1186. Note here and later the reaction of the poodle (Mephistopheles) to Faust's expressions of religious feeling.

1200–1. Are the "flowing sources" streams of heavenly peace? Is the "Fount of Life" God? Cf. 1217 ff.

1210–9. That is, the religious feeling that arises in the breasts of even the devout often runs dry very soon, and men find new inspiration ("compensation") in turning to the "supernatural," or written, revelation as it is found in the New Testament.

1224–37. Cf. the interpretation of this passage in the Introduction, p. xvii.

1258. As Faust is sure that a spirit is hiding in the poodle, he decides to call it forth by means of a spell. First he chooses a minor spell, "the Key of Solomon." A book of this name, *Clavicula Salomonis*, contains directions for exorcizing the spirits of the four elements, fire, water, air, and earth; cf. 1273–6. Solomon was a magician according to legend.

1258+. The "Spirits" are minions of Mephistopheles, who have come to help him, and do help him, in calling up a vision before Faust (1447–1505), but they do not venture into Faust's study as they wish to remain free from a captivity like that of Mephistopheles.

1273–6. The spirit of each of the four elements is commanded to act in characteristic fashion: fire to glow, water to move sinuously ("self-coiling" in our translation for the sake of the rhyme), air (which is transparent) to vanish, and earth to toil as kobolds, or gnomes, do.

1283–91. Faust now commands the four spirits to come forth, calling the kobold "incubus," here as a helpful house-spirit, one of the qualities ascribed to the kobold in German folk-lore.

1295. The spirit must be "hurt" in order to force him from his hiding-place.

1300. The "Sign" is one of Christ, perhaps the cross, perhaps a crucifix.

1306–9. Literally from the German: "the Never-arisen, the Unuttered, He who is diffused through all the Heavens, Who was criminally thrust through," cf. Eph. IV, 10; John XIX, 34; and Rev. I, 7.

1319. The sign of the Trinity.

1321+. By "travelling scholar" Goethe means *scholasticus vagans*, as a roving or vagabond student was called in the Middle Ages, who roved from one university to another, living by his wits. Faust uses *casus* (1324) in recognition of the Latin which was commonly employed by students of that time.

1331–4. Since the spirit was evoked by means of Christian symbols, Faust knows that a devil is facing him and therefore he suggests various names applied to the Devil; for "Liar" and for "Prince of Lies" (as Mephistopheles is called in 10995) cf. John VIII, 44; for "destroyer" cf. Rev. IX, 11; for "Beëlzebub" (which Goethe translates as "God of Flies") cf. Matt. XII, 24 and Mark III, 22.

1335–6. The destructive power which Mephistopheles exercises is called "Evil" by men, but Mephistopheles calls it "Good" because he thinks nothing ought to exist and the sooner all is destroyed, the better, as he says in the following lines.

1347–8. That is, man is such a fool as to think himself in miniature

(Microcosm) a reproduction or concentrated essence of the universe (Macrocosm).

1349–58. The conception underlying these lines may be sketched as follows: Mephistopheles sprang from Chaos (cf. the references to him as " Chaos' odd, fantastic son," 1384, and " Chaos' well-belovèd son," 8027); hence he speaks here as a Prince of Darkness. The creation of Light followed that of Chaos (or Night), and now we have an alternation of the two, or, as Mephistopheles contends, strife between the two. But it is a fact of physics that light is dependent upon bodies, it exists only through them and issues only from them, and therefore, since all bodies are doomed to dissolution, Mephistopheles can reasonably hope that light too will disappear.

1377. Fire is by its nature Mephistopheles's very own destructive element because life can not exist in fire.

1395–1412. The " witch's foot " or " pentagram " is a five-pointed star carved or painted or drawn somewhere in a house (here on the threshold) to keep away evil spirits. ☆ It may be a Christian symbol whose five points represent the five wounds of Christ. Goethe invents the ideas that the pentagram protects only if no point is left open and that spirits must come and go by the same route. It was " lucky " that an outer point of the pentagram was left open in this case so that Mephistopheles could come in.

1440–4. Mephistopheles promises that through the aid of his spirits Faust will enjoy actual physical pleasure, the gratification of his senses of sight, smelling, tasting, and feeling.

1446. Mephistopheles addresses his minion-spirits, those of 1259–70.

1447–1505. Faust seems, as the spirits sing, to fall asleep and to dream that the vaulted ceiling over him vanishes, revealing an open sky with suns and stars; angels seem to appear, luring Faust on to a landscape where lovers exchange vows and where streams of wine flow and broaden into lakes, flowing thence on and on toward Isles of the Blest, toward realms of supreme and eternal joy, of love and grace.

1513. An inner point of the pentagram must now be opened to permit Mephistopheles's exit.

1516–7. Mephistopheles appears as the master of parasitic, destructive animals here as in lines 6591+.

1520. Mephistopheles dabs the threshold with oil, presumably to attract a rat by the odour.

1526. " again ": a second disappointment following upon that with the Earth-Spirit.

STUDY
(1530–2072)

The calm mood in which Faust returned from his Easter Sunday walk has been followed by a new wave of the pessimism which was engulfing him in the first scene in which he appears. How long a time is supposed to have elapsed between the preceding scene and the present one Goethe does not indicate. It may be assumed as long, in order to allow for growing intimacy between Faust and Mephistopheles, or as brief, only long enough for a brooding Faust to pass from disappointment to a mood of despair in which he is ready to come to an understanding with the Devil.

1535. Mephistopheles appears in the guise which legend ascribes to him: a Squire dressed in red and black (that is, fire and darkness) with a cock's-feather in his hat.

1561. "life's grinning faces" are the petty, annoying distractions which seem to delight in destroying a man's peace of mind and in keeping him from positive accomplishment. Such distractions can not be escaped or controlled, cf. 1569.

1572. A reference to the night before Easter Sunday, which Faust does not heed, so that Mephistopheles refers to it again in 1579–80.

1573–8. That is, happy is the man who dies in a moment of supreme achievement or exaltation such as Faust felt in the presence of the Earth-Spirit.

1584. "A sweet familiar tone": the Easter music.

1587–1606. Faust points out those elements of life that make life seem beautiful, that keep us alive ("banned within this cave of sorrows"): self-confidence, fame, possessions, sensual pleasures, hope, faith, patience, but to Faust all these are an accursed illusion, "Patience most of all," in the mind of the plodding scholar. Faust has "destroyed the beautiful world," as the spirits sing in the next lines; he is ready to consider a proposition from the Devil. Cf. Carlyle's translation of 1585–1606, "Faust's Curse."

1607–26. Who are these spirits? Many guesses have been ventured but none is irrefutable. Mephistopheles claims the spirits as his "little folk" (1627–8) because they attend upon a work of destruction; their admonition to Faust to build a newer, "splendider" world within his own breast Mephistopheles interprets as advice to enter into the joys of the world. But their song can be said to read like the sincere lament and exhortation of kindly spirits, a dirge followed by urgent bidding to a new life.

1652. Not merely because someone begs him to do something "for God's sake!"

1660–70. An important passage in which Faust makes it clear that his interest is now concentrated upon the solution of the problem of earthly living. His attempts to establish contact with the world beyond have failed utterly.

1678–87. Faust enumerates stock jugglers' tricks that are only shams. Mephistopheles acknowledges them as such, and hence he promises "something good" (1691), that is, satisfying.

1692–1706. Cf. Introduction, p. xviii f.

1698. Faust holds out his hand and Mephistopheles shakes it ("Done!"); Mephistopheles then holds out his hand which Faust clasps in turn to show his acceptance of the agreement. Or, as this episode is sometimes presented: while their right hands are clasped, Mephistopheles slaps his left hand on their hand-clasp whereupon Faust slaps his own left hand on top of the three hands.

1705. "the pointer falling": a reference to medieval water-clocks whose hour-hand rose for twenty-four hours and then fell back, marking the end of a period.

1712. Goethe once planned a scene in which the acquisition of the Doctor's degree was to be celebrated by a banquet in accordance with German custom.

1716–33. Faust maintains that a man's spoken word should be considered as binding as his written word, but he acknowledges that the world clings to written rather than to oral agreements and so he consents to an agreement documented in any form.

1741–59. Faust assures Mephistopheles that since he deserves only to be guided by Mephistopheles (1745), he will follow that guidance absolutely and with zest.

1759. That is, a *real* man.

1765–75. Faust insists that while desiring all the experiences of this life, he demands "life's wildering whirl," but he does not expect any real " enjoyment " that is not accompanied by pain, by hate (of himself), or by vexation ("annoyment") that quickens him on to something else. Faust's longing for all-including self-expansion (1774) is referred to also in lines 641 and 3285. The expression of this longing came from Goethe's heart, for he wrote this and the subsequent lines in the midst of his Storm and Stress when he was twenty-four or twenty-five years old and when, with the vaulting aspiration of young manhood, he longed to encompass the universe.

1776–1802. Mephistopheles laughs at the idea that one man can have all the experiences of human life; the attempt to have them all would be like trying to digest a mass of old dough. Only a God can know the whole of life. Mephistopheles therefore advises Faust to identify himself with the hero of a poet who will make him all-things-in-one.

1804. " the crown of all mankind ": the sum of all that is humanly attainable.

1808: " ell-high socks ": Goethe is thinking of the Greek cothurni whose soles and heels raised the actor so high that he appeared much larger than normal men, cf. note to 10038+.

1816–33. According to Mephistopheles: the pleasures of life are the one object, so make use of anything you have. You have hands and feet, head and seed, also the powers of a horse or anything else that you can pay for! Away with arid speculation!

1838. " Master Paunch ": a name for a fat, dull, self-satisfied pedagogue.

1841. That is, if you did, you would be driven from your position for radicalism.

1853. The " Spirit of all Lies " is probably not Mephistopheles but Faust's illimitable aspiration and desire seeking help through " works of dazzling magic."

1866–7. Mephistopheles means that a man of such desires as those of Faust would have gone to ruin in any case.

1874. That is, have you called on anybody else?

1879. " abroad ": the student evidently comes from some other German state.

1911. Formerly every German student began his university career with a course concerning the logical processes of disciplined thinking.

1913. " Spanish boots " were instruments of torture favoured by the

Spanish Inquisition, consisting of long iron gaiters which were screwed tighter and tighter around the legs.

1935. In short: logic is only analytic, never synthetic; it only picks to pieces, it never weaves, never creates.

1940. *Encheirisis naturae,* "manipulation of nature" or "getting at nature's secrets by manipulation"; that is, logicians, like chemists, try to explain organic processes by taking things to pieces but they only destroy the vital elements, "the spirit's band"; the high-sounding title is a mockery.

1959. "paragraphs": that is, of the text-books which formerly afforded the starting-points of lectures.

1972–9. Mephistopheles laments the rigidity of laws and the fact that the law of one generation (for example, Roman law, formerly the basis of German jurisprudence) may be "nonsense" for later times or even harmful; the student of law does not study questions of justice or of natural rights.

1986–7. The "hidden poison": unorthodox views which the student may acquire from the study of church and dogma; the "medicine" or "cure" is the prescribed religious point of view of the church.

2026. Mephistopheles devilishly locates all the ills of woman in her sexual nature.

2029. "A title": the M.D.

2038–9. "grey," the colour of ashes and death; "green," the colour of the living tree.

2045. Autograph albums often circulated among students in Goethe's time.

2048. "Ye shall be as God, knowing good and evil"; cf. the serpent's promise in Gen. III, 5.

2049–50. That is, follow the wiles of the serpent as, for example, Adam and Eve did. Try to learn all you can; you will only be disappointed too.

2052. "The little world" of ordinary middle-class life, "the great world" at the Emperor's court.

2069. "fiery (inflammable) air": hydrogen; Goethe was probably thinking of the hydrogen balloon which had been invented in 1782.

AUERBACH'S CELLAR IN LEIPSIC
(2073–2336)

Auerbach's Hotel was a large inn with a wine-room in the "cellar" where students often assembled. As one of his intimate friends lived in the hotel when Goethe was a student in Leipsic, Goethe must have known the cellar well and must have often seen a wall-painting of Faust riding out of the cellar on a wine-cask, cf. 2329–30. This painting was executed certainly by 1625, possibly in the preceding century, and it is still extant as the wine-room which contains it was left intact when the rest of the building was torn away early in the present century in order to make room for a modern structure. Goethe wrote the scene originally in the early seventies of the eighteenth century when his memories of Auerbach's Cellar were still vivid; the Cellar is one of the few known localities that are specified throughout the whole of *Faust*. Goethe gave the incident its present form for the version of the play that appeared in 1790. The "Jolly Companions" are students.

" Frosch " is a designation of a young student in his first semester, and " Brander " suggests " Brandfuchs," a student in his second semester. Siebel and especially Altmayer are older. The hour is late and heads are growing heavy, so it is time for Frosch, the liveliest, to stir things up.

2088–9. Frosch and Altmayer sing a few notes by way of trying out their voices.

2090–1. The lack of unity in the Holy Roman Empire was frequently satirized in the eighteenth century.

2098–100. Students often elected a " Pope " to preside at such gatherings; the quality which made a man eligible for the office seems to have been a proof either of surpassing capacity in drinking or of potency as a male. In the second half of the 1760's when Goethe attended the University of Leipsic, the students there were vastly delighted by the republication (1765) of a pamphlet of 1565. This publication — a kind of play — depicted mock-seriously the legend of the elevation of a woman to the papacy, the discovery of the " pope's " pregnancy, and the resolution that henceforth no one should be elected as pope whose masculinity had not been attested by competent witnesses.

2105–7. That is, a lover entreats his sweetheart to admit him and to bolt the door when he departs at dawn.

2113. The Blocksberg (more usually called the Brocken) is the legendary gathering-place of witches riding on rams, he-goats, etc., cf. the introduction to the Walpurgis Night scene (3835–4398).

2172. " A little Paris ": a name applied to Leipsic in the eighteenth century on account of its air of Frenchified refinement and polish.

2180. The figure of the " screw " is taken from the thumbscrew used in torturing.

2184. Mephistopheles's limp is mentioned only here but his " horse's foot " which causes the limp is referred to in several later lines.

2189–90. Hans Arsch of Rippach was the stock name for a simpleminded, boorish person. Rippach is a village only a few miles southwest of Leipsic.

2237–8. That is, the middle-class jubilates over the fact that it is not affected by court conventions or by fawning upstarts at court.

2256. Altmayer suspects the strangers of being wine-connoisseurs from the Rhine.

2272. A mockery of extreme German nationalism and of German feeling against the French.

WITCH'S KITCHEN
(2337–2604)

Goethe wrote this scene of northern *diablerie* in the gardens of the Villa Borghese in Rome in 1788. He had found no model or inspiration for the scene in the stories of plays about Faust, and in writing it he had in mind perhaps only certain paintings by Teniers and Breughel and Luther's conception of apes as creatures of the Devil. Goethe called the scene " dramatic-humoristic nonsense," intending apparently that the jingles of the apes and the witch should not be taken seriously; he was amused by attempts to find sense in his "nonsense." Numerous incidents in the poet's life display Goethe's fondness for practical jokes and mystifications.

2338. Faust is seemingly to "get well" from the malady of advancing years.

2342. The Faust of the Gretchen episode appears as a young man who is approximately between twenty and twenty-five years old, a young man of the appearance and vitality of an age appropriate for the lover of a young woman such as Gretchen. If Faust is now in the Witch's Kitchen to be divested of "some thirty years," he must be between fifty and fifty-five years old. But it is Faust's *body* (or appearance) that is to be thus rejuvenated, not the learnèd, relatively inexperienced Faust. Like other mortals the man Faust remains as old as before and we shall see him going on and on until he becomes a hundred years old, cf. Palace, p. 318, and Introduction, p. xxvii.

2349. "another": that is, other than a book of magic.

2353–61. In other words: "live the simple life and you will remain young."

2369. In Germanic folk-lore the Devil is said to build bridges from good to evil, cf. "Devil's Bridge" in 10121.

2393. That is, thin stuff such as the general public likes best.

2394–401. A satire on the love of gambling. The ape complains (2397) that wealth is badly distributed and that he only needs money to be credited with having "good sense."

2416–8. The ancient art of divination by means of a sieve: if held loosely, the sieve was said to revolve when the name of a suspected criminal was uttered; also, a criminal could be detected by looking at the suspected wrong-doer through a magic sieve.

2427–8. Here and in 2448 a mockery of kingship.

2429–40. Faust sees a vision of ideal female beauty.

2442. A paraphrase of Gen. I, 31: And God saw every thing that he had made, and, behold, it was very good.

2450–60. The make-believe king is besought to mend the cracked crown, presumably with the "blood and sweat" of his subjects because the lines satirize the brittle nature of kingship. The satire then leaps to rhymesters, and the apes claim that if they only succeed in making jingles, a thought may creep in. In any case people will be apt to see meaning in their rhymes. Mephistopheles commends their frank honesty in 2463–4.

2462. Faust is ready for such an experience as that with Gretchen without the potion.

2491. The Christian Devil is accredited with having the two ravens, "Thought" and "Memory," of the Norse god Odin. These ravens appear in 10664.

2507–9. That is, the rationalists have assigned the Devil ("the Evil One") to the realm of fables but they can not deny that "evil ones" are still here.

2526. In accordance with Goethe's scheme of elaborate nonsense, Faust must be "prepared" by the incantations usual in such ceremonies.

2581. The "degrees" may mean that Faust is a man of experience or that he has many academic degrees or dignities.

2590. "Walpurgis Night": cf. the Walpurgis Night scene, 3835–4222 and note. According to German folk-lore it was customary for witches to be thanked by the Devil during Walpurgis Night for services rendered.

A STREET
(2605–2677)

The remaining scenes of the First Part of *Faust* constitute, in general, what is sometimes called "the Gretchen tragedy" when the speaker is thinking primarily of Gretchen's fate, sometimes "the Gretchen episode" in allusion to the fact that Faust's association with Gretchen is but one of the experiences with which Mephistopheles tempts Faust. Goethe composed almost all of the scenes (virtually as they stand in the final version) while still a young man in Frankfort, between 1771 and 1775, at a time when he and other young men were deeply offended by current abuses of social conventions and by the attitude of the world toward the young unmarried mother. The reader will see as the plot develops that this is not a drama of seduction. Gretchen is not a frivolous girl inquisitive about the mystery of sex and Faust is no libertine. Both are swept along by honest love. Gretchen's so-called "ruin" is but response to a God-given impulse and the normal consummation of love between man and woman.

Goethe uses the name "Margaret" in the following more serene, untroubled scenes, but, with the one exception of the Prison Scene (4405–4612), whenever the situation becomes overcast and more tragic, he employs the more sympathetic, more familiar, more tender "Gretchen."

2607. "lady": in the sense of one of better birth.

2623. Mephistopheles may be assumed to have spied out Gretchen and brought Faust here where he can see her. Mephistopheles's question in 2620 is hypocritical, cf. his further knowledge of Gretchen in 2668.

2652. An allusion to lubricious French and Italian stories.

EVENING
(2678–2804)

2706. An allusion to the custom of sprinkling sand on the floor after scrubbing and of tracing decorative patterns in the sand.

2737. That is, "one woman is as good as another in this 'play' of ours."

2759. Thule is the legendary northernmost Germanic habitation. Its people are credited with a faithfulness transcending death such as the poem celebrates.

2792. Even as late as the eighteenth century German municipal laws often regulated what kind of clothes and ornaments might be worn by the different classes of people, and Gretchen knows that only "a noble lady" might wear such jewels as she has found in the casket. Gretchen's brother tells her later that she will not be allowed to wear "a golden chain" (3756).

A PROMENADE
(2805–2864)

2826 and 2835. Cf. Rev. II, 17: To him that overcometh will I give to eat of the hidden manna.

THE NEIGHBOUR'S HOUSE
(2865–3024)

2868. The pun in the German is lost in our translation. Martha is a " grass widow "; the German calls her a " straw widow."

2895+. There is a peep-hole in the door with a curtain in front of it.

2974. Turkish pirates were common down into the eighteenth century and Christian crews often retaliated with equal piracy.

2981–4. That is, a courtesan who infected him with syphilis which the eighteenth century sometimes called " the Neapolitan malady."

A STREET
(3025–3072)

3030. Gypsies were said to brew love-potions, carry messages, and be of other uses.

3050–8. Faust can call Mephistopheles a " sophist " because Faust at least thought on the occasions cited by Mephistopheles that he was telling the truth, whereas Mephistopheles now wants Faust to subscribe to a conscious, deliberate lie. Mephistopheles retorts by denying that even Faust will think he is telling the truth when he swears eternal love to Gretchen.

3072. Faust's desire to know Gretchen is now so strong that it can not be restrained by scruples of conscience.

A GARDEN
(3073–3204)

The two couples have evidently been strolling together for some time.

A GARDEN HOUSE
(3205–3216)

On the stage this scene is usually played as part of the preceding scene but it is probable that a few days are supposed to have elapsed. In the German of the scene Margaret has taken a significant step in addressing Faust no longer as " you " but as " thou."

FOREST AND CAVERN
(3217–3373)

In this and the two following scenes the " Gretchen episode " reaches its climax. Faust has formerly communed with nature (cf. 386–97 and the effect of the Easter Sunday walk, 1178 ff.) and he now goes off into nature, seeking to get or keep his desire for Gretchen under control, but, partly under the influence of Mephistopheles, he surrenders at the last to the intensity of his passion.

3217. "Spirit sublime": the Spirit of the Universe.

3218. "Thou hast not," that is, as the Earth-Spirit did. "in vain": without effect, or result.

3238. The "forms" are spirits of bygone times which in the "silvery" moonlight turn Faust away from "contemplation."

3277. Perhaps a "Doctor" in pursuit of natural science, perhaps the brooding Doctor Faust.

3288. "six days' work": Creation.

3291+. Mephistopheles makes an obscene gesture.

3300. "again": as in lines 1544–1606.

3318. "Were I a little bird": the beginning of a familiar folk-song.

3334. "the Body of the Lord": possibly the holy wafer, possibly the crucifix.

3337. Cf. the Song of Solomon IV, 5: Thy two breasts are like two young roes that are twins, which feed among the lilies.

3363. Faust acknowledges that he can not conquer his desire.

GRETCHEN'S ROOM
(3374–3413)

Gretchen's lyrical monologue is to be taken as a companion-piece to the preceding scene. Faust, a more responsible agent, struggles for self-control and surrenders. Gretchen broods over her loneliness, then seems actually to see her lover coming nearer and nearer, and finally yearns to give herself to him. She longs to give herself to Faust consummately "in a blaze of glorious passion."

MARTHA'S GARDEN
(3414–3543)

3414. Goethe knew Faust's historical name as "Johann" (cf. Introduction, p. ix), but he changed it in the play to "Heinrich" because "Johann" had become vulgarized through various associations of the name.

3421–58. To Gretchen's simple piety religious belief means acceptance of churchly dogma, of what the "priest or sage" lays down. To Faust the phrase, "I believe in God," is not adequate. To him the question is: "What do you believe or think concerning Him? If in your acknowledgment of Him you are satisfied merely with His name — a name that is so worn out through repetition that it no longer means anything — you acknowledge nothing; but if, seeing the Infinite all about you, you *feel* His Being within you, then you can not fail to acknowledge Him." "Feeling is all in all." Faust's creed has much in common with that held by Goethe in 1772, according to the contemporary statement of one of Goethe's friends.

3469 ff. Note the irregularity of the metre when Gretchen in her agitation speaks of Mephistopheles.

AT THE WELL
(3544–3586)

Again some interval of time has elapsed. Gretchen's pregnancy is not yet generally known, but she is well aware of it and her serenity of mind is gone. She knows that what gossipy, scurrilous Lisbeth tells of Babbie will soon apply to her. Now she knows how the world will condemn her, however innocently she followed a natural impulse.

3546. " Sibylla " is the name of some other girl.

3569. Girls who had " fallen " were required to do penance by appearing before a church congregation in a sinner's smock. Goethe was largely responsible for the abrogation of this penance in the Duchy of Saxe-Weimar.

3575–6. A wreath could be worn only by a chaste bride; " chaff " or " straw ": the Germans call a bastard a " straw child."

THE RAMPARTS
(3587–3619)

The scene seems to be located in the narrow passage-way between the wall of the town and the nearest houses within, possibly between the inner and outer walls of the town. Gretchen is praying to an image of the " Sorrowing Mother " that is set in a niche in a wall. The Virgin is represented as bearing a sword thrust through Her heart and gazing upward at Her Son on the cross. The time is a few weeks later. Two similar crucifixion groups dating from the early 16th century and well known to Goethe from his earliest years are still extant in Frankfort.

NIGHT
(3620–3775)

Various items in this scene were derived from *Hamlet* or from *Romeo and Juliet*.

3634–7. " clink-clink ": the clinking of glasses in assent; that is, it is agreed that the challenge is accepted and that all of Valentine's companions agree that Gretchen is " the pride and ornament of all her sex! "

3650–1. The " sacristy " is probably a chapel (of the Cathedral in the following scene) with an altar-lamp burning night and day.

3661. Mephistopheles is enjoying the foretaste of the joys of Walpurgis Night, cf. the next scene but one.

3664–5. Faust sees a phosphorescent light near the ground, a sign (according to German folk-lore) that a treasure lies underneath.

3669. " lion-dollars ": coins minted first perhaps in Bohemia with the royal Bohemian lion stamped on them, perhaps first in Louvain which the Germans call " Löwen," " Lions."

3673. A German saying runs: " Pearls mean tears."

3682–97. Cf. Ophelia's song, *Hamlet* IV, 5. Goethe said to his secretary Eckermann (January 18, 1825), in reference to Byron's reproach that Goethe had taken the song from Shakespeare: " Why should I take the trouble to invent a song of my own when Shakespeare's was just the thing and said just what was needed? " In the same conversation with Eckermann Goethe said: " Walter Scott made use of a scene in my ' Egmont ' [in *Kenilworth*] and he was right in doing so and because he did it intelligently, he is to be praised."

3706. " duster ": an equivalent of German slang for " sword."

3714–5. Mephistopheles and Faust flee. Mephistopheles can " get on " with the police who dispose of minor offences, but the " assizes " (criminal courts) deal with cases of life and death, deriving their authority from God and thus barring the Devil's interference.

3756–7. Reminiscences of legal restrictions once placed upon girls of the lower classes and especially upon prostitutes, cf. above note to 2792.

CATHEDRAL
(3776–3834)

Gretchen is rapidly approaching her time of travail. In addition, she has used Faust's (or Mephistopheles's) opiate carelessly, thus killing her mother, and she has caused indirectly the death of her brother. The " Evil Spirit " gives voice to Gretchen's conscience and to all that her little world will say about her. A requiem mass is being celebrated in memory of some friend or acquaintance of Gretchen's, not of Gretchen's mother or brother.

3788. According to the Roman Catholic faith, the mother's soul must linger in Purgatory because she died without receiving extreme unction; the same is true of Valentine.

3798–9. " Day of wrath, that day shall dissolve the world in ashes ": the first lines of the dirge of the Judgment Day composed in the thirteenth century, probably by Thomas of Celano. The music which Goethe here had in mind was probably the standard or traditional melody used in requiem masses of the Roman Catholic Church as given, for example, in the Vatican edition of the Graduale Romanum. Rome. 1938.

3800–7. Gretchen is visualizing her resurrection.

3813–5. " When therefore the Judge shall be seated, whatever is hidden shall appear, nothing shall remain unpunished."

3821. " Hide thyself! ": if thou canst.

3825–7. " What then shall I, miserable one, say? Whom shall I call upon as my protector when scarcely the just man shall be secure? "

3834+. It may be imagined that Gretchen not only " falls in a swoon " but into the mental derangement in which she later drowns her child.

WALPURGIS NIGHT
(3835–4222)

Walpurgis Night is the night between the thirtieth of April and the first of May, a time when, according to German folk-lore, witches hold high carnival on the Brocken, a peak in northern Germany about 3600 feet in altitude, the highest in the Hartz Mountains. Witches are said to meet there at that time in defence of their claim to May 1st (a day when ancient Germanic tribes observed various religious customs) against the allotment of that day in the calendar to Walpurgis (or Walpurga), an English Benedictine nun long resident in Germany. The summit of the Brocken rises above the tree-line and is strewn with granite blocks, hence probably the popular name, " Blocksberg." Schierke and Elend are villages a few hours' walk below the summit. Goethe was in the Hartz Mountains three times, and he is said to have been the first man to climb the Brocken in winter. Faust and Mephistopheles do not reach the summit; they stop on a high plateau to take part in a dance. Goethe's own manuscript of this scene, preserved in the State Library in Berlin, indicates that the scene was written between November, 1800, and March, 1801. Cf. Shelley's translation of this scene.

3835–7. Cf. note to 3961.

3855. Mephistopheles can command will-o'-the-wisps because folk-lore regards them as evil spirits that lure wayfarers to their destruction.

3870+. "alternating song": who sings this or that stanza in lines 3871–911? Perhaps: the three — Faust, Mephistopheles, and the Will-o'-the-Wisp — unite in singing the first stanza (3871–5); Faust and Mephistopheles combine in the second stanza (3876–80); Faust sings a solo (3881–8); Mephistopheles likewise (3889–905); and Faust again sings a solo (3906–11).

3880. An allusion to two granite rocks called "the Snorers," near Schierke.

3889. The Germans call both the owl and its cry "Hoo-hoo" ("Uhu") and "Shoo-hoo" ("Schuhu").

3892–900. These lines contain various weird fancies. The climbers may only *think* they see salamanders and mice, although both are of the Devil's kingdom.

3915. "Mammon": gold. Cf. note to 3664–5. In 3932–3 Mammon, the New Testament lord of wealth, is personified, cf. Matt. VI, 24: Ye can not serve God and mammon.

3959. Urian: a Low German name for the Devil.

3961. The witches are supposed to ride on he-goats and rams and on pitchforks and broomsticks smeared with witch's salve (cf. 4008), also in troughs (4010). The use of dashes here and later (4138–9 and 4142–3) accords with the practice of the last edition of his works which Goethe supervised, but it is known that the dashes of that edition in line 3961 stood for the German equivalent of "makes wind."

3962. Baubo of classical mythology was famous for her bestial shamelessness. She herself may be introduced here in anticipation of similar figures in the Second Part of *Faust* or her name only may be given to a witch-in-chief in the present scene.

3968. The Ilsenstein ("Ilsa's Stone") is a tall cliff-like rock a few miles north of the Brocken.

3972. Some witch has scraped against the speaker and wounded her.

3977. That is, a pregnant witch and her unborn child, from the pressure of the crowd.

3977+. The "Wizards" are conceived as men who throng with witches. Goethe is flaying corruption in both sexes, ascribing to women greater readiness for evil, to men more energy in pursuing it.

3987–4007. Who these witches are or whether Goethe intended anything more than mocking mystification is not certain. The "Voices" (3987–9) *may* mean critics or prudes. The "Voice" (3996–9) *may* refer to Protestantism or science. The "Half-witch" (4004–7) *may* be half-developed and incapable of reaching the summit in time to satisfy her lust.

4023. "Voland" ("Evil Spirit") is another name for the Devil.

4037–40. Goethe once planned but never executed a scene (to be included as a part of the Walpurgis Night scene) in which Satan would hold high court on the summit of the Brocken.

4064. An allusion to the English Order of the Garter.

4072–95. Goethe turns aside from the witches' carnival to satirize members of another, older generation: the General and the Minister (of State) who have been thrust out of office; the Parvenu who wants the preservation of the former corrupt order through which he has come up; and the Author whose popularity has waned. Mephistopheles burlesques all four by pretending for a moment that he is one with them.

4095+. Faust calls the scene a " fair " (4115), hence the inclusion of a witch who offers various odds and ends for sale.

4110–1. Mephistopheles means that there are now less brutal and more effective ways for bringing people to destruction.

4119. Jewish tradition ascribes to Adam a first wife named Lilith. After the creation of Eve, Lilith is said to have become the mistress of a devil, seducing men and pursuing children. She has been identified with the " female " of Gen. I, 27, and with the " screech owl " (or " night monster ") of Isaiah XXXIV, 14. (Gen. I, 27: So God created man in his own image, in the image of God created he him; male and female created he them. Isaiah XXXIV, 14: the screech owl also shall rest there, and find for herself a place of rest.) Lilith is an embodiment of sensuality, a culmination of Walpurgis Night, of that phase of the Eternal-Womanly which degrades, the extremest opposite of the all-understanding, all-forgiving Virgin at the end of the play.

4120–3. German folk-lore ascribed especial power to witches' hair; in the trials of witches therefore their hair was shorn before the proceedings started.

4124. Is the Old Witch Mephistopheles's old friend of the Witch's Kitchen? Cf. 2503 ff.

4138–9. Cf. note to 3961. The dashes stand for " monstrous hole " (4138) and " huge " (4139); those in 4142–3 for " proper cork " and " a big hole."

4143+. The " proctophantasmist," or " rump-visionary," is Friedrich Nicolai who toward the end of the eighteenth century made himself ridiculous in advocating dry common-sense in literature and in opposing new ideas. He had angered Goethe first by writing a parody of Goethe's novel, *The Sorrows of Young Werther,* calling his own story *The Joys of Young Werther;* later he attacked Goethe's friend Schiller. Nicolai then committed an almost unbelievable indiscretion. The rumour had gone about in Berlin in 1797 that ghosts had appeared in the suburb of Tegel (cf. 4161), whereupon Nicolai prepared a paper which he read before the Berlin Academy of Sciences (published in 1799) in which he announced that he had been plagued by ghostly apparitions and that he had cured himself by applying leeches to his rump. Goethe now saw an opportunity to even up the score with Nicolai and he seized it, however out of place in *Faust* the castigation is. Even when the First Part of *Faust* was first published (1808), the references to Nicolai were fully appreciated by only a small proportion of Goethe's friends and readers.

4150. That is, he has to talk about everything that happens. In a vision called *The Judgment Day* (1799), Ludwig Tieck describes Nicolai with leeches clinging to his rump and condemns him to a sojourn of two thousand years in Hell where he must listen constantly to the devils' chatter and never say a word.

4155. In another work by Tieck, *Zerbino*, Nicolai appears as a miller who describes his mill at length. But it is also possible that the line (4155) refers to Nicolai's publications in which he repeats himself *ad nauseam*.

4159. " enlightenment ": Nicolai boasted that he was a leader of the " Age of Enlightenment."

4165–7. " spirit " in three senses: " ghost," " supernatural being," and " intelligence."

4169. An allusion to Nicolai's *Description of a Tour through Germany and Switzerland in 1781,* a work in twelve fat volumes which Goethe and Schiller had already chastised ferociously and ludicrously. Nicolai appears again as a traveller in lines 4267 and 4319.

4172. That is, where he will find leeches.

4179. A red mouse, according to German folk-lore, sometimes runs out of the mouth of a sleeping witch.

4181. Mephistopheles thinks that mice are usually grey; this one was at least not an ordinary mouse.

4190. " eidolon ": " phantom."

4194. Medusa whose serpent hair changed all who looked at her to stone and whose head Perseus struck off with his face averted, cf. 4208.

4211. " Prater ": a park in Vienna that was opened to the public in 1776 as a place of amusement.

4214. " Servibilis ": literally, " one ready to serve," here a stage employee.

4214–22. A mockery of dilettantism.

WALPURGIS NIGHT'S DREAM
(4223–4398)

This scene which is mentioned by way of anticipation in 4214–5 has nothing whatever to do with Faust. Faust may be looking on at its presentation, but he is in great distress of mind about Gretchen and he is therefore hardly following the scene. The scene consists of a collection of epigrammatic quatrains which Goethe called " Xenia," " gifts of hospitality," which he intended originally to publish as a work complete in itself. They are directed in many cases at outstanding figures in the life of Goethe's own time who express their reactions to the revels of Walpurgis Night and thus satirize themselves. The scene may be said to be placed properly beside the preceding scene, since all the figures are spirits and biting satire may be considered a devilish enterprise; the scene contains, moreover, very clever ridicule of individuals and types who are mischievously thrown into this mad environment. But the scene is not woven organically into the texture of the play as a whole and Goethe made a regrettable blunder in embedding the scene in his *Faust.*

The sub-title, " Oberon and Titania's Golden Wedding," suggested by Shakespeare's *A Midsummer-Night's Dream,* indicates the general background of the scene and prepares us for the reconciliation of Oberon and Titania after their quarrel. The second sub-title, " Intermezzo," was added at a time when Goethe planned to have Faust and Mephistopheles see this scene as an interlude while ascending the Brocken; the sub-title should have been omitted later because it had lost its meaning.

4223–50. These lines introduce the personnel of the theatre and the characters who form the centre of attraction.

4223–6. A simple stage-set has been put into place, leaving the Theatre-Manager and his scene-shifters with nothing to do. Mieding was Goethe's right-hand man in the presentation of plays in Weimar until Mieding's death in 1782. Mieding's " sons " are scene-shifters and the like.

4227–30. The Herald, in a kind of prologue, announces the reconciliation of Oberon and Titania as the primary cause of the gathering.

4235–42. Puck, who is borrowed from *A Midsummer-Night's Dream*, and Ariel, from *The Tempest*, appear as the leaders of comical and noble figures. By " frights " and " fair ones " Ariel means in each case spirits of both sexes, ugly, ludicrous ones and those with feeling and understanding for " pure and heavenly measures."

4251–4. The Orchestra describes its own make-up.

4255–8. It seems that a bagpipe comes along as a fitting addition to the orchestra and delivers a " solo " about itself; the German equivalent of " snecke-snicke-snack " is an onomatopoetic invention of Goethe's.

4259–62. These lines probably refer to the product of poetasters who attempt to combine the unrelated. The product still speaks with customary pride in its wings (its bit of poetic inspiration) and in the final form into which it will develop.

4263–6. Each one of a little pair of poets addresses the other in two lines each; they are modest and industrious in contrast with the arrogance of the preceding speaker.

4267–70. The " Inquisitive Traveller ": cf. note to 4143+.

4271–4. " Orthodox " is Count Friedrich Leopold von Stolberg who with the zeal of a fanatic accused Schiller of blasphemy when Schiller wrote his poem, " The Gods of Greece."

4275–8. That is, perhaps the North offers material for sketches but not for finished works of art as Italy does. Goethe may be thinking of himself as he was planning his own " Italian Journey " when he wrote these lines.

4279–82. The " Purist " stands for the rules of propriety in all places and all connexions.

4291–4. The " Young Witch " has caused a great stir and excitement in the orchestra so that the " Leader of the Orchestra " has to call its members to time.

4295–4302. The " Weather-vane " first praises, then condemns, in the manner of a turncoat, thus embodying a mockery of the unreliable.

4303–6. Goethe and Schiller wrote a great many Xenia which could be called " insects " on account of their stings. Some of the victims said the Xenia had been directly inspired by the Devil.

4307–18. August von Hennings published a collection of poems called *Der Musaget* (" Leader of the Muses ") and edited a journal called *Spirit of the Times* (later *Spirit of the Nineteenth Century,* hence " Quondam "). Hennings had attacked the Xenia violently.

4319–22. Nicolai again, but here he is talked about; one speaker explains another. Nicolai was a bitter enemy of the Jesuits.

4323–6. Goethe said to Eckermann (February 17, 1829) that the " crane " on the Blocksberg was his one-time friend Lavater, " a man of powerful illusions, who walked like a crane."

4327–30. Goethe dined with Lavater and another friend, Basedow, in 1774, an occasion which Goethe commemorated in his poem " Dinner at Coblenz ": " A prophet right, a prophet left, a worldling in between them." Goethe is the " worldling " here too.

4331–42. The " Dancer," the " Dancing Master," and the " Fiddler " announce and describe the coming of a group of philosophers, who, like philosophers in general (according to Goethe), differ and debate with each other endlessly and fruitlessly.

4343–62. Each philosopher in turn reflects upon the existence of devils in a manner typical of his school of philosophy: the " Dogmatist " does not accept the existence of the Devil on faith and trust, as we should expect, but argues that since he sees the " devilish " about him, the Devil himself must be a reality; the " Idealist," a follower of Fichte, true to the principle that the Not-Me is a creation of the Me, identifies himself with the revelry about him and naturally concludes that here he is " idiotic "; the " Realist," who still believes that experience through the senses affords the only solid foundation for life, can not now believe the testimony of his eyes and ears and therefore feels the ground unsteady beneath him; the belief of the " Supernaturalist " in a personal God and direct revelation finds in the existence of " devilish " spirits a confirmation of his belief in spirits of a higher order; finally, the " Skeptic " doubts everything and ridicules his predecessors and their hope of finding their beliefs confirmed in these surroundings.

4363–6. The " Leader of the Orchestra " again finds it necessary to ridicule his assistants and to call them to order.

4367–90. A concluding group appears, consisting of political figures: the " Adroit " who in revolutionary times change their opinions according to their personal advantage; the " Ne'er-do-wells," fawners at court, who bewail the loss of reward for their fawning; the " Will-o'-the-Wisps " who arose from the marshes and litter of revolution and play a brilliant role in the society of a new era; the " Falling Star " who probably symbolizes the meteoric career of men in public life; the " Heavy Ones " who are rabble bent upon the destruction of the existing. Puck wants to be the heaviest one now because everything in this spirit-scene should be light and airy.

4394. Ariel directs the spirits to Oberon's palace which was said to be situated on a " hill of roses."

A DISMAL DAY   A FIELD

(Pages 129–30)

The vision of Gretchen has gripped Faust and he is now speeding back to rescue her from prison if he can. As he and his comrade cross a " field " where no one else can hear him, he addresses Mephistopheles in impassioned prose such as Goethe wrote in his young manhood, in the days of his Storm and Stress. The time of the scene is evening twilight.

7. The " evil spirits " are such as the " Evil Spirit " in the Cathedral, cf. 3776–834.

NIGHT   AN OPEN FIELD
(4399–4404)

As Faust and Mephistopheles storm along on their black steeds, they pass an elevated stone-block, a place of execution known as the " Raven-stone." The spirits hovering around the Ravenstone, " strewing and dedi-cating," appear to Faust like kindly spirits or angels such as those, unknown to Faust, who will soon encamp about Gretchen and attend her as she rises to Heaven. Mephistopheles, however, can not and will not accept Faust's interpretation of the spirits around the Ravenstone. He tells Faust that the spirits are " a witches' guild," hence to be ignored and forgotten, and so he urges: " On! On! "

PRISON
(4405–4612)

4406. " the woe of human lot ": the woe of human existence, of living.

4408. Her crime was her simple faith that it was right for her to follow a natural impulse of love.

4412–20. In her intermittent madness Gretchen sings a coarse song as does Ophelia in *Hamlet*. The original story underlying Goethe's version of the song tells of a child whom a wicked stepmother kills and serves up as a meal for her husband; a stepsister gathers up the bones and lays them under a juniper-tree, but the bones vanish and a timid little bird flies up singing the whole sad story.

4436. Cf. note to 3575–6.

4448–50. Songs have always been frequently made up about recent events and one was perhaps made up about Gretchen which she now con-fuses with a similar, older song.

4512. " wet ": with the blood of Valentine.

4569. Gretchen means her mother's fatal drowsiness.

4590. The church bell was tolled when the culprit was on the way to the place of execution; after reading the death-sentence the judge broke a white wand as a sign that the culprit's life was forfeited to the law.

4599–600. Mephistopheles's magic horses can not stand the daylight.

4603. The place is " holy " because it is occupied by a person who is about to meet her God. Cf. note to 3714–5.

4611. Mephistopheles means that Gretchen is judged *and* condemned, but the " Voice (from above) " proclaims that she is saved. As Goethe im-plies at the end of the Second Part of *Faust,* Gretchen is saved because she has suffered and atoned.

Notes

TO THE SECOND PART
OF THE TRAGEDY

PREFATORY: Almost all of the Second Part of *Faust* was written between March, 1825, and the end of July, 1831, when Goethe was from seventy-five to very nearly eighty-two years old. It was not, however, written in its present sequence of Acts and Scenes. The first Scene of the First Act was composed by the end of 1826, also all of the Third Act except lines 8489–8802 which Goethe wrote in 1800; the Scenes at the Emperor's court as far as line 6036 were written in 1827; the remainder of the First Act and the Second Act as far as line 7004 in 1828 and 1829; the Classical Walpurgis Night (7005–8487) in the incredibly short time between the middle of January and the end of June, 1830, more than half of it indeed in less than a month; the greater part of the Fifth Act, revised and completed, in 1830; the remainder of the Fifth Act and all of the Fourth Act in the spring and summer of the following year. On July 22, 1831, Goethe wrote in his diary: "Das Hauptgeschäft zu Stande gebracht," "My chief task completed."

ACT I

A PLEASING LANDSCAPE
(4613–4727)

The time of this scene follows the death of Gretchen, but not very closely. Recovery from such distress as Faust has suffered proceeds slowly in real life, and at the end of this scene Faust is to be thought of symbolically as at least several years older and as freed from remorse over the past. He awakens refreshed and eager for new experiences. Ariel, Shakespeare's "airy spirit," has already appeared in the play as a charming singer (4239–42) and as a representative of "kind Nature" (4391).

4626. An allusion to the Roman *vigiliae* of three hours each, extending from six p.m. to six a.m.

4634–65. According to the composer Eberwein, each of the four stanzas of the chorus originally bore a superscription: "serenade" suggesting the hush of nightfall; "notturno," deep slumber; "mattutino," the coming of dawn; and "réveille," sunrise.

4666–71. This conception of dawn may have been suggested by Guido Reni's painting of the sun-god Helios in his chariot, preceded by Aurora and attended by the dancing "Hours." But the "Hours" are rather to be imagined as the goddesses who open and close the "rocky portals" when Phoebus

Apollo, the sun-god, begins his journey across the heavens in his sun-lit chariot.

4674. The elves are of a nocturnal kind; their ears can hear the whisperings of night, but they have never been able to bear the " tumult " of the break of day, so they must flee.

4679–4727. Goethe rarely employed *terza rima* (here ababcbcbcdcdedefef, etc.), " because," he said, " it never comes to rest," but he turned to it here, perhaps under the influence of Dante, perhaps to embody Faust's unresting spirit.

In these lines Faust comes with the dawning of a new day to a new view of life. Faust realizes (4702–27) that man can not know ultimate truth; he can not bear the light that comes from on high; he sees it only with a vision that remains baffled and clouded like that of youth. Man is destined to see light only in coloured reflection, only in that which light falls upon, namely, this phenomenal world, a manifestation of the divine and the only form in which the divine is knowable to man. With this new perception Faust will henceforth indulge in no vain attempts to solve the metaphysical; he will observe the world as it unfolds before him and he will finally lay stout hold upon the opportunity to do and serve which this world offers to him. As now, he will still believe that " the view beyond is barred to mortal ken " and that a man is " a fool who thither turns his blinking eyes " (11442–3), just as Goethe made no pretence of knowing the unexplorable and even in his scientific research confined his investigation strictly within the limits of the ascertainable. In his study on optics Goethe offered no theory about the origin and essence of light and called his famous treatise significantly, not " A Theory of Light," but " A Theory of Colour."

THE EMPEROR'S PALACE
(4728–5064)

The palace, as it is usually set forth on the stage, consists at first of a great formal throne-room and later of a spacious hall, a pleasure garden, a dark gallery, brightly lighted halls, and a hall of the knights. The present scene in the throne-room presupposes that Mephistopheles, who has promised to show the " great world " to Faust (2052), has told Faust of the decadent conditions prevailing at the Emperor's court and that after winning the favour of the Emperor he will introduce Faust there in the course of a masquerade. The Emperor, his court, and the attendant circumstances are modelled in part in consonance with Maximilian I (1493–1519) and his times. Maximilian too was very fond of amusement and always in need of money. But Goethe said to Eckermann (October 1, 1827) that he did not intend to depict Maximilian exactly but " a prince possessed of every possible capacity for losing his realm."

4743–50. " Genius," " money," " devil," and " fool " have been suggested as the answer to each of these questions, but " fool " seems the most satisfying whether referring to the court fool in general, to the old fool, or to the new fool.

4771+. The chancellor was also the Archbishop of Mainz. Later (10930+) he is called the Archbishop-Arch-Chancellor.

4811+. The Commander-in-Chief, or Master of the Army, is the equivalent of a modern Minister of War.

4829–30. He means that foreign princes, though friendly and in some cases subject to the Emperor, are not concerned about the internal condition of the Empire. Goethe is perhaps remembering satirically that foreign princes all too frequently meddled in affairs of the Holy Roman Empire.

4836–7. That is, " a new lord " has displaced a predecessor and insists on freedom from tribute to the Emperor.

4845. Goethe uses the names of the old papal (Guelph) and imperial (Ghibelline) factions as typical of the attitude of parties in general in the sixteenth century.

4859. " Allowances-in-kind ": food products paid by tenants.

4866. A wine-cellar was usually maintained in the town-hall of a medieval city.

4897. " Nature and Mind " mean heresy and atheism to the Chancellor. As a prelate of the church he wants men to rely on authority and faith.

4906. " the saints and knights ": the clergy and the nobility.

4913. " you " in this line is probably addressed to Mephistopheles, while " you " in 4915 is addressed to the members of the court.

4923. In this case " you " may refer to Mephistopheles or to the Chancellor, but the latter is certainly meant by " you " in 4924.

4931. " those fearful times ": a reference to the migrations of Germanic tribes, to the Hunnish invasion, and to other such events.

4938. Old German lawbooks prescribed that treasure buried beneath the reach of a ploughshare belonged to the Emperor.

4949. The celestial hemisphere of the astrologers was divided by concentric curves and radii into twelve " houses." When the hour of birth and the latitude and longitude of the birthplace were known, the astrologer could locate the sun, moon, planets, and signs of the zodiac in the different " houses " and cast a person's horoscope. Many a potentate of the sixteenth and seventeenth centuries had an astrologer in his retinue.

4955–64. The astrologers taught that the sun represents gold; Mercury, quicksilver; Venus, copper; the moon, silver; Mars, iron; Jupiter, tin; and Saturn, lead. This astrological jargon leads up to Mephistopheles's recommendation of himself (4969) through the mouth of the Astrologer. Luna's " whimsical humours " (4959) allude to the periodic changes of the moon.

4976. " he ": " the highly learnèd man " of 4969.

4979–80. Folk-lore tells us that the mandrake, a magic plant more or less like a small scarecrow, can be pulled up only by a black dog at midnight of the summer solstice; a human being would drop dead if he attempted it. In obtaining a mandrake the dog must be tied to a cord attached to the root of the plant and a piercing blast must be blown on a horn; the terrified dog will then pull up the screaming mandrake and immediately fall dead. The mandrake is said to confer health, wealth, control of wind and weather, and other pleasing properties. Mephistopheles jeers: " You believe in these things, why not in me? "

4981–92. Further banter of Mephistopheles: " Laugh as you will or cry ' Sorcery! ' — Still, what if your sole tickles or you do not stride as before?

Either sensation means that you are standing over buried treasure." " There lies the fiddler ": a reference to a proverb meaning that when the fiddler was alive, he made people happy, and so he does too in death; the place where he lies buried becomes a lucky spot, and when a man stumbles, he may be sure that he is stumbling over the fiddler's burial-place.

5006. An " aside."

5011–2. " He scratches saltpetre from an old clay wall for his cattle (who love to lick saltpetre) and behind the saltpetre, in a cavity in the wall, he discovers a roll of gold."

5026. Wine was said to deposit so much tartar on the sides of a buried wine-cask that the tartar would form a cask and hold the wine after the staves had rotted away.

5036. That is, colours can not be distinguished in the dark.

5040. " grow great ": become famous.

5041. Cf. the golden calf of Exodus XXXII, 3–4, as a symbol of great wealth: And all the people brake off the golden earrings which were in their ears, and brought them unto Aaron. And he received them at their hand, and fashioned it with a graving tool, after he had made it a molten calf: and they said, These be thy gods, O Israel, which brought thee up out of the land of Egypt.

5050. Mephistopheles urges through the mouth of the Astrologer that the carnival (when men's minds are distraught) take its course and that the digging be done in Lent. In reality no digging is to be done at all and Mephistopheles secretly intends to bring about the issuance of paper money on the basis of the treasure that supposedly lies buried – but where?

A SPACIOUS HALL
(5065–5986)

The Masquerade is supposed to take place in the Emperor's palace on Shrove Tuesday, thus representing the climax of pre-Lenten festivities. It is a kind of Roman Carnival which Goethe depicted in happy recollection of his sojourn in Italy in 1786–8. Considered as a part of a drama the scene may seem unduly long but no one can gainsay the wisdom and beauty of a great many of the lines. The scene gives Goethe an opportunity to show the people of the court both in the frivolous vanity of their amusements and in their shallow emotional reactions. Faust tries to elevate the crowd by showing them allegorically the intimate relation between wealth and art (5612–29 and 5689–708) and the blessing that follows upon high-minded activity (5449–56), but in vain; vainly too does he warn the Emperor that danger lies in the sudden acquisition of wealth (5926–69).

5066. The " Dance of Death " (*Totentanz* or *danse macabre*) has often been represented in pictorial art as a skeleton leading a troupe of people of all ages and occupations and both sexes.

5072–4. The Emperors of the Holy Roman Empire were formally crowned in Rome down to the end of the fifteenth century, revering the Pope by kissing the toe of his slipper as devout Roman Catholics still do.

5087+. The " flower girls," represented as coming from the city of Florence and hence a long way from home, wear and carry artificial flowers.

5116–7. That is, " Offer your flowers but don't haggle about the price." The flower girls then proceed to show off their wares, pretending that each flower is describing itself.

5128. Ceres: the goddess of the harvest.

5136. Theophrastus (born about 390 B.C.), a pupil of Aristotle, has been called the father of botany.

5143+. Rosebuds (5150) " challenge " the artificial " Fancy Nosegay," delighting in their own beauty and in the happiness they bestow throughout their gradual unfolding.

5157+. " theorbos ": lutes of lower tones than those of the mandolins. The gardeners address the flower girls and then urge the crowd to buy fruits instead of deceiving flowers, but later (5170–3) they court the favour of the flower girls.

5162. " Sun-burnt faces ": those of the gardeners.

5194. " Hindmost Man ": the name of a familiar social game.

5198+. The ending of this strange stage direction suggests that Goethe once thought of elaborating this portion of the scene.

5214+. " Pulcinelli," literally, " little chickens ": the name of clowns whom Goethe describes as jolly loafers and whom he contrasts with hard-working wood-cutters.

5236+. Fawning, hungry " parasites " appear often in ancient comedy. Here they try to insinuate themselves into the good graces of the wood-cutters (the " stout porters," 5237), acknowledging their own two-faced character but flattering the industry of the wood-cutters and hoping to share their hearty meal.

5290+. " Chorus ": friends in similar condition.

5294+. Goethe apparently intended to elaborate this scene too, as a satire on poets of his time who tried to please everybody.

5298+. In the second and third decades of the nineteenth century many gruesome stories were written in Europe; cf. John W. Polidori's novel *The Vampire* and E. T. A. Hoffmann's short story *A Tale of Vampirism*. Goethe said to Eckermann (March 14, 1830): " They introduce devils, witches, and vampires instead of the beautiful figures of Greek mythology." True to his conviction that the Romantic is sickly and the Classical is healthy, Goethe now proceeds to bring the Classical figures before us. The second of the three Graces is generally called " Thalia," but Goethe retained the name " Hegemone " which he took from his Classical source-book (Hederich: *Gründliches mythologisches Lexicon*, hsg. von Johann Joachim Schwabe. Leipsic. 1770), so that his readers might not confuse this Grace with Thalia, the Muse of Comedy. Hederich says: " The three Graces were goddesses of amenity, benefaction, and gratitude."

5304+. Goethe violates the common tradition concerning the Fates, altering the roles usually assigned to them. Here Atropos holds the distaff, Clotho guards the shears but in their sheath in order not to disturb the merriment of the Masquerade, and Lachesis winds the thread on a reel until in the fullness of time the Weaver (the Deity) takes the skein of the individual life and weaves it into the fabric of human history.

5317–24. Clotho claims that she has taken the shears from Atropos, their usual guardian, because Atropos lets worthless old people live on and cuts off promising young lives.

5357–80. Again Goethe uses figures of classical mythology to suit his own purpose. Instead of introducing the Furies as hideous hags with snaky hair (just as he transformed the *Macbeth* witches in Weimar performances into " beautiful young girls ") he now brings the Furies into this merry throng as young women whose office now is not to avenge blood-guiltiness but to arouse jealousy between lovers, to incite quarrels between man and wife, and to avenge marital infidelity.

5357. " What boots it that the Herald has warned you against us? "

5378. In the Book of Tobit, a Book of the Old Testament Apocrypha, III, 8, Asmodeus (who was originally an erotic demon of Persian mythology) becomes a part of the Jewish realm of ideas, at first as an " evil spirit," later as a fomenter of feuds between husband and wife; he is referred to in 6961 as a provocative spirit of strife in general.

5393–405. The Herald announces the approach of an elephant with Prudence (or Wisdom, " a dainty woman," 5399) seated on its neck, Victory (5401) standing on its back, and Fear and Hope (5403–4) fettered at its sides.

5421. In carnival time men everywhere would slay Fear.

5423–40. Hope knows that while the ladies are now absorbed by the present, she and they will soon resume their life together.

5444. " For the present you [the crowd] are not subject to Fear and Hope." Note the irony in the appearance of Prudence as a mistress of ceremonies in a " mad Carnival."

5455–60. Victory: successful activity as the result of strength guided by prudence (or wisdom).

5457–93. Zoïlo-Thersites: Goethe combines in one figure Zoïlus, a defamer of Homer, and Thersites who in the Second Book of the *Iliad* reviles the hero Agamemnon; thus Goethe created a marplot who seeks to degrade the great. Mephistopheles is to be imagined as inspiring the two-headed dwarf (with one face looking forward and one looking backward) and thus breaking into the pre-arranged sequence of the Masquerade. The indignant Herald strikes the creature, and he and the crowd are greatly surprised by the result.

5505–13. The Herald now sees something else that surprises him: a chariot driven by a Boy (who identifies himself in 5573 as " Poesy ") and occupied by Faust in the guise of Plutus, the god of wealth, and Mephistopheles in the guise of Avarice. The chariot contains a box of treasure.

5559. That is, than in mere having and enjoying.

5582–9. The Boy Charioteer seems to scatter jewels and flames, symbols of poetry, but the Herald soon sees the jewels turn into things of no worth. Poetry has no value for common folk.

5640–5. Mephistopheles who has been guarding the box of treasure in the form of Avarice (or Stinginess) is now described as a " Starveling," a fanciful contrast to Wealth (Faust) and Profusion (Poetry).

5648–65. " The Starveling " acknowledges that formerly he appeared as a woman when women were saving, but now that they have become spend-

[383]

thrifts, he has changed his gender and become an ally of husbands, changing from the feminine " *Avaritia* " to a masculine " Avarice." The German expresses it with more finish as a change from the feminine " *Avaritia* " to the masculine " *der Geiz.*"

5671. " wooden cross ": Mephistopheles's lean figure.

5685. It is a " marvel " (5688) that the dragons (" they ") who have no hands, have lifted the chest from the chariot with Mephistopheles seated on it and that they have brought it to Faust.

5706. Poetry is self-revelation.

5709–14. Faust proceeds to qualify as a magician.

5762. Faust draws the ring to keep the crowd back.

5782. Mephistopheles is moulding plastic gold, probably into the form of a phallus.

5797. Faust merely pretends that Mephistopheles does not know that the Emperor will soon appear in the mask of Pan.

5800. The Herald's wand imposes " mighty Law "; " mightier Necessity " makes room for Pan and his attendants.

5801–6. The " wild host " sings of itself in the third person as it does again in 5816–8 and as others do in later lines of this scene. The host knows that Pan masks the Emperor.

5809–14. Faust is saying that the wild host does not know that it has rushed into a magic circle that renders it subject to Faust and Mephistopheles.

5815. The wild host addresses the masqueraders outside of the circle.

5819–71. Fauns, Satyrs, Gnomes, and Giants appear in turn and describe themselves in the third person.

5841. Fauns like dancing and therefore want partners, but Gnomes work busily each for himself.

5848. " Good-men ": for the German " Gütchen," a popular name for Gnomes of kindly disposition.

5859. " wholesale murder ": war.

5860. " three commandments ": against theft and adultery (5857) and murder (5859).

5864–71. These " Wild Men of the Woods," familiar figures in North German folk-lore, are conceived as gigantic Fauns.

5869–70. " band ": " apron."

5874–5. Goethe's source-book says under " Pan ": " He is called by this name πάν, because he embodies the All of Nature."

5884–9. All nature did not stir while Pan slept at noon, according to the Greek myth. The Nymphs suggest that Pan will soon fall asleep and the merriment must cease.

5890–5. Panics were said to be caused by Pan, cf. 10002.

5906–7. Gnomes draw Pan's attention to a vein of gold in the magic chest.

5910–1. At some moment in the play a paper is presented to Pan (the Emperor) for his signature, perhaps at this moment, perhaps later, cf. 6068 and note.

5919+. Plutus maintains his hold on the magic staff in order to avert a danger that will threaten.

5920–43. The Emperor is led to Faust's magic chest of molten gold where he sees flames rising and falling. Suddenly his beard falls off and then flies back to his face, seeming to set him on fire. The fire quickly spreads throughout the halls. But Faust extinguishes the magic fire with magic rain and nobody of course is hurt. The scene is based on a story that Goethe read in his childhood and always remembered vividly. According to the story Charles VI of France, dressed in 1394 as a Satyr in a masquerade, was approached too nearly by the Duke of Orleans whose torch set fire to Charles's false beard, and Charles went hopelessly insane.

5962. " The mimic woods ": the foliage decorating the hall.

5970–84. Plutus (Faust) has saved the day, the Masquerade has ended happily, and Faust is established as the Emperor's indispensable *maître de plaisir*.

PLEASURE GARDEN
(5987–6172)

5990. Pluto: in classical mythology the god of the lower world, but the name has also been applied to the Christian Devil.

5998. " Peoples ": probably a reference to different nationalities subject to the head of the Holy Roman Empire.

6006–26. Mephistopheles urges the Emperor, now that he has " proved " fire to be obedient to him, to show himself master of another element, water. Air and earth are disposed of in 6027–30.

6022–6. Nereids: daughters of Nereus, " the old man of the sea." Thetis, one of these Nymphs, became, as the wife of Peleus, the mother of Achilles.

6033. Scheherazade: the inexhaustible story-teller of the *Arabian Nights*.

6068. This incident may be assumed as having taken place at lines 5910–1, cf. the note on those lines.

6072. " conjurors ": wonder-working printers with their new art.

6081. " The only letters now worth anything are those employed by the initials of your name."

6108. " girdle ": that is, his money-belt, by putting paper money into it instead of metal coins.

6121. People haggled much about coins of different mintages and dubious weight.

6148+. " Banneret ": a nobleman privileged to have a banner of his own in war.

6170. " Milord ": a title used in addressing a landed proprietor.

6172. " wit " in its usual meaning and in its old meaning of " intelligence."

The result of this orgy of paper money appears later in the Fourth Act.

A DARK GALLERY
(6173–6306)

The Emperor has been deeply impressed by Faust's skill in magic and he has expressed a desire to see ideal male and female beauty in the forms of Paris and Helena.* Mephistopheles tells Faust that he, a Christian devil, has no connection with Hades, the other-world of the ancients; he can only give Faust a key which in the hands of Mephistopheles is a useless thing but in the hands of Faust flashes with the light of idealistic promise. With this key Faust must go to a realm outside of time and space, to the realm of the "Mothers," a realm of "images of all creatures" (6289). These images Goethe calls "archetypes."

The realm of the Mothers should be conceived metaphysically rather than logically or psychologically. It corresponds to Plato's realm of Ideas in so far as it comprises the eternal and abiding essence of things, that innermost core of reality of which our world in time and space presents but the transitory manifestation. But whereas Plato regards the realm of ideas as in its very essence fixed and static, Goethe conceives this realm which he calls "the realm of the Mothers" as one of being and becoming. Hence Helena is eternal but she can also change and so, as we shall see in the Third Act, Helena appears with a capacity for easy, ready adjustment to Faust and association with him. Then, too, there issues from Helena, regarded as an archetype, a power far greater than that exercised by the Platonic idea of beauty.

Goethe drew the startling name "Mothers" from Plutarch, but this scene was conceived and executed in almost every detail as an invention of Goethe's.

6196. That is, "you have not yet fulfilled your obligations in regard to the paper money and now you want to assume another great responsibility."

6199–200. The German says literally "witch-monstrosities"; "changeling dwarfs" are the children of devils and witches.

6206–7. "You not only want me at the end of my earthly life, but you also want pay for each service in the course of it. Now you need only to utter some magic incantation."

6222–4. "No way" because the realm of the Mothers can never be explored by discerning mind, and imploring avails nothing either. That is, no discernible connexion exists between the empirical and the metaphysical.

6231–8. Faust seems to be talking about his life before our first meeting with him, when, as a lecturer, he may have aroused many disputes and often fled to nature to recover his peace of mind.

6250–1. "Mystagogues try to attract neophytes by telling them of coming wonders; you are trying to scare me off by telling of a terrifying Void."

6253–4. For this allusion cf. La Fontaine's *Fables* IX, 17.

6256. The realm of ideals (archetypes) means Naught to the sensualist Mephistopheles but naturally All to Faust the idealist.

6272. That is, awe in the presence of the incomprehensible. This idea, basic throughout Goethe's life for his attitude toward the world and the universe, is emphasized repeatedly in Goethe's writings and conversations, cf. his remark that a man is a fool who can not stand in awe, on whom the everlasting laws of nature do not make a powerful impression.

* The form "Helena" is used throughout the following pages, chiefly for rhythmic reasons, though it may be at variance both with the customary English "Helen (of Troy)" and occasionally with the form which Goethe uses.

6273. "Every-day life may dull a man's powers of reaction."

6283. The tripod, the source of the power of the Mothers, bestows the gift of evoking ideals, somewhat analogous to the sacred tripod at Delphi, associated with Apollo's power.

6290. An allusion to the old saying that all creatures recognize and understand only their own kind.

6291. "danger": that is, of being rendered senseless, as really happens at the end of this Act.

BRIGHTLY LIGHTED HALLS
(6307–6376)

A humorous interlude in which Mephistopheles prescribes magic remedies for various complaints.

6325. "cohobate": distil repeatedly.

6336. A hit at homeopathy and its *Similia similibus curantur*.

6357–8. Mephistopheles refers to the burning of witches and heretics.

HALL OF THE KNIGHTS
(6377–6565)

Faust has returned from the realm of the Mothers and now proceeds to evoke the archetypes of male and female beauty in the semblances of Paris and Helena. Faust has become aware of the creative power within him and he displays his skill before the court as a great creative artist reveals his images in art or poetry.

6394–6. The tapestries are rolled up on the right and left halves into which the end-wall is divided and the two halves part and fold back, revealing an inner stage.

6398. The Astrologer ascends to the front part of the inner stage in order to be near the prompter's box in the centre of the inner proscenium.

6399–400. An aside to the main audience — to us, as it were — not to the courtiers.

6433–6. The "Powers" preside over the destinies of life, allotting to some men and to some ideas the power to shine like stars (in the "canopy of day") and to live on before the eyes of men, sending others back for "transformation" in the realm of the Mothers whence they may be brought forth by the magician (or by the poet, the creative artist, as Goethe said in two earlier versions of 6436).

6442. The cloud gradually resolves itself into a pair which will become the semblances of Paris and Helena.

6447. That the temple embodies the Doric type of architecture is revealed by the mention of the triglyph, a tablet with vertical channels characteristic of the Doric frieze.

6459. "when a shepherd boy": that is, in his naïve state.

6481–3. The vision of Helena causes the Astrologer to forget his role as Mephistopheles's mouthpiece and to speak for himself: "And had I tongues of fire, I could not describe her."

6495–6. Probably an allusion to the vision in the Witch's Kitchen, 2429–40.

6509. Goethe owned a reproduction of Le Sueur's painting of Diana and Endymion in the pose here described.

6530. That is, from the time when Theseus is said to have fallen in love with her and to have carried her off.

6538. Cf. the dictum of the Trojan greybeards, *Iliad* III, 156–8: " Small blame is it that Trojans and well-greaved Achaians long suffer hardships for such a woman; marvellously like is she to the immortal goddesses to look upon."

6555. The " great twin-realm " that Faust will establish comprises both the ideal and the real worlds. He therefore tries to unite the two and to force the issue by laying hold on Helena.

6559. That is, " he who once has known the ideal."

6563. " it is done! ": a warning to the spectators.

Helena, the ideal, vanishes. The ideal can not be attained in a moment or by force and Faust must go through a long process of purification and organic development before he can become worthy of a union with Helena.

ACT II
(6566–8487)

A HIGH–VAULTED, NARROW, GOTHIC CHAMBER
(6566–6818)

Apparently not knowing what else to do with him in his swoon, Mephistopheles carries Faust back to his old study.

6593. " patron of yore ": cf. 1516–7, where Mephistopheles is welcomed as the patron of parasitic, destructive animals.

6597. The insects refer presumably to a former occasion when Mephistopheles wore the coat, cf. 1850+.

6634. Cf. John III, 1–21 where another, Biblical Nicodemus appears as a good-hearted, uneasy Pharisee.

6635. *Oremus*, " let us pray ": the Famulus is still frightened by the seeming earthquake and by the fact that the stranger knows his name, so he utters the verbal equivalent of a sign of the Cross.

6650–1. Cf. the words of Christ in Matt. XVI, 19: And I will give unto thee the keys of the kingdom of heaven: and whatsoever thou shalt bind on earth, shall be bound in heaven; and whatsoever thou shalt loose on earth, shall be loosed in heaven. Here " Lower and Upper " means the earthly and heavenly, or the material and spiritual, perhaps Heaven and Hell.

6667. The Famulus thinks the recent earthquake must have some astrologic connexion.

6689–806. The young Bachelor of Arts, the student of 1868–2048, is conceived (according to Goethe's remarks to Eckermann, December 6, 1829) as a personification of the fervour of youth and of youth's arrogant assumption that the world began with him and that everything exists for his sake; note especially the Bachelor's peroration, 6793–6806, one of the most deeply-felt and most poetical passages in the Second Part of *Faust*. In the same conversation Goethe told Eckermann the story of a man in the Orient who had gathered his people about him in the early morning and told them not to go to work until he had bidden the sun to rise, but he had wisely restrained his bidding till the sun was about to appear of its own accord.

6705. " long-beards ": professors.

6733–4. In German the expression " wore a queue " involves a pun since it refers to a man's braided hair *and* to old-fogyism. The Swedes set a fashion among European men in discarding the queue, and short hair became known as " the Swedish cut." The Bachelor of our play is supposed to be sporting a hair-cut of the latest style.

6736. " absolute " may involve a pun. Philosophically, it implies perfect, self-sufficing independence of experience and tradition, or up-to-date radicalism, but Mephistopheles may also mean: " Don't go home ' absolutely ' without any hair."

6758–61. The Bachelor sees philosophical worth only in the most recent systems of metaphysics.

6772–3. Mephistopheles oversteps the limits of the stage in addressing the audience in the main body of the theatre, a humorous device in Attic comedy, which Goethe uses more than once in the Second Part of *Faust*.

6791. This line may reflect Fichte's doctrine that the world exists only in so far as the ego thinks, or creates, it. Possibly the young man imagines himself the Creator; Mephistopheles promised him that he should be " as God " (2048).

LABORATORY
(6819–7004)

Mephistopheles finds Wagner attempting to make a man by means of chemical synthesis. He gives Wagner's experiment the finishing touch of successful creation (cf. 6684, 6885–6, and 7004), because he needs the assistance of some spiritual creature in dealing with Faust in Faust's present condition. A tiny spark of life, Homunculus, appears in the phial, who announces that he aims solely to be active and for this purpose to acquire corporeal form.

The initial conception of Homunculus was inspired by various forerunners of the poet who were deeply interested in the problem of the artificial production of life from inanimate matter, but Goethe added an all-important characteristic of Homunculus, his desire to commence corporeal existence. As we shall see, Goethe presents Homunculus as beginning life in the water in accordance with a theory which Goethe derived, at least in part, from a contemporary natural scientist, Oken, cf. note to 8435. But Goethe does not present Homunculus as beginning life in a human form; he suggests that Homunculus must go through all forms of living creatures until he develops into the form of a human being, in accordance with Goethe's theory of metamorphosis, cf. note to 8324. But this does not tell the whole story of Homunculus.

Homunculus's impulse to activity and his longing for a perfect existence correspond to the two impulses stirring Faust, and thus the two are deeply related and the Homunculus-action forms a fitting parallel to the main action of the play. Faust suffers from the limitations of space, time, and the flesh, and he is struggling out of a life thus conditioned toward a life that recognizes no limitations. Homunculus suffers as yet from no limitations but he wants to be limited, to be subject to space, time, and the flesh. Thus Homunculus figures in the drama as an element of contrast. In addition to this he plays an indispensable part in the development of the action of the drama. He is born with transcendent learning and by means of this he assists Mephistopheles and points out the way to Faust's recovery. But Homunculus — a spirit, in part, a product of Mephistopheles, in part, also a product of Wagner, note the name " Homunculus " — always exhibits feeling and aspiration, two of Faust's chief characteristics.

In the presentation of the drama Homunculus is usually represented as if contained in an electric bulb, with his voice coming from the wings of the stage. Goethe suggested that a ventriloquist might speak the lines attributed to Homunculus.

6819–20. The clanging which the Famulus and the Bachelor of Arts have heard seems to Wagner to announce the moment of triumphant success in producing life.

6853. " cohobated," cf. note to 6325.

6860. " crystallize ": assume definite form, as shaking causes freezing water to turn into ice, crystallization in contrast with organic or biologic process.

6864. A thrust at people who live mechanically, without capacity for development and unreceptive to new ideas, in other words, old fogies.

6873–4. Wagner's imagination leads him to think that he sees a manikin, but Homunculus must go a long way before he acquires a body.

6883–4. Two lines which embody a pet theory of Goethe's.

6885. Homunculus can claim kinship with Mephistopheles because, as Goethe said to Eckermann (December 16, 1829): " Such spirit beings as Homunculus which are not yet darkened and hemmed in by a complete assumption of human nature, were counted among the supernatural, daemonic spirits."

6903–20. By means of the superior capacities which enable him to see more than Mephistopheles can, Homunculus redes Faust's dream of Leda and the Swan, a reproduction in verse of Correggio's painting.

6916. " The swan-prince ": Zeus in the guise of a swan.

6924. Our conception of the Devil has come down to us, in general, as a product of the Middle Ages.

6935. " the most adaptable ": in adjustment to any situation.

6937–8. That is, " take each person to the environment which is most fitting or most attractive to him."

6947. " A genuine ghost must have a classical counterpart."

6952. Peneus, a river in Thessaly.

6955–7. Pharsalus consisted of two parts. There the great battle was fought between Pompey ("tyranny") and Caesar ("slavery"), cf. the introduction to the next scene.

6961. Asmodeus: cf. note to 5378.

6970. " Brocken-game ": fun in the style of the Brocken.

6976–8. If Mephistopheles can be said to be "free of squeamish twitches," the mention of Thessalian witches (Homunculus thinks) ought to win his consent to the journey. Lucan (*Pharsalia*, VI, 438 ff.) ascribes horrible powers and practices to these witches.

6992. " What " to put together and " How " to proceed.

6994–8. " the dot on the *i* ": the final touch, here the corporeal. Then Homunculus will attain to many things that men enjoy.

CLASSICAL WALPURGIS NIGHT
(7005–8487)

The primary purpose of the Classical Walpurgis Night, one of Goethe's most original, most inspired achievements, is to make ready for the Third, so-called "Helena," Act of the play by drawing the romantic, medieval world closer together with the classical world of the ancients. Goethe pointed out to Eckermann (December 16, 1829) that numerous lines in earlier portions of the play suggest the Classical and the Romantic, sometimes one or the other individually, sometimes through a fusion of the two: in the Masquerade (5065–986), in the evocation of Paris and Helena (6453–563), and in occasional remarks (6022–6, 6290, 6923–6, and 6946–63). This was done, Goethe said, to indicate that the action of the play proceeds upward as if on rising ground to Helena herself where both the Romantic and the Classical appear plainly and where a kind of equalizing balance or fusion of the two takes place. The Classical Walpurgis Night presents successive and final stages of this ascent. In its presentation Goethe invents a complement of the northern German Walpurgis Night of the First Part of the play; here in the Second Part the gathering represents an annual conclave of spirits of classical mythology who range from the most grotesque and hideous forms upward to supreme physical beauty, from beastly Griffins and semi-beastly Sphinxes up to Galatea who in her all-surpassing physical beauty represents the culminating approach to the physico-spiritual beauty of Helena who appears in the following Third Act.

The spirits of the Classical Walpurgis Night are assembling in the night before the ninth of August as the northern witches assembled in the night before the first of May (3952–4015). The present gathering has assembled now and here in order to celebrate the anniversary of the Battle of Pharsalus which Caesar and Pompey fought in 48 B.C., a battle of incalculable importance because Caesar's victory at that time enabled him to establish a dictatorship on the ruin of the former Roman Republic and to clear the ground for the empire of Caesar Augustus and his successors. The action in Goethe's play occurs on the broad plain of Thessaly and a neighbouring portion of the Aegean Sea, an extensive area offering varying backgrounds and room for the spirit figures of individual scenes: on the upper banks of the river Peneus (in two scenes): Griffins, Ants, Sphinxes, Pygmies, Dactyls, Cranes, Lamiae, Empusas, Phorkyads, Stymphalides, the Lernaean Snake, and Sirens; on the lower banks of the Peneus, nearer the Aegean Sea: Nymphs and Chiron; by and on the sea: Nereus, Proteus, Nereids, Tritons, Telchines, Psylli and Marsi, Dorides with Galatea.

Into this general environment enter the three figures which most concern the reader and student of *Faust:* namely, Faust, Mephistopheles, and Homunculus. Each of these " seeks his own adventures," that is, his own personal interests and intents, and yet each helps to supply dramatic content and cohesion to the Classical Walpurgis Night as a whole. Homunculus seeks the place where he can best begin corporeal existence; Mephistopheles roams around until he is entranced by examples of supreme ugliness; Faust seeks ideal, supreme beauty.

The Classical Walpurgis Night presents, most importantly, the ascent of Faust to Helena. Alighting on the Pharsalian Fields Faust awakens with the urgent query: " Where is she? " and thus he begins to seek the idol of his vision and his dream. The Sphinxes direct him to Chiron, and Chiron carries him to Manto who declares herself ready to escort Faust to the lower world where Faust (or she) will beseech Persephone (Proserpina) to allow Helena to return to a world of desire and ambition. (Goethe tells us later, in result though not in detail, that the mission of Manto and Faust succeeded.) Goethe thus expresses — through implication and symbolically, though perhaps too briefly — the gradual, organic development of Faust. Faust's union with Helena is not to be achieved by force, and therefore Helena vanished when Faust attempted to lay hold on her at the Emperor's court. Nature makes no sudden leaps, and man, a phase of nature, can not. The boundless aspiration and the passionate will to grasp which have always characterized Faust and which manifested themselves again at the Emperor's court must yield to a gradual, organic developing and maturing. In other words, Faust must traverse the path which the development of the Greek world pursued — though far, far more slowly — before he can attain to Helena. While remaining true to himself — in his urge to activity, in his all-encompassing desire and ambition — Faust becomes broadened in acquiring a knowledge of the Greek world and in becoming enriched in absorbing and assimilating the spirit of Greek antiquity. In the Classical Walpurgis Night Faust crosses the bridge to Helena.

Mephistopheles enters into a jesting give-and-take with Griffins and Sphinxes, then is lured by his innate, lustful curiosity into a pursuit of the Lamiae who tease him and sneer at him and destroy his pleasure in the new, ancient world which had attracted him. But since Faust will form a union with Helena in this new world, Mephistopheles knows that he must appear in a guise that will enable him to approach Helena and thus to assert some influence on the relation between Helena and Faust. This guise Mephistopheles finds among Phorkyads, fabulous figures of antiquity, human and most hideous in form. One of these forms Mephistopheles borrows from the Phorkyads. When Helena appears later as an embodiment of supreme beauty, Mephistopheles appears soon after as an embodiment of supreme ugliness.

Homunculus — Goethe's embodiment, or realization, of his idea of metamorphosis — does not know at first how or where he is to " come to be," to assume corporeal existence. But Homunculus finds two philosophers — Thales (c. 624–546 B.C.) and Anaxagoras (500–428 B.C.) — one of whom,

Thales, conducts him to ancient Nereus who, though half-heartedly, advises Homunculus to turn to Proteus, the greatest of all masters of metamorphosis. Proteus can indeed give Homunculus the desired information and, changing into a dolphin, he carries Homunculus out into the open sea where Homunculus can begin his new, corporeal existence. As Galatea approaches on her sea-borne throne, Homunculus is overwhelmed by ecstatic love for Galatea and by his desire to live. He hurls himself at the base of Galatea's chariot and sinks into water where (according to Goethe's scientific theories) he will begin to develop and "come to be." Therewith the Classical Walpurgis Night ends and ends with a twofold hymn, to Eros (Love), the source of all life, and to the four elements. Man does not now stand forth as the highest ultimate product of universal activity but Nature in all its manifold forms and in its ever-active omnipotence.

Another fairly extensive episode is bound up with Homunculus and his activities though of little connexion with the mythology of antiquity. Seismos, the spirit of earthquakes, heaves up a mountain which is at once populated by a host of little beings. The sage Anaxagoras advises Homunculus to become the king of these little folk, but the other sage, Thales, warns Homunculus against it, wisely, because a meteor soon falls and wipes out the little creatures.

Homunculus is thus confronted with the bewildering problem of creation in nature. Having witnessed new formation by means of volcanic forces, he next sees the varied life which arises in water. The Vulcanistic and Neptunistic philosophers in turn advise him as to the best way in which he should begin to be. Being a spirit, conscious of himself, Homunculus should and does make his own choice.

But Goethe may have inserted this episode in his *Faust* in order to express views which he held about various natural sciences, indifferent as to the possibility or probability that he might thus confuse his readers in their understanding of the Classical Walpurgis Night as a whole, but the beauty and wisdom of many lines cast a spell upon the sensitive, imaginative reader, and in the end such a reader would not willingly dispense with many of the lines.

However, since the reader can easily become bewildered by the frequent change of scene and by the more or less interlocking events of the Classical Walpurgis Night, he might read, first, the lines concerning Faust, then those concerning Mephistopheles, and, thirdly, those concerning Homunculus, reserving the remainder to the last and then reading the scene as a whole.

For Faust's adventures read 7005–79, 7181–213, and 7249–494.

For those of Mephistopheles: 7080–180, 7214–48, 7676–850, and 7951–8033.

For those of Homunculus: 7825–950, 8082–159, and 8219–487.

For the remainder: 7495–675, 7877–945, 8034–81, and 8160–218.

The verse-form of the Classical Walpurgis Night reproduces the trimeter and other metres of classical antiquity but Goethe also brings an astounding wealth and variety of romantic verse-forms into play. Many lines and stanzas not only vivify sensuous impressions for the eye; in the original they also complement and deepen these impressions through the ear by the melody of Goethe's language.

Goethe knew a great deal about classical mythology from his childhood on, but in composing the Classical Walpurgis Night he referred frequently — and most often, it seems — to Hederich (cf. 5298+) and to Dodwell (*A Classical and Topographical Tour through Greece*. London) in the original English version (1819) and in Sickler's German translation of Dodwell (Meiningen. 1821).

PHARSALIAN FIELDS
(7005–7079)

The spectacle begins with the appearance of Erichtho, a typical Thessalian witch (cf. note to 6976–8) who speaks in classical iambic trimeters.

7007–8. An allusion to scathing, grisly accounts of Erichtho by Ovid and by Lucan (died 65 A.D.) whose *Pharsalia* (Book IV, 507 ff.) was consulted by Goethe in the composition of these and other lines of the Classical Walpurgis Night.

7036–7. Lucan says that Erichtho avoided the living and dwelt in tombs.

7040–55. Cf. these stanzas with the alternating stanzas at the beginning of the northern Walpurgis Night (3871–911).

7077. Faust's soul is reinvigorated when his feet touch Greek soil, as the giant Antaeus always gained new strength from contact with his mother, Earth.

BY THE UPPER PENEUS
(7080–7248)

The Peneus, the principal and most beautiful river in Thessaly, winds through the gorge of the Vale of Tempe between the heights of Olympus and Ossa and flows on into the Aegean Sea.

7083–103. "Griffins": fabulous beasts with heads of birds and bodies of lions, who are described by Herodotus as greedy guardians of gold. The Griffin objects to "grizzly" because the word begins with *gr* as other disagreeable words do. "How is it with the *gri* in 'griffin'?" Mephistopheles asks, and the Griffin replies, with satirizing etymology, that *gri* in "griffin" is related to *gri* in "grip" and "gripper." The point is plainer and more effective in German: *Greif*, "griffin," *greifen*, "to grip," and *Greifer*, "gripper."

7103+. Herodotus tells of Ants bigger than foxes that lived in India and threw out gold-dust in making their burrows.

7106. "The Arimaspians": also according to Herodotus, a one-eyed race who fought the Griffins for gold.

7111+. Mephistopheles seats himself between the two Sphinxes, an Egyptian and a Greek (Theban), each of whom bears a woman's head and bust on the body of a lion.

7115. That is, "you coarsen them," the spiritual you make material.

7123. Vice appears as "Iniquity" in old English morality plays. In Ben Jonson's play *The Devil is an Ass* Vice calls himself "Vetus Iniquitas."

7130–1. Mephistopheles does not want to bother about the stars, so he asks the (Theban) Sphinx to suggest some of her famous riddles by way of amusement. It was the Theban Sphinx whose riddle was guessed by Oedipus.

7134–7. A definition of the Devil. The "pious" man needs the Devil as an object against which to exercise the rapier of his asceticism, the "wicked" needs him as an excuse, the pious and the wicked equally ridiculous in the sight of Zeus (God).

7151+. The Sirens, half bird of prey and half woman, are swaying in the poplars along the Peneus.

7184–90. These various beings of classical antiquity arouse heroic memories in Faust and make him feel that he is following the trail that will lead him to Helena.

7197–8. An invention of Goethe's, meaning: "Since Hercules who slew the last of us did not himself survive until the time of Helena, of course we have not known her."

7199. Chiron: according to Goethe's source-book (cf. note to 5298+), "a centaur, son of Saturn and Philyra, half man and half horse but such a good physician, musician, and astronomer that he instructed Hercules, Aesculapius, Jason, Achilles, and nearly all the young princes of his time in knowledge needful to them." Cf. 7337–40. The "young princes" included Helena's brothers Castor and Pollux. Chiron is said to have been the wisest of the centaurs who dwelt in the hills of Thessaly.

7206. The lying Sirens try to lure Faust by insisting that their repetition of Ulysses's stories would give him the information he wants.

7219–20. Alcides, another name for Hercules (grandson of Alcaeus), slew the Stymphalides, monstrous birds of prey with iron beaks and talons.

7227. Hercules cut off eight heads of the Hydra, the Lernaean snake, each in turn; a ninth head remained immortal.

7235. Again from Goethe's source-book: "The Lamiae were ghosts with an appetite for human flesh and blood, who therefore tried to entice young people with all sorts of lures. To this end they assumed the form of beautiful women who showed their white breasts to passers-by. . . . Further, they are considered ghosts of a very special kind, capable of transforming themselves into different shapes." The Lamiae will lure Mephistopheles later on (7696–790).

7241–8. That is, "You are sure to find us here." The lines 7243–4 refer possibly to a theory that the lines of Sphinxes in front of the Egyptian pyramids refer symbolically to the summer solstice; in this case the Sphinxes can call themselves rulers of the lapse of time, looking down on the changing world of man "with eternal changeless faces."

BY THE LOWER PENEUS
(7249–7494)

7249–56. The river-god Peneus is wakened by the first rumbling of the coming earthquake (7502+) and begs to be lulled to sleep again.

7276. "once before": cf. 6903–20. Faust seems to see his dream come true.

7329. Cf. note to 7199.

7342. Pallas Athena instructed Telemachus though he never seemed to profit greatly from his association with her, the goddess of wisdom.

[395]

7372. The sons of Boreas took care of their sister Cleopatra and rescued her husband from the Harpies (8819).

7382–94. Chiron is thinking of Hercules as an ideal of manly strength and noble character, not merely as a slayer of monsters.

7389. His cousin (not his " brother ") Eurystheus bade Hercules perform his twelve labours, but Goethe may be thinking of Admetus (cf. note to 9558), a " brotherly " friend of Hercules.

7390. Hercules spun in woman's clothes for love of Omphale, Queen of Lydia, but he loved a long list of other women too.

7391. Gaea: Earth.

7392. Hercules and Hebe were united as man and wife after his apotheosis.

7403–4. Chiron is comparing statuesque beauty with animate charm.

7415–6. Theseus is said to have fallen in love with Helena when he saw her, a child and dancing, in the temple of Diana in Sparta and to have carried her away and imprisoned her in Aphidnus's castle in Attica whence Castor and Pollux rescued her, cf. 8851–2. Chiron's part in the affair is only according to Goethe.

7435. Pherae: Goethe's source-book says: " Helena is also said to have been married to Achilles on the island of Leuce after her death and to have borne a son Euphorion to him. He (Achilles) had loved her when he was alive." Why Goethe substituted the name of a Thessalian city for Leuce is not known.

7451. Goethe makes Manto the daughter of the physician Aesculapius (not of the blind seer Tiresias, according to tradition) in order to credit her with the helpfulness that Faust needs.

7465. Chiron refers to the Battle of Pydna (168 B.C.) in which the Romans under the Consul Lucius Aemilius Paulus defeated King Perseus of Macedonia.

7488. An affirmation of the essence of Faust's character or, it might be said, of the whole of *Faust* condensed in a single line, cf. the initial paragraphs of these Notes, p. 349.

7492. Persephone is supposed to be an unwilling prisoner in Hades, ready to receive anyone from the upper world.

7493–4. Goethe invents the notion that Manto conducted Orpheus to Hades on his unsuccessful venture to bring Eurydice back to complete awareness.

Goethe wished and intended to write a scene in which Faust (or Manto) would successfully beg Persephone (Proserpina) to release Helena from the lower world. Goethe even outlined " what " would thereby take place but he never found the mood and power to tell the " how," cf. his conversation with Eckermann on January 15, 1827.

BY THE UPPER PENEUS AS BEFORE
(7495–8033)

The following scene presents the earthquake cited in the introductory note to the Classical Walpurgis Night, p. 393, and indicates implicitly Goethe's attitude toward a lively dispute of Goethe's later life about the origin of the earth's surface, whether the surface of the earth came about through volcanic (Vulcanist, Plutonist) origin or as a deposit of primeval seas, that is, was of Neptunist origin. Goethe stood with both feet on the side of the Neptunists since their theories coincided closely with his way of thinking and, believing in the quiet rule of nature, in its " gentle progress," he was deeply opposed to the violent and revolutionary. Water is therefore now praised as the creative power, and Homunculus throws himself finally into the sea as the place of places where he can " come to be," where he can develop a corporeal existence.

7498. " people ": probably those who live on land.

7513. " twofold ": in the sky and on the water.

7518+. Seismos, " earthquake," here personified as a giant pushing up out of the earth of the Vale of Tempe and thus forming a volcanic mountain. Valuable metals are thus exposed to the greed of the Ants and Griffins and Pygmies; only the " changeless " Sphinxes refuse to change their places " though all hell burst in their faces."

7533-5. The island of Delos was said to have been thrust up from the sea by Poseidon at the instigation of Zeus so that Leto might give birth to the offspring which Zeus had begotten with her; Hera had vowed that the pregnant goddess should not give birth in any place the sun had ever shone upon. Goethe ascribes the creation of Delos to Seismos.

7550-7. Seismos, in line with the so-called Plutonists, declares here in all formality that volcanic forces played a leading part in the shaping of the earth's crust, a doctrine opposed to that of the Neptunists who made the same claim for water.

7559. Out of Night and Chaos are Day and Cosmos (the organization of the world) said to have arisen, and this creation was followed by the action of Seismos when he heaved the mountains up out of the earth.

7561-5. According to the myth the giants piled Ossa and Pelion on Olympus in order to scale heaven, but Seismos says that he and the giants piled Ossa and Pelion " in wanton fashion " on Parnassus, thus giving Parnassus its " twin peaks." Seismos even claims (7568-9) that he heaved up Olympus too.

7569. " his lofty seat ": Olympus.

7601. The German uses the word " Berg," which usually means " mountain," but which in the lingo of miners means " rock that contains no ore, that is therefore valueless."

7605+. According to Homer the Pygmies carry on war with the Cranes; here too, but these Pygmies also govern a swarm of tiny earth-spirits very busily.

7621+. The Dactyls (" Fingerlings "), here the tiniest creatures who resemble human beings (cf. 7624), were known as very clever metal-workers who have to forge weapons for the Pygmies whether the Fingerlings wish to do it or not.

7643+. The Generalissimo of the Pygmies orders an attack on the Herons (7646), relatives and allies of the Cranes, in order to have decorative heron-feathers to put on their helmets, a conflict often referred to in medieval lore.

7659. " their ": the Pygmies'.

7659+. The Cranes of Ibycus, known (especially from a poem by Schiller) as instruments of vengeance, cf. the slaughter of their heron kinsmen; they are now said to fly away to summon other kinsmen, the Cranes of the sea, to wreak vengeance on the Pygmies, their legendary enemies. The outcome of their mission is told in 7884–99.

7680–2. " Ilsa on her Stone," " Snorers," " Elend ", cf. notes to 3968 and 3880 and the introductory note to the Walpurgis Night of the First Part of *Faust,* p. 371. A long wall-like stretch of rock on the Brocken is known as " Henry's Height."

7710–3. Mephistopheles identifies himself with men.

7716. That is, nothing wholesome can be expected of such a people.

7731+. Empusa: according to Goethe's source-book, a spook, some say, with an ass's foot. She is able to change into various forms and is therefore related to the Lamiae.

7777–8. " thyrsus pole ": a long wand used at festivals in honour of Bacchus, decorated with vine leaves and ending in a pine-cone.

7785–90. The Lamiae turn into bats and disappear.

7809–10. That is, " You can ride to the Brocken easily if you can take it with you and have it wherever you like."

7810+. An Oread, or mountain nymph, speaking from a rock not thrown up by the recent earthquake.

7814. Pindus: a mountain range on the border of Thessaly, the source of the Peneus.

7830. The beginning of the fate of Homunculus in his desire to " come to be."

7843–6. The " ghosts ": probably metaphysical philosophers, " ghost-hunters," perhaps hypotheses concerning natural sciences.

7850+. Anaxagoras, a Plutonist according to Goethe, and Thales, a Neptunist, the two " sages " of 7836, differ in their views of the way in which nature works. Cf. note to 7550–7 and the introduction to the Classical Walpurgis Night, pp. 391 ff. Anaxagoras was an Athenian philosopher, a friend of Pericles and a teacher of Thucydides and Euripides. Thales, also a philosopher, advocated the theory that the earth floats on primeval waters which gave and give birth to all beings and all life.

7853–4. A figurative but highly fitting way for the Neptunist to say that he can be won over by gentle, rational argument but that he can not debate with rugged, unyielding prejudice.

7861–4. Goethe's own creed, cf. the paragraph introducing the Notes to this scene, p. 396 f.

7866. " Aeolian ": Aeolus imprisoned the wind in his cave and when it escaped, it burst forth with all the more violence.

7870. That is, a volcanic mountain which does not arise from orderly development stands merely as an isolated fact and means nothing.

7873. " Myrmidons ": perhaps from *myrmex,* " ant "; in any case the word here means " ant-like people."

7875. " fingerlings ": the Dactyls of 7622–5.

7901–29. Anaxagoras, the Plutonist, naturally sympathizes with the little inhabitants of the earth's interior and wishes to protect them from the vengeance of the Cranes (7884 ff.); he offers to make Homunculus king of the little folk, perhaps because he recognizes a certain kinship between the ants and Homunculus, cf. 7876 and 7878, " active little things " and " hermit-like." But Homunculus has found his mentor in Thales who will lead him to his destiny; he refuses the kingship, and the little folk are crushed by a falling meteorite. Thinking that he has conjured the moon from the sky, Anaxagoras falls on his face in terror, and in his agony for aid to avenge the slaughter of his little folk, he appeals to threefold Hecate, " threefold " according to Hederich (cf. 5298+): " Luna in the heavens, Diana on earth, Hecate (Persephone, Proserpina) in the lower world," hence three heads attributed to her.

7909. " without magic ": without the incantations with which Thessalian witches were said to draw the moon and the stars down from the sky, cf. 7920–3 and 8034–6.

7946. That is, a swiftly passing phenomenon.

7958+. " Dryad " (from a Greek word meaning " oak "): a tree-nymph.

7967. " Phorkyads," daughters of Phorkyas, also called *Graiae*. According to Goethe's source-book: " They were grey old women. . . . They had one eye and one tooth in common which they gave to each other in turn when they wished to see or to eat something. . . . Furthermore, they dwelt in a place which neither sun nor moon shone upon." Cf. note to 8735.

7989–91. Rhea and Ops: originally two deities, Greek and Latin respectively. Later they were identified as one, the mother of Zeus (or Jupiter), hence one of the most ancient. Mephistopheles pretends to be of equal antiquity, also to have known the Fates. Goethe specifies the Fates, the Phorkyads, and the Devil, all of them as manifestations of the ugly, as children of Chaos, primeval ugliness. Cf. 8028 and 1384.

Mephistopheles has now assumed the form of a Phorkyad and thus he ends the role he plays in the Classical Walpurgis Night, but he reappears as a hideous, ancient Phorkyad-stewardess in the palace of Menelaus and Helena in Sparta in the Third Act. This will then be the role in which the northern Christian Devil will find a place for himself and where he can associate with Faust and Helena.

ROCKY COVES OF THE AEGEAN SEA
(8034–8487)

The climax and ultimate content of the Classical Walpurgis Night appear in the worshipful adoration of nature in this final scene. The demons and semi-deities of antiquity who consider Homunculus one of themselves, dominate the scene. Characteristically for Goethe, the scene begins with paeans, then soon turns from semi-irony to the dignity of a solemn celebration, and closes with the overwhelming harmony of all the participants. The Sirens, more or less like a Greek Chorus, exalt their deities in song and they describe and determine the progress of the celebration. The deities who are honoured, are Luna (by the Sirens, 8034–43, 8078–81), Helios (the sun-god, by the Telchines, 8289–302), and the Cabiri (ancient, storied deities, by the Sirens, 8070–7, 8206–9, 8212–8).

As in the masquerade of the First Act, the scene varies or develops with the appearance of various personages or deities: the Sirens who do not remain alluringly on their cliffs or reefs; the Nereids and Tritons who dash off to Samothrace to fetch the Cabiri to the celebration; the metal-working Telchines of Rhodes, not to mention the Cyprian snake-charming Libyan Psylli and Marsi who guard and attend the pearly chariot of Galatea. The Dorides, tender-hearted mermaids who care for shipwrecked mariners, form a part of the retinue of Galatea who enters the scene triumphantly as the Goddess of Love on Aphrodite's chariot.

Meanwhile the incarnation of Homunculus has brought Thales and Homunculus to Nereus and Proteus, two sea-gods famous for their wisdom and good counsel. Nereus holds back his advice for various reasons, but Proteus is well known as a master of metamorphosis which makes him an ideal adviser for Homunculus and he favours the Neptunist theory in accord with Goethean ideas and outlook in more than one respect. Hence Proteus now takes the form of a dolphin and bears Homunculus on his back to the chariot of the approaching Galatea. There in an ecstasy of adoration Homunculus hurls himself at the base of Galatea's chariot and begins a transformation — " to begin to be " — in the water, the progenitor of all true life.

The scene as a whole thus presents the joy of living in all of living's active, multiform potentiality. The sea becomes a symbol of the cosmos. But water appears not merely as a colourless producer of life; it is made radiant and glamorous by Eros himself, the element of elements in the production of life. The scene ends in a paean of praise to Father Ocean, to Galatea (the " ruler who all hath begun "), and to the all-embracing four elements.

All this does not merely present a mythological phantasmagoria of Goethean conception. It embodies Goethe's profound homage to nature in its eternal, procreative, and sustaining potentialities. Combine the ending of this Second Act with the ending of the final Fifth Act, and we have Goethe's ultimate philosophy of life. On the one hand, Goethe could but accept as his own the realistic, philosophic conception of life which the Greeks held and which was based on the immutable laws of the natural sciences. On the other hand, Goethe could but adopt in his theory and practice of life the love and brotherhood of man implicit in Christianity. In the fusion of these two basic elements of Goethe's thinking and conclusions lies Goethe's whole philosophy of the origin, meaning, and purpose of life. It is his " Weltanschauung."

8034–6. Cf. note to 6976–8, also 7920–3.

8043+. The daughters of Nereus are mermaids, and the followers of Triton, the ancient sea-deity, are mermen.

8070–7. The Nereids and Tritons speed away to the island of Samothrace to enhance the festival with the presence of the " Mighty Cabiri." These deities (their name means " the Great, or Mighty ") were originally Phoenician gods; they were worshipped on the island of Lemnos and later on the island of Samothrace which lies near the mouth of the Peneus. There the mysteries attendant on the worship of the Cabiri were of very great importance, since they now were said to have been the rulers of earth and sea and to have been the starting-point of all Greek mythology. Very, very little is known of their cult and rites, but they did in some way combine the ideas of immortality and metamorphosis. Perhaps for this reason Goethe introduced them here rather than merely in order to satirize the attempt of the philosopher Schelling to credit the Cabiri with extraordinary attributes and powers, cf. *Sitzung der Bayerischen Akademie der Wissenschaften am 12. Oktober 1815*. The number of the Cabiri is stated differently by different scholars but Goethe accepts eight as correct. They were pictured in the form of a small clay pot with a head superimposed.

8082. Nereus: the character and career of this sea-god Goethe drew from his usual source-book, except that he makes Nereus " sour " because men have not followed the advice he has given them.

8121. " Pindus' eagles ": the Greeks.

8122–5. This prophecy was invented by Goethe.

8123. Homer says that the Cyclops, the "round-eyed," giants of the Sicilian coast, had their one eye in their foreheads.

8127. " friendly shore ": the land of the Phaeacians who received Ulysses hospitably and took him home.

8137. Goethe follows his source-book in distinguishing between the Dorides, daughters of Nereus and Doris, and the Nereids, daughters of Nereus and some other wife.

8138. " your soil ": all Greece.

8146. The cult of Aphrodite (also known as Cypris and as Venus) was chiefly that of a land-goddess, although Aphrodite was born of sea-foam. Nereus may well say that Aphrodite " turned her face " from her kindred of the sea. Galatea, the loveliest of the Dorides, takes the place of Aphrodite, according to Nereus (Goethe), as the centre of the cult at Paphos on the island of Cyprus.

8152. Nereus is said to have been able to change his form, but he wisely directs Homunculus (who must proceed through many changes on his way to corporeal existence) to Proteus, the greatest of all masters of metamorphosis.

8165. " transfigured ": as proud escorts of the Cabiri.

8170. Chelone, a nymph, was changed into a huge tortoise because she ridiculed the marriage of Zeus and Hera. She is now bearing the Cabiri to the festival.

8174–7. Through their Phoenician origin the Cabiri were known as guardians of mariners whereas the song of the Sirens lured seafarers to their destruction.

8182–5. The Sirens, enemies of sailors, acknowledge their inferiority to the Cabiri.

8186–205. Perhaps mockery over the quarrel between Schelling and other scholars as to the number of the Cabiri.

8194. G. F. Creuzer (*Symbolik und Mythologie der alten Völker*, II, 303 ff., 1811) numbered the Cabiri as seven in which case the eighth would have been Phthas, the god honoured in Memphis in Egypt.

8197. Schelling associated the Cabiri with the gods on Olympus.

8201. That is, " ready " to travel.

8203–5. Schelling claimed that these deities were subject to a metamorphosis and evolution to a higher and higher form.

8216. Perhaps further mockery of Schelling: " In capturing the Cabiri (that is, in telling so much that you think you know about them) you have captured a prize even greater than the Golden Fleece."

8218. " We " is said by the Nereids and Tritons, " Ye " by the Sirens.

8221. " wise men ": German scholars.

8232. Proteus's " curiosity " was invented by Goethe.

8258. " As soon as he arrives at the place where his corporeal existence is to begin, the question of his sex will be easily solved."

8274+. According to Goethe's source-book, the Telchines of Rhodes, sons of the sea, " first created statues to the gods (cf. 8299). . . . Others say they were good artists . . . at any rate to have learned first how to work in brass and iron and to have made Neptune's trident." The hippocampi combined the forepart of a horse and the tail of a dolphin.

8283. " Wherefore ": because the trident " assuages the wildest of billows " and the sea must be placid to assure a perfect festival.

8285. Goethe " dedicates " the Telchines to the ministry of the Rhodian Helios, or sun-god.

8289–90. Diana and Apollo.

8295–300. Rhodes exulted in the topographical features cited here as well as in its many statues.

8311. An earthquake destroyed the Colossus of Rhodes in 224 B.C.

8324. Goethe's theory of metamorphosis: that in the simplest form conceivable, in the original animal or plant form, lies the possibility of development into any form of the species.

8332. Man stands at the end of metamorphic development.

8341. The doves of Aphrodite are accompanying Galatea.

8348. A " ring " around the moon.

8355–8. " One ought not to be too rationalistic," says Thales; " it is a good thing, as you are doing, to cherish the idea that you are seeing the doves of Venus and not what rationalists might call an ' atmospheric phenomenon.' "

8358+. The Psylli (of Libya) and the Marsi (of Italy): snake-charmers whom Goethe locates on the island of Cyprus as attendants upon the seaborne Aphrodite.

8370–8. They do not worry about, nor are they worried by, the Romans (the eagle) or the Venetians (the wingèd lion) or Christians or Mohammedans, each of whom at some time conquered and overran the island.

8379–90. The influence of Raphael's fresco of Galatea in the Villa Farnesina in Rome is latent in these lines. Goethe had seen the original fresco and engravings of it. Engravings of frescoes by the Carraccis are still to be found in Goethe's collection at Weimar.

8398. " light ": life.

8431. " whole long year " of separation.

8435. The summation of Goethe's theory of the origin of life. Goethe came to this conclusion, at least in part, through talks with Lorenz Oken, Professor of Natural Philosophy in the University of Jena, cf. above p. 389, introduction to "Laboratory." Oken believed that life arose in water and, like Goethe, he viewed nature as a process of metamorphosis; in natural philosophy he saw evidence of ever-continuous transformation and of the manifestation of God in the world.

8469–71. "swayed": Thales disapproves the sacrifice by Homunculus of his free, spiritual existence for the fetters of existence as a corporeal man; he foresees that Homunculus will know the anguish of being a man.

8472–3. Homunculus is assured that he has now found the place where he should begin existence, and Thales sees him, thrilled by love and beauty, hurl himself into the sea against Galatea's chariot.

8479. According to Plato, Eros (Love), the first of the gods, came forth at once from Chaos.

8480–7. The concluding chorus celebrates the four elements — water, fire, air, and earth — in all of which Eros is at home. Through Eros all life arises, from its first rudimentary forms up to supreme beauty.

ACT III

(8488–10038)

The Third Act marks a long stride forward in the development of Faust. Faust has been prepared for union with Helena by his course through the Classical Walpurgis Night and he now becomes united with her. Helena herself, coming from that realm of the ever-being and ever-becoming, feels drawn to Faust at once and soon adapts herself to him. Thus Helena becomes a reality to Faust and they dwell together in love; cf. "Introduction," p. xxv f.

Goethe composed the first and last parts of this Act (8488–9191 and 9939–10038) with deliberate and glad intent to reproduce the atmosphere of Greek drama as far as possible without pedantry and without sacrificing the vital connection between this and other episodes in Faust's career. Greek influence therefore appears repeatedly: in the use of out-door scenes, in the small number of chief characters, and in the Chorus. Greek metres are also used freely, especially the iambic trimeter, giving way symbolically in the course of the Act to modern metres and rhymes. In the use of Greek devices Goethe wished to make the spectator or reader think and feel himself in the presence of an ancient Greek drama.

BEFORE THE PALACE OF MENELAUS IN SPARTA
(8488–9126)

With the aid of Manto Faust has secured the release of the shade of Helena from the lower world, and we now see this phantom of supreme beauty standing before her former home in Sparta. With striking aptness, in the manner of Greek drama, in a kind of prologue, Helena announces her repute and name and then relates the events preceding the present situation as she thinks they have occurred.

8491. " Eurus ": the east wind.

8492. The " plain " of Troy.

8494. " on the shore ": at the mouth of the Eurotas.

8497. The " hill " of Pallas Athena.

8498. Tyndareus: the husband of Leda. Tyndareus is sometimes said to have begotten Helena, but (according to the myth) Helena was really procreated by Leda and Zeus when Zeus came to Leda in the form of a swan. At that time Zeus is said to have begotten either Castor or Pollux or both in addition to Helena, cf. note to 6903–20. In 8647 Helena calls herself " the child of Zeus." Tyndareus is said to have been in Aetolia at the time of Leda's *affaire* with Zeus.

8511. Goethe's source-book says that Helena went to the island of Cythera out of curiosity to see Paris and that she was sacrificing there in the temple of Artemis when Paris ("the Phrygian") first saw her and whence he carried her away.

8538. Eurotas: the chief stream in Lacedaemon (modern Laconia).

8570–7. The tripods were intended for the incense, the ewers of water for the priest's ablutions, the other vessels for the victim's blood and for the wine and barley-meal that were sprinkled on the parts to be burned.

8649. " Fright ": an Homeric figure, one of many monsters accounted as offspring of Night, herself a daughter of Chaos.

8653. " the Stygians ": gods of the lower world, so-called from the river Styx.

8685. " thalamos ": sleeping-chamber.

8697. The Chorus speaks in the singular — " I " — as often in Greek tragedy.

8700. " Ilion ": Troy.

8705. " Strife ": an Homeric personification.

8735. Cf. note to 7967. Goethe's source-book says that the Graiae took their name from a word meaning " an old woman " because they were reputed to be grey old women from birth.

8762. " Orcus ": the lower world.

8772. " Maenads ": a kind of Bacchantes, called Maenads, " raving women," because they went into a frenzy in their worship of Dionysus.

8810–25. Members of the Chorus vie with Phorkyas in hurling epithets to and fro about the ugliness and antiquity of the other's ancestors. The lines constitute a brilliant use of stichomythy, a favourite device of Greek dramatic technique.

8812. Erebus ("Darkness"): like Night, an offspring of Chaos and hence of ancient birth.

8813. Scylla: known as a sea-monster, a combination of girl and dog, a symbol of shamelessness.

8817. That is, only the blind seer Tiresias of Thebes would be attracted by them. Tiresias was said to have lived through nine mortal generations. Cf. note to 7451.

[404]

8818. Greek mythology does not name the nurse of Orion, the ancient giant and famous hunter, but Phorkyas must have come to birth long, long ago if she could be considered the great-great-grandmother of Orion's nurse.

8819. Harpies: monsters in the form of birds (with the faces of women) that scattered filth about them.

8821. That is, " you belong in Hades because the shades there long for the taste of blood."

8822. The Chorus conceives Phorkyas as a Thessalian witch (cf. 9963) and therefore ascribes to her the fondness for corpses which Erichtho is said to have had, cf. the introductory note to the Classical Walpurgis Night (p. 391 ff.) and the note to 7036–7.

8848–52. Cf. note to 7415–6.

8855. Pelides (" son of Peleus "): Achilles.

8858. Lacedaemon with its capital Sparta was given to Menelaus by Tyndareus.

8860. A reference to the assumption that Menelaus was an heir of his grandfather Creteus.

8864. This fictional origin of Phorkyas — that, born in Crete, she was seized by Menelaus in connexion with his voyage to that island — accounts for Helena's not knowing her now, since Helena was captured by Paris during that absence of Menelaus from Sparta.

8872–3. A later version of the Helena myth says that Paris carried only a phantom of Helena to Troy as Hermes had spirited the real Helena away to Egypt and that in Egypt she was restored to Menelaus.

8876–8. Cf. note to 7435.

8880. Since both Achilles and Helena appeared and acted as phantoms, their union could only have been a dream, as indicated by the repetition of the word " phantom."

8890. " three-headed monster ": Cerberus who watches over the entrance to the lower world.

8936+. Phorkyas reveals the Mephistopheles behind her mask; that is, Mephistopheles summons his own minions, the " dwarfish figures " ever ready for works of destruction. Mephistopheles could not command the Trojan maidens, so he summons helpers from his northern realm, but being disguised, they retain a kind of mythological neutrality.

8969. Cf. note to 7989–91.

8994–8. Phorkyas is describing Arcadia, identifying Faust (9006–16) with one of the Frankish knights who took possession of a large portion of Greece in the thirteenth century. Parts of the Peloponnesus remained under the rule of the successors of these knights down into the fifteenth century.

8996. Taygetus: a range of mountains, the highest (about 7500 feet) in the Peloponnesus.

9000. " Cimmerian night ": according to legend the darkness of the land in the far north or west of Europe peopled by the ancient Cimmerii.

9009. The early " free gifts " became in feudal times exacted tribute.

9020. Cyclops, cf. note to 8123. Cyclopean structures were said to consist of huge irregular masses of rock put together without mortar, whereas the masonry of Gothic buildings exhibits horizontal and vertical lines.

9030. " scutcheons ": the Greeks did not display coats of arms in a technical sense, but Phorkyas can explain the word by referring to the devices on Greek shields. Ajax was acclaimed as the mightiest hero at Troy with the one exception of Achilles.

9032. " The Seven against Thebes ": Polynices and six other heroes who attempted to wrest the sovereignty of Thebes for Polynices from his brother Eteocles.

9054–8. From his source-book Goethe drew the details that after the death of Paris Deïphobus took possession of Helena and that Menelaus later ordered that the ears of Deïphobus be cut off, then his arms, his nose, and finally all his other external members.

9062+. The sound of the trumpets is to be ascribed to the magic of Phorkyas (Mephistopheles), so too in 9424.

9117. Hermes conducted souls to Hades, waving his " golden wand " before them.

THE INNER COURT OF THE CASTLE
(9127–9573)

Helena and the Chorus have arrived in the courtyard of Faust's rambling, medieval castle far to the north of Sparta in the highlands of Arcadia. At one end of the courtyard a flight of steps appears, soon descended by a procession of pages and finally by Faust himself.

Goethe's use of metre and rhyme from this point on to the end of the Act presents in highly artistic and at the same time symbolical fashion both Helena's organic development and her adjustment to Faust. The metres — at first Greek, then modern — always remain in keeping with the nature and mood of the speaker and with the situation. For example, Faust speaks first (9192–9212) in modern blank verse to which Helena at once conforms. She then hears rhyme for the first time and it charms her so much that she requests Faust to teach her how to speak in rhyme. She learns her lesson thoroughly, speaking in rhyme thenceforth in perfect formal as well as spiritual harmony with Faust until she feels herself recalled to the lower world (9939–44) when she voices and thus symbolizes her farewell in Greek iambic trimeter.

9135. " Pythoness ": Helena refers to Phorkyas. Goethe took his word " Pythonissa " from the French and used it, as was done in antiquity, to indicate a prophetess or wonder-working woman at Delphi. Phorkyas has not revealed her name, although the Chorus suspects it (8728–35). It seems that Goethe does not allow Phorkyas to appear in this scene, partly, in order to keep the number of actors at a minimum in accordance with Greek dramatic technique, partly, because the presence of Phorkyas would disturb the perfect accord of the first meeting of Faust and Helena.

9146. A reference to the mixture of architectural styles common in medieval castles.

9162–4. An allusion to the apples of Sodom which were found to be full of dust if they dried on the trees. The Chorus fears that the attractive pages will come to be phantoms like themselves.

9172–9. As Helena ascends to a throne that has just been placed, a canopy appears over the throne forming a cloudlike wreath over Helena's head; the Chorus is bidden to stand " gravely aligned " up the steps of the throne.

9217+. Lynceus: " the lynx-eyed," the name of the warder of Faust's castle, a namesake of the pilot of the Argonauts (cf. 7377–8), who could see through earth, sea, and sky by day and by night.

9218. Up to this point the verse-forms of the whole of the Third Act have been those of ancient Greek drama, but Lynceus now speaks in rhymed quatrains. Helena soon feels the exotic charm of Lynceus's speech, and Faust leads her to the lesson in rhyming which symbolizes her readiness of adjustment to Faust as well as her perfected, all-inclusive union with him.

9235. That is, " What were these things to me then? "

9252. We may think here, in turn, of Theseus, Paris, Hermes, and Phorkyas.

9254–5. These lines can be interpreted differently but one may argue reasonably that Helena is referring to the fame of her beauty, to the part she played in the Trojan War, to her appearance in Troy and Egypt (cf. 8872–3), and to the trouble she has just caused between Faust and Lynceus.

9273–80. An illustration of beauty-worship characteristic of medieval chivalry.

9281–96. Lynceus seems to identify himself with the migrations of the races rather than with the knights of the thirteenth century.

9341. The flashing gems may *seem* to live, though they are really " lifeless."

9363. " limitless ": that is, the realm of beauty.

9385–410. A poem in celebration of marriage, an epithalamium, more or less in the classical style.

9411. " so far away," that is, as belonging to a world many centuries before the time of Faust, yet " near " in love. Note the use of both medial and final rhymes through 9418.

9415. " lived-out ": she feels that her life lies in the past.

9417–8. " Don't try to find out the content and meaning which this destiny of ours contains; our duty bids us to take each hour as it comes and to realize its opportunities without brooding." The German says " moment," a much more emphatic, more effective word than " hour." Even in such a moment of bliss Faust emphasizes significantly his conception of life as a field of conscientious activity.

9419–28. The approach of Menelaus is merely threatened as he is still pent in the lower world.

9432. " trash ": in the German, literally, " light ware." The Chorus is meant, cf. 8928–9.

9442–81. Faust reassures Helena as well as himself in regard to their safety and he then proceeds to divide lands that are to be conquered as lands were divided in the thirteenth century, cf. note to 8994–8.

9452–3. The reader expects " Ye come, ye stride " since Faust is addressing the leaders as representatives of the hosts that are marching past.

9454–5. Pylos: an important seaport of the Peloponnesus, now known as Navarino, once the home of wise old Nestor. Since Nestor and the heroes of old had died long before, Faust asserts that he and his " free hosts " encountered little difficulty in seizing the country.

9466. " German ": used as the name of a tribe.

9467–76. Corinth, Achaea, Elis, Messenia, Argolis, Sparta, with Arcadia at the centre: different portions of the Peloponnesus.

9480–1. The districts are allotted as fiefs, in medieval fashion.

9511–3. The Peloponnesian peninsula (" half-island ") is attached to the " last link of Europe's mountain-chain " by the " green hills " of the Isthmus of Corinth.

9514–55. A picture of Arcadia, a plateau in the middle of the Peloponnesus, praised of yore as a land of blissful happiness.

9526–8. That is, the peaks are still covered with snow and are unaffected by the cool air of spring, but lower-lying rocks offer some verdure. From this point on the eye travels farther and farther down to fertile, habitable regions.

9552. Under these conditions they resemble immortal gods, living on and on in their descendants and their own achievements.

9558. When a youth, Apollo was forced to tend the herds of King Admetus in Thessaly for a year because he had slain the Cyclops.

9561. Gods become as men and men as gods, forming a single and united world.

9565. The " primal world " of gods and heroes.

9573. " free ": as in the earliest times and unfettered by the conventions of later culture.

THE SCENE CHANGES (ARCADIA)
(9574–10038)

This scene presents the birth, life, and death of Euphorion together with the return of Helena to the lower world. The *Faust* chap-book (cf. Introduction, p. x) ascribed a son to Faust and Helena, and the Greek myth gave the son of Achilles and Helena the name Euphorion, the " lightly borne." Goethe invests the figure with symbolic meaning. He said to Eckermann (December 20, 1829): " Euphorion is not a human but only an allegorical being. He is a personification of poetry that is not bound to any time or place or person," meaning " poetry " not in any technical sense but as an imaginative comprehension of the world. As a child of Faust and Helena, Euphorion represents a product of the union of the classical (antique) and romantic (modern) worlds, inheriting his beauty and a consciousness of supremacy from his mother, from Faust his impulse to aspiring activity. To this inheritance from his father Euphorion adds intensified ardour for mankind and readiness to sacrifice himself for the good of his fellowmen. Since he acts in unrestrained, youthful impetuousness, he can not help others; he can only destroy himself. His aim of purposeful, altruistic enterprise remains to be achieved by his father. Thus Euphorion is closely related to Faust, uniting in himself elements of the Faust of the First Part of the play and elements of the later Faust.

In regard to the relation between Euphorion and Byron cf. note to 9902+.

[408]

The style and technique of Greek tragedy prevail in this scene through 9678. An operatic form is then introduced, continuing through 9938 in duets and trios with and without attendant choruses; Goethe specified that all this was to be sung with orchestral accompaniment, thus anticipating later music drama. In this way poetry was to be glorified and a requiem celebrated in honour of Lord Byron as a prototype of poetic genius. (Byron had died in 1824 to Goethe's profound regret, about three years before Goethe composed this scene.) Beyond 9938 Goethe employs Greek unrhymed metres again.

9574-9. An ironical address to the audience in the main part of the theatre, reminiscent of ancient comedy in form and mood. The expression "long-beards" is aimed at men who made up the audiences in Greek theatres. Cf. note to 6772-3.

9592. That is, for the birth of Euphorion.

9645-78. The Chorus gives a description (based primarily on Lucan) of the babyhood of Hermes, the child of Zeus and Maia (a daughter of Atlas), setting it off against the babyhood of Euphorion. Hermes too was begotten and born in an Arcadian grotto.

9678+. Goethe here wished that he might have music by Mozart but since Mozart had died, Goethe was thinking of Meyerbeer or Rossini.

9691-4. The happiness of deep personal feeling, though the world may deny the reason or even the existence of our feeling.

9707-9. Euphorion symbolizes to the Chorus the happiness of a marriage of many years. Time is again assumed to have elapsed symbolically since the preceding scene as at the beginning of the Second Part of the play.

9815. From this point on to the end of the dirge (9938) the lines contain almost constant suggestions of Byron and of the struggle of the Greeks for independence from Turkey (1821-9) which led indirectly to the death of the English poet, cf. note to 9902+.

9824. That is, the Peloponnesus.

9850. "it": the combat or what I am undertaking or what they are undertaking, an obscure passage.

9863-9. The Chorus addresses Euphorion in his character as a symbol of poetry, urging him to poetic heights, not (by implication) to combat, but he soon insists on playing the part of a warrior.

9873. He means that great deeds done "in spirit" are a proof of manhood even before they are done in fact.

9884. Here theoretically and dramatically, the conflict between the champions of Menelaus and those of Faust, in Goethe's mind one of the battles in the Greek struggle for independence of Turkey.

9901. The Chorus is reminded of Icarus who flew too near the sun so that his wings that were fastened on with wax were melted off and he fell into the sea.

9902+. "a familiar form": that of Byron whom Goethe identified with Euphorion "as a representative of the most recent era in poetry." Goethe said to Eckermann (July 5, 1827): "I could use no one but him (Byron) who is to be regarded without doubt as the greatest talent of the century.

And then Byron is not antique and not romantic, but like the present day itself. Such a one I had to have. Moreover he suited my purpose completely on account of his unsatisfied temperament and his warlike tendency which led to his death at Missolonghi." — Euphorion's aureole symbolizes supernatural genius, cf. 9623–4.

9907–38. A passage that is often accepted as Goethe's tribute to Byron.

9924. That is, Byron as well as Euphorion ran into a " net " of complications which each of them could have avoided; the " net " itself remained " without a flaw."

9927. Both Byron and Euphorion resolved to help the Greeks.

9930. Byron died (1824) of a fever before he could strike a blow for Greece.

9938+. The operatic Euphorion scene which Goethe conceived as being sung or at least accompanied by music comes to an end. Cf. the Stage Direction after 9678.

9945–53. These lines may be taken merely as a fine tribute to the culture of the ancient Greeks. But Mephistopheles may be thinking that he can use Helena's garments in later, grandiose temptations of Faust.

9955–61. A mockery of poetasters of some technique but no ideas.

9962–5. Panthalis thinks of Phorkyas as a witch and naturally associates her with Thessaly as the home of witches. The hideous features of Phorkyas, the romantic music, and the rhymed verse have offended Panthalis's Greek spirit.

9969. " the Inscrutable ": Persephone (Proserpina).

9975. The asphodel is often thought of as the pale flower of Hades.

9981–4. These lines express Goethe's serious belief in immortality: specifically, that the personal immortality of a man depends on the character of his life in this world, on his showing faithfulness (loyalty, steadfastness) or on his proving that he has converted his potentiality into actuality. As her companions in the Chorus have thought only of their own selfish, individual existence, not of loyalty to their queen, Goethe's inventiveness had Panthalis bid them seek a further life in the elements. Thus they gladly prefer some other fate rather than that of a return to Hades, some turning into tree-nymphs or dryads (9992–8), some into echo-nymphs or oreads (9999–10004), others into brook-nymphs or naiads (10005–10), and the remainder into spirits of the vine or bacchantes (10011–38). As early in his life as December 3, 1781 (in a letter to a friend) Goethe expressed the belief, or conviction, that only through steadfastness and faithfulness in this life do we make ourselves worthy of a higher after-life whether the new after-life be temporal or eternal. The " personality " (also " persons," 9986) means that the individual is to continue in name and character. Goethe's last words are said to have been not " Mehr Licht " (" More Light ") as people often say but " Nun kommt die Wandlung zu höheren Wandlungen " (" Now comes the change to higher changings ").

10030–8. A picture of an orgy or bacchanal such as those of Dionysus, the god of wine.

10033. The ass on which Silenus rode brayed so loudly that it frightened the giants.

10038+. "cothurni," or buskins, of Greek tragedy gave the wearer an appearance of great height. By descending from the cothurni and casting aside his mask and veil Mephistopheles marks the end of Faust's experience in Greece. The epilogue that is mentioned was never written.

ACT IV

(10039–11042)

Faust has lost Helena but his experience with the beautiful and sublime inspires him to try to attain power and to have effect and influence in the world. Entering the service of the Emperor he uses the magic of Mephistopheles in winning a victory for the Emperor over an enemy who has threatened to dispossess the Emperor of his realm. Faust receives as his reward and as his own all the land that can be wrested from the sea along the Emperor's coast. Faust will thus be enabled to rule not over land that constitutes a part of the Empire but land which he will himself create. Create for whom? At present he thinks chiefly of his own personal "lordship" (domination), of "possession," of the satisfaction to be gained from effective activity ("deed"), but Faust's latent altruism will come to the fore. Unfortunately Goethe never executed the scene in which the Emperor was to bestow on Faust the right to the barren seashore.

A HIGH MOUNTAIN RANGE
(10039–10344)

10039–66. Still under the spell of the antique, Faust speaks in classical iambic trimeters.

10058–66. Faust sees a vision of Gretchen.

10075–86. Another presentation of the Plutonist theory that mountains are thrust up by explosions within the earth, cf. note to 7550–7. The first lines refer to Lucifer and his rebel angels.

10089–90. Irony directed against Alexander von Humboldt and other Plutonists who believed that volcanic rocks once lay lower than granite, whereas Goethe held the opposite view. The Plutonist theory therefore seemed to Goethe to turn things topsy-turvy.

10092. "excessive": as compared with their previous close quarters. The Book of the Ephesians (II, 2) speaks of the Devil as "prince of the power of the air."

10094. The Biblical reference here and the one after 10131 were inserted in Goethe's manuscript by his secretary Riemer; Ephesians VI, 12: For we wrestle not against flesh and blood, but against principalities, against powers, against the rulers of the darkness of this world, against spiritual wickedness in high places.

10097–10104. Cf. Goethe's remark: "According to my view the earth develops itself out of itself," that is, in the process of becoming without being affected at all by other, external forces.

10109. This conception of Moloch, the Biblical " god of the Ammonites " (cf. Lev. XVIII, 21), was drawn from Klopstock's *Messias* (II, 352 ff.) where Moloch appears as a warring spirit who piles up mountains to ward off attacks by Jehovah, cf. also Milton's *Paradise Lost*, I, 392 ff.

10111. The " masses " are the " erratic boulders " which were deposited by primeval glaciers, but which Mephistopheles ascribes to his own primeval explosions. Mephistopheles proceeds to praise the common people for giving the Devil the glory for things they do not understand and for naming them accordingly.

10127. Mephistopheles's " sign " (or proof) is the mountain range and the rocks strewn around.

10131. Matt. IV, the story of the temptation of Christ, especially Verse 8: Again, the devil taketh him up into an exceeding high mountain and sheweth him all the kingdoms of the world, and the glory of them.

10159. That is, if people learn (especially, to think for themselves), they turn into rebels. Goethe is probably thinking here of the abuses of the French Revolution of 1789.

10160–9. A suggestion of the palace and gardens of Versailles and imitations of them in Germany.

10176. Sardanapalus: a type of luxury-loving despot, revived in people's memories by Byron's tragedy, *Sardanapalus*.

10187–8. Basic lines for the understanding of Faust at this stage of his development: " lordship " (domination) and " possession " through activity and through the use of his powers, through " deed."

10198–233. Faust's prophetic vision of a great undertaking which he might accomplish.

10218–9. Again an expression of Goethe's whole view of nature, a purposeful progression based on natural laws.

10228–9. The joy of creation.

10252–9. The theory of benevolent despotism, a political ideal which often occupied Goethe's thinking.

10285–8. " like priestcraft ": like working for one's own ends under the pretence of acting in the interest of public welfare. Since the Church saw its possessions threatened by anarchy, it aided rival emperors more than once during the Middle Ages.

10294. That is, in this particular case, " if we save him now, rebellious spirits will hesitate much longer before they try again to overthrow him."

10302–3. Mephistopheles evidently thinks that the end justifies the means.

10315. The German word " *Kriegsunrat* " means both " lack of counsel in war " and " evil of war," a pun lost in the translation.

10321–2. Like Peter Quince in *A Midsummer-Night's Dream*, Mephistopheles has selected the quintessence or extract of a large group of people, in this case three members of a mountain-folk who now appear as " Mighty Men," such as helped David against the Philistines. According to 2 Sam. XXIII, 8–9 the Biblical names were: The Tachmonite that sat in the seat, chief among the captains; . . . Adino the Eznite: *he lift up his spear* against eight hundred, whom he slew at one time. And after him *was* Eleazar . . . *one* of the three mighty men with David. In *Faust* the Biblical names are replaced by " Fight-hard " (Youth), " Get-quick " (Manhood), and " Hold-fast " (Age).

10327–30. Goethe is satirizing the Romantic period's delight in stories and plays of knighthood.

ON THE HEADLAND
(10345–10782)

Goethe follows an old tradition in having Faust aid the Emperor by means of magic.

10366. The Generalissimo expects his solid phalanx to break through the enemy's centre.

10389. " many " refers to princes and leaders.

10392. " Inner ferment ": trouble at home.

10395–6. The Emperor apostrophizes the rebel leaders.

10409. " I put on armour only to appear in military fashion, not that I myself expected to fight."

10412–4. " You shielded me by advising that I tilt at a ring instead of at some knight, but I felt the lack of danger and longed for a real joust."

10417–20. The Emperor refers to an incident in the Masquerade when he first really felt himself as Emperor and ruler of the world, cf. 5926–30.

10425. Folk-lore attributes to mountain-people especially close relations with the spirit-world on account of their close association with nature. From folk-lore sources Goethe drew his dealings with these mountain-people, with the witch's foot (1395), with Homunculus (6879), and with " changeling dwarfs " (6200).

10439–54. Faust wants to make it easy for the Emperor to accept the aid of the mountain-folk, so he ascribes his own presence to a Sabine wizard living in the mountains of Norcia in central Italy. Faust says that the wizard has sent him to aid the Emperor out of gratitude for a former act of the Emperor's. Faust now reminds the Emperor of this act: on his coronation day in Rome, Faust says, the Emperor pardoned the wizard after the clergy had condemned the wizard to die at the stake.

10467. That is, a real man relies on himself, " I am going to fight this out myself."

10475. The especial adornment of the helmet signifies the value of the head it protects.

10497. " Your best men have wished that your challenge be rejected."

10553+. " the knowing ones " are the spectators who, in Goethe's time, used to read many tales about supernatural beings.

10576. The sky is also becoming red.

10581–2. The illusion that Fight-hard's " one arm " seems to have become a " dozen " is explained as a mirage, a " fata morgana."

10594–6. The flashes of light are so-called " St. Elmo's fires " which appear on the mast-heads of ships and, when in pairs, were called Castor and Pollux.

10606. The Norcian wizard is meant here and in 10615.

10624–5. The Eagle symbolizes the Emperor, the Griffin his rival. The Griffin of heraldry is of legendary origin (10627) and consists of a bird's head and a lion's body (10636), cf. note to 7083–103.

10664. Folk-lore accredited ravens to the Christian Devil, cf. note to 2491.

10742. " Master ": Lucifer.

10772. Cf. 4845 and note. The very suits of armour, once worn by Guelph and Ghibelline, renew the old factional fighting.

THE RIVAL EMPEROR'S TENT
(10783–11042)

This is the last scene that Goethe wrote in the composition of *Faust*. About two months before his death in March, 1832, Goethe took out and looked at his manuscript of the Second Part of the play, apparently considering the possibility of elaborating this scene, of depicting the investiture of Faust with the barren seashore, of filling in other gaps in the play, but Goethe, now in his eighty-third year, never found the time or the mental energy or the inspiration to achieve this final purpose.

10816+. " our ": in distinction from the pretender.

10857–64. The Emperor is convincing himself and others that the battle has been won through bravery and happy chance rather than through the aid of magic.

10873–930. The Emperor proceeds to invest four generals with the ceremonial offices which the Golden Bull (established by Charles IV in 1356) assigned to the four lay electors of the Holy Roman Empire. According to the Bull the Duke of Saxony was appointed Arch-Marshal, the Margrave of Brandenburg Arch-Chamberlain, the Count Palatine of the Rhine Arch-Steward, and the King of Bohemia Arch-Cupbearer. The other three electors of the Empire were the Archbishops of Mainz, Trier, and Cologne, but Goethe combines the three in one and has him appear now in the one and now in the other of his dual capacity as Archbishop (10951 and later) and Arch-Chancellor (10961). Both the content and the form of the scene parody the stiff formality and the love of pomp at the court of the Holy Roman Empire as well as those at " our " Emperor's court.

10921. The Middle Ages believed that Venetian glass had the miraculous power of revealing poison in wine and of averting intoxication.

10931. We meet again the Chancellor of 4772 and of later lines in the First Act of the Second Part of *Faust*.

10947. Sovereign princes exacted pay for safe-conduct through their territories.

10960. The election of the present Emperor's successor.

11035–6. We may infer from this remark of the Archbishop that a stretch of seashore has been conferred upon Faust. (A sketch of a scene in which Faust was to receive this seashore was found among Goethe's papers, and this sketch has been presented in Weimar in performances of *Faust*.) Faust now has a chance to convert his vision of 10198–209 and 10212–33 into reality.

ACT V

(11043–12111)

The Fifth Act offers the solution which Faust finds for the problem of living.

When the Act opens, Faust has been working for years, pushing back the sea, draining marsh-land, and transforming barren soil into a fertile, habitable abiding-place for many people.

OPEN COUNTRY
(11043–11142)

This scene presupposes that before Faust began his work, an old couple, who resemble Philemon and Baucis of classical mythology, occupied a cottage near the sea. There they once saved the life of a young seafarer who now returns to thank them again.

11071–2. Philemon lighted a fire and rang a chapel bell to warn and guide the stranding vessel.

11123–30. Baucis thinks that the work done by day amounted to nothing, that the real work was accomplished at night with the aid of evil spirits, and that human lives were sacrificed.

PALACE
(11143–11287)

Faust's palace lies at a distance from the sea and is approached by a canal on which barges bring the booty of ships which Mephistopheles has commanded during their expeditions. Goethe may have had in mind any one or several cases of canalization or of wresting land from the sea on a large scale, especially the achievements at Venice and in Holland. But the important element of Faust's present activity does not lie in the object of the activity but in the idealism of the deed, in its creativeness and its influence and effect, in the subjugation of nature to the control of the human will and to the service of works of civilization and culture. Mephistopheles and his magic have played a part in this achievement, but Faust conceived it and it has been achieved mainly by Faust. We are to think of Faust (according to Goethe's direction) as being now just a hundred years old. For the name Lynceus cf. note to 9217+.

11149. Lynceus apostrophizes Faust.

11162. Faust is not contented with what he already possesses; he demands everything in sight and with the hope of attaining it he will soon make himself a party to indefensible wrong-doing, cf. 11275.

11177. " free " from prejudice such as regard for other people's property.

11217. " the gay birds ": wenches or ships.

11222. That is, land and tide are no longer battling with each other.

11266–8. The " first bath " probably refers to the infant's baptism in church. To Mephistopheles the ringing of the bell seems to mark all that life holds of the constant and real, that all that happens between the peals of the bell is worthless and unreal like the happenings of a dream.

11287. Cf. 1 Kings XXI for the story of King Ahab's appropriation of Naboth's vineyard by means of the arts of Queen Jezebel, an episode similar to that in the foregoing lines of *Faust*. But Faust orders the seizure of the property of others which Ahab does not do, and Ahab rejoices in his stolen goods while Faust curses the seizure of his.

DEEP NIGHT
(11288–11383)

11288–303. One of the last poems Goethe ever wrote. Though coming from the mouth of a character in *Faust*, the poem may be taken as an expression of Goethe's own view of life in his advanced old age. In its summation of the beauty of the world and the preciousness of life, also as coming from Goethe at the height of his wisdom, the poem delivers one of Goethe's most inspiring, most stimulating messages. The name Lynceus does not identify this warder with another warder of Faust's, cf. 7377–8 and 9217 with note. In each case the name merely denotes a warder of extraordinarily penetrating, comprehensive vision.

11290. That is, pledged by oath to the duties of a warder, cf. 9243.

11298–9. "In so far as they have pleased me, I am pleased with myself; it is my fault, not theirs, if I fail to see the grace, or beauty, of the cosmos."

11309. The darkness, already prevailing, is doubled by the foliage of the lindens.

11339. Faust sees that the cottage can not be saved.

11375–7. That is, "stake your all in the service of a powerful master and don't bother about consequences."

MIDNIGHT
(11384–11510)

The symbolism inherent in the "Four Grey Women" of this scene offers at least one difficulty whether we consider the figures according to their German or their English names. The "First" and "Fourth" ("Want" and "Distress") certainly refer to material circumstances, and since neither want nor distress exists in Faust's present life, neither of these figures can approach Faust or exercise any effect on him. The "Second" figure baffles interpretation most elusively, as the German word "Schuld" means in both German and English either "Debt" in a financial sense or "Guilt" in a moral sense. If this "grey woman" symbolizes "Debt," of course she can not gain access to the wealthy Faust, but such an interpretation does not satisfy, being too obvious as well as being highly unpoetic. The figure probably means "Guilt" and the question arises: "Why in view of what has just happened, can she not lay hold on Faust?" Goethe seems to answer: "Of course Faust was guilty; Faust was never an ideal, faultless hero, but a man who, with all his aspiration and his nobility of purpose, was plentifully endowed with human weaknesses. He is now again only human in that his guilt does not appear so great that ' Guilt ' can take possession of him and smother his determination to complete his great undertaking. Faust can not brood over the errors of his past, however great or many, if he is to arrive at his goal." The " Third Grey Woman," stealthy, insinuating " Worry," has long been a familiar spirit of Faust (cf. 644–51) and she can find the way to him and does. Faust can fear, or " worry," lest much will happen to defeat his ultimate purpose. But Faust will not listen to Worry's dronings. Though she blinds him, she can not dampen his ardour or halt his progress. (Numerous Goethe scholars will not agree with the above interpretation of the symbolism of the " Four Grey Women." The present translator-commentator merely offers the above interpretation as the one which now seems to him the most fitting and satisfying.)

11403–7. Faust now longs to be free from all magic, to be " only a man " but all that being a *man* implies. To realize the great change which has been wrought in Faust, cf. his attitude here with that expressed in 392–7, 614–22, 1074–88, and 1768–75.

11414–8. " We think ourselves rational beings, but superstition still lingers in our blood and we feel helpless in the presence of ominous portents."

11433–40. Faust's career since making the wager with Mephistopheles.

11443–6. One of Goethe's final bits of philosophy, cf. his remark: " It is the fairest happiness of a thinking man to have fathomed the fathomable and calmly to revere the unfathomable."

11444. Not a denial of God but a protest against the anthropomorphic conception of the Deity.

11456. " A man who is the victim of Worry is not even aware of the change of day and night."

11481. " rolling on ": like a ball, with no power or will of self-determination.

11482. " He finds it painful to cease activity and yet he is loath to submit to his sense of duty."

11492. " Spirits once invoked cling fast to a man."

11497–8. Faust has not been blinded spiritually, but Worry thinks that physical blindness will check Faust's impulse to activity, as physical limitations usually hamper and halt men.

GREAT OUTER COURT OF THE PALACE
(11511–11603)

Mephistopheles summons a band of Lemurs ("wicked dead ") to dig what might be called a trench for the furtherance of Faust's undertaking but they are coming really to dig Faust's grave, for his death is drawing near.

11516. The Lemurs are said to hear badly and to forget quickly.

11531–8. In part a translation, in part a remoulding, of the Gravediggers' song in *Hamlet* which Shakespeare borrowed from an earlier poem. Goethe probably knew both versions.

11541. That is, to reconcile or bind together the old earth and that taken from the sea.

11547. Mephistopheles characterizes Neptune as a devil on account of his destructiveness.

11567. The " hill " means a great dike, " mighty " in its power to resist the sea.

11572. Faust means communal, public spirit.

11575–6. Again Goethe's optimistic emphasis on the boon of life: that he only deserves life and freedom who through fighting for them has a claim to have and enjoy them.

11577–8. In 10187 Faust envisaged his own personal " lordship, possession " as his aim. He now, with great significance, substitutes altruistic activity as his (and man's) ultimate goal, that is, communal, coöperative activity.

11581. " might ": not a dubitative but a potential subjunctive, meaning not " I might possibly " but " I would have the capacity, the power, the right, I could."

11589–90. " Even in this vile moment of incipient dissolution the poor wretch wanted to live on."

11594. Cf. note to 1705.

11595–603. Mephistopheles as a devil naturally objects to the suggestion that all is at an end with Faust. " If a man's death in this world, after so short an existence, is the end, what is the sense in creation? If this is the end, it would be better that a man never lived at all, and I'd prefer the utter uniformity of the Eternal Void. However, life goes on as if it were something."

Mephistopheles thinks or pretends to think that he has won the wager with Faust and that he will possess Faust in the life beyond. But he has obviously lost. Cf. Introduction, p. xxix.

To some readers it may seem strange and even flat that Faust should find his highest happiness in a more or less prosaic engineering project. Goethe apparently chose this particular solution for various reasons, spiritual and physical.

The reader can easily imagine the spiritual effect of Faust's endeavour and achievement on his immediate fellow-men: on their receptiveness, on their sense and appreciation of inventiveness, of leadership, foresight, genius of organization, and of daring, coöperative activity. These forces would naturally produce a deeper feeling of freedom through breaking down the walls of confinement built up by nature, through the substitution of active individualism in the place of stagnation, through the realization that real and lasting freedom can be preserved only through constant watchfulness and coöperative activity and the realistic application of ideals.

To these spiritual reasons certain physical reasons may be added for Goethe's choice of his solution of Faust's problem. To Goethe's fellow-countrymen as well as to other Europeans confined within a comparatively limited space, the acquisition of new land on which men can live and prosper has long loomed large as a vital problem. In Europe the infinite possibilities in conquering the sea strike home, far more deeply than can yet be the case in America where vast tracts of land still await occupation and development. To understand the situation in Europe one needs to refer only to the deep impression which Venice made on Goethe and to the gigantic undertaking that has been in progress in Holland in the conquest of the Zuider Zee.

BURIAL
(11604–11843)

With this scene Goethe swings into line with the medieval conception of the struggle between devils and angels for the soul as it leaves the body.

Mephistopheles's long speech (11612–75) is based primarily on details in the frescoes of the Campo Santo at Pisa. Goethe never saw the original frescoes but he studied them in reproductions, making use of many details, and he knew other similar scenes, not to mention Dante's *Inferno*.

11604–7. A free use of the third stanza of the Grave-diggers' Song in *Hamlet*. The single Lemur speaks in the name of the dead man. The inherent idea of the lines denotes the "house" as the grave, life as a passing feast.

11610–1. That is, "earthly possessions were yours only for a short time; the living now have a claim to them and there are many such creditors."

11614. Mephistopheles refers especially to those who deny the existence of the Devil; to them he has no claim.

11616–7. "the old way" concerns people who promised their souls to the Devil in return for the pleasures of this life and who were snatched away at the end of a fixed period in fulfilment of a bargain, of a *quid pro quo*. The "new way" of fighting the angels in a disputable claim for the soul of a man does not appeal to Mephistopheles.

11623. One of the Pisan frescoes pictures the soul of a dying man as escaping from his mouth in the form of a little wingèd sprite.

11626–9. Death is not certain until decomposition has set in.

11631–3. "tiresome queries": *when* death takes place, *how* the soul parts from the body, *where* the soul leaves the body, even *whether* death has really set in or only apparently; probably to be taken as a parody, or as a thrust at scholastic questionings.

11635+. Mephistopheles proceeds to command his minions like a sergeant or corporal directing a squad of soldiers.

11638. A metaphor taken from the mint: "you genuine devils."

11639. The devils are credited with the power of producing the maw of Hell in any place.

11640–3. "We have been using many maws of Hell in accordance with the different earthly ranks and dignities of people, but the world is becoming more and more democratic and soon one maw will suffice for all."

11644. "Tusks": those of the "hyena" in 11650.

11650. The jaws of Hell were often portrayed graphically in medieval mystery plays. In this passage the "hyena" seems to have been suggested by a monster in a Pisan fresco, whose jaws constitute the maw of Hell. The damned are imagined as swimming in the fiery lake within until with the hope of escape they reach the jaws, but just as they draw near, the jaws snap to.

11659–60. Mephistopheles identifies the phosphorescent light appearing in decomposition with the soul which the Greeks conceived as having the form of a butterfly (Psyche).

11661. Mephistopheles wants the entire soul, especially the wings with which it ascends on high.

11662. Cf. the " mark of the beast " in Rev. XVI, 2, and XIX, 20: there fell a noisome and grievous sore upon the men which had the mark of the beast and upon them which worshipped his image . . . them that had received the mark of the beast and them that worshipped his image. These both were cast alive into a lake of fire burning with brimstone.

11670–3. The tall devils with long arms and crooked horns may, by threshing the air, seize the soul if it escapes the short devils who are bending low over the body.

11676–84. Angels appear in a flood of light proclaiming themselves as bearers of forgiveness, resurrection, and love.

11680. That is, awakening the souls to a new life.

11691–2. " the shamefullest ": probably the crucifixion of Christ.

11695. Mephistopheles charges the angels with as much hypocrisy as the devils possess.

11698+. The angels have received the roses from holy penitent women (cf. 11942) and strew them now as symbols of divine love.

11718–25. Heavenly roses turn into stinging, burning flames when they touch the devils; heavenly love becomes a " voluptuous glow."

11732. Goethe uses " ether " here and later in the sense of " heavenly pure atmosphere," in this line the ether in which the angels are soaring.

11745–8. " What " and " it ": the soul and its message of love.

11749–50. " If heavenly love is to have any effect in opposition to the powers of Hell, we must fight hard."

11756–8. Perhaps addressed only to Mephistopheles's minions who have plunged into the maw of Hell and are gazing backwards, perhaps, with a wider bearing, addressed to all spurned lovers.

11759–800. Purifying, heaven-sent love becomes only an impulse to sexual perversion in Mephistopheles.

11759. " I too am affected as my minions are."

11760–1. " its " and " it ": heavenly love.

11785–6. That is, his whole being burns so hotly with perverse love that he scarcely feels the external burning of the roses.

11814. Mephistopheles feels a sense of triumph, being convinced that evil outweighs the good.

11818–20. That is, " those who on earth are surrounded by the glow of heavenly love enjoy a heavenly bliss even in their mortal lives."

11823–4. The odours of Hell have fled; Faust's soul can breathe freely.

Mephistopheles is forced to acknowledge his defeat but he must explain it to himself, which he does by ascribing his defeat to hypocritical craftiness on the part of the angels. Mephistopheles has lost himself in lascivious gazing at the angels and since Faust's soul has therefore eluded and escaped him, he finds now at the end that he has only been fooled after all, that he is now only a stupid, deluded devil, a very different figure from the arrogant, self-assured Mephistopheles who appeared first in the " Prologue in Heaven " (271–353). In this scene in which he appears for the last time Mephistopheles may be said to represent utter sexuality — an un-procreative sexuality which means nihilism — as contrasted with the creative and elevating love which Faust has experienced and will experience.

[420]

MOUNTAIN GORGES
(11844–12111)

The title of this scene applies appropriately only to the beginning as the action ascends from the earthly habitations of pious hermits to the heights of Heaven. These hermits, or anchorites, are imagined as men of the first Christian centuries who devoted themselves to acts of penance in order to mortify the flesh and thus to achieve a mystic union with God, Christ, and the Virgin Mary. They were later enrolled among the saints.

In clinging so closely to Christian tradition Goethe visualizes for us not only Faust's assumption and his own conception of an afterlife; he also completes the circle of the drama by ending it in Heaven where it began. The Heaven of this scene does not, however, convey the austerity of the Prologue in Heaven; it presents a realm of ceaseless, loving activity. The First Part of the play ended in a prison, the Second Part ends at the feet of the Virgin. The Second Part begins and ends with manifestations of altruistic love.

Goethe confidently looked forward to activity in the life beyond. He said to Eckermann (May 2, 1824): " I am firmly convinced that our spirit (mind) is a being whose nature (essence) is absolutely indestructible, a being that continues to be active on and on, from eternity to eternity; it is like the sun which only to our earthly eyes seems to set, which, however, never really sets but shines unceasingly." Thus what we call death appeared to Goethe as but a transition.

11844–53. The Chorus and Echo are to be taken as unseen heralds of the nature and spirit of the first portion of this scene.

11850. The friendly lions and other features of the landscape were probably drawn from a picture of St. Jerome in the Wilderness, attributed to Titian or one of his school.

11853+. The patres of this scene represent typical early Christian Fathers in different stages of their dedication of themselves to the worship of the Deity. The Pater Ecstaticus who wavers between the joys of martyrdom and the yearning for a perfect union with the divine has already overcome in large part the weight of gross earthly flesh and so he " hovers up and down."

11866–89. To the Pater Profundus who bears a name given to Bernard of Clairvaux, the chasms, streams, and trees embody, like everything else on earth, immanent manifestations of God. Feeling his limitations, the Pater Profundus longs to understand all of these manifestations and thus to attain to divine truth.

11887. The " chains " of physical limitations are conceived as cramping and smarting.

11890–3. The Pater Seraphicus, as St. Francis of Assisi was called, dwells upon a still higher plane. He has come into touch with heavenly spirits, and all that he knows and has experienced he can share with others if they can learn life and the world through his eyes. He knows nothing of the conflicts and agonies of the Pater Ecstaticus and the Pater Profundus and, like St. Francis, he leads a contented existence based on the " revelation of endless loving " (11924).

11893+. The Blessèd Boys are the spirits of children who died before they were baptized and before they knew the world and sin. They have inherited original sin, however, and therefore they occupy a place between men and angels. Before they can enter Heaven, they must be purified and instructed, as they are now being instructed by the Pater Seraphicus. The condition of the Blessèd Boys resembles that of Faust and for this reason he is later associated with them.

11894–933. The Blessèd Boys are received at first only as " blessèd " on account of their inexperience with the world, but the more they believe in God, the more they are strengthened through " God's high presence " and through " the revelation of endless loving," the more ready will they be to soar upward, bearing Faust's immortal part into a realm where they are assured they will see Him Whom they yearn to see.

11898. It was believed that infants " born at midnight " did not live long.

11903. " One who loves ": the Pater himself.

11906–13. Goethe read in Swedenborg the assertion that spirits entered into Swedenborg's body in order to be able to see earthly things.

11934–41. Goethe said to Eckermann (June 6, 1831): " In these lines lies the key to Faust's salvation: in Faust himself an ever higher and purer activity to the end and eternal love coming from above to aid him. This harmonizes perfectly with our religious ideas according to which we are saved not only through our own strength but through the freely bestowed grace of God." Goethe placed the quotation marks around 11936–7 in order to emphasize them. The lines are Goethe's own.

11937. What is " salvation "? Formerly it could be interpreted as negative, as liberation from the Devil and Hell. With Goethe it was far more personal, more intimate, more essential, namely, positive; it meant eternal life and activity. Thus a basic idea of Goethe's *Faust* consists of a continuation on and on, embodying the very essence of Goethe who said to Eckermann (February 4, 1829): " The conviction that we shall live beyond this life arises in my mind from my idea of activity." In this ascension into Heaven this (aspiring) activity becomes an ever purer, ever more intensive contemplation and penetrating understanding of God.

11954–65. That is, the " more perfected angels " would still feel the stain of earth clinging to Faust's immortal part even if it had gone through the purification of fire and flame, but when strong spiritual forces unite with earthly forces as is now happening, only an angel can separate the earthly from the heavenly; only " Eternal Love " can succeed in achieving this.

11983–4. " The fact that this aspiring spirit is entrusted to us implies a pledge that we shall enjoy the bliss of the angels."

11985. " flakes ": dross, the covering of the chrysalis.

11988+. Doctor Marianus: a name given to various mystics and applied here to one who introduces and teaches the worship of the Virgin with which the scene closes. The remainder of the play is surcharged with intercessions and petitions in behalf of Faust, and for this reason they are directed primarily to the Virgin, the embodiment of forgiving mercy. And now the Mater Gloriosa soars into view, attended by Dr. Marianus, the holy instructor of the love of the Virgin and of the love of God. The Mater Gloriosa does not appear here as the Virgin of the Immaculate Conception but as the guardian of love. Dr. Marianus pleads first for Faust, then for Gretchen, and, finally, for three sinning women, Mary Magdalen, the Woman of Samaria, and Mary of Egypt. Gretchen's prayer of despair before the image of the Mater Dolorosa (3587–3619) is now transformed into a hymn of praise at the feet of the Mater Gloriosa. Gretchen's despair has become transfiguration. But the action of the play goes on and on, as it were, into faraway eternities. Goethe's play never really ends, it only vanishes in dim distance because our senses are not capable of following its ultimate reaches. The last we hear is the message of the members of the Mystic Chorus who have become one with God.

11994. "star-crowned": with a halo of stars.

11999. What Goethe may have had in mind in "mystery" is not apparent. We might only assume that it was some element of the divine beyond all human perception and understanding.

12020–3. The Virgin is immaculate but she is nevertheless not unapproachable; all women who have sinned may draw near to her, confident of her grace.

12052+. Mary of Egypt is associated with Mary Magdalen and the Woman of Samaria because all three had committed the sin of sensuality. According to the *Acta Sanctorum* Mary of Egypt led a life of excess for seventeen years. At the festival of the Elevation of the Cross she tried to enter the Church of the Holy Sepulchre in Jerusalem but an invisible hand thrust her back. In answer to her prayer of remorse to the Virgin she was lifted up in miraculous fashion and borne into the church where a voice commanded her to go and find peace on the shore of the Jordan. There in the desert she did penance for forty-eight years and when she reached the point of death, she wrote in the sand a request to the monk Socinius that he bury her body and pray for her soul.

12076–7. The tutelage of the Blessèd Boys has already developed the members of Faust's new spiritual body.

12104–11. In other words, Goethe seems to mean: All that is earthly is only a symbol of the eternal and divine. Earthly activity is never sufficient in itself, but if it was activity with aspiring purpose, it is recognized in the life beyond and there made sufficient. What is past human grasp and understanding (or "indescribable," as Goethe says, literally), namely, the transition from earthly life to the life beyond, is accomplished here, in the case of Faust, through the grace of an understanding love that is divine in its essence and in its workings. We know such love in its purest, most selfless form only in womanhood, whether incorporated in earthly woman or imagined in its highest perfection in the Virgin. Such love is the supreme, uplifting power. The Eternal-Womanly leads us upward and on, closer and closer to God.

FINIS

[423]

Bibliography

English books concerning Goethe and his works have increased with considerable rapidity in recent years so that it is feasible to name only a few here, but perhaps a small, selected list of such books will be welcome to the reader of these pages. Each of the books named below has merits, as the translator knows to his profit, and each will in some way further the reader's knowledge and understanding of Goethe and his *Faust*.

BIBLIOGRAPHIES

Brown, P. Hume: *Life of Goethe*. London, 1920.

Lewes, George Henry: *The Life and Works of Goethe*. 1855. Everyman's Library, No. 269.

Nevinson, Henry W.: *Goethe*. New York, 1932.

Robertson, J. G.: *The Life and Work of Goethe*. New York, 1932.

Thomas, Calvin: *Goethe*. New Edition with an Introduction by Robert Herndon Fife. New York, 1929.

There are also excellent English translations of German biographies by Bielschowsky, Düntzer, Ludwig, and Meyer, and of the Danish biography of Goethe by Brandes. It is a pity that the biographies by Gundolf and Witkowski are not available in English.

ESSAYS

Arnold, Matthew: *Mixed Essays*. New York, 1924.

Carlyle, Thomas: *Essays on the Greater German Poets and Writers*. The Scott Library, No. 83. London.

Croce, Benedetto: *Goethe*. New York and London, 1923.

Eliot, George: *Essays*. London and New York, 1924.

Emerson, R. W.: *Representative Men*. " Goethe, or the Writer." Everyman's Library, No. 279.

Fairley, Barker: *Goethe as revealed in his Poetry*. Chicago, 1932.

Santayana, George: *Three Philosophical Poets*. "Goethe's Faust." Cambridge, Mass., 1922.

Seeley, J. R.: *Goethe Reviewed after Sixty Years*. London, 1894.

Further information about the historical Faust and the Faust chap-books and puppet-plays can be found in:

Dr. Johannes Faust. Puppet-Play. Now first done into English. Mediaeval Legends. London, 1893.

The History of the Damnable Life and Deserved Death of Doctor John Faustus. Both modernized and edited by William Rose. Broadway Translations. London (1925).

Rose, William: *Men, Myths, and Movements in German Literature*. New York, 1931.

Two English books are devoted exclusively to a commentary on *Faust*:

Coupland, W. C.: *The Spirit of Goethe's Faust*. London, 1888.

Stawell, F. M., and Dickinson, G. Lowes: *Goethe and Faust*. London, 1928.

But the reader who is seeking further light on the interpretation of *Faust* is advised to consult also:

Boyesen, H. H.: *Goethe and Schiller: Their Lives and Works.* New York, 1882.

Goethe's Conversations with Eckermann. Everyman's Library, No. 851.

Various translations with notes are helpful, especially those by

Latham, Albert G.: Parts One and Two. Everyman's Library, No. 335.

McLintock, R.: Part One. London, 1897.

Swanwick, Anna: Parts One and Two. With an Introduction by Karl Breul. Bohn Library. London, 1928.

Taylor, Bayard: Parts One and Two. With an Introduction by Robert Herndon Fife. The Modern Readers' Series. New York, 1930.

Goethe's original text with notes in English has been edited by

Thomas, Calvin: Parts One and Two. Boston, Mass., 1892 and 1897.

Goebel, J.: Part One. Revised Edition. New York, 1910.

The best German editions of *Faust* with notes in German are those of

Beutler, Ernst: *Goethe: Faust und Urfaust.* Sammlung Dieterich, Band 25. Leipsic, 1939.

Petsch, Robert: *Goethes Werke*, Vol. 5. Leipsic.

Schmidt, Erich: Jubiläumsausgabe, Vols. 13 and 14. Stuttgart.

Schröer, K. J.: *Faust von Goethe.* Sixth Edition. Two volumes. Stuttgart, 1926.

Trendelenburg, Adolf: *Goethes Faust.* Two volumes. Berlin and Leipsic, 1921–2.

Witkowski, Georg: *Goethes Faust.* Ninth Edition. Two volumes. Leiden, 1936.

Two outstanding German works devoted exclusively to a commentary on *Faust* are those by

Rickert, Heinrich: *Goethes Faust.* Tübingen, 1932.

Traumann, Ernst: *Goethes Faust.* Two volumes. Munich, 1919–20.

PRINTER'S NOTE

The text of this book is set in Caledonia, a Linotype face designed by W. A. Dwiggins. The larger type used in the headings, etc., is Bulmer, produced by the American Type Founders Company. Both Caledonia and Bulmer belong to the family of printing-types called " modern face," a term used to mark the change in style of type-letters that occurred about 1800.

Mr. Dwiggins contrived the typographic scheme and designed the binding and jacket. The book was composed, printed, and bound by The Plimpton Press, Norwood, Massachusetts.

Photogravure from an oil painting by J. K. Stieler.

In personal appearance Goethe was impressive, rather than handsome. He had the bold, high brow that denotes intellect, and the strong, well-set features that are the outward signs of a firm character. The accompanying picture is the reproduction of a painting made when the author of " Faust " had passed the prime of life, and it is said to be the best likeness of him that is now existing. It is the face of a man who has seen life in all its beauty and ugliness, in all its pathos and sublimity. As in his writings there shines forth, now and then, a ray of the Great Thought that is beyond human ken, so in his countenance there is the reflected sadness of human experience, of human frailties and passions.